# ENGLISH ON COURSE

## THE COMPLETE STUDY GUIDE FOR GCSE

# RHODRI JONES

Heinemann Educational Books

Heinemann Educational Books Ltd
22 Bedford Square, London WC1B 3HH
London   Edinburgh   Melbourne   Auckland
Singapore   Kuala Lumpur   New Delhi
Ibadan   Nairobi   Johannesburg
Kingston   Portsmouth (NH)

Jones, Rhodri
    English on course: the complete study guide for
    GCSE.
    1. English language—Grammar—1950–
I. Title
428        PE1112

ISBN 0 435 10502 7
Copyright © 1988 Rhodri Jones
First published 1988

Printed and bound in Great Britain by
Butler & Tanner Ltd., Frome and London

# Contents

# Introduction

## For the teacher

This course provides a comprehensive preparation for the four components of the GCSE examination in English – writing, reading, oral communication and coursework. It is based on a close study of the syllabuses of the five examining boards and on the National Grade Criteria.

In GCSE pupils are required to show an ability in a range of different kinds of writing – from personal writing to giving instructions, from narrative to describing an event. They should be able to use formal and informal language as appropriate. They should have a sense of the audience for which they are writing. They should be encouraged to plan, draft and redraft.

In their reading, pupils should be able to detect bias, assumptions, illogical arguments and hearsay evidence. They should be able to distinguish between fact and opinion. They should be able to evaluate an argument and reformulate information in a given piece of writing for another purpose. They should be able to comment on the significant features of a text, recognise the author's standpoint and indicate the thematic development of a text.

In oral communication, pupils are required to show ability in a range of oral situations – from group and class discussion to role-playing, from interviews to giving instructions. They need to be able to speak and listen effectively. They need to be able to distinguish between formal and informal registers and the occasions when each is appropriate. They need to be able to distinguish between the power of expression and the force of the ideas expressed.

In their coursework, pupils will have to show a response to reading, to both literary and non-literary texts, including whole texts. They will have to produce examples of their best work which indicate their ability in a range of different kinds of writing.

All of these aspects – and much more – are covered in this course.

The work is arranged in fifteen units, one for each month of the five-term course. Each unit contains guidance on and practice in particular aspects of writing, reading, oral communication and coursework. Generally speaking, the work becomes progressively more difficult, following the requirements of the National Grade Criteria from Grade G to Grade A.

After each third unit, there is a test paper based on the types of examinations set by different examining boards, which provides practice for those pupils who are required to sit a written examination. Appendices covering such points as spelling, punctuation, figurative language and sentence structure are included for reference and revision.

It is possible for teachers to use the book unit by unit in the confidence that every aspect of the GCSE examination has been covered. Alternatively, they may prefer to use those sections that they feel are particularly relevant to the needs of their classes in the order that they choose. For this purpose, each section within each unit is designed to deal with a particular topic and to be largely independent. It is also possible for pupils to study individual sections on their own.

## What is GCSE English?

In the fourth and fifth years of their secondary schooling, most pupils study for the GCSE examination in English. This book, covering two years' work, is designed to help you understand what is required of you in GCSE English and therefore to meet the challenge of the course with greater success.

The first point to make about GCSE English is that it is a single unified course, involving both language and literature, speaking and writing. There is a separate English Literature examination, but candidates in English are also expected to read widely both literary and non-literary material.

The second point about GCSE English is that the course is meant to provide you with an opportunity to show what you know, understand and can do. You are unlikely to be faced with a situation where you can do nothing. The questions and tasks set offer starting points that should be accessible and comprehensible to all. You will therefore have the chance to demonstrate your achievements and abilities positively. The necessary skills can be developed over the two-year course.

Language, spoken and written, is a form of communication. It can be used for many purposes – to inform, instruct, persuade, divert, convince, interpret, evaluate, express, explain, speculate, and even (unfortunately) mislead. How you use language is therefore important. The aim of GCSE English is to provide opportunities for you to develop and demonstrate your ability to communicate. This includes communicating your ideas, knowledge, feelings and points of view orally and in writing; understanding and responding appropriately to others; reading, enjoying and responding to literature in a wide variety of ways; speaking and writing effectively and accurately.

There are four main elements in GCSE English – Writing, Reading, Oral communication and Coursework.

# *Introduction*

## For the pupil

## Writing

You will be expected to show your ability to write in a variety of styles and situations. Some of these situations may be called 'closed' – for example, the writing of letters, reports and instructions where certain information is given and conditions are set. Others will be in what may be called 'open' situations, such as narrative and imaginative and personal writing where you are free to choose. You will also have to show in writing a response to what you have read. This may be factual or imaginative. The ability to use the conventions of paragraphing, sentence structure, punctuation and spelling will be taken into consideration.

## Oral communication

You will be expected to read widely both literary and non-literary material. Literary texts include novels, short stories, poetry, plays, autobiographies. Non-literary material includes newspapers, advertisements, reports and information leaflets. You should show an ability to respond in a variety of ways to what you read.

## Reading

Speaking and listening are both part of oral communication. You will be expected to show that you can communicate effectively and appropriately in spoken English in a wide range of situations. Some of these include activities such as group discussion, giving a talk, reading aloud, role-playing, telling a story, giving a report. Others will take the form of discussion in the course of other work, such as exploring a poem or a story, discussing a topic, preparing a statement summing up your findings.

Your ability to listen carefully may be assessed by a separate aural test in which you will be asked to respond in writing to a recording of spoken material.

## Coursework

This consists of pieces of writing done during the two-year course and submitted for assessment. It should represent your best work. Requirements differ slightly between examining boards, but generally writing that displays a range of styles is required. For instance, one board specifies the following five pieces:

o   writing that shows an understanding of non-literary material and that has been produced in controlled conditions in class
o   two pieces of writing in 'closed' situations
o   two pieces of writing in 'open' situations.

Evidence of reading one whole work of literature will also be required.

Another board specifies the following four pieces of work:

o   one piece of personal, descriptive or narrative writing of at least 400 words
o   one piece of argumentative or informative writing
o   two pieces showing a response to your reading during the course.

## Assessment

In GCSE English, you will be assessed in one of the following ways, depending on the syllabus you are studying:

o   a written paper (50%) testing reading and writing plus coursework (50%)
o   coursework (100%)
o   an aural test (20%) plus a written paper (50%) plus coursework (30%)
o   an aural test (20%) plus coursework (80%)
o   written papers (80%) plus coursework (20%)
o   written papers (100%) – for 'external' candidates.

According to your ability and achievements, you are awarded Grades from A to G. The assessment for oral communication is compulsory, but it is assessed separately. It appears on the certificate as a Grade from 1 to 5. Oral communication and coursework are assessed internally (that is, by your teacher).

Syllabuses vary in their schemes of assessment, so it is important to seek guidance from your teacher about the syllabus you are studying and the scheme of assessment that applies.

There is a lot of information here to be digested, and the various points may take some time to get into focus. But don't worry, everything should become clearer as you work through the course. Refer back to this introduction from time to time to check that you understand what GCSE English is about.

# Unit One

# 1.1 Writing about personal experience

Personal experience means those things that have happened to you. The most obvious feature about an account of personal experience is that it is written in the first person. 'I was five minutes late.' 'I didn't like the way he was looking at me.' 'We all agreed it was the best party we had ever been to.'

It can be about general things such as the kind of person I am, my earliest memories, my favourite hobbies, or it can describe one particular occasion such as my first day at school, the time I got into trouble, when I was caught in a storm.

Everyone lives through similar experiences as they grow up. Yet everyone's life is different, and everyone sees and experiences events differently. For instance, everyone knows what it is like to go to school for the first time, but different things happen to different people. And even where two people experience the same thing, they will remember it and describe it differently.

When you write about your experience, you will be describing something that only you can describe. It will be unique. That is what gives writing about personal experience its freshness and interest.

When you write about personal experience you are in a sense reliving it. This can give to your writing a vividness and genuineness you may find harder to achieve when you are making up stories or outlining an argument.

What you should be aiming at then in personal writing is freshness, interest, vividness and genuineness.

But it must also be *coherent*. That means your account of personal experience must be clearly told so that a reader can easily understand and follow it. The purpose is to share your experience with the reader so that the reader knows what you went through, what your feelings were, and what it was like for you. Your account should hang together as a piece of writing and have some kind of unity.

● Here are two accounts of personal experience. In the first, David Dekon writes about himself. He was eleven at the time.

# ME

When anyone asked me to write a story or a poem or a play I always sit for such a long time thinking what to write about and in the end, if it's at school I get into trouble because I left it so long I don't write anything and if I do write I spell it all wrong and get into trouble for that, so it's just as bad anyway.

I've been kept behind at school today because I do not attend to my teacher during lessons. He told me I must write two hundred lines of three words. Look Listen and Learn. It's on the blackboard so I can spell it right. Look Listen and Learn Look Listen and Learn Look Listen and Learn Look Listen and Learn. I'm fed up. Each time my teacher said Look Listen and Learn he hit me on the head with his knuckles. That is to make it sink in. If I looked and listened all day and night I would not learn because I am a dope.

I start off listening because my teacher has a loud voice and you can't help listening to it and if he thinks I'm not listening he bangs on his desk and makes me jump and I look because sometimes his false teeth drop down a bit on some words and he makes a little slurruppy sound when he catches them up with his tongue. I long for them to fall right out on to his desk and sometimes he thinks I am interested in the lesson because I look for ages to see them drop out but he always manages to catch them up in time.

He's got hairs sticking out of his ears and when he scratches his chin they waggle in and out. I am the awfullest boy in the world because I would much rather look at his teeth drop and his hairs waggle than look at the blackboard.

My teacher is like the vicar I used to know in Kent, always on about going to heaven. I do not think I shall go to heaven because my friend isn't going. Johnny wants to see the devil and if he doesn't go to heaven I won't. Johnny is a bit more wicked than I am, sometimes I hate him and we fight but he is my best friend.

I wish there would be a power cut then I would not have to do these lines but nothing ever happens the way I want it. I have a lucky charm on a chain round my neck but it doesn't work. I always get caught out in things but Johnny never does. Once I found a shilling in the garden when we lived in Kent. I thought it was some buried treasure but I dug a big hole and did not find any more. Mom was mad about the hole, it was where she put the seeds. People get mad very easy. I expect I will have to stay in again tomorrow night because I just saw my teacher go home and I am going because there's Just William on the T.V. and he's my favourite.

━━━━ David Dekon ━━━━

1   Do you get a clear impression of the kind of person David is from this piece of writing? Sum up what you learn about him.
2   Look at each paragraph in turn, and sum up the subject matter of each. Would you describe this as a *coherent* account of personal experience? Justify your answer.
3   How would you rate this piece of writing for freshness, interest, vividness and genuiness?
4   How does the fact that the writer was eleven at the time affect your opinion of this piece of writing?

● In this account of personal experience, Esther-Yanne Lee-French writes about a house she lived in. She too was eleven when this was written.

# 35 PORTMAN STREET

We were aroused by the sound of squabbling. To see better we poked our heads through the stair banisters. Further on down we could perceive Mrs Kinti a quite attractive, tall Gambian woman shaking her fist at Birdie our West Indian ground floor neighbour.

Mrs Kinti's skin shone like polished ebony in the dim light given to her by an unshaded light bulb swinging on the landing. Her handsome face was contorted into an ugly scowl. 'How dare you, you ignorant bitch, you flea bitten monkey!'

'Ha you talk about me! You daughter of a pig, stinking de house up wid your cooking stink, stink, de place up!' Birdie retorted back. 'Always bringing de binpan when I have my meal.'

'You forget yourself, you bitch.'

Birdie forgot herself and poured out a torrent of swear words and other things to the like.

Birdie advancing on Mrs Kinti, brandishing a bottle, spurred my interfering mother into action. Between her and Mrs Kinti, the two were somehow separated and hustled into their flats like sulky children – a harmless end to a noisy quarrel (preceding ones had come to blows and pepper-throwing). Those were the great days of quarrels! – Mrs Kinti and Birdie; Mrs Kinti and Mr Kinti with knife and the police; Birdie and the Nigerian landlord, screaming insults at each other; my mother and us children – everyone quarrelled at No. 35 Portman Street!

Other memories? Jumbled they come out like this: Birdie's soup with yam and green bananas, goat's meat and dumplings; Birdie's front room crammed with frilly ornaments and gilded photographs, crucifixes and 'The Lord is in this room listening to you' notices; Birdie's shining hall – then upstairs, halfway, African rice, an indignant Mrs Kinti and an ancient leaking boiler in the bathroom; at the very top – us in a dingy leaking attic full of dark corners and posters, views down into a litter-strewn street with overgrown gardens on one side and trees – a street where half the world seemed to live and worship, opposite a Sikh temple in a crumbling house, up and down the street West Indian children, Indians, Poles, Hungarians and poor white people like us!

Yes, I can still quite easily remember No. 35 Portman Street, the road with its dirty red-brick houses, and tiny overgrown front gardens, the reddish brown of the walls contrasting with the brilliant greens of the larger back gardens across the road. Piles of dust and dirt along the roadside, rubbish fluttering in the gutters and clogging up the drains.

Inside number 35 it was no better, damp peeling wallpaper, rubbish under the bath, flaking plaster, mice, cockroaches, no hot water, I suppose it had none of the luxuries of modern life. We lived in the tiny attic with two fairly large rooms but with low ceilings. Our bedroom was at the front, and our combined kitchen, dining-room, and living-room, overlooked the spacious back garden, or jungle, which it more closely resembled, being terribly overgrown and undercared for.

We loved the kitchen, my mother would turn the gas stove on, and slowly it would heat the room until we were practically basking in the warmth, and it was possible to dream of rolling in sand on a tropical island.

It was beautiful at night to look out of the kitchen window and see a view of trees and gardens, housetops and far away lights, to see silent trees casting their ghost-like shadows onto the window pane, to watch cats flit or sneak from garden to garden like burglars on velvet paws.

The bedroom was not quite so cosy as the kitchen, although in some ways it reminded me of a hay loft because of the way the ceiling slanted down as it ran parallel with the roof. The room was absolutely cram-packed with furniture and odds and ends although surprisingly enough there was about enough room to allow four people to sleep quite comfortably. Often though when it rained we would have little streams trickling down the walls and onto the floor.

I don't miss 35 Portman Street, but it was an interesting experience.

■■■■■■■ Esther-Yanne Lee-French ■■■■■■■

5   Divide this account into different sections according to the subject matter. Give each section a heading or sub-title. Say whether you think this is a coherent account of personal experience and justify your answer.
6   What is the writer's attitude to the quarrels, the people, the area and the tiny attic?

7   How would you rate this piece for freshness, interest, vividness and genuineness?
8   Do you think the last sentence makes an effective ending to this account? Suggest an alternative last sentence.

As well as describing personal experience, it is possible to *reflect* on it. That means that you think more deeply about it. You compare your feelings now with what they were then. You see meanings in the events that you weren't aware of at the time. You draw conclusions from what happened to you.

Look again at 'Me' and '35 Portman Street'. To what extent do the writers reflect on their experience, and to what extent do they simply describe what it was like at the time?

● Now read the following piece. In the days before comprehensive schools, children aged eleven sat the eleven-plus exam to decide who went to grammar schools. The exam still exists in some areas. Lynette Halewood was sixteen when she wrote this piece.

# ■ ELEVEN PLUS AND MINUS ■

It was an ordinary, blustery day, that could have belonged to any season of the year. The village was curled up like a cat in its basket, one eye open. It was just an ordinary anything day, and I did not hurry, since it was early yet. Kicking at pebbles and watching the disconsolate seagulls drift by, I idly went on my way.

School, when I arrived, seemed somehow more alive than usual. There was an excited, expectant buzz in the playground. Suddenly, three boys came rushing out of the doorway at the bottom of the boys' stairs, screaming, 'They've come, they've come!' 'I've passed!' and creating an immediate stir.

'What's happened?' I yelled at them. They were in my class, so it was all right, I could talk to them.

One of them stopped, generously, even though I was a girl, and said, 'The eleven plus results – you've passed, too.' For a moment I stared at him, wondering if I dared trust him. Then I walked around the corner, leaving the playground to the ten-year-olds and their gossip, and, as soon as I was out of sight, pelted up the outside iron stairs that the girls had to use (the boys had a different, inside stairway) faster than any eleven-year-old had gone before.

Mrs Horton was sitting in her chair, beaming maternally. 'You've passed,' she boomed out, with a great quivering of chins, before being inundated with thousands of questions from newly-arrived pupils.

All my friends had passed too. The shock and the sudden joy hit us, and quite literally knocked us silly. Shrieking and giggling, we passed the news around, yelling over the pandemonium that existed in our normally quiet, orderly classroom. As usual, more girls than boys had passed ... what grammar school would we go to, we wondered.

Not everyone shared in this rejoicing. Those who had known from the outset that they would never pass shrugged their shoulders philosophically and took advantage of the disorder to throw pieces of chalk at the blackboard and each other. And, of course, there were the in-betweens – the ones who might have passed.

Michael Hamilton was one of these. At the moment he was perched on the windowsill, sullenly watching the seagulls. He had not passed; his friends had. They were joining in the general merriment.

He turned his head and deigned to notice me. He had always disliked me, because I was a girl. Last summer, when the girls had gathered in corners to tell secrets, to giggle and pass round the discreet booklets that Brenda's mother had given to her, explaining 'Where babies come from' (we were unimpressed, as I remember), we laughed at the boys in their goose-berry-bush ignorance, and told them to go away. We were children, just beginning to grow, and we loved to tease with childish spite, or perhaps with the beginnings of the feminine love of being knowingly, secretively superior to the opposite sex.

Michael was furiously angry, but did not know what to say. Looking back now I can see how every laugh in the room must have seemed to be directed at him: at the time, with a child's simplicity, I thought it was just because he was a boy being beaten by a girl.

'You're snobs!' he called out, shrilly.

So, now a second great division had opened up between us. I was a snob: all grammar school children were snobs, automatically. 'Snobs!' he yelled accusingly, and other voices joined in.

His friends did not join in the shouting. You cannot play with your friends in future, if they have been proved cleverer than you, if they go to the grammar school and you to the secondary school. It was an unwritten, unbreakable law: the thing lay between you, like an ocean, but with frozen waves of broken glass, uncrossable.

'Who wants to go to a grammar school?' he yelled, scornfully, defiantly. He did. I said nothing: I stared at him, knowing it, and he stared at me, knowing it too.

I did not understand until some time later why he ran away, out of the claustrophobic classroom, just then. Being a boy, he should not have cried; that was a feminine luxury. I had yet to learn that such rules as these may apply in public, but not in private.

■■■■■■■■■ Lynette Halewood ■■■■■■■■■

9   What view of the eleven-plus exam and its effect do you get from this account?

10  Explain how the title sums up what happens in this piece of writing.

11  Look at the description of Mrs Horton. It is short and yet the writer gives the reader a vivid account. What do you learn about her?

12  Pick out some of the words and descriptive phrases the writer uses to describe the feeling of excitement.

13  Point out the sections of this account where the

writer reflects on her experience. What things does the writer see in the experience which she didn't realise at the time?

It is possible that none of these pieces of writing is true. The writers may have made it all up. But the writing certainly gives the impression of being about real experience and personal thoughts and feelings. Perhaps things or people or places weren't exactly as the writers describe them. Perhaps the dialogue the writers use wasn't exactly like that. It doesn't matter, so long as the writing makes the experience come over vividly and convincingly.

There are suggestions in these accounts that could help you in writing about your own personal experience:

o   try to see it as it was
o   picture it in your mind as you write
o   describe the people and the places, your feelings and thoughts
o   use detail to make it convincing and real
o   use dialogue (but not too much) to bring it alive
o   use words and comparisons to create the right images
o   make sure your account is planned and coherent
o   where appropriate, reflect on the experience.

 ### 1.1.1 Writing about personal experience – coursework

Write about one of the following:

1   'First Day' – it might be at play-group, infant school, junior school, secondary school, a part-time job. We all experience a series of first days. *Either* describe one of your own 'first days', remembering what you thought and felt at the time and how you coped with the situation. *Or* recall a number of your first days, describe how they went and reflect on whether they become easier through experience.

2   Were you ever lost as a child? What happened and how did you feel? Write a detailed account.

3   Anger, jealousy, joy, sorrow, malice, disappointment, envy, pride. *Either* choose *one* of these emotions and describe an occasion when you experienced it. *Or* choose *three* of these emotions and describe your experience of them. Try to recall your feelings and thoughts at the time. What situations called forth these particular emotions and how were the situations resolved?

4   'A Helping Hand'. Write an account of an occasion when you helped someone or when someone helped you, and say how that affected your relationship with that person.

5   Think about a place or places you have a particular affection for. It may be a house you have lived in or somewhere you have visited or an area that has special associations for you. Describe the place or places fully, other people connected with them, and explore why you feel the way you do.

# 1.2 Presentation of coursework

You must be very careful to keep all the written work you do during the two-year course because towards the end of the fifth or beginning of the sixth term you and/or your teacher will be required to make a selection of your best work for assessment.

The kind of work selected will depend on the syllabus you are following. Make sure you are clear about its requirements. Check with your teacher. The more pieces you have written, the more you have to choose from, and the bigger chance there is of making a selection that shows your capabilities. If you do not present the required amount of coursework, you will automatically lose marks.

When the final selection is made, your pieces of writing will be tagged together with a front sheet supplied by the examining board. On this front sheet, you will have to give details of the titles of the pieces, the type of assignment, and the authors and titles of texts referred to. You will also have to detail the conditions under which the writing was produced (e.g. in class/for homework), the date on which the piece was written or handed in, and the time allowed, or taken, for the task.

The work submitted must be in your own hand-writing. It must be the version given to the teacher for marking and must have evidence of the teacher's assessment. Fair copies, rewritten after the teacher's marking, will not be accepted unless accompanied by the original work. You will have to sign a declaration that the work presented is your own unaided work.

Details vary slightly from syllabus to syllabus. Again, check with your teacher.

It follows from all this that the way you set out your work is important. It is probably best to use A4 file paper. On every piece of written work you do, put the date, your name, the title and type of assignment, the conditions under which it was written and the time taken. Get into the habit of doing this regularly or it could lead to confusion and difficulties.

Above all, keep your written work in a file or somewhere safe. It could be disastrous if you were to lose it.

o   Make sure you understand these instructions and requirements.
o   Make a summary of the coursework requirements and presentation details specified by the syllabus you are taking.

# 1.3 The basics of writing

Since writing is a form of communication, it is important to make sure that you get rid of any obstacles that threaten effective communication. Such obstacles include bad spelling, poor sentence structure, inadequate punctuation and non-existent paragraphing.

## 1.3.1 Spelling

The spelling of English words is difficult – partly because of the way words have developed, and partly because so many words have come into English from other languages. There are some rules, but also many exceptions. Pronunciation doesn't always help. But it is not impossible to learn to spell correctly.

First of all, get to know how to spell the words you use. On average, you might use three thousand words regularly in your writing. Does that sound a lot? It isn't really. Some of these words you will use only occasionally; others you will use time and time again. With care and concentration, it should be possible to learn how to spell these words and get them right every time.

Secondly, get to know the words you usually get wrong. All of us have words we are unsure about. We write down a version that we hope will be right and leave it at that. But that's not good enough. Find out the correct spellings and learn them. Then every time you use those words in the future, stop and think and write down the correct version.

The important thing is to use your eyes. Really see the words on the page when you are writing and when you are reading.

Equally important is to use a dictionary. Helping as it does with spelling and shades of meaning, a dictionary is an essential tool in English. It is as important to a writer as a slide rule is to an architect.

Finally, learning to spell demands effort. Many people find it difficult. They have to work at it. There are some rules, but for the most part you just have to sit down and learn it.

(For a reminder of the basic rules of spelling, see Appendix A.)

## 1.3.2 Sentence structure

When we speak, we often hesitate and break off in the middle of an idea and repeat ourselves and get lost in our line of thought, but usually we speak in statements that other people can understand. We may not always speak in sentences, but what we say usually makes sense and is communicated to a listener.

It is this idea you should try to develop when you are writing. As you write, catch the tone of voice you are using, say the words to yourself, and listen to the 'soundtrack' in your head. Then, as one statement is completed, use a full stop to show that it is completed, before going on to the next one.

When you are talking, it is unlikely that you will rush on without pause from one idea to another, from one statement to another. You will need to pause to take breath, or to emphasise what you are saying. You will need to pause to show that you are moving on to a different statement or idea. These pauses are full stops.

If by any chance you do rush on headlong without pausing when you talk, a listener will probably have difficulty understanding you. It is the same in writing. A piece of writing without pauses or full stops is difficult to decipher.

● Look at the following passages. Because the sentences are not clearly indicated by full stops, it takes effort to make out the meaning. Try to establish the tone of voice the writer is using, say the words to yourself, listen to the 'soundtrack' in your head. Then rewrite the passages using full stops and other punctuation marks where appropriate.

## A

I was feeling nervous I didn't know what I was doing well it was the first time I'd been to a disco and as if that wasn't enough Loretta was going to be there the very thought made my head spin would she let me dance with her would she let me buy her a Coke would she let me walk her home afterwards probably not I'd be lucky if she even spoke to me

## B

If you travel up Barnet Hill and turn left at the church you come to Arkley the village popular with commuters who want to combine the tranquillity of the countryside with easy access to London borders the main road between Barnet and the A1 running into this main road on either side are lanes and avenues and around them lies farmland with uninterrupted views across open countryside many of the houses are indeed what may be called desirable residences looking across the green fields dotted with cows and horses it is difficult to realise that the centre of London is only thirteen miles away

(For a reminder about sentence structure, see Appendix B.)

### 1.3.3 Punctuation

As with sentence structure, using punctuation correctly helps the reader understand more easily what you have written. Again, it is a case of listening to the 'soundtrack' in your head, and knowing when the pauses and changes in emphasis require a comma or a semi-colon or a colon in order to make sure that what you want to say is clear to the reader.

● Sometimes, inadequate punctuation results in ambiguity, and the reader can't be sure what you (the writer) mean. Look at the following examples. How could punctuation help to make the meaning clear?

1  The shop sold bread rolls and pastries.
2  She was horrified to hear there was a man eating tiger in the area.
3  Next time I go to the library, I'm going to see if Jane Eyre is there.
4  The artist said the critic was better at oils than at watercolours.
5  This painting cost me £20 more than I am likely to get if I try to sell it.
6  Joe the milkman has forgotten to leave two pints this morning.
7  Outside the house appeared to be in good condition.
8  Jean is studying English history and physics at A level.
9  To Tony Boyle's Law is a complete mystery.
10  Look at the top of the hill there is a tower.

● The following examples are also inadequately punctuated. Rewrite them so that they make sense.

11  John stopped at the pavement and carefully looked both ways the road was empty.
12  The man the one with the rolled-up newspaper was hurrying across the street.
13  You need some help it was a question not a statement.
14  Stop that at once roared the shop-keeper.
15  The contents of the box were as follows four moth-eaten books with faded covers a heap of magazines with loose pages a notebook of some kind that had worn leather binding a sheaf of closely-typed pages dog-eared and smudged.
16  It was raining hard, we didn't have an umbrella.
17  The exhibition contained many fine paintings. Ranging from the eighteenth-century to the present.
18  One of the most famous lines in all Shakespeare said the teacher is To be or not to be.
19  My next-door neighbour who has always been very pleasant has suddenly stopped talking to me.
20  English contains words from many different languages Greek Latin French Italian Spanish and so on.

(For a reminder of the use of punctuation marks, see Appendix C.)

### 1.3.4 Paragraphing

It is very off-putting for readers to be faced with page after page of uninterrupted type or writing. Readers need to have what they are reading broken down into smaller more manageable sections or paragraphs so that it does not appear too demanding. At the same time, paragraphing can help readers follow the writer's line of thought.

Paragraphs indicate stages in an argument or a dramatic situation. When the writer moves on to another aspect of the argument or a new idea or the next step in a story, a new paragraph should be used. This is a way of alerting the reader. It allows the reader a moment's pause to take stock of what has just been read before going on to the next paragraph, knowing that the argument or the narrative is being advanced.

● Look at the following passages. Divide each of them into three paragraphs and justify the way you have divided them.

### ━━━━ A ━━━━

He moved carefully round the garden. The darkness hid his movements, and there were no unexpected obstacles to block his way. Yet, he went carefully, making sure his footsteps made no noise and keeping under cover of the trees. The house was still some distance away, but he was slowly advancing on it. There were no lights showing at the windows, and no noise came from within. All was dark and quiet. The building, now almost within touch, was a silent shadow against the night sky. And then the front door suddenly burst open, and light splashed out onto the forecourt.

### ━━━━ B ━━━━

Even today, with women's lib, housework is definitely considered to be women's work. Sometimes a man will help, but even in families where husband and wife both have jobs, responsibility for looking after the home still usually rests with the woman. A recent survey showed that 90% of all housework is still done by women. It is a job that has many disadvantages. For a start, it is a solitary occupation. There are none of the social compensations that people get from even the most repetitive jobs outside the home. The hours are unsocial (you never finish!). You don't normally get paid for it. All you get is your board and lodgings and some money to help you do the job. Where men do give a hand in the home, it is by doing specific jobs such as bringing in the coal or cleaning shoes or DIY jobs. They do things like change plugs or clean cars. They may cook one particular meal a week or help with the weekly shopping. But they don't hoover, dust, polish, change sheets, wash clothes, iron, wash dishes, or in general cook meals. Most men would feel insulted to be asked to do so. Such things are not man's work.

(For guidelines on paragraphing, see Appendix D.)

#  1.4 Reading – the main ideas in a text

When you are looking for the main ideas in a text, you have to weigh up one statement against another. You have to distinguish between main statements and illustrative examples. You have to decide whether one statement is simply putting the idea in a different way or whether it is introducing an important new idea.

The *title*, if there is one, can give you a clue.

*Paragraphing* can be a guide. Usually, when writers move on to a new idea, they move on to a new paragraph.

*Topic sentences* can help. A topic sentence is a sentence in a paragraph which in a way announces or sums up what the paragraph is about. It can often be the first or the last sentence of the paragraph, though not all paragraphs have topic sentences.

1  Consider the following passages. State the main idea or ideas in each. Say whether there is a topic sentence.

### ━━━━ A ━━━━

Sarah's whole body was tense and listening. It was very dark in the room but a faint line of sunlight showed through the weave of the blanket at the top of the window. She heard a rumble in the distance, a great wave of sound that came sweeping towards her, engulfing everything in its path, drowning Catherine's cries. Sarah blundered towards the fragile edge of light as the blast struck the house.

Roof tiles smashed and the windows were blown inward. Books and ornaments and light fittings crashed and fell in the upstairs rooms. In the howling darkness the mattress sagged and the bookcase started to topple. The black human shape that was Veronica screamed at her to help. But Sarah was already there, moved by her instinct, exerting force against force. The blanket tore at its nails, came loose at one corner. Heat screamed through the crack. Sarah had one brief glimpse of devastation, a hurricane of tearing trees and whirling leaves, the sky gone dark and lurid with fire, before the wind passed over them and things sank back into stillness.

■ From Louise Lawrence, *Children of the Dust* ■

## B

### Brakes fault on death bus

A WORN rubber seal in a school bus's br aking system could have been to blame for a teenager's death, an inquest heard yesterday.

Doctor's son Kes Somasunderam, 13, died after the 14-year-old runaway coach ploughed into him at a bus stop in Nether Hampton, near Salisbury.

His school friend Sorrel Marchant, also 13, was injured. The Salisbury inquest was told the bus's brakes failed, although they had been checked a few weeks beforehand after earlier trouble.

Verdict : Accidental death.

## C

### Boring sport

I am writing to complain about the lousy trick the BBC has just pulled on the long-suffering public, including me. You publish RADIO TIMES one week in advance with all the programmes laid out ready for us to plan our week's viewing, then almost without warning the BBC cancels shows which we wanted to see and substitutes instead boring sport.

I am complaining about the postponing of the film *Blood Money* on 7 February (BBC1). If cricket fans wanted to sit up all night to watch the match, they were welcome to do so, but why knock films off in order to start sport earlier?

(Mr) C. Orunn

Barnsley, South Yorkshire

2 Look at the following extract. What are the main facts and main ideas? (The answer could be written or oral.)

Only the unemployed can really describe what they feel. In a society dedicated to work, it is obviously a blow to pride, to self-esteem and to people's sense of identity to be jobless. There is also a financial problem involved. Unemployment pay, in the overwhelming majority of cases, is less than the wages people would have earned had they been working. In turn, this means that they cannot buy things that other families have; be they food, clothes, drink, holidays, cars, fridges, or television sets. Nowadays such items are not luxuries and people believe that they have a right to them. In other words, the unemployed are cut off from the normal expectations of society.

As the entire social system is work-orientated, so, being without work often leads to loss of purpose. Too many people feel useless and of no value to society, and this feeling grows stronger the longer unemployment lasts. Initially there may be a sense of freedom and, if there is a redundancy payment, some available cash, but once a holiday or house decorating or car repairs are done, depression sets in. Indeed, real clinical depression may result.

Research in the USA by Dr Harvey Brenner, which is being repeated in Britain, suggests that there is a significant connection between some forms of ill-health and unemployment. Alcoholism, cirrhosis of the liver, heart disease, and mental hospital admissions, all rise in times of high unemployment. Serious crime may increase also. Families come under strain too. This is caused partly by inadequate income, partly because people are with each other all the time, with little respite, and partly because of depression.

Society is very work, not leisure orientated, so that there is not very much the unemployed can do – even if they have money. Many leisure activities, cinemas or pubs for example, require money and many sports need a lot of equipment. In any event, the attitude of the British is so work conscious that leisure, in the words of an unemployed young man from Newcastle, 'is a waste of time'. This is compounded by people getting many of their social contacts and outlets through work. In pre-industrial days leisure and work were mixed. Today, leisure is increasingly pursued within the home, especially watching TV. Unemployment cuts a person off from the elements which, in years gone by, he or she would have had alternative means of reaching.

An unusually high percentage of men die within one year after retirement, and it is often suggested (though never proved) that this is because they then feel useless. Work becomes a yardstick by which people measure their position in society. The unemployed face similar problems. Young men and women today are brought up with the idea that they will spend their life working. Clearly, for these young people there are psychological as well as financial difficulties to being without a job.

Boredom, resentment and humiliation would seem to sum up the effects of no job. The riots in the British inner cities of Toxteth, Brixton and Moss Side in the spring of 1981 were the symptoms of this underlying disease. Older people have already felt the weight of life's disappointments, younger ones have not, and are both less resigned and have more energy. Their loss of ideals can lead to violence. Perhaps the surprise is not that these riots took place, but that they took so long in coming, given the importance of believing that work is almost everything.

From Barrie Sherman, *Freedom from Work*

3 Discuss the ideas given here in groups or as a class. How convincing do you find them? What are your own views on unemployment? You could think about the following:

a What is the employment situation in your area?
b Why do you think so many people are unemployed?
c Are unemployed people just work-shy?
d What problems might an unemployed person face?
e Do you know people who are unemployed? What do they feel and how do they cope?
f What do you know about 'the Puritan work ethic'?
g What do you understand by 'the dignity of labour'?
h Is 'enforced leisure' a good idea?
i Do you think your prospects of getting a job are good or not?
j What do you think can be done to create more employment?

◀ *This could be used for oral assessment.* ▶

# 1.5 Reading – kinds of writing

Writing can be broadly divided into three categories – writing that has an expressive intent, writing that has a persuasive intent and writing that has an expository intent.

Writing with an *expressive* intent originates in the imagination and feelings, and acts on the imagination and feelings. Examples of this kind of writing are novels, short stories and poems.

Writing with a *persuasive* intent is writing that attempts to influence your views and opinions. Advertisements, newspaper editorials and political manifestos are examples.

Writing with an *expository* intent deals with facts and information. Examples are news reports, travel guides, cookery books and information pamphlets.

It is important to be aware of the differences between these three types of writing, to be able to distinguish between fact and fiction and between news and opinion.

1 Give further examples of types of writing that could be called expressive, persuasive and expository.

2 Look at the following passages. Say what type of writing you think each comes from and to which of the three categories – expressive, persuasive, expository – each belongs.

## A

When Lila went out on the beach it was so early in the morning that there was no one else there. The sand was washed clean by last night's tide and no one had walked on it except the birds that fished along the coast – gulls, curlews and sandpipers. She walked down to the sea with the small basket she carried on the flat of her hand, filled with flowers she had plucked from the garden around their house – scarlet hibiscus blooms, sweet-smelling spider lilies and bright butter-yellow allamanda flowers.

From Anita Desai, *The Village by the Sea*

## B

**6.35** **Crossroads** Sam Benson seeks out Nicola Freeman in the hope that impending expulsion from the motel will rekindle their dead romance.

**7.00** **This Is Your Life** Eamonn Andrews goes to Hollywood clutching the red book, and searching for English actor victims.

**7.30** **Coronation Street** Lover Alan Bradley makes a belated discovery that it is Rita Fairclough's birthday. She goes coy about her age and declines a present but gracefully allows him to cook her a meal.

From TV guide, *London Daily News*

## C

# All those in favour of keeping the dog licence sign here:

According to the latest figures, an estimated 200,000 dogs are registered as strays each year: over 40% are destroyed. So, lack of Government action will condemn to death another 80,000 unwanted dogs in the next 12 months.

Now the Government intends to abolish the dog licence as part of new legislation currently going through Parliament.

Don't let the Government turn its back on the stray dog problem. Support the RSPCA's Charter for Responsible Dog Ownership. For your free Information Pack, simply fill in the coupon and return it to: RSPCA, FREEPOST, Northampton, NN4 0BR. Or better still, telephone (0604) 767676 now.

RT5
I want to know more about the RSPCA's Charter for Responsible Dog Ownership. Please send me my free Information Pack.

Name:_____

Address:_____

_____

_____ Postcode_____

RSPCA, FREEPOST, Northampton, NN4 0BR. Freepost means we pay the postage but if you could use a stamp more of our precious funds will be available to prevent cruelty to animals.

Registered Charity No. 219099

**D**

# Pensioner dies alone without a scrap of food

HOUSEBOUND pensioner Doris McKone died alone in her one-roomed New Barnet flat without a scrap of food—five weeks after her worried landlord had begged social workers to help her.

Miss McKone, 64, was found lying in her Warwick Road flat surrounded by rubbish and next to a bucket she had been forced to use as a toilet because she was too frail to tackle the three steps to her bathroom.

And this week landlord David Edgecumbe demanded to know why his pleas for help in the month before she died went unanswered by the Barnet social services.

He told The Press he had repeatedly asked staff in the council's Lytton Road office in New Barnet to contact him and arrange for a home help and meals on wheels for Miss McKone.

**E**

# PRESS OPINION

LANDLORD David Edgecumbe is a very bitter man this week.

And he has every reason to be. With the best of intentions he did all he could to help a frail old woman, only to be frustrated by red tape.

Understandably he's angry and feels that Barnet social services should shoulder the blame for her sad and lonely death in a bedsit.

But council spokesman Bill White explained that social workers can't force their attention on people. Whatever their plight, individuals still have the right to say no.

But it still raises the question of what sort of society allows its old folk to end their days as did Doris McKone.

It's a sad fact of modern life that, to many families, the elderly are an embarrassment, to be shunned or put away.

For a supposedly civilised society, we could learn a lot from the Hindus and Muslims in our midst. They look after their old folk in a way that puts the rest of us to shame.

# 1.6 Oral assessment

Your oral skills will be assessed by your teacher. Over the two years of your course, you will be given many opportunities to show your skills in oral communication in a wide range of situations and assignments. Your teacher will be making notes and reports on these and assessing them so as to arrive at a final grade for you.

Different teachers have different ways of keeping records. The kinds of skills required vary from one oral assignment to another. But over the whole range of oral communication, all teachers will be looking for and judging the following aspects:

○ content and presentation of ideas
○ delivery
○ interaction with others
○ appropriateness
○ relevance
○ ability to listen and respond appreciatively
○ ability to communicate ideas and feelings
○ ability to tell a story
○ ability to present a point of view
○ ability to discuss a point of view
○ ability to ask questions
○ ability to answer questions
○ ability to describe a process.

1  Explain in your own words what each of these means and the difference between them.
2  Which of these aspects do you think are particularly relevant to group discussion?

●  It could be useful to tape, transcribe and assess your own group discussion or to present your group discussion to the class for comment, using the guidelines set out above.

# 1.7 Group discussion

In group discussion, you will be expected to discuss a subject with four or five other pupils for about fifteen minutes.

Pupils may choose their own groups or these may be organised by your teacher. Each group should be representative of the class as a whole. The best arrangement is for the group to sit in a circle so that everyone can see everyone else – perhaps round a table in the library or round desks pushed together. The subject chosen must be one that members of the group know something about. It can help if you do some research so that you have ideas to contribute – find topical examples in newspapers, keep an eye on TV news reports and documentaries, check reference books in the library, and note down points that may be useful. Always remember that group discussion is a cooperative activity in which every member of the group must share.

Here are some suggestions that could help you:

o  make sure that what you say is relevant
o  give illustrations, examples and personal experiences that support your arguments
o  listen to what others say
o  respond to what others say
o  don't monopolise the discussion or allow others to do so
o  where appropriate, take the lead or move the discussion on to another aspect of the subject
o  question statements that are not clear.

Use this checklist to assess your own performance and that of your group.

● Form groups of five or six. Three of you choose one of the following subjects while the rest make notes with reference to the checklist above on how the talkers perform. Then swop round and choose a different subject. You might consider the best and worst points of each speaker.

1  Space exploration
2  Conservation
3  The role of the police
4  Local amenities for young people
5  Women's lib
6  The value of television

Prepare your chosen subject. Discuss it in your group.

◄  *This could be used for oral assessment.*  ►

# Unit Two

 # 2.1 Writing narrative

A narrative is a story, a fictional account of events. Usually, these events are presented in a way that convinces the reader that they could actually have happened, although sometimes stories can be deliberately absurd or fantastic. In most stories, there are three important elements – characters, setting and plot.

*Characters* These are the people the story is about; the people involved in the events, who set them in motion and influence the direction they take; the people who are affected by what happens and who change as a result (or fail to change).

*Setting* This is where the events of the story take place – the background, which can have an effect on the events and the characters involved in them.

*Plot* This is what happens in the story – the events, the action, the stages of development. Many plots are based on conflict, contrast, action and reaction, cause and effect.

For a story to be interesting and for it to achieve what the writer intended, it must be plausible. This means that you have to make the reader believe in the characters, the setting and the plot of your story. How do you achieve this?

For other people to 'see' and 'know' the characters and setting you describe in your story, you must yourself 'see' and 'know' them. The more you have thought about your characters and setting, the more you know them in real detail, then the more you will be able to persuade others to see them as well. (One well-known writer of short stories, William Trevor, often writes seventy pages about his characters before reducing these to the ten pages of the final story.)

The easiest way to make your story plausible is to write about something that you already know. Base what you write on people you know, set them in places that are familiar to you, use incidents that have happened to you. You don't have to follow all the real-life details slavishly: simply use some of them as a starting-off point and develop them in your own way.

Before you write, think about the following:

○ What are you trying to do in your story? In a sense, when you write a story, you are saying something to your readers. It could be a moral point about which you feel strongly. It could be about how you think certain people would react to a particular situation. It could be something you think is amusing. Be clear about what the 'point' of your story is.

○ What kind of story is it to be? There is a wide variety of types of stories to choose from: realistic, comic, horror, science fiction, satirical, romantic, etc. Be clear about the kind of story you are planning to write.

○ From whose point of view is the story to be told? Will the events be seen through the eyes of:

One particular character (in which case, will you use the first person: 'I knew something disastrous was going to happen. . .'; or the third person: 'She knew something disastrous was going to happen. . .'?)
More than one character (shifting from one person's point of view to another's)
An objective detached observer (in other words, you describe the events as if you were looking at them from the outside, not through the eyes of anyone in particular)?

Be clear from whose point of view you are telling the story, and stick to it.

○ Think carefully about the three elements of your story:
*Characters*: Make them interesting, show what their thoughts and feelings are, provide a rounded picture of them. (For further advice on describing people, see section 5.1.)
*Setting*: Make it relevant to the story, bring it to life. This can be done as easily in a few words or lines as it can in long descriptions. (For further advice on describing places, see section 6.1.)
*Plot*: Keep it simple and plausible, think about conflict, action and reaction, why one thing causes a person to act in a certain way, etc. (For further information on describing events, see section 7.1.)

 ### 2.1.1 Writing narrative – coursework

Choose one of the following:

1 Write a story which begins: 'How could she ever forgive him?'
2 Write a story in which a particular character is important. It could be an old man or a tiresome child or a treacherous friend.
3 Write a story in which the setting is important. It could be about someone starting at a new school or someone visiting a strange town or someone leaving to move to a new house.
4 Write a story based on one of the following:

a Conflict (for example, a story about a daughter and her father who disagree about a friend she has made)
b Contrast (for example, a story involving someone who is well off and someone who is poor)
c Action and reaction (for example, a story about someone who shoplifts and gets caught)
d Cause and effect (for example, a story about someone who tells a lie and the effect of that on someone else).

5 Write a story with the title 'What a thing to say!' or 'On Second thoughts' or 'A hollow victory'.

 # 2.2 Writing – beginning and ending

How you begin and end a piece of writing is important. This is true not just of stories but of any kind of writing. (It applies also to many aspects of oral communication.)

If you want people to read what you have written, you have to catch their attention at the very beginning. Think it out first. Get to the point straightaway. Say something that will tickle the readers' curiosity and make them want to read on.
Here are some suggestions for beginnings:

○ a question
○ a quotation
○ a piece of dialogue
○ a striking image
○ a controversial statement
○ a dramatic description
○ an anecdote.

● Comment on each of the following beginnings to newspaper articles and say whether or not you think each is effective. What do you think these articles are about?

1 'Jack Solomons used to have a clause written into world title fight contracts that the participants were not allowed to drive a car in the week before the championship bout.' (John Rodda, *The Guardian*)
2 'My grandson, Charlie, aged six, is much given to using the word wicked, pronounced wick-id, when expressing enthusiasm for something or someone.' (Beryl Bainbridge, *The London Evening Standard*)
3 'If we strip cricket back to its bleached bones and abandon the frills and fripperies of marketing, then there can be no finer sight in the game than a great fast bowler in full cry.' (Mike Selvey, *The Guardian*)
4 'When Henry Ford created his first mass-produced car he offered his customers a choice. "You can have any colour you like," he said, "as long as it's black."' (Deirdre McQuillan, *The Telegraph Sunday Magazine*)

● Each of the following is the beginning of a story by Katherine Mansfield. Say whether or not you think each is an effective beginning. Speculate on what each of these stories may be about.

6 'Something's happened to me – something bad. And I don't know what to do about it.'

7 'He really was an impossible person. Too shy altogether. With absolutely nothing to say for himself.'

8 'In the afternoon the chairs came, a whole big cart full of little gold ones with their legs in the air.'

9 'She was just beginning to walk along a little white road with tall black trees on either side, a little road that led to nowhere, and where nobody walked at all, when a hand gripped her shoulder, shook her, slapped her ear.'

10 'It was his fault, wholly and solely his fault, that they had missed the train.'

● Suggest an opening sentence for each of the following and indicate why you think each of your suggestions is effective:

11 An essay on pollution;
12 An account of a tennis match or an athletics event;
13 A story about a lost child;
14 An essay supporting or attacking corporal punishment;
15 A review of a novel or a film.

When you end a piece of writing, you want to leave the readers feeling that the effort of reading has been worthwhile and leave them thinking and reflecting over what they have read. The way you end a piece of writing is vital in achieving this effect. Don't simply repeat what you have already said in a kind of summing up.

Here are suggestions for endings:

○ a question
○ a surprise
○ a point that prompts further thought
○ a sudden stop that brings the readers up short and makes them reconsider what they have read
○ a statement that implies rather than states
○ a quotation
○ an image that stays in the mind and epitomises the feeling of the story.

● Comment on each of the following endings to newspaper articles and say whether or not you think each is effective. What form do you think each of these articles may have taken?

1 'In a run-up to a general election when 6.2 million young people will be voting for the first time, the government would do well to listen to us.' (Vicky Phillips, President, National Union of Students, *Today*)

2 'Then that sad, world-weary look came back into his eyes once more.' (John Blake, *Daily Mirror*)

3 'To sum up, there is a clear-cut case for contemplating investments on the Spanish stockmarket, but it would be as well to keep in mind that to be abroad is great but to risk going overboard would be quite another matter.' (Bill Richards, *The Guardian*)

4 'A climate of private affluence and public squalor is not much of a memorial for any Chancellor to leave behind him.' (*The Observer*)

● Each of the following is the ending of a story by Katherine Mansfield. Say whether or not you think each of them makes an effective ending. Speculate on what each of these stories may be about.

5 'The box that the fur came out of was on the bed. She unclasped the necklet quickly; quickly, without looking, laid it inside. But when she put the lid on she thought she heard something crying.'

6 'The voices murmured, murmured. They were never still. But so great was his heavenly happiness as he stood there he wished he might live for ever.'

7 'Blushing more crimson than ever, but looking at her severely he said, almost angrily: "Excuse me, Mademoiselle, you dropped this."
And he handed her an egg.'

8 'Then she got up, changed the plates, and went to the larder for the pudding. Do you know what the pudding was? Well, of course, it wouldn't mean anything to you. It was my favourite – the kind she only made me on special occasions – honeycomb cream. . .'

9 'Then both were silent once more.'

● Suggest an ending for each of the following and indicate what effect your ending has in each case.

10 An essay on newspapers.
11 A description of a country walk.
12 A story about a child who has stormed out of the house after a quarrel but who decides to go back.
13 An essay supporting or attacking school uniform.
14 An account of your favourite hobby.

 # 2.3 Reading – making a summary

Making a summary is similar to picking out and restating the main points (see section 1.4), but in this section the passages are longer and the final result should be a polished piece of writing. When in 'real life' do you think it could be useful to make a summary?

When making a summary, careful reading of the original piece of writing is essential. It should be read once straight through to get the general meaning. Then a second time, and possibly a third, following the argument or exposition step by step. You should now be able to isolate the main points of the piece from other material which may be padding or repetition, supporting evidence or digression. During the next reading, write down the main points in note form. Numbering them as you go along may help.

You now have to reproduce the main points in a piece of writing of your own. The points should be clearly presented, but your piece should also read well in its own right. Using linking devices (see section 5.3) could help to make your writing flow more smoothly.

*Don't add any ideas of your own.* The point of a summary is to reproduce accurately what the writer is saying but in a shorter form. It is not an excuse for you to show off your own knowledge.

As far as you can, *use your own words.* This is not always possible, especially if the piece uses technical words or phrases which it would be difficult or awkward to express in any other way. But one of the aims of an exercise like this is to test whether or not you have understood the piece of writing. If you simply stitch together phrases here and there from the original, it is difficult to know how much you have really understood.

1   Read the following piece of writing. It is an introductory article about a TV *Horizon* programme that appeared in *Radio Times.* Make a summary of the main points, using between 100 and 120 words.

# Earth in Peril

When the world's environmental experts met in London earlier this year for a debate on the state of the planet, *Horizon's* cameras were there to record the arguments. GEOFFREY LEAN recalls the proceedings and the verdict

THE ARGUMENTS were over, the evidence in and our eyes turned to the Bench for a pronouncement of innocence or guilt. But the verdict was broader. 'What has become very clear,' said the judge, 'is that all of us are on trial.'

Not a common confession from a judge, but this was no ordinary hearing. We had been called to a special tribunal to learn the fate not of a lone figure in the dock, but of Planet Earth itself.

The charge was murder, the slow, relentless destruction of the life-support systems that sustain our small blue-green oasis in the limitless black wilderness of space.

We witnesses were called from 40 countries to the appropriately pompous leather and marble council chamber of London's County Hall by the United Nations Environmental Programme.

The evidence was devastating. It takes at least 3,000 years to form fertile topsoil, but we are turning it rapidly into dust. By the end of the century a third of it will be gone.

By then, too, said another expert, a fifth of the world's species of animals and plants will be extinct, tearing a hole in the web of life that could be as significant to mankind as a potential nuclear holocaust.

Thor Heyerdahl warned that the oceans were in peril, 'having spent a good deal of time on the ocean, with my nose very close to the surface, sometimes much closer than I would have liked.'

David Attenborough estimated: 'We have something like 20 years before there is a major catastrophe.' And Sir Peter Scott, the elder statesman of wildlife conservation, said: 'Man is the ultimately endangered species.'

But the evidence was not only one way. A Japanese told how a public revolt about the air pollution in Tokyo had led to it becoming one of the world's cleaner big cities.

And plenty of Third World spokesmen described effective campaigns by the poorest of the poor. There was Sunderlal Bahuguna, an unstoppable Gandhian who has marched thousands of miles through the Himalayas chanting folksongs, persuading the people of the area to hug trees to stop foresters cutting them down. When trees go, the fertile topsoil is washed away, water sources dry up and the hills become barren.

For me, two points became clear. The first was that only public pressure would stop the assault on Planet Earth, for left to themselves governments have an abysmal record.

The second was that, despite the assertions of some rich-country speakers, the Third World could become more prosperous without damaging vital life-support systems.

At any rate, it all made for two days of sometimes heated debate, which has been edited down into a pithy programme.

And the verdict on humankind? Innocent or guilty? Or perhaps guilty, but insane? Well, that's for you to decide.

**2** Summarise the main points in the following profile of the Pakistani squash player Jehangir Khan. Use between 180 and 200 words.

# Too young to last?

AT THE age of 18, Jehangir Khan is a sporting phenomenon. By winning the world open squash championship for the second year running he is well on the way to being considered the greatest player of the game ever. He is, at the moment, simply unbeatable.

A measure of Jehangir's dominance of the game is that, in the five matches before last week's final, his opponents were able to squeeze a total of only 25 points out of him, and though he did concede one game in the final against the Australian Dean Williams, it was only the fifth game he has lost since April 1981.

All this has been achieved at an incredibly early stage in his career. As a complete unknown, he won the world amateur title in Australia at the age of 15. He turned professional at 16, and won his first world championship at 17. No one has got so far so young. Jonah Barrington and Geoff Hunt, two previous champions, were well into their twenties before they reached the top. The legendary Hashim Khan was in his mid-thirties.

But it is Jehangir's early success which may yet deny him the chance of achieving true greatness. Jehangir's life has been as keenly programmed as an East European gymnast's. After his victory on Tuesday he told spectators that every day he runs ten miles, does ten 440-yard sprints and spends five hours on the squash court.

Watching him play last week, Jonah Barrington, himself no mean fitness expert, expressed reservations about so taxing a programme. "The fact is that to put as much strain as this on a body before it has stopped growing could be damaging. He may be overdoing it."

It was hard to see any sign of this last week, however. Racing tirelessly around the court, pressurising his opponents by standing right up near the front where he can cut off shots early, and then hitting the ball hard into the unreachable back corners, Jehangir looked devastating.

He was born to his career as much as a Rothschild is born into banking. The family interest has been squash ever since the mid 19th century when British soldiers, having learned to play the game at their public schools, took it to what was then India to while away their off-duty hours. The Khans learned fast. At the age of 76, Abdul Majeed Khan, one of Jehangir's relatives, could give the local British champion six points start and beat him 9-6. Jehangir's father, Roshan Khan, and his cousin, Hashim Khan, continued the remarkable family dominance after the Second World War and, with ancestors such as these, and with other family members to guide him, it was only a matter of time before Jehangir emerged as a champion.

Why are the Pakistanis so consistently good? "They have based their games on hitting to a grinding length", observes Barrington. "Hunt upped the pace by taking the ball on the volley. I varied it more, putting the ball up into the air, lobbing it to the back of the court. Jehangir embraces the lot.

He applies intense pressure and hits an excellent length. His hitting to the back of the court is more severe than anyone."

It does not make for sparkling squash. Only occasionally does Jehangir play drop shots to lure his opponents to the front of the court. He relies, instead, on power play. Some players suggest that this ability to out-hit everyone else could be a weakness. When he is confronted by an opponent who plays a lot of short drop-shots, Jehangir can be thrown off balance. Under Hunt's guidance, Dean Williams did this in the second game of the final, moving the Pakistani from side to side. His reward was four successive points and the second game.

But if there was one moment when Jehangir confirmed his promise, it was now. He is mentally tougher than many talented Pakistanis, and now, in addition, he remained absolutely cool as the crowd roared on the excited Australian. He started the third game in a whirlwind, made only one mistake and took the game from the fast-tiring Australian in 15 minutes. The fourth game lasted only eight minutes.

So how good is he? Is he as good as Hashim Khan, who used to give some of his fellow professionals an 8-0 start, play them for the price of a cup of tea, and still defeat them 10-8? Is he as good as Hunt, who last year won his eighth British Open, the de facto world title?

Only time will tell. But in tournaments nowadays Jehangir's nonplussed rivals are simply reduced to asking: "Who's going to come second?"

John Hopkins, *The Sunday Times*

# 2.4 Reading – words in context

What do you do when you come across a word in your reading that you haven't met before? Do you just give up and stop reading? Do you rush over it and pretend it doesn't matter? Do you get out your dictionary and look it up? Do you make a wild guess and hope for the best?

Looking words up in a dictionary is a good idea. You can get to know new words that way and make them part of your vocabulary. But sometimes it is a pity to interrupt your reading to reach for a dictionary. Often you can work out the meaning of the word from its context – from the way the word is used, from the other words around it and from the general sense of the sentence.

1 Work out the meanings of the *italicised* words in the following:

  a Although her neighbours tried to comfort her, Martha remained *inconsolable*. Nothing could compensate for the loss of her only son.

  b The *authoritarian* rule of the president aroused more and more opposition. People resented the restrictions on free speech and personal liberty that he imposed.

  c You will never achieve anything by *coercion*. The only way you will get people to do what you want them to do is by persuasion.

  d She was so *fastidious* that the merest suggestion of anything improper would make her screw up her face in distaste and disapproval.

  e I have told you again and again how to do it. I find it *inconceivable* that you do not understand.

  f When he heard that he had passed his exam, he was filled with *exhilaration*. He gave a mighty cheer and went whirling and dancing round the room.

  g Leave them alone. If you interfere, you will only *exacerbate* matters. If you ask me, they seem to enjoy having rows.

  h It is perhaps understandable that many *affluent* people fail to appreciate the problems of the unemployed since they themselves never have to worry about bills coming in or where the next meal is coming from.

  i The *frustration* the child felt at not being able to get his own way made him roar and kick the door in fury.

2 Check the meaning of the following words in a dictionary and then use each of them in a context like the examples in the previous exercise. Try to make interesting contexts from which someone could deduce the meaning of the words. Don't just say, 'Andrew was being ostentatious again'.

  | | |
  |---|---|
  | a ostentatious | f conglomeration |
  | b dawdle | g incredulous |
  | c cryptic | h scamper |
  | d disaffected | i translucent |
  | e exuberant | j parsimonious |

3 You probably know some interesting words yourself. Put some of them into contexts and see if your neighbour can work out their meanings. The point of this exercise is to see if your neighbour can work out the meaning of the words from your contexts, not to try to baffle him or her.

4 In the following passage, certain words have been blanked out. Examine the context and try to work out which words fit best into the blanks. In some cases it is possible that a number of different words would be suitable. Justify the choices you make.

  The complete passage is given at the end of this unit. Compare the words you chose with those the writer actually used. What differences in shades of meaning are there?

It was mid-morning and the open-air pavement terrace attached to the New Stanley Hotel was —————— with tourists dressed for Africa. Bush-shirts and sun hats banded with leopard skin of synthetic garishness were everywhere in ——————. Cameras and binoculars dangled from sun-tanned ——————. German, French and American —————— rang in the air. Out on the street was parked a —————— of zebra-striped Volkswagen vans. The smell of safari – of tented bush, of elephant, of ——————, of lion – suffused the bright morning. Noisy traffic —————— the broad expanse of Kenyatta Avenue. —————— dressed blacks streamed along the pavements, the men —————— briefcases, the women —————— handbags. Nairobi —————— with cosmopolitan splendour. A —————— beggar, his knees —————— with foam rubber, his hands —————— in sandals, —————— nimbly on the periphery of the terrace. 'Jambo . . . jambo . . .' The waiters, —————— dressed in white and green tunics, —————— him at bay. A thorn tree, centrally from the terrace, threw a dappled green —————— across the metal tables.

Without —————— if they could, two Americans came over and —————— down at my table. They were an oddly —————— pair. One was well —————— six foot tall, slope-shouldered and concave-stomached. His hair, frizzed and —————— out in 'Afro' style, formed a dark, —————— halo; his skin, bronzed and —————— by exposure to the sun, was leathery in ——————. The other was at least six —————— shorter and anaemically ——————. He had lank, shoulder-length ——————. His pale blue ——————, unfocused and restless, hinted at a kind of semi-idiocy. The tall one —————— a roll of cigarette —————— and a —————— of loose tobacco.

■■■ From Shiva Naipaul, *North of South* ■■■

# 2.5 Speaking

If you have something to say, then you ought to say it in such a way that people can hear it. Can you remember times recently when you have had to ask someone to speak up or when you yourself have been asked to repeat something because the person you were speaking to couldn't grasp what you said?

Getting the *volume* right is important. The loudness or quietness with which we use our voices depends on the occasion and situation. If we want to attract the attention of someone on the other side of the road, we shout. When we get angry, we usually raise our voices. If we are talking intimately to someone and don't wish to be overheard, we whisper.

Similarly, in oral assignments you have to *modulate* your voice according to the occasion and situation. If it is a one-to-one interview in a small room, then normal conversational volume will be appropriate. If you are addressing thirty other pupils in a large classroom, then a much bigger volume is necessary. In order to achieve this greater volume, you have to use more breath and raise the pitch of your voice slightly. Don't shout. Aim at the back wall of the room and get the sense of your voice bouncing back off it. This is known as *projection*.

But it is not just a question of volume. It is also a question of *articulation*. Your words should be separate and distinct, not blurred and run together. The *rate* at which you speak can help here. You may have to slow down from your normal rate of speaking in order to make sure your words are clear. Remember that words have further to travel in a large room than they would have if you were speaking to someone sitting next to you.

The rate at which you speak also affects the quality of what you say. There will be times when it would be effective to slow down or speed up. The sense of what you say will demand it.

You should also vary the *tone* and *pitch* of your voice. If everything is spoken on the same unrelieved level, your audience will soon become bored and stop listening. There are times when the voice naturally gets higher – when asking questions for instance. There will be times when you want to hold your audience's attention by speaking quietly or in hushed tones so as to draw the audience towards you. There will be other times when you want to pound out the words to show that what you are saying is important.

These are some of the ways in which you can give *emphasis* to your words. Not all words or sentences are of equal importance. Some will be of greater importance in getting across the points you are making. Varying your pace, tone and pitch, stressing certain words, are various means you can use to indicate the relative importance of what you say to your audience.

Another means to consider is the *pause*. You shouldn't just rattle off everything breathlessly. There will be moments in your talk or speech when you will want to pause – to give emphasis to what you have just said, to allow your audience time to think over what you have said, to show that you have come to the end of one section and are about to move on to another.

There is a difference, of course, between pauses and *hesitation*. If your speech is full of 'ums' and 'ahs', then it breaks up what you are saying and makes it difficult to follow. Your audience may also feel you are not sure about what you are saying. You have to give the appearance of being confident, even if you are not, and that you know what you are talking about.

When speaking, you want to sound as natural as possible. Don't put on an artificial or affected voice. Speak in your usual voice. There is nothing wrong with speaking with the accent of the place in which you were born and/or brought up. But you must make sure that your accent doesn't obscure what you want to say to your audience and prevent understanding.

There may be occasions when you want to use *different voices* – for indicating different speakers in a story, for instance, or quoting someone. Get the voices clear in your mind and be consistent. Differences of pitch or accent can help here. But make sure you don't overdo it or exaggerate. If you are a boy quoting the words of a woman, for instance, there is no need to use a very high-pitched voice. Simply use a slightly higher, lighter tone.

Use this checklist to assess your own spoken performance, and that of others:

o  get the volume right for the occasion and situation
o  articulate words clearly
o  select the right pace at which to speak
o  vary the pace, tone and pitch of your words according to the meaning and the intention behind them
o  give appropriate emphasis to your words by stress, pause or pitch
o  be confident without hesitation
o  be natural, even when using 'different voices'.

●  See how many different ways you can say each of the following and describe how the meaning changes according to the way it is said:

**a** Come and help me put this up.
**b** That was very clever.
**c** What a lovely day this has been!
**d** There's going to be an accident.
**e** Let me see that.

Think up some other examples which can be interpreted in different ways depending on how they are spoken.

# 2.6 Reading aloud

One of the oral skills you ought to be able to demonstrate is the ability to read aloud effectively. Normally, you would have the opportunity to prepare a piece for reading aloud. Here are some points to help you.

o  Be ready to present your reading e.g. saying why you chose it and where it is taken from, and to answer any questions about it.
o  By holding the book in one hand and marking your place with the other you will be able to glance up at your audience from time to time as you read.
o  Let your posture and facial expressions match the tone of what you are reading. You might feel like making an occasional gesture for emphasis, but don't overdo this.

There are certain obvious vocal requirements. You have to use a voice that is loud enough for everyone to hear. You have to articulate the words clearly enough for your audience to be able to understand them. You should read at a reasonable speed which people can follow – almost certainly more slowly than normal speech. You should breathe in the right places (at ends of phrases or sentences where there is a natural pause), emphasise the right words and phrase so that what you read makes sense.

But there are more subtle matters of *tone* and *interpretation* as well. The tone you choose depends on the piece of writing. Is it light-hearted or serious? Is it intended to amuse or move, or what? The answer to those questions will indicate the kind of tone you should adopt.

*Pace* and *variety* are other important considerations. Should some phrases or sentences be read more quickly or slowly than others? When would it be effective for the voice to rise or fall? Are there words or phrases that should be given a greater emphasis? Are there places where pauses would add to the dramatic effect?

Where necessary, for instance in the case of dialogue, you should use slightly *different voices* for the speech of the different characters so that listeners can distinguish between them.

Some people may find it helpful to pencil in notes and reminders on the reading. For instance, they may put in a line where a breath is necessary or effective. In poetry, they may link one line to the next with an arrow to indicate that the sense runs on and no breath should be taken at the end of the first line. They may underline words that need special emphasis. Or they may underline sections of direct speech with different colours for different speakers as a guide to the kind of voice to use. They may put notes in the margin – 'slow', 'faster', 'long pause', 'look up', 'hesitate', 'laugh' – as reminders of what they are to do. But be careful not to cover the piece with so many notes and symbols that it becomes confusing!

There are different opinions about whether poetry should be read in a different way from prose. Because poetry describes heightened experience and uses words in a more concentrated way, a slightly more intense tone may be appropriate, and it may help if you read poetry more slowly than prose.

Use this check-list when preparing your own reading (or assessing other people's readings):
o prepare your reading well, including your introduction and answers to possible questions
o maintain eye contact with your listeners
o posture, facial expression and gesture should be appropriate
o use your voice effectively to convey the meaning
o make notes on your text if this is helpful (in pencil).

● Here are some exercises on reading aloud:

1 Prepare two pieces of your own choice for reading aloud. One should be prose (about 500 words), and the other verse (at least twelve lines). Say why you have chosen these two pieces.
2 Choose a piece of prose or a poem that would be appropriate for an anthology on the subject of the seasons, or conflict, or men and women. Justify your choice.
3 Choose two short pieces of prose (about 200 words each), one in formal language and the other informal. Explain clearly the difference between them.
4 Prepare one of the prose extracts used in this book for reading aloud and say why you have chosen it.
5 Prepare one of the poems used in this book for reading aloud and say why you have chosen it.
6 Introduce and read an extract from a book you have enjoyed. Your extract should be about two pages long and should be chosen with the idea of encouraging others to read the book.

◄ *This could be used for oral assessment.* ►

● This is the extract from *North of South*, used in section 2.4 'Reading – words in context', as the author Shiva Naipaul wrote it:

It was mid-morning and the open-air pavement terrace attached to the New Stanley Hotel was crowded with tourists dressed for Africa. Bush-shirts and sun hats banded with leopard skin of synthetic garishness were everywhere in evidence. Cameras and binoculars dangled from sun-tanned necks. German, French and American voices rang in the air. Out on the street was parked a convoy of zebra-striped Volkswagen vans. The smell of safari – of tented bush, of elephant, of hippopotamus, of lion – suffused the bright morning. Noisy traffic choked the broad expanse of Kenyatta Avenue. Fashionably dressed blacks streamed along the pavements, the men carrying briefcases, the women swinging handbags. Nairobi vibrated with cosmopolitan splendour. A crippled beggar, his knees padded with foam rubber, his hands encased in sandals, crawled nimbly on the periphery of the terrace. 'Jambo ... jambo ...' The waiters, smartly dressed in white and green tunics, kept him at bay. A thorn tree, rising centrally from the terrace, threw a dappled green shade across the metal tables.

Without asking if they could, two Americans came over and sat down at my table. They were an oddly contrasting pair. One was well over six foot tall, slope-shouldered and concave-stomached. His hair, frizzed and teased out in 'Afro' style, formed a dark, woolly halo; his skin, bronzed and toughened by exposure to the sun, was leathery in appearance. The other was at least six inches shorter and anaemically white. He had lank, shoulder-length hair. His pale blue eyes, unfocused and restless, hinted at a kind of semi-idiocy. The tall one produced a roll of cigarette paper and a packet of loose tobacco.

# Unit Three

# 3.1 Written response to reading – general

You will be expected to do a lot of reading during your course, and you will be expected to write about what you have read. It is a good idea to keep a reading diary. You can jot down your reactions to a book, during the course of your reading and at the end. These notes could include first impressions, an account of the parts you enjoyed and those parts you found difficult or unconvincing, any episodes that reminded you of personal experience, your response to the characters, an account of what you think the author was saying, reasons why you would or would not recommend the book to others.

People read for all sorts of reasons – to get information, to pass the time, to increase their knowledge, to keep up with what is happening in the world, to gain a spiritual or artistic experience, to enable them to cope with living in society.

Reading material can take many shapes – newspapers, novels, advertisements, timetables, poems, telephone directories, income tax forms, application forms, magazines, guide books, recipes, DIY manuals, the Bible, textbooks, cereal packets, sauce bottles, menus, knitting patterns, Ceefax and Oracle.

● Consider these questions about your own reading.

○ Do you read a daily newspaper? If so, which one and why? If not, why not?

○ Which magazines do you look at regularly and why?

○ Do you go to your local library? If not, why not?
○ What kind of stories and novels do you read?
○ How much reading do you do in the course of a typical day? Make a list of all the different kinds of reading material you encounter.

Some of your response to reading will be oral – in comments, in answer to questions, in discussion. But much of your response to reading will be concerned with expressive writing, and may take one of three main forms:

1 It may act as a stimulus for your own creative work. A story or poem may give you an idea for a story or poem of your own on a similar theme. A piece of writing about childhood or experiences at school may suggest things about your own childhood or school life that you would like to write about.
2 Reinterpretation or extension. You may give an account of the events of a story as seen through the eyes of another character. You may retell an episode from a play as it might have appeared on the front page of a newspaper. You may write another adventure that the characters in a story might have been involved in.
3 Critical and analytical. You may write an account of a novel or a play, saying what it is about, describing the characters, explaining what you think is good and bad about it. You may write about why you think science fiction is popular, drawing examples from your reading. You may write about a poet whose poems you have enjoyed and try to explain why you like this poet's work.

Examples of all of these can be found in the course of this book.

Try one of the following assignments. It is important to remember two things. First, since this is an opportunity to respond to your reading, you must refer to things you have read. Describe them, quote from them, comment on them. Secondly, what is wanted is *your* response. Be honest and genuine about your reactions and opinions. Don't say how much you enjoyed a particular novel simply because you think someone will be impressed, if you actually found the novel boring. Your real feelings often make themselves known even if you try hard to disguise them. Choose something you can enthuse about naturally.

### 3.1.1 Written response to reading – coursework

1 'I read the ——— newspaper because...' Write about the newspaper which you read regularly. Explain why you read this particular newspaper. You might consider such things as its approach to the news, its features, its use of illustrations, its coverage of the arts and sport and women's affairs, its advertisements. You may also like to say why other newspapers don't appeal to you.
2 Do you regularly read a magazine which has a specialist appeal? It might be a magazine devoted to football or pop music or fashion or dance or mechanics. Describe the magazine and say what it is that you enjoy about it. What improvements, if any, would you suggest?
3 Suppose you were consulted about a new magazine for people your age. What kind of magazine would you like to see and what suggestions would you make? Think about the different kinds of regular features the magazine might have. Would there be news items and interviews? Would there be an 'agony column' and reviews? How often would it appear? How much would it cost?
4 Is there a book that has impressed you and remained in your memory? It may be a book which you read when you were much younger. Give an account of the book and say what impressed you about it and why you still remember it.
5 Have you ever seen a film or television version of a book you have read, or read a book which you have seen in a film or television version? Compare the two. Which do you think was the more successful? What was gained and what was lost? *Or* compare your impression of a play you have read with the effect it had when you saw the play performed in the theatre.
6 Suppose an author were to ask you for advice on the kind of novel to write for people of your age. What suggestions would you make? Think about the kind of characters, the setting, the plot, the length, the style.

# 3.2 Controlled classroom conditions for coursework

Some pieces of writing you submit for your coursework may have to be written in controlled classroom conditions. These are not the same as examination conditions. The term simply means that the writing has been produced wholly in the classroom under the supervision of your teacher. Controlled classroom conditions provide a quiet atmosphere in which you can work. You can use such books as you require for reference. There may not be a specified time limit within which the work has to be completed.

The work produced is also clearly your own unaided work. This does not prevent you from discussing the assignment or preparing for it before you begin – though this would have to be stated on your work. But once you start writing, you are on your own.

● Here are some suggestions for personal writing or narrative writing. You may if you wish discuss them first in groups or as a class. You may also care to revise Personal Writing (section 1.1) and Writing Narrative (section 2.1). You should write about 500 or 600 words. You should take about one hour over the actual writing.

1 'Would daylight never come?' Use this as the opening sentence of your writing.
2 'A Shiver of Fear'.
3 Write about someone who makes an unpleasant discovery about his or her character, perhaps by overhearing what someone else says, or by being told directly in anger or scorn, or through thinking about something he or she has done.
4 'Never Keep a Pet'. Write about how a pet causes havoc or disagreements or disappointments. This could be real or imaginary, comic or sad.
5 Write a story or an account of personal experience that would be suitable for an anthology on the subject of young people today.

 # 3.3 Tone in writing

In speech, the word 'tone' is used to describe the way words are said and the feeling behind them – sadly, cheekily, brightly, sarcastically, and so on. The word 'tone' can also be applied to writing. It describes the writer's attitude towards both the subject written about and the audience written for. The tone can be aggressive, hostile, neutral, ingratiating, enthusiastic, passionate, arrogant, sincere, polite, and so on.

In speech, tone is indicate by the words used and the way they are spoken. In writing, the tone is indicated by the way the subject matter is presented, the choice of words and the sentence structure. To assess the tone and the feeling behind the words, imagine how you would say the words aloud.

1 Look at the following examples. How would you describe the tone of each of them? Give reasons for your views.

## A

# Trespassers will be prosecuted

## (Official notice)

## B

□ LAST Monday I was disgusted that my friends' children had to leave school at 1 pm because of the so-called strike and yet the same day my friend who works as a barmaid in a pub in Kennington was inundated with teachers drinking when they were supposed to be on a march. There were 35 teachers in the pub while she had to pay someone to look after her kids.

## C

She tore the envelope open and removed a folded sheet of lined paper.

'Who is it from?' her mother called back over her shoulder, as she carried the breakfast dishes into the kitchen. 'Anybody I've ever heard of?'

'No,' Julie said. 'Nobody you know.'

With slowly growing horror she stared at the letter, at the one black sentence that peered up at her from the smudged paper.

I'm going to be sick, she thought.

Her legs felt weak, and she reached out and caught hold of the edge of the table to steady herself.

It's a dream, she told herself hopefully. I'm not really awake and standing here in the dining room at all. I'm lying in bed upstairs, asleep, and this is only a nightmare like the ones I used to have back in the beginning. I'll close my eyes, and when I open them I will wake up. It will be gone – the paper will be gone – it will never have been.

So she closed her eyes, and when she opened them again the paper was still there in her hand with the short sentence printed on it –

'I KNOW WHAT YOU
DID LAST SUMMER.'

From Lois Duncan, *I Know What You Did Last Summer*

## D

# The Philadelphia Story
*1940 (3.0-4.50 BBC1)*
MGM's glorious, smart comedy about a socialite wedding that runs amok thanks to the presence of the bride's ex-husband. Timing is exquisite and the cast approach perfection. Katharine Hepburn repeats the stage role tailored to her special talents; Cary Grant cuts a splendid sardonic figure as the bride's ex-husband (played on Broadway by Joseph Cotten).

**E**

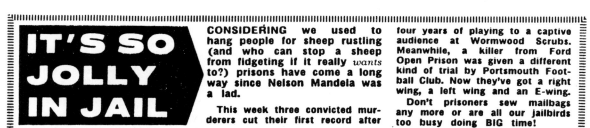

**F**

Keep tone in mind when you are doing your own writing. Try to use words that create the right mood for what you are writing and the audience for whom you are writing.

2   Choose three or four of the following 'tone' words and write a short paragraph for each which uses the appropriate tone:

| | | | |
|---|---|---|---|
| a | angry | f | neutral |
| b | sarcastic | g | enthusiastic |
| c | sad | h | cool |
| d | hostile | i | understated |
| e | critical | j | arrogant |

# 3.4 Reading – speculating, predicting, reviewing and modifying responses

As we read, we don't just think of the meaning of the words immediately in front of us. We also keep in mind what we have just read and think about what is to come. This is particularly true of expressive writing.

As we read a short story or a novel or a poem, we build up all sorts of impressions in our minds about the characters or the ideas and what is going on. On the basis of what we have read so far, we speculate about what is going to happen next. We may think we can predict the course of events, and we may be right. But sometimes a story or a poem can take an unexpected turn, and we are surprised. Our first impressions have to be reviewed and modified.

A short story or a poem has a kind of unity so that we can go backwards and forwards as we read and hold it all in our minds at the end and see how the various ideas and characters and events have evolved and been reinforced or qualified and modified and altered. The same is true of a novel though it is larger in scope of course. As we read a novel, our views of the characters change as they develop and relate with other characters. At the end, we can look back and see the whole pattern of the novel – the significance of this event and the importance of that character.

Reading expressive writing is a kind of creative process. In a sense, the reader is recreating in his or her mind the process the writer has gone through. The reader is sharing the writer's thoughts.

● Read the following story and answer the questions step by step as indicated.

# THE SHAVE

He came into town riding fast and firing his guns at the blue sky. He shot a chicken in the dust and kicked it around, using his horse as a mauler, and then, reloading and yelling, his three-week beard red and irritable in the sunlight, he rode on to the saloon where he tethered his horse and carried his guns, still hot, into the bar where he glared at his own sunburnt image in the mirror and yelled for a glass and a bottle.

1  What impression do you get of the man from the way he acts in the first paragraph?
2  Does this first paragraph suggest anything to you about what is going to happen in the rest of the story?

The bartender slid them over the edge of the bar and went away.

The men along the bar moved down to the free lunch at the far end, and conversation withered.

'What in hell's wrong with everyone?' cried Mr James Malone. 'Talk, laugh, everyone. Go on, now, or I'll shoot your damn eyebrows off!'

Everyone began to talk and laugh.

'That's better,' said James Malone, drinking his drinks one upon another.

He rammed the swing doors of the saloon wide and in the resulting wind stomped out like an elephant into the afternoon street where other men were riding up from the mines or the mountains and tying their horses to the worn hitching poles.

The barber shop was directly across the street.

Before crossing to it, he rechecked his bright blue pistols and snuffed at them with his red nose, saying Ah! at the scent of gunpowder. Then he saw a tin can in the talcumy dust and shot it three times ahead of him as he strode laughing, and the horses all along the street jumped nervously and flickered their ears. Reloading again, he kicked the barber shop door wide and confronted a full house. The four barber chairs were full of lathered customers, waiting with magazines in their hands, and the mirrors behind them repeated the comfort and the creamy lather and the pantomime of efficient barbers.

Along the wall on a bench sat six other men waiting to be cleansed of the mountain and the desert.

3  How does this section reinforce the impression of Malone made in the first paragraph?
4  Do you think the writer intends Malone to be a sympathetic or an unsympathetic character? Justify your answer.
5  What bearing do you think the nature of Malone is going to have on what happens to him in the story?
6  In view of what has already happened, what do you think Malone is going to do when he finds the barber shop full?

'Have a seat,' said one of the barbers, glancing up.

'I sure will,' said Mr James Malone, and pointed his pistol at the first chair. 'Get out of there, mister, or I'll sew you right back into the upholstery.'

The man's eyes were startled, then angry, then apprehensive in turn above his creamy mask, but after a long hesitation, he levered himself up with difficulty, swiped the white stuff off his chin with the apron, flung the apron to the floor, and walked over to shove in and sit with the other waiting men.

James Malone snorted at this, laughed, jounced into the black leather chair, and cocked his two pistols.

'I *never* have to wait,' he said to no one and everyone at once. His gaze wandered over their heads and touched on the ceiling. 'If you live right, you don't have to wait for anything. You ought to know that by now!'

7  Do you think Malone would really have shot the customer if he hadn't vacated his chair?
8  How does the customer react? How would you have reacted?
9  'I *never* have to wait.' What aspect of Malone's character does this illustrate?

The men looked at the floor. The barber cleared his throat and put an apron over Jamie Malone. The pistols stuck up, making white tents underneath. There was a sharp click as he knocked the pistols together, just to let everyone know they were there, and pointed.

'Give me the works,' he said to the barber, not looking at him. 'A shave first, I feel itchy and mean, then a haircut. You men there, starting on the right, tell jokes. Make 'em good jokes. I want entertainment while I'm being shorn, ain't been entertained in months. You, there, you start.'

The man who had been evicted from his comfortable chair unfroze himself slowly and rolled his eyes at the other men and talked as if someone had hit him in the mouth.

'I knew a gent once who . . .' he said, and word by word, white-faced, he launched himself into a tale. 'That gent, he . . .'

To the barber, James Malone now said, 'Listen, you, I want a shave, I want a beautiful shave. But I got a fine-skinned face and it's a pretty face with the beard off, and I been in the mountains for a long time and I had no luck with gold-panning, so I'm feeling mean. I just want to warn you of one little thing. If you so much as nick my face once with your straight razor, I'll kill you. You hear that? I mean I'll kill you. If you so much as bring one little speck of blood to the surface, I'll plug you clean through the heart. You hear?'

10  What explanation is given for Malone's behaviour? Is it a justification?
11  Do you think Malone means it when he says he'll kill the barber if he so much as nicks his face?
12  How do you think the barber will respond to that?

The barber nodded quietly. The barber shop was silent. Nobody was telling jokes or laughing.

'Not one drop of blood, not one little cut, mind you,' repeated Mr James Malone, 'or you'll be dead on the floor a second later.'

'I'm a married man,' said the barber.

'I don't give a damn if you're a Mormon with six wives and 57 children. You're dead if you scratch me once.'

'I happen to have two children,' said the barber. 'A fine little girl and a boy.'

'Don't hand me any of that,' said Malone, settling back, closing his eyes. 'Start.'

The barber began to get the hot towels ready. He put them on James Malone's face, and under them the man cursed and yelled and waved his pistols under the white apron. When the hot towels came off and the hot lather was put on his beard, James Malone still chewed on his profanity and threats, and the men waiting sat white-faced and stiff with the pistols pointing at them. The other barbers had almost stopped moving and stood like statues by their customers in the chairs, and the barber shop was cold for a summer day.

'What's wrong with the stories?' snapped James Malone. 'All right, then sing. You four there, sing somethink like *My Darling Clementine*. Start it up. You heard me.'

13  What impression do you get of the barber from this section? Is he afraid of Malone?
14  Is sympathy for Malone increased or decreased in this section?

The barber was stropping his razor slowly with a trembling hand. 'Mr Malone,' he said.

'Shut up and get to work.' Malone tilted his head back, grimacing.

The barber stropped his razor some more and looked at the men seated all around the shop. He cleared his throat and said, 'Did all of you gentlemen hear what Mr Malone said to me?'

Everyone nodded mutely.

'You heard him threaten to kill me,' said the barber, 'if I so much as drew a drop of blood to his skin?'

The men nodded again.

'And you'd swear to it in a court of law, if necessary?' asked the barber.

The men nodded for the last time.

15  Why do you think the barber wants the other men to confirm that Malone has threatened to kill him?

'Cut the malarkey,' said Mr James Malone. 'Get to work.'

'That's all I wanted to be sure of,' said the barber, letting the leather strop fall and clatter against the chair. He raised the razor in the light and it gleamed and glittered with cold metal there.

He tilted Mr James Malone's head back and put the razor against the hairy throat.

'We'll start here,' he said. 'We'll start *here*.'

━━━━━ Ray Bradbury ━━━━━

16  What do you think happens?
17  What are your feelings about it?
18  From the rest of the story do you think it was inevitable that something like this would happen to Malone?
19  Does what happens alter your views of Malone and the barber?
20  Given the time and place in which the story is set and the way the story has been developed, do you think what happens is believable?
21  The writer doesn't actually say what happens. Does that make the ending of the story more or less effective?

 # 3.5 Listening

In any oral situation – conversation, interview, talk, speech – the listener is almost as important as the speaker. Without a listener, there would be no point in speaking. But the listener is not just a passive participant. How the listener responds can affect the quality of what is said. For instance, if a friend is eager to tell you something, and you are bored or not interested or in a bad mood, then your friend has to work harder to arouse your interest. It is the same when you are listening as a member of a group or audience.

Your ability to be a good listener will be assessed as part of your course. This assessment may be direct (as in an aural test – see 4.7) or incidental, based on evidence built up in the course of oral assignments.

An important element of listening is *concentration*. Keep your eyes on the speaker. Follow his or her movements if there are gestures or if your attention is directed to a diagram on the board. Keep track of the various stages of the point of view or instructions, or the description being given.

In your listening, you don't just take in the words and the ideas. You should also be listening to how the words are said and *interpreting* what effect that has on the meaning. For instance, is the speaker being sincere or only pretending? Is the speaker trying to make the words amusing or is the comic effect only accidental? Things like these can influence the meaning you get from the words.

One way you can demonstrate your ability to listen is by the questions you ask and the comments you make. Refer to things the speaker has said. Agree with or dispute statements made. Criticise where you think the speaker has been misleading or misinformed. Expand on areas where you feel the speaker has not gone into sufficient depth, giving your own examples and indicating your own knowledge.

Another way your ability to listen can be revealed is by your physical response. How you sit can show whether you are paying attention and listening. So can other signs. You may nod your head in agreement or frown or shake your head at some comment that you disagree with or disapprove of. You may smile or laugh at something amusing or at some ironic comment.

● Here is a check-list of points to remember:

○ concentrate on what is being said
○ interpret what is being said
○ respond to what is said by questions and comments
○ show by your physical response that you are listening.

● Here are some exercises on listening:

1 Find a short passage in this book (about 150 words) that provides information. Read it to a friend and then ask questions about it and see how much your friend is able to remember.

2 Find a short news item from a newspaper in this book. Read it to the class and then test the class on it by asking questions.

#  3.6 Telling a story

There are two elements to telling a story of whatever kind – the content of the story, and the way it is told. Both are important, though many comedians, for instance, would claim that it's not so much what you say, it's the way you say it! Performance, or getting the story or joke across, is a vital ingredient.

● Look at the following story.
1 a Read the story to yourself silently.
  b Listen to it as a prepared reading.
  c Listen to it as someone retells it, more or less as it is, but without using the printed text.

2 Analyse what the differences are between the three versions with particular reference to the effect, the use of voice and the visual presentation.

# ▬▬▬▬ THE TWINS ▬▬▬▬

There were two brothers who were identical twins. Sometimes even their own mother had to study them hard before she could tell t'other from which. Anyway, when they got to school age, they were sent off to different schools so that nobody would have trouble mixing them up, you see.

Both lads turned out to be quite bright, clever chaps who learned their lessons easily. Trouble was, the teacher of one of them didn't care much for him and was always looking for a chance to bring the lad down a peg or two.
Well, one year, after the exams, this brother got better marks than anybody else, and a lot better than the teacher wanted him to have.

'Before I'll let you be top of the class,' said the teacher, 'you'll have to answer me three questions. You can have till tomorrow morning to think about them. The questions are: What is the weight of the moon? What is the depth of the sea? And, last, what am I thinking?'

The lad went off home and that night he wouldn't play with his brother because he was puzzling over the answers to the teacher's questions. In the finish, his brother asked him why he was so long in the face.

'Teacher's given me three questions before he'll let me be top of the class and I can't think of the answers,' he said.

'What're the questions?' his brother asked.

When he told them, his brother said, 'Never mind about the questions. Just you let me go to your school tomorrow instead of you, and you go to mine. Our mates will tell us where to sit.'

So in the morning both brothers went to each other's schools. And after a bit, the teacher told the twin to stand up.

'Now,' he said, 'what about my questions? What weight is the moon?'

'A hundredweight, sir,' said the lad.

'How do you make that out?'

'Well, sir, there's four quarters in a hundredweight and four quarters in the moon.'

'Very good,' said the teacher. 'And what do you think is the depth of the sea?'

'A stone's throw, sir.'

'Why's that?'

'When you throw a stone it goes straight to the bottom, sir.'

'Well done,' said the teacher. 'Now for the third and hardest question. What am I thinking?'

'Please, sir,' said the lad, 'you're thinking I'm our Bobby, but I'm not. I'm his brother, Tommy.'

▬▬▬▬▬▬ Aidan Chambers ▬▬▬▬▬

The following check-list will help you when telling a story:
○ Plan your story beforehand – how you are going to present it, the way the story will be developed, the use of dialogue and different voices, the ending or punch line. It may help to write it out first, but your story must be *told*, not read.
○ Listen to how people tell jokes and anecdotes on television and radio, and analyse their technique.
○ Use simple and direct language.
○ Use dialogue if appropriate to create variety and dramatic effect.
○ Make sure you have an effective ending, especially if you are telling a joke.
○ Use your voice and body to communicate your words effectively.
○ Tailor your story to the audience it is being presented to.
○ Avoid racist or sexist jokes and stories – for instance, Irish jokes and stories about mothers-in-law.

● Here are some exercises in story-telling:

1 Tell a story round the class with each member contributing a sentence or two before the next one takes it up.
2 Tell your favourite joke.
3 Tell a story that you have heard from one of your parents or grandparents about something that happened to them or something that happened to you when you were a young child.
4 Tell a story about something that happened at a well-known house or place in your area.
5 Tell a myth or legend. It could be from Greek, Roman or Norse mythology, or one of the Indian or African myths.

6 Tell a religious story, taken from any religion.
7 Tell a fairy story or a folk tale. This could be from any country.
8 Tell a story that illustrates a proverb such as 'A stitch in time saves nine', or 'Too many cooks spoil the broth', or 'A rolling stone gathers no moss'.
9 Tell a story that you have made up yourself.
10 Record a story to be played to a 6-year-old child.

◀ *This could be used for oral assessment.* ▶

# Test Paper 1

Time allowed: two hours.

The question paper consists of two sections, Section A and Section B.

Dictionaries may be used.

Section A consists of compulsory questions.

Section B consists of a choice of questions. Candidates are required to answer ONE question.

## Section A

Read this piece of writing and answer the questions which follow.

### THE PICTURES I SEE IN ═══ MY FIRE ═══

Every winter my mother complained that our house was so damp that you could grow mushrooms on the mattress in the back bedroom. My father said it was a blasted lie and that there was
5 nothing structurally wrong with the place, just a matter of a few window frames that needed replacing – and we all knew why he couldn't afford to do that, didn't we? We knew all right; it was on account of Bob Ward.
10 It was Bob Ward's fault too, economically speaking, that though we had other rooms downstairs – euphemistically referred to as the dining room and the lounge – we could only ever use the kitchen, which my mother called the
15 morning room. The back kitchen, in that it had a cooker, was called the scullery.

The morning room, though hardly larger than a butler's pantry, never reached maximum warmth until it was almost time to go to bed.
20 There would be an hour, perhaps, of delicious comfort and then Father would rewind his muffler about his neck and go out into the scullery to fetch the kettle to douse the fire. Before that happy hour – while we ate our tea,
25 when we slumped over our homework – we kept our coats on. When it was very cold my brother wore a balaclava, but then, he wasn't in all that often because as he grew bigger there wasn't room for him.
30 It was during those sacred sixty minutes of blissful heat, when the shadows licked across the wallpaper patterned with overblown roses, that Bob Ward was most likely to join us round the fire. Sometimes he slipped in unnoticed, and
35 sometimes you could sense his presence outside in the dark little hall, hear his breathing above the ticking of the grandfather clock long before he made an entrance.
I always sat under the table. There wasn't
40 room for another chair and besides my mother said it looked tidier if I was out of sight. Made wanton by the leaping flames in the grate, my mother and father in their respective armchairs on either side of the fender would stretch out
45 their legs across the rug with the ship in full sail that my mother had woven, and grow so intimate as to let their slippers mingle. My father would remark that it was a grand fire. Grand. My mother would agree. Then perhaps my
50 father would mention that he had met Johnny Henderson or Frank Bigerstaff or one or other of his business cronies while travelling on the train that morning. Mother would murmur, oh yes,

55 and what did he have to say for himself, and father would reply, nothing much. Next my mother would venture the opinion that she had never thought much of Mrs Henderson or Mrs Bigerstaff or whoever, that the woman had never had any sense of style. But *he's* a good sport, my

60 father would say, and then they would both fall silent and stare mesmerised into the fiery heart of that grand conflagration. So far, so good. One of my mother's slippers might even have fallen off, and now she was holding the pom-pom of

65 my father's slipper between her bare toes, tugging at it playfully, her eyes closed, her cheeks rosy from the flames. At such times, if only for moments, it seemed to me that 'morning room' was an apt name, for I sat there

70 surrounded by roses in bloom and felt the sunlight.

Then, one or other of them would mention money, usually Mother. Perhaps the fire made her reckless as well as reflective. And off they

75 would start on that ding-dong slope that led from percentages and lost commissions, past rotten window frames and deliberate omissions, directly to Bob Ward who was always waiting below.

80 I didn't understand all of it; I couldn't follow the bits about the tram ride or the meeting at the shipping office, or the lost pair of gentlemen's gloves that fastened with buttons – they were mentioned every time – or the snapshot of a

85 picnic in a field with my mother with a bandeau round her head. But I understood about the party.

My mother had been asked out by my father; they were engaged to be married. She had a ring

90 and everything. My mother said he couldn't see her that particular night because she'd promised her friend Dorothy that she'd go and visit her. Dorothy and she did flower pressing together in an album, and that was their night for doing it.

95 There was an argument because my father said that was the first he'd heard of any flowers, or any album for that matter. He went off in a huff. Later on, he just had to see her and make up and so he went round to Dorothy's house, and there

100 was a party in full swing. A proper one with dancing and the carpet pushed back in the sitting room, so he knew it wasn't impromptu. And guess who Mother was dancing with? Father was so upset at the deception that he

105 couldn't concentrate on his business for months, and he lost an important shipping assignment, and then the slump came.

When they got to this bit my mother always shouted out, 'Don't talk soft. You can't blame

110 the slump on Bob Ward.' Then she'd struggle into her slipper in an offended manner and Father would flounce out into the scullery to get the kettle and swoosh it so hard over the coals that smoke billowed up to the ceiling and a little

115 flood of sooty water trickled under the fender and dripped onto the ship sailing across the rug.

Now I have a room of my own with windows that close properly, and shutters, and plenty of coal, enough to make a fire that roars up the

120 chimney every winter night and sets the walls spinning with light. Sometimes, when I look into the flames long enough, I think I see fragments of pictures; long blades of grass and a girl sitting with a bandeau round her hair; two

125 gleaming rails with a crooked tram spitting sparks; the shape of a hand with a scarlet button glowing at the wrist. And sometimes I catch myself looking into the far corners of the room, just in case it's Bob Ward hovering there, come

130 back to warm his bones.

■■■■■■ Beryl Bainbridge ■■■■■■

---

You are advised to spend approximately one and a quarter hours on this section.

1  Look at lines 1–29. Describe the writer's family and home when she was a child. (5)
2  Look at lines 30–71. Describe the effect of the fire on the writer and her parents. (4)
3  What impression do you get of the relationship between the mother and father from lines 39–67? (3)
4  What effect does the mention of money have on the situation? What suggestions are there earlier that money is a problem? (4)
5  Explain the part played by Bob Ward in the life of the mother and father and their subsequent family life. How does the writer make the presence of Bob Ward felt? (5)
6  Look at lines 117–130. Why does the writer see these pictures in the fire? Why does she look round to see if Bob Ward is 'hovering there'? (4)
7  This piece of writing was printed originally as an advertisement for 'real fires and real fire heating appliances' by the Solid Fuel Advisory Service. Comment on how effective you think this piece of writing is as an advertisement for this purpose. (5)
(Total 30)

# Section B

You are advised to spend approximately three-quarters of an hour on this section. Answer only ONE of the questions in this section. Twenty marks are allocated to each question.

Write approximately two sides on one of the following subjects. If your handwriting is unusually large or small, you should make some adjustment in the amount you write. It is assumed that average handwriting produces about eight words per line.

8  'Memories'. Write an account of how memories of events in your childhood are brought back to you by some situation or object as they were for Beryl Bainbridge in 'The pictures I see in my fire'.

   Here are some suggestions you may use, if you wish. You may have come across an old photograph, or you may have met another member of the family whom you have not seen for some years, or you may have revisited a house or street where you once lived.

9  Write about an occasion when you experienced the contrasted effects of cold and heat.

   Here are some suggestions you could use, if you wish. You trudge home through the snow from school or an early morning paper-round to the comfort of home, or you plunge into the chilly sea after sunbathing, or a sports activity on a blazing hot afternoon is followed by a cool shower.

10  'The Misunderstanding'. Write a short story in which there is a misunderstanding like the one that occurred in 'The pictures I see in my fire' between the mother and father over Bob Ward.

11  'How people lived then'. Using your own knowledge and what older people such as your parents and grandparents have said, write about what life was like thirty or forty years ago compared with what it is like for you today.

12  Look at the photograph below. Write about it in any way you wish.

(If you are not required to sit a written examination, this could be part of your coursework.)

# Unit Four

# 4.1 Expressing a point of view in writing

In some of your writing you will be asked to express a point of view. This means putting a case for and/or against a particular argument. For instance, you may be asked to agree or disagree with fox hunting.

First, you have to decide what your point of view is. One way is to jot down any ideas that come to you. You could put them in two columns, for and against, and see which side appears to be stronger.

Another way is to find evidence. Consider the following:

o   topical references in the news, on television, in your locality

o   different approaches, for example, historical, social, geographical, ecological, scientific, religious, economic, political

o   research in the library – find facts, figures, statistics, examples, comparisons, illustrations, quotations, references

o   other people – talking about a subject can produce ideas.

Sometimes attack is the best form of defence. Think of arguments that could be used against your point of view and work out ways in which these arguments could be undermined or shown to be unconvincing.

You now have to organise your notes and evidence in the most effective and persuasive way to support your point of view. Think about the following:

o   make sure statements are supported by convincing evidence

o   present your points in the most effective sequence

o   link your ideas together so that one flows into the next

o   work out an effective beginning and ending.

● Look at the points given below about killing animals for sport and consider the following questions:

1 Which points are in favour and which are against? What further arguments either for or against can you think of?

2 Can any of the arguments given here be countered by other arguments?

3 What evidence – facts, figures, etc. – do you know of to support or refute the arguments given here? Or can you find evidence that would do this?

4 Which side of the general argument do you think is stronger and why?

5 If you were writing in support of your point of view, what order would you put the arguments in? How would you begin and end?

a By hunting animals, people release aggressive instincts and therefore are less likely to be violent towards others.

b In hunting animals, people face dangers just as great as those faced by the animals.

c By hunting animals, people destroy the balance of nature.

d Animals are a lower order of creation than human beings and therefore a fit subject for hunting.

e Good sportsmen and women always give the animals they hunt a 'sporting chance'.

f Nature is itself cruel, and people are simply conforming to the natural order of things when they catch fish or shoot game.

g All creatures are the creation of God and therefore are holy and should be protected.

h The hunting of animals causes unnecessary pain and suffering.

i The killing of some animals (such as foxes) for sport is not even justified by the argument that they provide food.

j Hunting brings people into close and pleasurable contact with open air and the countryside.

k Hunting helps to keep down pests which attack farm animals and crops.

l Hunting is an invigorating and enjoyable pastime.

m Animals hunt each other, so why shouldn't people hunt animals?

n Hunting animals provides food for people without which they would not survive.

● Read the following article in which Peter Bradshaw gives his views on shooting and fishing.

# BUT DOES HE GET BY WITHOUT HIS RABBIT PIE?

### By Peter Bradshaw

" I have a deep and genuine love for the countryside and all the things it contains. I also shoot and fish, two abiding interests which entail the killing and cutting-up of creatures which in life are magnificent and in death are delicious. Can that be such an incredible contradiction? I think not.

There has been much coverage in newspapers and on television in recent weeks of the abhorrence and revulsion which some people feel for those who participate in so-called "blood sports" the "killing for fun brigade". Particular emphasis has been placed upon those brigade members of noble birth. It is true that money buys the best fishing, game and pheasant shooting, and most people traditionally associate such pursuits with the privileged classes.

However, thousands of people, rich and poor, shoot and fish in this country, and I believe that most of use share similar opinions. I certainly feel no shame in expressing mine.

I detest any form of cruelty, to animals or to people, but I do not like hypocrisy either. There are millions of people in our civilised Britain who eat meat. My meat comes both from the butcher's shop and from the carcases of animals, birds and fish I kill and prepare myself. I derive great pleasure from my own ability to use a gun and cast a fly line, and being surrounded by the majesty of unspoilt countryside heightens that pleasure. When I see a salmon leap or watch hares grazing, hear the trumpeting of wild geese, marvel at the plumage of a cock pheasant, or listen to wood-pigeon cooing in a summer copse, I am awestruck and fulfilled by nature's beauty and complexity.

I often wonder how many of our ardent and vociferous anti-blood sport campaigners are vegetarian. They seem to regard only wild creatures as having a right to live, but what of cows, pigs, lambs and domestic fowl? They too appear to most of us as endearing and possessed of some kind of beauty, but they are killed, butchered and eaten in their thousands every day. No one cares because no one sees the blood and agony which are very much a part of these animals' demises. The abattoirs see to all of that, conveniently out of sight.

For those who use the argument "It's all done so humanely", I ask them to visit a slaughterhouse. The sight would come as a real shock. Veal, for instance, comes from little Bambi-eyed calves. It is very pale, tender meat, because veal calves are bled to death. Do people really believe that chickens are born in deep-frozen portions and that pork chops, legs of lamb and rump steak grow on trees?

I laugh when I see the shooting fraternity described as "Country-side Ravagers". I am a conservationist. Anyone whose quarry exists as a wild animal *must* be: if the countryside dies, so does shooting.

I do not kill for the sake of it and I do not kill creatures which I cannot use as food. Neither do I shoot because I am poor and cannot afford to buy meat. No one *has* to eat turkey at Christmas, but a lot of birds get their throats cut all the same. I find it incredible that rebuke is heaped upon a certain Princess for shooting a stag, but at the same time it is acceptable to everyone for our supermarkets to stock game soup containing venison. When it is alive it is deer; when it is dead it is venison.

Before you dismiss my views, please spare a thought for the pig from whence your breakfast bacon came. He was probably castrated without anaesthetic, and the same is probably true of the lamb or bullock which died in the interests of your lunch.

I can look at a wild creature without wishing to kill it, fully appreciative of its splendour. I can also kill such a creature and feel completely honest and guiltless in the knowledge that it is food. It is Sunday: shall we practise what we preach?

1 How effective do you think the beginning and ending of this article are?

2 What are the main points the writer makes in favour of his sport?

3 How much of this article is based on personal experience? Does that make it more convincing?

4 Attack is the best form of defence. To what extent does the writer argue his case by attacking the opposite view? Give examples.

5 How much of the writer's arguments depend on fact and how much on opinion?

6 Are there any points in the argument that could be considered contradictory?

7 Are there points the writer carefully avoids?

8 Do you think the writer makes a convincing case for his point of view?

---

◄ *This could be discussed in groups or as a class and could be used for oral assessment.* ►

---

### 4.1.1 Expressing a point of view – coursework

Write an essay on one of the following:

1 Do you think the motor car has done more harm than good?

2 Defend or attack the view that private schools should be abolished.

3 What arguments are there for and against shops opening on Sundays? What are your own views?

4 Argue for or against the view that the United Kingdom should be a nuclear-free zone.

5 Justify the view that every school should have its own school council of elected pupils.

# 4.2 Coursework – response to reading: the short story

The short story has already been discussed in the Writing sections of Unit 2 (2.1, 2.2). Check back on what was said there. When reading a short story and considering your response to it, you go through much the same kind of procedure that you do when you plan and write your own stories. You need to think about the characters, the setting and the plot, and the way they interrelate. The following questions provide a guide to the kind of thing to look for. They don't all apply to all stories.

○ What impression do you get of the main characters? How does the writer help you to get to know them – by description, dialogue, action, the response of other characters? Are the characters convincing and true to life? What part do they play in the plot? Are there comparisons or contrasts between characters and their positions in life or their attitudes or feelings? Are there conflicts? Have the characters changed in any way by the end of the story? If so, why?

○ Is the setting appropriate to the characters and events of the story? Does it play any part in the events – having an effect on the characters, making them react in a particular way, reflecting their lives in some way?

○ What actually happens in the story? Is it concerned mainly with action or mood or feeling? Are there contrasts or patterns in the events of the story? Is the plot built on some kind of conflict of characters or attitudes? Is there an action and a reaction of some kind? How are things different at the end from what they were at the beginning? Are you convinced by what happens in the story?

○ From whose point of view is the story being told? Why does the writer choose this point of view? Is this point of view convincingly conveyed?

○ What kind of language is the story told in? Is it appropriate to the story and the point of view? Are words used interestingly? Is it free of clichés? Does the writing move the story along at a pace appropriate to the events of the plot?

○ What is the point of the story? What impression does the writer want to leave you with at the end? Did you find the story interesting? Did you enjoy reading it? What did you particularly like about it? Has the story left you with any new knowledge or insight into people and how they feel and behave, or about life? Has it reminded you of something in your own life or character and made you see it in a new light?

● Read the following story carefully.

## ▬ LIFE OF MA PARKER ▬

When the literary gentleman, whose flat old Ma Parker cleaned every Tuesday, opened the door to her that morning, he asked after her grandson. Ma Parker stood on the doormat inside the dark little hall, and she stretched out her hand to help her gentleman shut the door before she replied. 'We buried 'im yesterday, sir,' she said quietly.

'Oh, dear me! I'm sorry to hear that,' said the literary gentleman in a shocked tone. He was in the middle of his breakfast. He wore a very shabby dressing-gown and carried a crumpled newspaper in one hand. But he felt awkward. He could hardly go back to the warm sitting-room without saying something – something more. Then because these people set such store by funerals he said kindly, 'I hope the funeral went off all right.'

'Beg parding, sir?' said old Ma Parker huskily.

Poor old bird! She did look dashed. 'I hope the funeral was a – a – success,' said he. Ma Parker gave no answer. She bent her head and hobbled off to the kitchen, clasping the old fish bag that held her cleaning things and an apron and a pair of felt shoes. The literary gentleman raised his eyebrows and went back to his breakfast.

'Overcome, I suppose,' he said aloud, helping himself to the marmalade.

Ma Parker drew the two jetty spears out of her toque and hung it behind the door. She unhooked her worn jacket and hung that up too. Then she tied her apron and sat down to take off her boots. To take off her boots or to put them on was an agony to her, but it had been an agony for years. In fact, she was so accustomed to the pain that her face was drawn and screwed up ready for the twinge before she'd so much as untied the laces. That over, she sat back with a sigh and softly rubbed her knees. . . .

'Gran! Gran!' Her little grandson stood on her lap in his button boots. He'd just come in from playing in the street.

'Look what a state you've made your gran's skirt into – you wicked boy!'

But he put his arms round her neck and rubbed his cheek against hers.

'Gran, gi' us a penny!' he coaxed.

'Be off with you; Gran ain't got no pennies.'

'Yes, you 'ave.'

'No, I ain't.'

'Yes, you 'ave. Gi' us one!'

Already she was feeling for the old, squashed, black leather purse.

'Well, what'll you give your gran?'

He gave a shy little laugh and pressed closer. She felt his eyelid quivering against her cheek. 'I ain't got nothing,' he murmured. . . .

The old woman sprang up, seized the iron kettle off the gas stove and took it over to the sink. The noise of the water drumming in the kettle deadened her pain, it seemed. She filled the pail, too, and the washing-up bowl.

It would take a whole book to describe the state of that kitchen. During the week the literary gentleman 'did' for himself. That is to say, he emptied the tea-leaves now and again into a jam jar set aside for that purpose, and if he ran out of clean forks he wiped over one or two on the roller towel. Otherwise, as he explained to his friends, his 'system' was quite simple, and he couldn't understand why people made all this fuss about housekeeping.

'You simply dirty everything you've got, get a hag in once a week to clean up, and the thing's done.'

The result looked like a gigantic dustbin. Even the floor was littered with toast crusts, envelopes, cigarette ends. But Ma Parker bore him no grudge. She pitied the poor young gentleman for having no one to look after him. Out of the smudgy little window you could see an immense expanse of sad-looking sky, and whenever there were clouds they looked very worn, old clouds, frayed at the edges, with holes in them, or dark stains like tea.

While the water was heating, Ma Parker began sweeping the floor. 'Yes,' she thought, as the broom knocked, 'what with one thing and another I've had my share. I've had a hard life.'

Even the neighbours said that of her. Many a time, hobbling home with her fish bag, she heard them, waiting at the corner, or leaning over the area railings, say among themselves, 'She's had a hard life, has Ma Parker.' And it was so true she wasn't in the least proud of it. It was just as if you were to say she lived in the basement-back at Number 27. A hard life! . . .

At sixteen she'd left Stratford and come up to London as kitching-maid. Yes, she was born in Stratford-on-Avon. Shakespeare, sir? No, people were always arsking her about him. But she'd never heard his name until she saw it on the theatres.

Nothing remained of Stratford except that 'sitting in the fireplace of a evening you could see the stars through the chimley,' and 'Mother always 'ad 'er side of bacon 'anging from the ceiling.' And there was something – a bush, there was – at the front door, that smelt ever so nice. But the bush was very vague. She'd only remembered it once or twice in the hospital, when she'd been taken bad.

That was a dreadful place – her first place. She was never allowed out. She never went upstairs except for prayers morning and evening. It was a fair cellar. And the cook was a cruel woman. She used to snatch away her letters from home before she'd read them, and throw them in the range because they made her dreamy. . . . And the beedles! Would you believe it? – until she came to London she'd never seen a black beedle. Here Ma always gave a little laugh, as though – not to have seen a black beedle! Well! It was as if to say you'd never seen your own feet.

When the family was sold up she went as 'help' to a doctor's house, and after two years there, on the run from morning till night, she married her husband. He was a baker.

'A baker, Mrs. Parker!' the literary gentleman would say. For occasionally he laid aside his tomes and lent an ear, at least, to this product called Life. 'It must be rather nice to be married to a baker!'

Mrs. Parker didn't look so sure.

'Such a clean trade,' said the gentleman.

Mrs. Parker didn't look convinced.

'And didn't you like handing the new loaves to the customers?'

'Well, sir,' said Mrs. Parker, 'I wasn't in the shop above a great deal. We had thirteen little ones and buried seven of them. If it wasn't the 'ospital it was the infirmary, you might say!'

'You might, indeed, Mrs. Parker!' said the gentleman, shuddering, and taking up his pen again.

Yes, seven had gone, and while the six were still small her husband was taken ill with consumption. It was flour on the lungs, the doctor told her at the time. . . . Her husband sat up in bed with his shirt pulled over his head, and the doctor's finger drew a circle on his back.

'Now, if we were to cut him open *here*, Mrs. Parker,' said the doctor, 'you'd find his lungs chock-a-block with white powder. Breathe, my good fellow!' And Mrs. Parker never knew for certain whether she saw or whether she fancied she saw a great fan of white dust come out of her poor dear husband's lips. . . .

But the struggle she'd had to bring up those six little children and keep herself to herself. Terrible it had been! Then, just when they were old enough to go to school her husband's sister came to stop with them to help things along, and she hadn't been there more than two months when she fell down a flight of steps and hurt her spine. And for five years Ma Parker had another baby – and such a one for crying! – to look after. Then young Maudie went wrong and took her sister Alice with her; the two boys emigrimated, and young Jim went to India with the army, and Ethel, the youngest, married a good-for-nothing little waiter who died of ulcers the year little Lennie was born. And now little Lennie – my grandson. . . .

The piles of dirty cups, dirty dishes, were washed and dried. The ink-black knives were cleaned with a piece of potato and finished off with a piece of cork. The table was scrubbed, and the dresser and the sink that had sardine tails swimming in it. . . .

He'd never been a strong child – never from the first. He'd been one of those fair babies that everybody took for a girl. Silvery fair curls he had, blue eyes, and a little freckle like a diamond on one side of his nose. The trouble she and Ethel had had to rear that child! The things out of the newspapers they tried him with! Every Sunday morning Ethel would read aloud while Ma Parker did her washing.

'DEAR SIR, – Just a line to let you know my little Myrtil was laid out for dead. . . . After four bottils . . . gained 8 lbs. in 9 weeks, *and is still putting it on.*'

And then the egg-cup of ink would come off the dresser and the letter would be written, and Ma would buy a postal order on her way to work next morning. But it was no use. Nothing made little Lennie put it on. Taking him to the cemetery, even, never gave him a colour; a nice shake-up in the bus never improved his appetite.

But he was gran's boy from the first. . . .

'Whose boy are you?' said old Ma Parker, straightening up from the stove and going over to the smudgy window. And a little voice, so warm, so close, it half stifled her – it seemed to be in her breast under her heart – laughed out, and said, 'I'm gran's boy!'

At that moment here was a sound of steps, and the literary gentleman appeared, dressed for walking.

'Oh, Mrs. Parker, I'm going out.'

'Very good, sir.'

'And you'll find your half-crown in the tray of the inkstand.'

'Thank you, sir.'

'Oh, by the way, Mrs Parker,' said the literary gentleman quickly, 'you didn't throw away any cocoa last time you were here – did you?'

'No, sir.'

'*Very* strange. I could have sworn I left a teaspoonful of cocoa in the tin.' He broke off. He said softly and firmly, 'You'll always tell me when you throw things away – won't you, Mrs. Parker?' And he walked off very well pleased with himself, convinced, in fact, he'd shown Mrs. Parker that under his apparent carelessness he was as vigilant as a woman.

The door banged. She took her brushes and cloths into the bedroom. But when she began to make the bed, smoothing, tucking, patting, the thought of little Lennie was unbearable. Why did he have to suffer so? That's what she couldn't understand. Why should a little angel child have to arsk for his breath and fight for it? There was no sense in making a child suffer like that.

. . . From Lennie's little box of a chest there came a sound as though something was boiling. There was a great lump of something bubbling in his chest that he couldn't get rid of. When he coughed, the sweat sprang out on his head; his eyes bulged, his hands waved, and the great lump bubbled as a potato knocks in a saucepan. But what was more awful than all was when he didn't cough he sat against the pillow and never spoke or answered, or even made as if he heard. Only he looked offended.

'It's not your poor old gran's doing it, my lovey,' said old Ma Parker, patting back the damp hair from his scarlet ears. But Lennie moved his head and edged away. Dreadfully offended with her he looked – and solemn. He bent his head and looked at her sideways as though he couldn't have believed it of his gran.

But at the last . . . Ma Parker threw the counterpane over the bed. No, she simply couldn't think about it. It was too much – she'd had too much in her life to bear. She'd borne it up till now, she'd kept herself to herself, and never once had she been seen to cry. Never by a living soul. Not even her own children had seen Ma break down. She'd kept a proud face always. But now! Lennie gone – what had she? She had nothing. He was all she'd got from life, and now he was took too. Why must it all have happened to me? she wondered. 'What have I done?' said old Ma Parker. 'What have I done?'

As she said those words she suddenly let fall her brush. She found herself in the kitchen. Her misery was so terrible that she pinned on her hat, put on her jacket and walked out of the flat like a person in a dream. She did not know what she was doing. She was like a person so dazed by the horror of what has happened that he walks away – anywhere, as though by walking away he could escape. . . .

It was cold in the street. There was a wind like ice. People went flitting by, very fast; the men walked like scissors; the women trod like cats. And nobody knew – nobody cared. Even if she broke down, if at last, after all these years, she were to cry, she'd find herself in the lock-up as like as not.

But at the thought of crying it was as though little Lennie leapt in his gran's arms. Ah, that's what she wants to do, my dove. Gran wants to cry. If she could only cry now, cry for a long time, over everything, beginning with her first place and the cruel cook, going on to the doctor's, and then the seven little ones, death of her husband, the children's leaving her, and all the years of misery that led up to Lennie. But to have a proper cry over all these things would take a long time. All the same, the time for it had come. She must do it. She couldn't put it off any longer; she couldn't wait any more.... Where could she go?

'She's had a hard life, has Ma Parker.' Yes, a hard life, indeed! Her chin began to tremble; there was no time to lose. But where? Where?

She couldn't go home; Ethel was there. It would frighten Ethel out of her life. She couldn't sit on a bench anywhere; people would come arsking her questions. She couldn't possibly go back to the gentleman's flat; she had no right to cry in strangers' houses. If she sat on some steps a policeman would speak to her.

Oh, wasn't there anywhere where she could hide and keep herself to herself and stay as long as she liked, not disturbing anybody, and nobody worrying her? Wasn't there anywhere in the world where she could have her cry out – at last?

Ma Parker stood, looking up and down. The icy wind blew out her apron into a balloon. And now it began to rain. There was nowhere.

■■■■■■■■ Katherine Mansfield ■■■■■■■■

1 Consider the characters. What impression do you get of them? Do you find them convincing? Which is the main character? What part do the other characters play in telling you about the main character?

2 Consider the setting. Do you get a clear picture of where the story takes place? Are any contrasts intended? Does the setting tell you anything about the characters?

3 Consider the plot. What actually happens in the story? Do you think enough happens to make the story interesting? Is the plot based on contrast and/ or action and reaction?

4 From whose point of view are most of the events of the story seen? Why does the writer choose this point of view? Is the language appropriate to this point of view? Are there other points of view? If so, why?

5 What do you think the writer was particularly interested in in telling this story? Is the writer *telling* the reader anything? What is the point of the story?

6 a Now write an account of the story in which you describe what it is about, comment on the writer's approach to character, setting and plot, give your views on how successful the writer is in achieving what she set out to do, and say whether you found the story interesting and moving.
   Or
   b What do you think Ma Parker eventually does? Continue the story from where Katherine Mansfield finished.
   Or
   c Write a story about another character who feels pain at the loss of someone dear.

## 4.2.1 Further reading

*Collections of short stories by individual authors*

Achebe, Chinua, *Girls at War*. Heinemann Educational Books.
Barstow, Stan, *The Human Element*. Longman.
Bradbury, Ray, *The Day it Rained Forever*. Penguin Books.
Chaplin, Sid, *The Leaping Lad*. Longman.
Dahl, Roald, *A Roald Dahl Selection*. Longman.
du Maurier, Daphne, *The Birds and Other Stories*. Longman.
Glanville, Brian, *Goalkeepers are Crazy*. Longman.
Gordimer, Nadine, *Six Feet of the Country*. Penguin Books.
———, *Some Monday for Sure*. Heinemann Educational Books.
Greene, Graham, *Twenty-one Stories*. Penguin Books.
Hardy, Thomas, *The Withered Arm and Other Wessex Tales*. Heinemann New Windmill.
Hemingway, Ernest, *A Hemingway Selection*. Longman.
Jacobson, Dan, *A Way of Life*. Longman.
Lawrence, D. H., *Selected Tales*. Heinemann New Windmill.
Lessing, Doris, *Nine African Stories*. Longman.
Maugham, W. Somerset, *The Kite and Other Stories*. Heinemann New Windmill.
Naipaul, V. S., *Miguel Street*. Penguin Books.
Naughton, Bill, *Late Night on Watling Street*. Longman.
Ngugi wa Thiong'o, *Secret Lives*. Heinemann Educational Books.
Norris, Leslie, *Sliding*. Longman.
O'Connor, Frank, *My Oedipus Complex and Other Stories*. Longman.
O'Flaherty, Liam, *The Wave and Other Stories*. Longman.
Sillitoe, Alan, *A Sillitoe Selection*. Longman.
Wells, H. G., *Selected Short Stories of H. G. Wells*. Penguin Books.

*Anthologies of short stories*

Ash, Ranjana (ed.), *Short Stories from Pakistan, India and Bangladesh*. Nelson Harrap.
Barnes, Douglas R. (ed.), *Short Stories of Our Time*. Nelson Harrap.
———and Egford, R. F. (eds), *Twentieth Century Short Stories*. Nelson Harrap.
Crowe, Frances (ed.), *Irish Short Stories*. Longman.
Fain, M. T. (ed.), *Four Modern Story-tellers*. Heinemann Educational Books.
Jackson, David and Pepper, Dennis (eds), *Story: the Third Book*. Penguin Books.
Jones, Rhodri (ed.), *Heinemann Short Stories*, Books 4 and 5. Heinemann Educational Books.
———, *Story Plus*, Books 4 and 5. Heinemann Educational Books.
Marland, Michael (ed.) *Caribbean Stories*. Longman.

# 4.3 Writing – a clear train of thought

For a reader to be able to follow your train of thought and understand what you are saying step by step, it must be clear in your own mind as you write. Plan your writing carefully and check that what you write is logical and has a definite sequence or order.

● Look at the following paragraphs. They have been printed in the wrong order. Reorder them so that the sequence of ideas makes sense. What clues are there in the subject matter and in the phrasing to help you decide which paragraph follows which? Begin with paragraph one.

**A** In terms of English teenagers, Teddy Boys were the start of everything: rock'n roll and coffee bars, clothes and bikes and language, jukeboxes and coffee with froth on it – the whole concept of a private teen life style, separate from the adult world.

**B** Drapes apart, they wore tight drainpipe jeans, tapered to the ankle, and luminous yellow socks; creepers, large crêpe-soled shoes like boats; brass rings on several fingers, worn both for ornament and for destruction; riverboat gamblers' bootlace ties; and often, in the back jeans pocket, a flick-knife.

**C** They were hooligans. They were kids with money and time to waste and nothing to do. They were bored and malcontent, and they formed themselves into gangs. Sometimes they only roamed the streets and brawled a bit and made noise; sometimes they got involved in real crime. But they didn't break laws for profit, or not primarily – the attraction lay in the excitement, the sense of action. The word 'kicks' was used a lot and it meant something, anything that made time pass.

**D** The reason for this lack of identity was simple: they had no money to spend. They were apprenticed or they were on the dole or they gave their wages to their mothers. In any case, they had no means of rising up and running amok.

**E** By the middle fifties, the gap would be filled. Catching on fast, businessmen began to bombard the market with gimmicks and a whole new industry was launched.

**F** This style was known as the duck's arse and variations were a diamond-shaped crewcut on top, with the rest hanging down from the crown, and the Boston, cut straight across at the back, above a shaved white neck.

**G** Before the war, working-class, and most middle-class kids had shared everything with their parents. They had danced to the same music, sat through the same films, worn the same clothes. 'In the thirties, being a teenager meant a pound a week and acne,' says John Taylor, who edits *Style Weekly*. 'They tried to dress like their fathers, they wore tweeds and smoked pipes. It was like lamb dressed as mutton and, even if they tried to be different, all they could get was a sixpenny tie from Woolworths.'

**H** That wasn't all. The draped jackets would be black or maroon or sometimes powder blue, and there might be a flash of fancy waistcoat as well. Altogether, the effect was one of heroic excess: garnish, greasy and quite magnificent.

**I** The first Teds emerged in the East End and in North London, around Tottenham and Highbury, and from there they spread southwards, to Streatham and Battersea and Purley, and westwards, to Shepherds Bush and Fulham, and then down to the seaside towns, and up into the Midlands until, by 1956, they had taken root all over Britain.

**J** But when the Teds first started, around 1952, they had none of this. They existed in a vacuum, without any kind of sponsorship and/or exploitation. They rode bikes or went to the movies or hung around in arcades. Mostly, they stood on street-corners, watching.

**K** Even after the war, things stayed tight. But by the early fifties, the austerity was ending and it was possible to experiment. For the first time, teenagers found themselves making proper money, anything up to £20 a week, and they started looking for things to spend it on.

**L** They also had a standardized face, which was pinched and underfed, a bit ratty, and they tended to pimples and acne. But their greatest glory was their sideburns, which had to sprout well past the ear-lobe, and their hair, which was worn long and swept up in a quiff at the front, then dragged back at the sides and slopped down heavy with hair-oil.

**M** Essentially, their uniform was a bowdlerization of the Savile Row Edwardian Look, hence the name Teddy Boys, but they also used elements of the zoot suit, with a very long and loose-draped jacket.

**N** In the beginning, this wasn't easy. Since the adolescent market had always been minimal, there were no businessmen aiming for teenage custom. There were no teen clubs and no teen music, no teen foods or clothes. Nothing that didn't apply equally to adults.

■ From Nik Cohn, *Today there are no Gentlemen* ■

### 4.3.1 Linking words

Certain words and phrases are very useful in giving the reader clues that one event follows another or that one part contrasts with another. That is, they help the reader to follow your train of thought.

● Here are examples of linking words and phrases. In each case, write two sentences, beginning your second sentence with the linking word or phrase. For instance:

> After fighting the fire for two hours, I had to move away from the heat and the smoke and rest. *By now*, the fire had spread through three fields and was threatening the copse by the side of the mill.

1 On the other hand . . .
2 Nevertheless . . .
3 Even so . . .
4 In spite of this . . .
5 It was at this point that . . .
6 Another reason is . . .
7 However . . .
8 Some time later . . .
9 Some people . . . others . . .
10 Of course . . .
11 But . . .
12 In addition . . .
13 Afterwards . . .
14 Before I could . . .
15 Certainly . . .

# 4.4 Reading – formal and informal language

There are different kinds of English, ranging from the formal to the very informal. Look at these words:

| | | | |
|---|---|---|---|
| gentleman | man | chap | geezer |
| police officer | policeman | copper | fuzz |

'Gentleman' and 'police officer' are very formal, and would be used on very formal occasions – if someone were trying to be especially polite, or in official or public situations, for example, at a formal dinner or in court.

'Man' and 'policeman' are Standard English, the words that would normally be used by the majority of educated English-speaking people.

'Chap' and 'copper' are colloquial. They are the kind of words people might use in ordinary speech but would not necessarily use in a formal letter.

'Geezer' and 'fuzz' are examples of slang. They are even less formal than 'chap' and 'copper'. Slang can sometimes be like a secret language, which a certain group of people understand, but others find incomprehensible – like 'schoolboy slang' and 'Cockney rhyming slang'.

Dialect is another form of informal English, and is the language spoken by people in a particular area or belonging to a particular social group. Different areas in the UK have different dialects. So too do different parts of the English-speaking world. A West Indian speaker, for instance, might use 'guy' for 'man' and 'bullman' for 'policeman'.

All these forms of English are valid. It is a matter of choosing the appropriate language form for different circumstances and purposes. You are doing this all the time – as you chat informally to your friends and family, or speak more formally to, say, your friends' parents or in class discussion, etc.

It is probably true that Standard English is more widely useful than other forms, and is more commonly used in writing. Standard English is used for world-wide communication and official business. It is used in official reports, business letters, news reports in 'serious' newspapers, the narrative of most novels and short stories, most poems. But informal language is used too in most modern plays, the speech in novels and stories, some newspapers and some poems.

You have to be able to write, speak, read and understand Standard English. You also have to be able to use the form of language that is appropriate to particular situations.

● Some questions to think about:

1 Can you give other examples of formal and informal words which refer to the same thing? Think of the different words for 'drink', 'drunk', 'arrested', 'money'.
2 Can you give examples of dialect used where you live or which you know?
3 Would it be fair to consider American as a dialect of English? What differences are there between American English and Standard English?
4 Consider occasions where particular types of language would be appropriate.

● Examine the kind of language used in each of the following. Say what kind of English it is and consider how appropriate and effective it is, taking into account what the writer is trying to do.

## ═══════════ A ═══════════

She was a bit of a drip was old Myra, but absolutely gone on me. If she hadn't have been I don't suppose I'd have looked on the same side of the street she was on, let alone take her out. But I'm like that I am. I can't turn my back on a woman who looks up to me and thinks I am somebody, even if, what you might say, I can't bear the sight of her otherwise. I must admit a bit of the old flannel goes a long way with me, especially if a woman tells me I dress well. I do like anything like that. Another thing I've got to have is a woman around that I can be off-hand with, blow my top with if I feel like it, and generally say what I want to, clean or dirty. Most women won't stand for it, because they ain't got the savvy to see it don't matter, and that once you've said what you want and done what you want, all the best what was underneath is on top. But them dames that can see it can make a bloke feel at home. Not that I like to go regular with that sort of woman – because as a rule they're on the scruffy side, and a bloke can't show 'em off to his mates in the dance hall or in the pubs, which I like to do with a woman – but if they ain't good enough for a steady, I do like to have one on the side as a fill-in.

From Bill Naughton, 'Spiv in Love'

## B

**Yuh Hear Bout?**

Yuh hear bout di people dem arres
Fi bun dung di Asian people dem house?
Yuh hear bout di policeman dem lock up
Fi beat up di black bwoy widout a cause?
Yuh hear bout di M.P. dem sack because im refuse fi help im coloured constituents in a dem fight 'gainst deportation?
Yuh noh hear bout dem?
Me neida.

Valerie Bloom

## C

This book is an attempt to explore a strange and rather exotic new area of modern life. It is about the way many of us are being influenced and manipulated – far more than we realize – in the patterns of our everyday lives. Large-scale efforts are being made, often with impressive success, to channel our unthinking habits, our purchasing decisions, and our thought processes by the use of insights gleaned from psychiatry and the social sciences. Typically these efforts take place beneath our level of awareness; so that the appeals which move us are often, in a sense, 'hidden'.

Some of the manipulating being attempted is simply amusing. Some of it is disquieting, particularly when viewed as a portent of what may be ahead on a more intensive and effective scale for us all. Cooperative scientists have come along providentially to furnish some awesome tools.

The use of mass psychoanalysis to guide campaigns of persuasion has become the basis of a multimillion-dollar industry. Professional persuaders have seized upon it in their groping for more effective ways to sell us their wares – whether products, ideas, attitudes, candidates, goals, or states of mind.

From Vance Packard, *The Hidden Persuaders*

## D

THE FIRST CAMERA DESIGNED FOR THE BRITISH SUMMER.

This is the Olympus AF-1 and it makes sure that your holiday snaps won't ever be a wash-out.

For a start, it's impervious to dust, sand and the odd downpour.

On dull overcast days, or long summer evenings it'll decide for itself whether you need a flash.

Even in broad daylight, it can detect whether you need flash for fill-in on back-lit shots.

It's loaded with other features, too.

Automatic focusing, exposure and film loading, built-in winder and self-timer.

In fact, it's one of the smallest auto-everything compacts around, so it won't make much of a bulge in your raincoat pocket.

Not surprisingly, the reviewers have showered praise upon it.

Camera Weekly said it was "The perfect compact." Amateur Photographer said it was "the most enjoyable compact I've ever used."

Don't let dodgy weather or a dodgy old camera spoil your shots again.

Slip on your wellies and splash out on a new AF-1.

Please send me more information about the AF-1
To: Olympus Optical Co. (UK) Limited, 2-8 Honduras St. London EC1Y 0TX Telephone: 01-253 2772.

NAME

ADDRESS

**OLYMPUS AF-1**

# 4.5 Body language

Body language, or non-verbal communication, is the name given to the way our bodies 'speak' and indicate our feelings and attitudes. When we speak to someone, our bodies reinforce or contradict what we say with eye movements, gestures, changes in posture and facial expression. It is the same when we listen to someone. Body language therefore has an important role to play in oral communication.

## 4.5.1 Speaking

*Eye contact* Eye contact with the person you are speaking to or your audience is vital. It is one of the ways by which you hold attention and emphasise what you are saying. If you look down at the floor or gaze into the middle distance, your listeners will lose interest and not feel involved.

If you are speaking to a group of people or to a class, don't just fix one or two people with a stare. Move your gaze round regularly to take everyone in, to make them feel they are all included.

*Gestures* These can be used to emphasise or echo what you say – a shrug, for instance, pointing, jabbing the air, raising the hands palms upwards, clenching a fist, nodding or shaking the head, waggling a finger. But gestures should be deliberate and not overdone. When you use them, you should know that you are using them and why.

*Posture* This should be appropriate to the situation. In an interview, you might sit back comfortably in your seat to show that you are relaxed, and lean forward when you have points you want to emphasise. In group discussion, you might lean forward and turn your body round to take in the other members of the group as you speak. When giving a talk, you should probably stand up reasonably straight, with your hands free to use gestures. You would be well balanced so that you can lean forward and draw your audience in towards you. You might even take a few steps. Variety in posture can show confidence and provide a change of view for the audience.

*Facial expression* Relate your facial expression to what you are saying. Whether you are being serious or frivolous should be reflected in your face – though sometimes a joke can be more effective if told with a 'dead-pan' expression. Raised eyebrows, eyes closed for reflection, sudden widening of the eyes, clamping the lips together, a wink, a smile, a rueful grin, a look of surprise – all these are things you might use.

*Listeners' body language* Be aware of the body language of your listeners. If you find signs of inattention and loss of interest (eye contact straying or eyes closing, heads lowering, fidgeting, shuffling of feet), then you have to try to do something about it – move on quickly to another aspect of the subject, for instance, or bring in a visual aid, or ask a question.

## 4.5.2 Listening

Revise the 'Listening' section in Unit 3 (3.5).

● Here are some exercises on aspects of body language:

1 Describe the body language you might expect if someone is telling you a lie, or trying to sell you something, or asking a favour, or telling you off, or getting annoyed with you, or showing off superior knowledge, or showing contempt for you. Think of the use of the eyes and the mouth, the facial expression, the position of the head, the way the body is held, the use of gesture and touching. In pairs, demonstrate one of the situations outlined above.

2 Make a list of as many variations of the following as you can and the feelings or attitudes they suggest:
a Use of the eyes (for example, lowering the eyes might suggest shame)
b Position of the head
c The way the body is held
d Use of the mouth and lips
e Facial expression
f Hand and arm gestures
Talk about them and demonstrate them to the class.

3 'What's my job?' Perform an action typical of a particular job. See if the class can guess what job it is.

4 'Guess the title'. In pairs or groups, choose the title of a book, a film or a television programme and prepare a mime that illustrates the title, taking it a word or a syllable at a time. See if the class can guess the title.

5 Imagine you are in a foreign country. You can't speak the language, and no one can speak yours. The only way you can communicate is by facial expression and gesture. In pairs, work out an encounter between yourself and an inhabitant of this country. You might be trying to buy food at a market stall, or seeking directions on how to get to the local theatre or art gallery, or trying to get assistance with your car which has broken down. Discuss which aspects of body language are most useful in a situation like this.

6 'The interview'. In pairs, work out and show an interview without using words. It might be between a policeman and a suspect, an employer and an applicant for a job, a manager and a member of the work force who is being disciplined.

# 4.6 Aural test

The aural test which may be part of your examination is designed to test your ability to listen and concentrate. It will probably take the following form.

A recording of spoken material will be played to you. You will be expected to listen carefully to the way the speakers talk, the kind of language they use and the way they respond to each other, as well as to what they say.

The recording will be played twice. The first time you simply listen. Concentrate on getting as full a picture as you can of what is going on and who is taking part. You need to get a clear image of the different speakers and their contributions, and what the talk is about. It may be relevant to work out where the talk is taking place. If an argument is involved, you need to decide which speaker is on which side and to follow the points being made.

After the first playing, you will be allowed to look at a transcript of the recording and the questions set. You will have three minutes to look at this before the recording is played again.

Study the questions so that you have some idea what to look for during the second playing, when you may make notes. Check particularly for any question which asks about the attitude or relationship of speakers. These can be conveyed by tone of voice as much as by words. Make careful notes on this aspect during the second playing. This is the last chance you will have of *hearing* the words spoken. Many nuances of meaning may be missing when you simply have the words printed on the page. Listen to how words are said and the tone used. Note whether speakers at particular points are angry or amused or hesitant or whatever. Are they hostile to each other, or friendly or indifferent or what?

After the second playing you will be allowed three minutes to complete your notes. Use this chance to annotate the transcript. Work out what information the questions need and find it in the transcript. Underline it, circle it, number it, use arrows to link points. Use any visual means which help you isolate and clarify the material you need. Jot down brief notes outlining the points to be covered.

You then have fifty minutes in which to write your answers to the questions. Be sure you know what the questions are asking. Check that you have given all the information available in the transcript and in the notes you made.

● Here is a specimen aural test. (If an aural test is not part of your examination, you can use it as a comprehension exercise.)

Do *not* read the following transcript and questions until you have heard a reading or a recording of it.

1  You are about to hear part of a radio programme about consumer research. First you will hear the interviewer. The others taking part are Margaret Harshaw, editor of *Consumer Research Guide*, Mrs Hilary Kane, a consumer, and Mr Hamish Morrison, Chairman of Consumer Research Services.
2  The recording will be played *twice*: the first time for listening and the second time for note-making.
3  When you have heard the reading or recording for the first time, you will be allowed to look at the transcript and the questions. You will be allowed three minutes to read the questions and then you will hear the passage again.
4  As you listen to the piece for the second time, you should make notes on the transcript and sheet of paper provided. After the second reading, you will be allowed three minutes to complete your note-making.
5  Attempt *all* questions. You will be allowed fifty minutes in which to write your answers.

INTERVIEWER Market research seems to be a growing industry. Many of you must have been stopped in the street or had people knocking on your door to ask you questions about what television programmes you watch or which brands of soft drinks you buy or what soap powder you use and why. The information obtained in this way is studied, and manufacturers modify their products accordingly. They change the shape or the formula. They change the colour or the packaging. They choose one advertising approach instead of another. But now there is a new development. People are being interviewed in groups. They are being asked to go to reception rooms in hotels or to hired halls where their opinions on certain products are asked, or they are invited to test new products about to be launched on the market. They don't get paid for this, but any travelling expenses are covered. Researchers feel that it is valuable to get consumers together to discuss products. The interplay of one consumer with another and one opinion with another can often provide more insight into the value of the product and how to market it than any amount of carefully filled-in questionnaires. We asked Margaret Harshaw, editor of the *Consumer Research Guide* about this new development.

MARGARET HARSHAW Yes, I think, that's true. The feeling now is that people are usually more candid discussing something in a group than they would be when answering questions put to them by a researcher. Frequently, there is the danger that the consumer will simply give the answer that the researcher seems to be wanting, no matter how impartial the researcher tries to be. Evidence suggests that the results of questionnaires are not always to be trusted. Group interviews might not give you the same statistical information as the analysis of one-to-one interviews, but it can often suggest more interesting lines for developing or marketing products.

INTERVIEWER And this kind of approach is becoming more common?

MARGARET HARSHAW Yes, I think so. People are sometimes reluctant to stop and answer questions in the street, or to spend time with someone going door to door. But if they are asked to come to a specially arranged meeting, with transport laid on, they usually take it much more seriously. I suppose they feel flattered that their opinion is being asked, in a way that they wouldn't be if they were simply stopped in the street or had someone who was knocking at every door in the street.

INTERVIEWER But would this approach still produce a representative sample?

MARGARET HARSHAW More so, because the researchers could do much more research into the backgrounds of the people they select. They could do much more to ensure a balanced group. The answers they get won't necessarily be the last word. There will still be advertising campaigns based on this kind of information which will fail. Producers will still get the product or the price or the packaging wrong. But it's the best approach we've got.

INTERVIEWER One person who has had experience of this new approach to consumer research is Mrs Hilary Kane. She was asked by Consumer Research Services to attend a meeting at the Hillier Hotel in London to discuss and comment on a new product she had tried out.

HILARY KANE I was pleased to be asked at first. I had the time to spare and I'm interested in consumer advice and guidance. A car was sent to collect me, so transport was no problem. It was when we got to the hotel that things started going wrong. I'd been told that the meeting would be tape recorded. Well, that was all right by me. But when I got to the hotel, I was shown into the wrong room by mistake, and there was a video recorder. I was shaken when I saw it. Tape recording's one thing, but video recording's another. I didn't want my every move and expression recorded. I went into the meeting, but I couldn't say a word. I was so disgusted with the way I had been misled and so worried about my every word and gesture being recorded on film. What were they going to do with it, I kept asking myself. I hadn't agreed to them having a copy of me on film. And then at the end someone asked, 'Where's the tape recorder?' Well, I'd been looking around too. 'It's not a tape recorder,' I said. 'It's a video recorder. And it's behind that mirror.'

INTERVIEWER We asked Mr Hamish Morrison, Chairman of Consumer Research Services about his use of video recorders for consumer sessions of this kind.

HAMISH MORRISON There is nothing sinister about it. We need to record these meetings, and it is easier and more effective to have a video recording than to have a secretary trying to take down everything that is said in shorthand.

INTERVIEWER But are all the people who take part aware of this?

HAMISH MORRISON Of course. We make it quite clear that all meetings will be recorded.

INTERVIEWER Do you specify that it will be a video recording? People we have spoken to are under the impression that it will be a tape recording, not a video recording. In fact, some of them have said they were specifically told it would be a tape recording.

HAMISH MORRISON Well, I don't know where they can have got that impression from. Nowadays, if we say 'recording', we automatically mean a video recording. Everyone knows that.

INTERVIEWER Then why make such a secret of it? Why hide the video recorder behind a mirror?

HAMISH MORRISON It's obvious. We don't want people to be put off by seeing the video camera and being aware they are being recorded. We want them to behave and react naturally so we keep the video recorder out of sight. It usually works out very satisfactorily.

INTERVIEWER So says Mr Hamish Morrison. But it didn't work out that way with Mrs Hilary Kane. I asked Margaret Harshaw about this use of video recording.

MARGARET HARSHAW It is certainly becoming more common. There are advantages to consumer research firms in using video recording. You don't just get the words. You get the reactions as well. It makes a big difference to know whether someone is leaning forward eagerly when he is saying something or whether he is sitting back relaxed and uninvolved. You get a lot of information from the way people behave which you can't get from a transcript of the spoken word. But, of course, people taking part should always be informed that they are being video-taped, and they should always be asked to give their permission first.

---

**a** Describe three methods referred to in this interview that are used by researchers to gain information from consumers.

**b** What advantages does Margaret Harshaw see in group interviews that are video-recorded?

**c** Why was Mrs Hilary Kane unhappy about being video-recorded?

**d** What impression do you get of Mr Hamish Morrison and his defence of using video recording?

**e** Is the interviewer totally neutral or can you find an example or examples of bias?

**f** Basing your ideas on what you have heard, write two paragraphs, one outlining the advantages of consumer research to manufacturers, and the other considering how effective such research is. Together, your two paragraphs should be between 100 and 150 words long.

# Unit Five

# 5.1 Writing – describing a character

● Read the following description of Mr Slope.

Mr Slope is tall, and not ill made. His feet and hands are large, as has ever been the case with all his family, but he has a broad chest and wide shoulders to carry off these excrescences, and on the whole his figure is good. His countenance, however, is not specially prepossessing. His hair is lank, and of a dull pale reddish hue. It is always formed into three straight lumpy masses, each brushed with admirable precision, and cemented with much grease; two of them adhere closely to the sides of his face, and the other lies at right angles above them. He wears no whiskers, and is always punctiliously shaven. His face is nearly of the same colour as his hair, though perhaps a little redder; it is not unlike beef – beef, however, one would say, of a bad quality. His forehead is capacious and high, but square and heavy, and unpleasantly shining. His mouth is large, though his lips are thin and bloodless; and his big, prominent, pale brown eyes inspire anything but confidence. His nose, however, is his redeeming feature: it is pronounced, straight and well-formed though I myself should have liked it better did it not possess a somewhat spongy, porous appearance, as though it had been cleverly formed out of a red coloured cork.

I never could endure to shake hands with Mr Slope. A cold, clammy perspiration always exudes from him, the small drops are ever to be seen standing on his brow, and his friendly grasp is unpleasant.

■■ From Anthony Trollope, *Barchester Towers* ■■

1   What *kinds* of information are you given about Mr Slope?

2   Look at the use of comparisons. How do these help to make the description of Mr Slope more vivid?

3   Do you think the choice of the name for the character is appropriate?

4   Sum up in your own words the impression you get of Mr Slope.

Mr Slope is a character in a long leisurely novel, so the writer has plenty of room to expand and give a detailed description. In a short story or a character sketch, it may not be appropriate to give such a full account. Nevertheless, the description gives some ideas about the approach you might take in your own description – for example:

o   factual description of physical appearance
o   the use of comparisons to make it more vivid
o   the choice of a name that suits the character.

● Compare the description of Mr Slope with the following.

# ▬▬ THE DEVIL DEALER ▬▬

When Mr Howard passed along the streets of Belmont* mothers hastily dragged their children indoors. The whole district knew that Mr Howard dealt with the devil.

He was a tall, lanky individual with a hoarse, colourless, funereal voice. Everything about him was lean. His face was thin and pale, almost yellow, under his brown skin. His arms were long, almost seeming to go past his knees, and his hands were bony with veins running over the back of them like worms. He had a fine, scattery moustache like a youth growing into manhood and a small, sparse beard. He always looked sallow, dirty, and his clothes rumpled as if he slept in them. His eyes were bright like the eyes of a bird. It was rumoured that he was very rich.

He lived alone in a huge house which was once brown but from which the paint peeled off in strips, as if changing its skin. It stood on the fringe of the village, isolated, at the far end of two acres of a wild, tangled garden that ended abruptly on the edge of a precipice below which a river ran that was dry for six months of the year.

*Belmont is part of Port of Spain, the capital of Trinidad.

From Barnabas J. Ramon-Fortuné,
▬▬▬ 'The Devil-Dealer' ▬▬▬

5   What *kinds* of information given here are similar to those used in the description of Mr Slope?

6   What *other* kinds of information are you given about Mr Howard?

7   Look at the comparisons. Comment on how effective they are.

8   Does the account of where Mr Howard lives tell you anything about him?

9   What impression of Mr Howard do you think the writer is trying to give? Does he succeed?

This description of Mr Howard is the beginning of a short story. It is told from the point of view of an 11-year-old boy. He and his older brother try to steal fruit from Mr Howard's garden and are caught. Since it is a short story, the writer has to concentrate on aspects of the character relevant to the plot. He has to pick out these details that create the impression he wants to give. He uses the following:

o   factual description of certain aspects of physical appearance that build up a particular impression
o   comparisons
o   what other people think of the character and how they behave towards him
o   where the character lives.

● Here is a description of another character, Mrs Gargery.

▬▬▬▬▬▬▬▬▬▬▬▬▬▬▬▬▬▬

My sister, Mrs. Joe Gargery, was more than twenty years older than I, and had established a great reputation with herself and the neighbours because she had brought me up 'by hand'. Having at that time to find out for myself what the expression meant, and knowing her to have a hard and heavy hand, and to be much in the habit of laying it upon her husband as well as upon me, I supposed that Joe Gargery and I were both brought up by hand.

She was not a good-looking woman, my sister; and I had a general impression that she must have made Joe Gargery marry her by hand. Joe was a fair man, with curls of flaxen hair on each side of his smooth face, and with eyes of such a very undecided blue that they seemed to have somehow got mixed with their own whites. He was a mild, good-natured, sweet-tempered, easy-going, foolish, dear fellow – a sort of Hercules in strength, and also in weakness.

My sister, Mrs. Joe, with black hair and eyes, had such a prevailing redness of skin that I sometimes used to wonder whether it was possible she washed herself with a nutmeg-grater instead of soap. She was tall and bony, and almost always wore a coarse apron, fastened over her figure behind with two loops, and having a square impregnable bib in front, that was stuck full of pins and needles. She made it a powerful merit in herself, and a strong reproach against Joe, that she wore this apron so much. Though I really see no reason why she should have worn it at all: or why, if she did wear it at all, she should not have taken it off, every day of her life.

Joe's forge adjoined our house, which was a wooden house, as many of the dwellings in our country were – most of them, at that time. When I ran home from the churchyard, the forge was shut up, and Joe was sitting alone in the kitchen. Joe and I being fellow-sufferers, and having confidences as such, Joe imparted a confidence to me, the moment I raised the latch of the door and peeped in at him opposite to it, sitting in the chimney-corner.

'Mrs. Joe has been out a dozen times, looking for you, Pip. And she's out now, making it a baker's dozen.'

'Is she?'

'Yes, Pip,' said Joe, 'and what's worse, she's got Tickler with her.'

At this dismal intelligence, I twisted the only button on my waistcoat round and round, and looked in great depression at the fire. Tickler was a wax-ended piece of cane, worn smooth by collision with my tickled frame.

'She sot down,' said Joe, 'and she got up, and she made a grab at Tickler, and she Ram-paged out. That's what she did,' said Joe, slowly clearing the fire between the lower bars with the poker, and looking at it, 'she Ram-paged out, Pip.'

'Has she been gone long, Joe?' I always treated him as a larger species of child, and as no more than my equal.

'Well,' said Joe, glancing up at the Dutch clock, 'she's been on the Ram-page, this last spell, about five minutes, Pip. She's a-coming! Get behind the door, old chap, and have the jack-towel betwixt you.'

I took the advice. My sister, Mrs. Joe, throwing the door wide open, and finding an obstruction behind it, immediately divined the cause, and applied Tickler to its further investigation. She concluded by throwing me – I often served her as a connubial missile – at Joe, who, glad to get hold of me on any terms, passed me on into the chimney, and quietly fenced me up there with his great leg.

'Where have you been, you young monkey? said Mrs. Joe, stamping her foot. 'Tell me directly what you've been doing to wear me away with fret and fright and worrit, or I'd have you out of that corner if you was fifty Pips, and he was five hundred Gargerys.'

'I have only been to the churchyard,' said I, from my stool, crying and rubbing myself.

'Churchyard!' repeated my sister. 'If it warn't for me you'd have been to the churchyard long ago, and stayed there. Who brought you up by hand?'

'You did,' said I.

'And why did I do it, I should like to know?' exclaimed my sister.

I whimpered, 'I don't know.'

'I don't!' said my sister. 'I'd never do it again! I know that. I may truly say I've never had this apron of mine off, since born you were. It's bad enough to be a blacksmith's wife (and him a Gargery) without being your mother.'

■ From Charles Dickens, *Great Expectations* ■

10  How much are you told about Mrs Joe's physical appearance?

11  What do you learn about Mrs Joe's present and past life in this extract?

12  Choose one comparison from the passage which you think is particularly effective, and explain how it works.

13  What do you learn about Mrs Joe from her attitude towards Joe and Pip?

14  What do you learn about her from what she says and how she says it?

15  Look again at what Mrs Joe actually does in this extract. What does that tell you about her?

This extract demonstrates some further pointers about how to set about describing a character:

o  give information about past and present life
o  show the character in action that is typical and revealing
o  give the character speech that shows what she or he is like.

When you are writing a story, it is important to give the reader an impression of the people you are writing about. This need not be full and expansive. Selecting a few relevant details as in the extract from 'The Devil-Dealer' page 49 provides sufficient physical description to create a picture of the character in the reader's mind, especially as you are probably going to show the character in action and in dialogue that will reinforce this first image in the rest of your story.

You need to think about the following:

o  select specific details of physical appearance that are relevant
o  use comparisons to make those details more vivid
o  describe the character's attitudes and opinions
o  say what other people feel about the character and how the character reacts towards other people
o  give information about the character's past and present life
o  describe where the character lives or works
o  show the character in action that is typical
o  use dialogue to reveal the character's feelings and views.

## 5.1.1 Describing a character – coursework

1  Write a character sketch of a neighbour, real or imaginary. You could call your piece of writing 'The perfect neighbour' or 'Who needs neighbours?' or 'The mysterious neighbour' or 'The new neighbour'.

2  Write a description of one of the following: 'The shopkeeper', 'The bus-conductor', 'The crossing attendant', 'The park gardener', 'The nurse', 'The librarian'. You could base your writing on someone you know or have seen several times.

3  Write a character sketch of someone who is a bully or someone who is accident-prone or someone who is always cheerful no matter what happens.

4  Write a character sketch of someone you know well.

5  Choose one of the following three pictures and write a description of the character depicted. Alternatively, you could write your account as 'an interior monologue', that is, the thoughts and ideas that go through the character's mind that reveal the kind of person he or she is.

**A**

**B**

**C**

# 5.2 Coursework – response to a non-literary text (1)

Generally speaking, literary texts consist of expressive writing – short stories, poems, novels, plays; non-literary texts consist of persuasive and informative writing – newspaper and magazine articles, advertisements, DHSS leaflets, instruction manuals, guide books, and so on. Literary texts tend to be of a higher quality, written with greater care for words and ideas, and as something that will have lasting value.

In many ways, the response to both literary and non-literary texts is similar. You need to examine what is said and how it is said.

In your coursework you will probably have to include pieces that show a response to non-literary as well as literary texts.

● Here is an example of a non-literary text. Read it carefully several times.

## ■ A READ IS A READ IS A . . . ■

A row has broken out in the cloistered world of the public libraries. And by row I mean literally a noise, clamour or commotion as defined by that pit-prop of the reference shelves, *The Shorter Oxford Dictionary*.

The sound that offends the bye-laws on silence and the non-commitment of nuisances is the bleep and burp of Space Invaders machines, those electronic Goths and Vandals which in their relentless march through our civilisation have now infiltrated the central library of the ancient diocese of Guildford.

Nor is that all. (Well, it wouldn't be, would it?) The county librarian, John Saunders, who as you gather is a bit of an innovator, has further scandalised parents and teachers by scrapping the children's section of the library.

His view is that modern ten- to twelve-year-olds are inhibited about using the children's section and that they should have wider access to the shelves. He believes furthermore that while children's requirements are changing, many of their parents still regard libraries as institutions which should be immune to change.

Many librarians feel as Mr Saunders does (although many do not) and they are supported by progressive educators, councillors, social workers, and other municipal oddballs who call the public libraries all sorts of nasty names like elitist, la-de-da and fuddy-duddy, and demand change.

This change usually consists of making the libraries look as little like libraries as possible, for fear that children who don't like reading will not have their stomachs churned by the sight of a book.

Swimming-baths without water will be the next logical step, I suppose. Meanwhile some public libraries feature more technological hardware than the average nuclear submarine, and it will not be long before library assistants glide to the Return Fiction shelves and back on fluorescent roller-skates, to the sound of piped music.

I will tell you where I stand on this controversy. I am so deeply conservative about what a public library should look like (the reading room of a gentleman's club), what it should sound like (a cathedral on early-closing day), and even what it should smell like (Mansion polish) that if my attitude on this were projected into general life, I would be somewhat to the right of the National Front.

A public library should be a place where people go in pursuit of reading matter. It should not be a leisure centre where they go to play games, or a 'communications' centre where they go to press buttons. A library should consist not of 'materials' – i.e., video-tapes, micro-film, language laboratories, etc – but of books. If it does not consist of books then it is not a library.

It is no use telling me that times have changed and that there are now more sophisticated means of storing knowledge. It is not the function of a library to supplement its stock of books with so-called visual aids any more than it is its function to provide practical teaching aids so that if you were studying, say, carpentry, there would be a corner of the library where you could saw bits of wood in half.

What is more – and this is why any librarian introducing Space Invaders machines should be burned in effigy – children should be brought up to respect their public libary, not to regard it as an adjunct of the Golden Nugget amusement arcade. Indeed, I would go so far as to say they should not only respect it, they should live in terror of it.

Mr Saunders speaks of youngsters being 'inhibited' about using the children's library. He does not know the meaning of the word. When I was a kid, our local branch librarian had us so inhibited that we used to stand outside cowering with fear for five minutes before we dared go in.

Before you were allowed past the counter – the equivalent, to us, of the frontier post in the Berlin Wall – your hands were inspected on both sides for signs of germ-carrying dirt. If you had not scrubbed them raw you were sent home.

Then the books you were returning were minutely examined as if you were suspected of being a diminutive drugs-runner. Any traces of jam, cocoa or pork-dripping and you got a monumental dressing-down.

The rules specified no talking, no coughing, no squeaky boots, no sweet-eating, no loitering and no giggling – and we loved the place.

You could not keep us out of it. I got through five books a week and would have devoured more but for the prevailing notion (which seems to be back in favour) that too much reading is bad for you.

We knew, and it was a source of great security in our lives, that a library is a library is a library as a rose is a rose is a rose or a dog is a dog is a dog. The librarian who tinkers with this profound truth does so at his peril.

■ From Keith Waterhouse, *Waterhouse at Large* ■

● Think about and discuss the following points.

**1** What is Keith Waterhouse objecting to in this article?

**2** How would you describe the way he outlines the new suggestions he is attacking? Does he play fair? (Look at his comments on 'other municipal odd-balls', 'swimming pools without water', 'library assistants . . . on fluorescent roller-skates').

**3** How serious do you think he is being? Are there signs that the article is meant to be humorous – at least to some extent?

**4** What evidence is there that the writer is aware that his own views are extreme?

**5** What do you think of the writer's idea of what a library should be like? What do you feel about libraries? Do you have any suggestions as to how they could be improved and made more attractive, or do you like them the way they are?

**6** Now write an account of this article in which you cover the following:
  **a** What the article is about;
  **b** How the writer attacks the new ideas and presents his case;
  **c** What you think of the views expressed and the way they are expressed;
  **d** Your own views on libraries.

You should write at least 300 words.

This work should be done in controlled classroom conditions. Allow about one hour for the actual writing.

# 5.3 Writing – variety of sentence length

If you are trying to create a feeling of excitement in a story, short sentences can help to build up a breathless effect and a sense of speed and urgency. Also when you are trying to get across information or instructions or reporting facts and events, short sentences can often be more effective. Shorter sentences may be easier to read and take in. You need to think of the audience you are writing for.

Longer sentences that flow more may create a better effect in a description or in the evocation of a calmer mood.

Too many short or long sentences can be monotonous, so vary the length of sentence in your writing. A sequence of long sentences followed by a short sentence as a kind of summing up or contrast can work. Similarly, short sentences followed by a long one can introduce a change of pace.

Some people find it difficult to construct long sentences. The main devices used to link ideas and help form longer sentences are *conjunctions* and *participles*. (For a reminder about these, and other parts of speech, see Appendix E.)

**1** Rewrite the following using conjunctions, participles and other methods to make more complex and more interesting sentences.

  **a** He found the door was unlocked. He pushed it open. He went inside.

  **b** The race was over. She found she had come second. She was disappointed.

  **c** You are going out. You can buy a paper. It will save me the trouble.

  **d** The dog was barking loudly. It was normally quiet. It knew there was someone outside.

  **e** The sparrow picked up a scrap of bread. It flew with it to a safe patch of the lawn. It ate the bread on the lawn.

  **f** He didn't want to watch television. The programmes were boring. He picked up a book and read.

  **g** There was a ring at the door. She hurried to answer it. She found a man standing on the doorstep. She had never seen him before.

  **h** The pole vaulter was hailed as a world beater. He lived up to his reputation. He created a new record.

  **i** The boy had lost his mother. He couldn't stop crying. The staff tried to comfort him. They tried to find his mother.

  **j** The man seized his opportunity. He was at the back of the crowd. He pushed his way forward. He began to shout at the speaker. The speaker was on the platform. The speaker was startled. The man's attack was ferocious.

**2** Write a few sentences for each of the following, paying particular attention to the kind of sentence you use and the variety of your sentences.

  **a** Instructions on how to play a particular game of cards or a party game.
  **b** Arguments for or against arming the police
  **c** Someone feeling panic
  **d** A mood of sadness
  **e** A description of a bird or an animal.

# 5.4 Reading – the effectiveness of an argument

In order to judge the effectiveness of a writer's argument, you have to examine carefully everything that is said and the way it is said.
Consider the following questions:

○ What main points does the writer make? Are they convincing?

○ What evidence does the writer produce to support the arguments?

○ Does the writer provide personal experience that supports the arguments, or make assumptions and generalise from this personal experience?

○ Are any of the writer's arguments illogical or contradictory?

- o Does the writer give examples and illustrations or parallels that convincingly support the arguments?
- o Does the writer make a false and sentimental appeal to the emotions instead of relying on the facts?
- o Does the writer exaggerate in order to win support?
- o Does the writer deliberately (as far as you can tell) omit aspects of the argument that would be damaging to his or her point of view?

- o Does the writer use facts and reasons for disagreeing with an opposing view, or simply abuse or ridicule or deliberately distort an alternative view?

1 Examine the effectiveness of Andre Drucker's argument in the article, 'Is work good?'. He is now a writer and self-employed shopkeeper. This fact may have some relevance on how you view his argument.

# IS WORK GOOD?

## By Andre Drucker

If you cannot beat unemployment, join it. It promises you freedom from toil, bosses and sulky workers. You can live like a civilised person, dreaming of high achievements. And you can smile at the naive clichés declaimed by MPs and union leaders about unemployment. They are simple people. They believe that man's destiny, except theirs, lies in clocking-in.

They talk with a quiver in their voices about our working class being thrown on some kind of giant "scrap heap", a grim Goyaesque vision of bones and skulls. They talk of workless people spending their days in "utter frustration", dragging themselves in pitiful queues to pubs and bookmakers. They talk of the "human tragedies" of the "victims of monopoly capitalism", pushing their high-piled supermarket trolleys across to their cars, cat and dog-food tins uppermost. And then they come to the most poetic phrase of all: "What has happened to the Dignity of Labour"?

I appreciate this question because I have been in and out of so many jobs. I have worked in a cotton mill, a silk-weaving mill and a spinning mill. Rain or shine I have cycled to work, clocked in, taken my place behind my machines for eight hours a day: crunch-crunch went the shuttles, zimm-zimm went the spindles, the foreman threw his bulky weight about, everybody was kept strictly to himself. At the end of the day I was deaf and dumb and my mind crippled. Aye, dignity of labour.

I have worked also in offices adding up long columns in ledgers; down, up, down, carry over, eight hours a day, the manager's eyes in my back.

At the end of the day I was devastated by boredom and emptiness. Dignity, my foot.

At other times I have worked in studios doing advertising layouts and visualising full pages, half pages and two-inch singles, for boats, cough pastilles, ladies' compacts, foundry sands, toys, Morris motors, pots and pans, seriously discussing the finer points of impact, the psychology of my slogans, the balance of lettering, chewing the pencil earnestly. An earnest cog in a business machine. Another bow-tie in a phoney business.

I worked as a van driver, up at 5.30 a.m., tram ride to depot, at 7 a.m. loading up crates, bags, bales, drums; hot bacon sandwich, tea-stained newspapers and obscenities at transport caff; unloading crates, bags, bales, drums and loading up crates, bags, bales, drums again for the next delivery and the foreman messing me about. Tram home and falling asleep over dinner. Fagged out, in full dignity.

Shall I go on?

Our politicians want everybody to get mangled in the mill of employment. They arrange fist-waving marchers behind wind-blown banners, shouting for work, the poor puppets. What is so wonderful about work? Not the pay. It is never good enough. Perhaps the actual work? Work in a factory is the biggest waste of an intelligent mind. Work in an office? Only if you wish for a complete degeneration of your brain cells.

Ah, it is the brotherhood, the comradeship of work. Have a fellow-worker set above you and the brotherhood goes out by the ventilator.

No. It is unemployment which opens the door to freedom and dignity. You can at last enjoy being a victim of monopoly capitalism. You can walk in a typically British upright cloth-capped and pipe-smoking attitude for your dole and collect what is rightfully yours and increased every Budget Day.

You can say goodbye, or a similar word, to your trade union bosses and to management bosses, to subservience, yes sir, no sir, go slow, strikes. At last you can get usefully unemployed.

There is a great future in unemployment, none in dignity. And who knows, if the worse came to the worst, you could even spend your time working at the things you really liked doing – and try to get others to pay you for it.

2 Compare the view of work (or unemployment) given above with that given in 'What it's like to be unemployed' in Unit 1 (1.4). Discuss both views.

◄ *This could be used for oral assessment.* ►

# 5.5 Reading – facts and opinions

In your reading, can you distinguish between facts and opinions? A fact is something for which there is evidence and which can be verified by research or experiment. An opinion is a view expressed that may or may not be true. It is a judgement or belief for which there is inadequate proof or which there is no way of proving, or which is merely the personal view of the speaker or writer. For instance, 'The temperature is 25°C today' is a fact. If a pupil says, 'It's too hot to work today', and the teacher says, 'No, it isn't', they are both expressing opinions.

Often statements that are opinions are presented as though they are facts, and often people accept them as facts without questioning them or examining them to see whether there is any evidence to support them.

Most critics, for instance, when reviewing a book or a film or record are expressing opinions. Whether you are prepared to accept what they say depends on the amount of evidence they produce for their views and on your previous experience of what they have said. In the 1660s, the diarist Samuel Pepys wrote that Shakespeare's *Twelfth Night* was 'but a silly play' and one of the weakest that he ever saw. *A Midsummer Night's Dream* was even worse, 'the most insipid, ridiculous play that ever I saw in my life', and he made a vow never to see it again. Yet both plays are still being performed and enjoyed today.

1 Examine the following and say whether they are facts or opinions, explaining the reasons for your answer.
   a Jack is the best sprinter this school has ever produced.
   b Last night's performance must have been the worst ever given of this play.
   c Last night's performance was the worst I have ever seen.
   d Too much money is being spent on education.
   e Not enough money is being spent on education.
   f I can't write poetry.
   g It is right that children should always obey their parents.
   h The population of the world is increasing every year.
   i Everyone knows that stealing is wrong.
   j God is good.

2 Write down five statements which are facts and five statements which are opinions.
3 Examine the following three letters carefully, pointing out when statements are opinions being presented as facts.

## A

**Disaster**

After all the publicity which heralded director Giles Foster's television version of *Northanger Abbey* what a disaster it turned out to be! I have often wondered what would happen if Jane Austen was subjected to the Ken Russell treatment. Now I know. I can only assume that since his beautiful rendering of *Silas Marner* for the small screen, Mr Foster has done a crash course in the Russell technique, and watched the new film *Gothic* .

Jane Austen was completely drowned in Mrs Radcliffe's early brand of 'Hammer horror', to the accompaniment of wailing refugees from a well-known chocolate commercial. This singularly inappropriate music was not only extremely irritating, but made Miss Austen's humour just ridiculous and completely ruined the period atmosphere . . .

## B

**Insights**

. . . *Northanger Abbey* was 90 minutes of the most exquisite television I have seen in a long time. Though I would not disagree that it did not follow the book exactly and scenes were changed, none the less, in the short time allocated, it not only told the basics of the story, but gave the viewer wonderful insights into the habits of Bath society often not fully explained in the pages of the book (eg the scenes in the baths and the Assembly Rooms). The acting, settings and haunting music were a delight from start to finish . . .

## C

Dear Editor,

I wish to remonstrate against the low moral standard of young people today. As a member of the older and wiser generation, I feel that I have a public duty to do so. If young people go on behaving the way they are doing, then this country's future is in grave jeopardy.

You only have to go into our city centres or travel on public transport to see the signs of this moral decay. Graffiti of the most obscene kind is splattered everywhere. Young people parade the streets in the most bizarre and outlandish costume. They sport punk hair-cuts and weird make-up. They behave on buses and underground as though they are in a children's playground. They are insulting to transport officials and cheat the companies out of their fares. This overwhelming evidence proves how degenerate young people are today. They show no respect for law and order, no respect for their elders and betters, no respect for authority. They are only interested in having a good time and show no thought for tomorrow. I shudder to think what this country will be like when the time comes for these people to take over the reins of government.

It is the same with education. Instead of valuing the opportunities they are being given, thanks to the sacrifice of hard-pressed taxpayers, they regard schools and education with derision. Instead of studying hard and spending their evenings doing their homework, they are out on the streets spoiling the pleasure of decent citizens. Or else they fill cinemas showing smutty violent films which are supposed to pass for entertainment today. Or else they cavort at discos which are nothing but centres for vice, drugs and sexual licence. Is it any wonder that headteachers deplore the plummeting standards of behaviour and academic achievement? Is it any wonder that examination results get worse and worse? Is it any wonder that the crime rate is soaring?

The only answer to this moral degeneracy is firm discipline. The reintroduction of national service is what is needed to bring the younger generation to its senses. I know this is so because I went through national service, and I know the value of it in giving young people moral fibre and a realisation of their duty. It made a man of me. It is the only hope if our once proud country is not to sink into utter degredation and ruin.

# 5.6 Oral communication – expressing a point of view

You have the opportunity to express your point of view on a variety of topics in group and class discussions. But you may also have the opportunity to do this in the form of a speech.

In many ways, the approach is similar to expressing your viewpoint in an essay (see 4.1). But there are obvious differences. You have to *speak* your point of view, not *read* it; you have to use your voice and body to give dramatic effect to what you say; and you have to be prepared to answer questions and respond to comments from your audience.

It can help to have notes which you can refer to while you speak. These should be brief – headings of your main points in the order in which you intend to make them, reminders which can help you to recall what you have prepared. Your preparation should include answers to any possible questions that may be asked.

● Express your point of view on a subject to the class. The subject you choose should be something about which you feel strongly. It could be a school issue (for example, a decision to abolish school uniform), or local issue (for example, the building of a bypass), or an issue of general interest (for example, proportional representation in Parliament).

◄ *This could be used for oral assessment.* ►

# 5.7 Oral communication – formal and informal language

In the preface to his play *Pygmalion*, George Bernard Shaw says, 'It is impossible for an Englishman to open his mouth without making some other Englishman hate or despise him.' It is true that people often judge others by the way they speak.

Basically, the way we speak depends on a number of factors – our family background, the social group we belong to, the area we were brought up in, the education we receive. But most of us employ a number of different ways of speaking, with varying degrees of formality and informality, ranging from Standard English to broad dialect. When we use a particular kind of spoken English will depend on the person we are speaking to and the situation. These different ways of speaking are called 'registers'.

There is no reason to think that one kind of spoken language is better than another. What matters is whether or not it is appropriate to the situation. But being able to speak Standard English is important. There are many official and formal occasions when the ability to communicate in Standard English could be an advantage. (See also section 4.5.)

● Questions to think about and discuss:

1 To what extent do you judge someone according to his or her accent?
2 Do you think some accents are more 'acceptable' than others?
3 Do you speak in exactly the same way when you are speaking to your parents, your friends, your headteacher, your doctor, a police officer, a stranger?
4 Do you think figures in authority (police, magistrates, teachers, employers) behave towards people differently according to the way they speak? Have you any personal experience of this?
5 Think about the way people talk on radio and television (for example, newscasters, disc jockeys, comedians, politicians). Comment on the different kinds of language they use and its appropriateness.

● Further questions and role-playing activities:

6 Make a list of situations where a formal register would be appropriate and where an informal register would be appropriate.
7 In groups, work out a situation where colloquial language or slang would be appropriate. Then act it again using Standard English and see what the difference is. Or you could write two versions of the same dialogue.

8  In pairs, work out an encounter between people who speak different kinds of language, for instance an American tourist and a Cockney, or a magistrate and a defendant. Try to avoid too stereotyped a view of your characters.

9  Look at the following dialogue. What points are these girls making about different ways of speaking? What do you think about the points they make? Can you parallel their experience with your own?

# WHY CAN'T WEST INDIANS ━ TALK WEST INDIAN? ━

MERYL If my mum heard me talking like that she'd bust my little ass. Your mum would as well?

AUDREY Yes, she'd say 'You're in England now, so talk English.' My dad's really got the Jamaican accent.

MERYL If you were to say 'what a rass hole' and all this stuff at home would your mum start . . .

ELEANOR But this is swearing isn't it? I mean if you're just talking properly like 'dey' instead of 'they' you know, there's nothing wrong in that but if you're swearing and ting you can understand them being angry and frustrated.

MERYL When you say 'dey' and 'tree' and all that instead of 'three' and all that, don't they say it's not 'tree' it's 'three'?

ELEANOR No because they know what I'm talking about, they're used to it. The majority of families say 'tree' instead of 'three'. I can't help saying 'tree' instead of 'three' because it's just, I don't know, it's just natural.

MERYL My parents talk like that but when I do it they try and stop me.

ELEANOR Well I don't really see why they should stop you because it's natural. There's nothing wrong with it.

MERYL No, there's nothing wrong with it.

ELEANOR Well I don't know . . .

SONYA Maybe they think, maybe the parents think that if my children go around speaking like that, then all the other people will think bad of them.

ELEANOR Maybe the only disadvantage of it is when you're coming for a job.

AUDREY Yeah you've got to talk all posh. You can't really talk West Indies to them because they wouldn't know what the heck you're on about. They'd go what, what?

ELEANOR Anyway I think West Indian dialect is very good. I like it.

# 6.1 Writing – Describing a scene

Describing a scene requires much the same procedure as describing a character: a factual account of physical appearance; the selection of significant details; the use of interesting adjectives and comparisons to bring the scene alive; and references to the past and present. When describing a character, you have to consider what you are doing and why. Is it a detailed description suitable for a long novel? Or an account of a few vivid features to help the reader visualise a character in a story? Is it an extended character sketch? The same kind of analysis is needed when describing a scene.

● Look at the following description of the city of Palma in Majorca which is taken from a holiday guide.

Palma de Mallorca, to give it its full title, is the capital of the whole group of Balearic Islands as well as of the island of Majorca itself. It has around 150,000 inhabitants – which is getting on for half the total population of the island.

As a city it is not as old as the island's history: the Romans, and others before them, may have used its fine natural harbour, but the Roman capital of Majorca was up in the north, at what is now called Alcudia.

It was the Moors (or Arabs, or Moslems, or whatever you like to call the invaders from North Africa) who developed what is now Palma, and when young Jaime I, the Spanish king, brought Christendom to the island he landed a few miles to the west of Palma, at Santa Ponsa, very near Paguera where a lot of tourists now spend the first night of their holidays. King Jaime then advanced for about nine weeks until Palma was his and then set about making it a Christian capital.

Like all cities which have grown with changing history, Palma presents a somewhat bewildering mixture. There are different bits of Palma, some on high ground and some at sea-level. There are slummy outskirts: the drive into the city from the airport, for example, is not exactly encouraging. Arriving by sea is better, for then, as you edge into the harbour, the fine green backcloth of wooded hills behind the city, with the lofty towers of the Bellver castle protruding through this greenery like a mushroom, lends a third dimension to your view: and away to the left, to the west you get a notion of the fine curving sweep of the *Paseo Maritimo*, a broad palm-edged waterfront running between the sea and the luxury hotels and restaurants.

Gradually, as you wander in the city, you begin to get the hang of so much hotch-potch: the wide Paseo Generalisimo Franco (for long and still known as the Paseo Borne), which has traffic running either side of a pedestrians' promenade lined on both sides by enormous trees whose shade, in summer, almost darkens the thoroughfare even at high noon; the great Gothic cathedral, the second largest in Spain; the *Almudaina*; the quiet, traffic-less shopping streets such as the Calle de Jaime I; and above all perhaps in sheer beauty the preserved stately homes and palaces of nobles who grew rich on trading in a maritime age and who did not abuse their wealth but spent it on exquisite buildings.

■■■ From Christopher Sidgwick, *Majorca* ■■■

1 What kinds of information does the writer give you in this description?
2 Considering the amount of space at his disposal, do you think the writer gives a reasonably full and comprehensive account of Palma? Justify your answer. Is there any information you think he could have given but doesn't? Do you think he has the balance right?
3 Point out examples of where he generalises about what Palma or parts of it are like, and where he gives more specific detail.
4 Comment on the kind of language the writer uses, particularly his use of adjectives and comparisons. Is the language appropriate for this kind of wrting?
5 Sum up in three or four sentences the impression you get of Palma from this description.

● Compare the description of Palma with this description which comes from a 500-page novel.

It was nearly midnight on the eve of St Thomas's, the shortest day in the year. A desolating wind wandered from the north over the hill whereon Oak had watched the yellow waggon and its occupant in the sunshine of a few days earlier.

Norcombe Hill – not far from lonely Toller-Down – was one of the spots which suggest to a passer-by that he is in the presence of a shape approaching the indestructible as nearly as any to be found on earth. It was a featureless convexity of chalk and soil – an ordinary specimen of those smoothly-outlined protuberances of the globe which may remain undisturbed on some great day of confusion, when far grander heights and dizzy granite precipices topple down.

The hill was covered on its northern side by an ancient and decaying plantation of beeches, whose upper verge formed a line over the crest, fringing its arched curve against the sky, like a mane. To-night these trees sheltered the southern slope from the keenest blasts, which smote the wood and floundered through it with a sound as of grumbling, or gushed over its crowning boughs in a weakened moan. The dry leaves in the ditch simmered and boiled in the same breezes, a tongue of air occasionally ferreting out a few, and sending them spinning across the grass. A group or two of the latest in date among the dead multitude had remained till this very mid-winter time on the twigs which bore them, and in falling rattled against the trunks with smart taps.

Between this half-wooded half-naked hill, and the vague still horizon that its summit indistinctly commanded, was a mysterious sheet of fathomless shade – the sounds from which suggested that what it concealed bore some reduced resemblance to features here. The thin grasses, more or less coating the hill, were touched by the wind in breezes of differing powers, and almost of differing natures – one rubbing the blades heavily, another raking them piercingly, another brushing them like a soft broom. The instinctive act of humankind was to stand and listen, and learn how the trees on the right and the trees on the left wailed or chaunted to each other in the regular antiphonies of a cathedral choir; how hedges and other shapes to leeward then caught the note, lowering it to the tenderest sob; and how the hurrying gust then plunged into the south, to be heard no more.

The sky was clear – remarkably clear – and the twinkling of all the stars seemed to be but throbs of one body, timed by a common pulse. The North Star was directly in the wind's eye, and since evening the Bear had swung round it outwardly to the east, till he was now at a right angle with the meridian. A difference of colour in the stars – oftener read of than seen in England – was really perceptible here. The sovereign brilliancy of Sirius pierced the eye with a steely glitter, the star called Capella was yellow, Aldebaran and Betelgueux shone with a fiery red.

To persons standing alone on a hill during a clear midnight such as this, the roll of the world eastward is almost a palpable movement. The sensation may be caused by the panoramic glide of the stars past earthly objects, which is perceptible in a few minutes of stillness, or by the better outlook upon space that a hill affords, or by the wind, or by the solitude; but whatever be its origin the impression of riding along is vivid and abiding. The poetry of motion is a phrase much in use, and to enjoy the epic form of that gratification it is necessary to stand on a hill at a small hour of the night, and, having first expanded with a sense of difference from the mass of civilized mankind, who are dreamwrapt and disregardful of all such proceedings at this time, long and quietly watch your stately progress through the stars. After such a nocturnal reconnoitre it is hard to get back to earth, and to believe that the consciousness of such majestic speeding is derived from a tiny human frame.

From Thomas Hardy,
*Far from the Madding Crowd*

6  How much factual description of the scene does the writer give?

7  Sum up what aspect of the scene is being described in each paragraph, using one sentence for each.

8  Pick out some of the comparisons the writer uses and comment on their effectiveness.

9  In what ways could it be said that the writer is describing a living being?

10  Comment on the way the writer makes use of the senses in his description.

11  What part do the imaginary spectators in the last paragraph play in the effectiveness of the description?

●  Towns and countryside are not the only suitable subjects. Scenes can also involve people, crowds of people as in the following.

A stout man with a pink face wears dingy white flannel trousers, a blue coat with a pink handkerchief showing, and a straw hat much too small for him, perched at the back of his head. He plays the guitar. A little chap in white canvas shoes, his face hidden under a felt hat like a broken wing, breathes into a flute; and a tall thin fellow, with bursting over-ripe button boots, draws ribbons – long, twisted, streaming ribbons – of tune out of a fiddle. They stand, unsmiling, but not serious, in the broad sunlight opposite the fruit-shop; the pink spider of a hand beats the guitar, the little squat hand, with a brass-and-turquoise ring, forces the reluctant flute, and the fiddler's arm tries to saw the fiddle in two.

A crowd collects, eating oranges and bananas, tearing off the skins, dividing, sharing. One young girl has even a basket of strawberries, but she does not eat them. 'Aren't they *dear*!' She stares at the tiny pointed fruits as if she were afraid of them. The Australian soldier laughs. 'Here, go on, there's not more than a mouthful.' But he doesn't want her to eat them, either. He likes to watch her little frightened face, and her puzzled eyes lifted to his; 'Aren't they a *price*!' He pushes out his chest and grins. Old fat women in velvet bodices – old dusty pin-cushions – ; lean old hags like worn umbrellas with a quivering bonnet on top; young women, in muslins, with hats that might have grown on hedges, and high pointed

shoes; men in khaki, sailors, shabby clerks, young Jews in fine cloth suits with padded shoulders and wide trousers, 'hospital boys' in blue – the sun discovers them – the loud, bold music holds them together in one big knot for a moment. The young ones are larking, pushing each other on and off the pavement, dodging, nudging; the old ones are talking: 'So I said to 'im, if you wants the doctor to yourself, fetch 'im, says I.'

'An' by the time they was cooked there wasn't so much as you could put in the palm of me 'and!'

The only ones who are quiet are the ragged children. They stand as close up to the musicians as they can get, their hands behind their backs, their eyes big. Occasionally a leg hops, an arm wags. A tiny staggerer, overcome, turns round twice, sits down solemn, and then gets up again.

'Ain't it lovely?' whispers a small girl behind her hand.

And the music breaks into bright pieces, and joins together again, and again breaks, and is dissolved, and the crowd scatters, moving slowly up the hill.

From Katherine Mansfield, 'Bank Holiday'

12  Pick out some of the descriptive detail that you find particularly vivid.

13  The writer describes individuals in the crowd rather than the crowd itself. Do you think this is an effective way of describing the crowd?

14  What do the scraps of conversation add to the general impression?

15  Look at the sentence structure. How would you describe it? Is it appropriate and how does it contribute to the effect of the description?

Here are some further points then to remember in your own descriptions involving people:

o  select vivid details
o  pick out individuals in a crowd
o  quote what people say
o  the kinds of sentences you use can have an effect.

## 6.1.1 Describing a scene

1  If appropriate, write a description of where you live that could be used in a guide book of the area for visitors.

2  Describe a scene that you find mysterious or strange or a scene that gives an impression of heat or cold.

3  The same area can have different moods. Describe a scene at different times. It could be the sea when it is stormy and when it is calm. Or a town centre at midday and at midnight.

4  Describe an amusement arcade, or a crowded supermarket, or the first day of the sales, or a concert, or Guy Fawkes' Night.

5  Write a description of one of the pictures opposite.

A

B

C

#  6.2 Coursework – response to reading – poetry

Poetry demands concentration. It demands that the reader or listener gives up everything for the duration of the poem so that the meaning of the poem can be communicated.

Because of its concentrated form – a few words on the page compared with a story or a novel – it can have great intensity and a powerful effect. Because the words are restricted in number and have to fit a pattern, they have to be chosen with care so each one carries a weight of meaning. A poem can pack a punch in a way that prose can't.

When responding to a poem or writing about it, you need to get to know the poem thoroughly, reading it several times. Try to work out what the poem is about. What events or feelings are being described? What is the point of the poem? What is the poet trying to say?

The poet may not say directly what the point is. You need to explore all the methods the poet uses in the poem – the language, the imagery, the rhythm and rhyme, the verse form and organisation, the tone, the overall effect of the poem.

Having got to know the poem, you can now express an opinion on it. Does the poem work? Do all the parts fit together to say what the poet wants to say? Or are there things which jar or undermine the impression the poet is trying to make? Has the poet said something worth saying? Has the poet made you see something in a new and fresh light?

● Read the following poem several times and discuss it on the lines suggested above. You may find the questions that follow more specific and more helpful.

## ■ MR BLEANEY ■

'This was Mr Bleaney's room. He stayed
The whole time he was at the Bodies, till
They moved him.' Flowered curtains, thin and
    frayed,
Fell to within five inches of the sill,

Whose window shows a strip of building land,
Tussocky, littered. 'Mr Bleaney took
My bit of garden properly in hand.'
Bed, upright chair, sixty-watt bulb, no hook

Behind the door, no room for books or bags –
'I'll take it.' So it happens that I lie
Where Mr Bleaney lay, and stub my fags
On the same saucer-souvenir, and try

Stuffing my ears with cotton-wool, to drown
The jabbering set he egged her on to buy.
I know his habits – what time he came down,
His preference for sauce to gravy, why

He kept on plugging at the four aways –
Likewise their yearly frame: the Frinton folk
Who put him up for summer holidays,
And Christmas at his sister's house in Stoke.

But if he stood and watched the frigid wind
Tousling the clouds, lay on the fusty bed
Telling himself that this was home, and grinned,
And shivered, without shaking off the dread

That how we live measures our own nature,
And at his age having no more to show
Than one hired box should make him pretty sure
He warranted no better, I don't know.

*Philip Larkin*

1. What part does quoted speech play in the poem?
2. How does the poet convey an impression of the room? What impression do you get of the room?
3. What change takes place after nine and a half lines?
4. What do you – and the poet – learn about Mr Bleaney from the first five verses?
5. Look at the sentence structure of the last two verses. How does it differ from the rest of the poem? Why do you think this is? The main statement or main clause 'I don't know' is held back until the very end. What effect does this have?
6. Is there a difference in the poet's thoughts about Mr Bleaney in the first five verses and in the last two?
7. Explain in your own words what the poet is saying in the last two verses.
8. The poet says 'how *we* live measures our own nature'. Could it be said that his position – or our position – is similar to Mr Bleaney's?
9. The poet's tone is informal and colloquial. Give examples. Why do you think he chooses this kind of language?
10. How would you describe the general mood of the poem and the conclusion the poet comes to?
11. a Write an account of your response to this poem. Say what the poem is about. Comment on how the poet gets his points across and on how successful you think this is as a poem.

   Or

   b Suppose the poet becomes tired of hearing the landlady talking about Mr Bleaney. Describe the row they have about it. You could write this as a play.

   Or

   c Imagine you have left home. Describe how you find a bedsitting room to live in and your feelings during your first days there.

## 6.2.1 Further reading

Some individual poets whose work you may find interesting are: W. H. Auden, John Betjeman, Edward Brathwaite, Emily Dickinson, Douglas Dunn, Robert Frost, Thom Gunn, Thomas Hardy, Seamus Heaney, Ted Hughes, Elizabeth Jennings, Philip Larkin, D. H. Lawrence, Adrian Mitchell, Wilfred Owen, Sylvia Plath, Siegfried Sassoon, Dylan Thomas, Edward Thomas, R. S. Thomas, Derek Walcott.

Here are some anthologies:

Baldwin, Michael (ed.), *Billy the Kid*. Hutchinson.
Berry, James, (ed.), *Bluefoot Traveller*. Nelson Harrap.
Black, E. L. (ed.), *Topics in Modern Poetry*. Murray.
Blackburn, Thomas and Cunningham, W. T. (eds), *Reach Out*. Nelson.
Boagey, E. J. (ed.), *Changing Islands*. Bell & Hyman.
Finn, F. E. S. (ed.), *Voices of Today*. Murray.
Foster, John L. (ed.), *Standpoints*. Nelson Harrap.
Hughes, Ted (ed.), *Here Today*. Hutchinson.
Jones, Rhodri (ed.), *One World Poets*. Heinemann Educational Books.
————, *Themes*. Heinemann Educational Books.
O'Malley, Raymond and Thompson, Denys (eds), *Rhyme and Reason*. Collins.
Summerfield, Geoffrey (ed.), *Voices*. Penguin Books.

# 6.3 Writing – formal and informal language

The language we use in writing can be formal or informal to varying degrees. (See 4.5.) The type of language you choose will depend on the audience you are writing for and your purpose in writing. A letter to the council complaining about the state of local roads is likely to be written in a different kind of language from that used in a letter to a friend describing a holiday.

1 Give examples of other kinds of writing and the type of language that would be appropriate for them.

Having decided on the kind of language that is appropriate, be consistent. Of course, there are times when you deliberately change style to achieve a particular effect. For instance, in a story you might use Standard English for the narrative and colloquial language or dialect for the dialogue. You might write the whole story in colloquial language or dialect if this were appropriate to the person from whose point of view the events were being seen.

2 Rewrite the following in Standard English as it might be written by a solicitor acting for the narrator, as part of the evidence for a case. You do not need to keep exactly to the same word order. What difference in effect is there between the solicitor's version and the original?

I was down the pub one day on my jack when this geezer came up to me and started getting dead friendly. He went rabbiting on about this and that like we was long-lost brothers or something. Then he started asking about some of the layabouts around the manor and I could smell something fishy. I soon tumbled to what he was up to. He was a nark trying to pump me about my mates. Well, I wasn't standing for that. I told him where he could stick his hooter. He never said another dicky-bird after that.

3 Rewrite the following as it might be written by a school pupil using colloquial English. What difference in effect is there between the school pupil's version and the original?

The school has a very low reputation among people who live in the neighbourhood. They see pupils coming out of the school at the end of the day behaving in a rowdy and ill-mannered way. There are frequent complaints about the behaviour of pupils towards other pedestrians and about the offensive remarks that pupils make. One person who lives near the school was knocked over by a mob of pupils racing along the pavement. When he protested, he was subjected to a torrent of abuse. Another cause for disquiet is the number of fights that occur at the front gates. Huge crowds collect to watch and cheer on the combatants. They spill out into the road and obstruct the traffic. It is highly probable that someone will be injured unless something is done to control the behaviour of these young, ill disciplined people.

4 Choose one of the subjects listed below and write two short paragraphs about each in different kinds of English. You could write from two different points of view. For instance, if you choose 'Football hooliganism', you could write from the point of view of a football fan and from the point of view of a leader written in a 'serious' newspaper.
   a Football hooliganism
   b A strange encounter
   c Science fiction
   d Lost
   e After the party

# 6.4 Reading for information

In reading for information, you select from a piece of writing the points relevant to the particular aspect of the subject you are interested in. In everyday life, you may check a bus timetable for the time of a bus that is convenient for you, or look at the television listings to find a programme you want to watch, or scan the football results to see how your team has done.

When it comes to more demanding tasks, the procedure is similar to that used in making a summary (see section 2.3). But instead of summarising *all* the points the writer makes, you are concerned only with the information relevant to the task set. You need to:

○ read the piece of writing carefully to get an overall impression
○ have the set task clear in your mind
○ isolate those sections that relate to that task
○ make notes of the relevant points
○ reproduce them in your own words in a fluent form.

1 Using only the information given in this newspaper report, write a paragraph on the various incentives used by local education authorities to attract teachers to their areas.

# £500 allowance to lure new staff

### ~ by TES reporters

Teachers taking up jobs in the London borough of Brent are to receive a £500 "relocation allowance" even if they already live in the area. The money will go to all new Scale 1 and 2 teachers.

The allowance is seen by the Labour-controlled authority as a crucial part of its campaign to recruit more teachers. In April, there were 155 vacancies in Brent schools. By last week the figure had fallen to 30.

Yesterday the authority interviewed another 40 applicants and it hopes to have filled most posts by Christmas. The remaining vacancies are in the national shortage subjects – CDT, maths, physics and RE.

Brent has advertised for teachers in the local and ethnic press, as well as in the national newspapers. About 20 of the recent appointments are black and at least half are women.

Mr Ron Anderson, the education committee chairman, said: "The £500 has obviously helped but we also stressed in our adverts the high level of in-service training provided in our schools, our strong advisory team and small class sizes."

Extra incentives offered by local education authorities to lure more teachers into their classrooms are increasing.

Earlier this summer, Labour-controlled Ealing decided to hire extra staff to work in its primary schools for the last few weeks of term – so it could put them on the payroll through the summer holidays instead of hiring them from September, as is traditional. The plan also helped newly-qualified teachers become familiar with their schools before the autumn term started.

In Waltham Forest, teachers were given priority on the council housing list – and supply staff have been offered permanent Scale 2 appointments.

All three authorities became Labour-controlled following May's council elections.

In Conservative-controlled Surrey, county councillors attempted to persuade people who had opted for early retirement from industry to take up teaching posts in a bid to overcome its staff shortages. Recruits will be starting their training with the authority on Monday week.

2 Using only the information given in this extract, write an account of the superstitions American children believed in a hundred years ago.

Huckleberry came and went, at his own free will. He slept on doorsteps in fine weather and in empty hogsheads in wet; he did not have to go to school or to church, or call any being master or obey anybody; he could go fishing or swimming when and where he chose, and stay as long as it suited him; nobody forbade him to fight; he could sit up as late as he pleased; he was always the first boy that went barefoot in the spring and the last to resume leather in the fall; he never had to wash, nor put on clean clothes; he could swear wonderfully. In a word, everything that goes to make life precious, that boy had. So thought every harassed, hampered, respectable boy in St Petersburgh.

Tom hailed the romantic outcast:

'Hello, Huckleberry!'

'Hello, yourself, and see how you like it.'

'What's that you got?'

'Dead cat.'

'Lemme see him, Huck. My, he's pretty stiff. Where'd you get him?'

'Bought him off'n a boy.'

'What did you give?'

'I give a blue ticket and bladder that I got at the slaughterhouse.'

'Where'd you get the blue ticket?'

'Bought it off'n Ben Rogers two weeks ago for a hoopstick.'

'Say – what is dead cats good for, Huck?'

'Good for? Cure warts with.'

'No! Is that so? I know something that's better.'

'I bet you don't. What it is?'

'Why, spunk-water.'

'Spunk-water! I wouldn't give a dern for spunk-water.'

'You wouldn't, wouldn't you? D'you ever try it?'

'No, I hain't. But Bob Tanner did.'

'Now you tell me how Bob Tanner done it, Huck.'

'Why he took and dipped his hand in a rotten stump where the rain water was.'

'In the day time?'

'Certainly.'

'With his face to the stump?'

'Yes. Least I reckon so.'

'Did he *say* anything?'

'I don't reckon he did. I don't know.'

'Aha! Talk about trying to cure warts with spunk-water such a blame fool way as that! Why that ain't a-going to do any good. You got to go all by yourself, to the middle of the woods, where you know there's a spunk-water stump, and just as it's midnight you back up against the stump and jam your hand in and say:

Barleycorn, Barleycorn,
    Injun-meal shorts,
Spunk-water, spunk-water,
    swaller these warts

and then walk away quick, eleven steps, with your eyes shut, and then turn around three times and walk home without speaking to anybody. Because if you speak the charm's busted.'

'Well that sounds like a good way; but that ain't the way Bob Tanner done.'

'No, sir, you can bet he didn't, becuz he's the wartiest boy in this town; and he wouldn't have a wart on him if he'd knowed how to work spunk-water. I've took off thousands of warts off my hands that way, Huck. I play with frogs so much that I've always got considerable many warts. Sometimes I take 'em off with a bean.'

'Yes, bean's good. I've done that.'

'Have you? What's your way?'

'You take and split the bean, and cut the wart so as to get some blood, and then you put the blood on one piece of the bean and take and dig a hole and bury it 'bout midnight at the crossroads in the dark of the moon, and then you burn up the rest of the bean. You see, that piece that's got the blood on it will keep drawing and drawing, trying to fetch the other piece to it, and so that helps the blood to draw the wart, and pretty soon off she comes.'

'Yes, that's it, Huck – that's it; though when you're burying it if you say "Down bean; off wart; come no more to bother me!" it's better. That's the way Jo Harper does, and he's been most everywheres. But say – how do you cure 'em with dead cats?'

'Why you take your cat and go and get in the graveyard 'long about midnight when somebody that was wicked has been buried; and when it's midnight a devil will come, or maybe two or three, but you can't see 'em, you can only hear something like the wind, or maybe hear 'em talk; and when they're taking that feller away, you heave your cat after 'em and say "Devil follow corpse, cat follow devil, warts follow cat, I'm done with ye!" That'll fetch any wart.'

'Sounds right. D'you ever try it, Huck?'

'No, but old mother Hopkins told me.'

'Then, I reckon it's so. Becuz they say she's a witch.'

'Say! Why, Tom, I *know* she is. She switched Pap. Pap says so his own self. He came along one day, and he see she was a witching him, so he took up a rock, and if she hadn't dodged, he'd a got her. Well that very night he rolled off'n a shed wher' he was a layin' drunk, and broke his arm.'

'Why that's awful. How did he know she was a witching him?'

'Lord, Pap can tell, easy. Pap says when they keep looking at you right stiddy, they're a witching you. Specially if they mumble. Becuz when they mumble they're saying the Lord's Prayer back-ards.'

'Say, Hucky, when you going to try the cat?'

'Tonight. I reckon they'll come after old Hoss Williams tonight.'

'But they buried him Saturday. Didn't they get him Saturday night?'

'Why how you talk! How could their charms work till midnight? – and *then* it's Sunday. Devils don't slosh around much of a Sunday. I don't reckon.'

'I never thought of that. That's so. Lemme go with you?'

'Of course – if you ain't afeard.'

'Afeard! 'Tain't likely.'

━━━━━ From Mark Twain, *Tom Sawyer* ━━━

3  Using only the information in the table below, write a short paragraph about the life expectancy of women throughout the world.

## Life Spans (2)

**Human life spans** Humans are among the longest-lived of all animals. Many people live to over 70, and at least one man has lived 118 years. Life spans are longest where people are well fed and medicine prevents and cures disease. In such lands life expectancies are three times longer than in Stone Age times.

| 1 | Chad 35 years | 6 | USSR 70 years |
|---|---|---|---|
| 2 | India 45 years | 7 | UK 72 years |
| 3 | Bolivia 49 years | 8 | USA 74 years |
| 4 | Turkey 54 years | 9 | Japan 76 years |
| 5 | Brazil 60 years | 10 | Netherlands 76 years |

**Life expectancies** (right)
Shown in this diagram, and listed above it, are the average number of years that people in different countries can expect to live. These figures refer to a person's life expectancy at birth. People in the richer countries have a much better chance of reaching 70 than people in the poorer ones.

**Male/Female life spans** (right)
In most countries, average life expectancy at birth is higher for females than for males. We give three examples (**a-c**). India (**d**) is one of very few exceptions.
a  UK: men 69, women 75
b  Bolivia: men 47, women 51
c  Chad: men 33, women 36
d  India: men 46, women 45

**Rising life expectancy** (right)
As a person gets older his or her life expectancy increases. (People who survive into older age groups tend to be stronger than those who die young.)
A  At birth: expectancy 71 years
B  At 25: expectancy 73 years
C  At 55: expectancy 78 years
D  At 75: expectancy 83 years

Average male and female

Male and female

0 years  10  20  30  40  50  60  70  80

# 6.5 Reading – recognising a point of view

Much writing seeks to present or argue a point of view. It may be persuading you to buy something or hoping to influence your opinion or stating a strongly held principle. Before you can consider how effectively the point of view is expressed, you have to be able to work out what that point of view is. This requires careful examination of the facts, the evidence and views put forward and the tone used in the writing.

● Study the following passages.

1 State the point of view presented or argued in each. Be as precise as you can.

## A

Childhood was a totalitarian regime from which I was very glad to escape. Still, we sentimentalise that time, remembering it as so many sandcastles and party balloons. Too often we remember ourselves running through long grass in slow-motion, with a dog at our side, like in those lyrical television commercials for cornflakes. Yet childhood was a time of indignities and injustice. A few days ago I saw a typical scene. A mother was dragging a tired child through a big store and he was lagging, dragging. Whereupon she suddenly flared and belted him repeatedly on the backside, causing his weariness to become tears and cries of outrage. Needless to say this embarrassed the mother all the more, so she hit him harder.

That was one of the worst aspects of childhood, the fact that a kid was property. Indeed, the dominant memory of childhood was being ordered about by parents, teachers, prefects, bullies. What were school assemblies but miniature Nuremberg rallies where pompous, petty officials could indulge their egos? I well remember the way the more paranoid teachers lorded it over their diminutive, powerless populations dressed in their compulsory uniforms.

But it was just as bad at home. One was ordered to wash one's hands, clean one's teeth or to kiss some overscented friend of mummy's whose gush of affection was manifestly insincere. Then there was the way you were sent to bed just when things were getting interesting or were forced to endure the ignominy of short pants. Don't ask silly questions. Just do what you're told. Don't answer back. How dare you talk to your mother like that? If children were to be seen and not heard, adults were to be obeyed and not questioned.

■ From Phillip Adams, *The Unspeakable Adams*■

## B

My time for registering came in the spring of 1940. France was falling, and on the morning when I had to go to the Labour Exchange, I'd read of the German units 'seeking to make contact' with the fleeing French: and I remember thinking *that* was such a friendly phrase for such a murderous activity: and I remember, too, the shock of knowing that France was finished, and the voice within me saying, 'You can't . . . you can't not be in it, now. Not now they've done this to France.'

But all that literature of disgust I'd read, bitter fruit of the Great War (as we'd called it till this greater war came) . . . the horror of it, the rejection it expressed, had run in my veins, until I could not think of fighting without a sense of shock. It had been horrible, they had all hated it, those chroniclers of the first world war, and one couldn't, having supped of their anger and revulsion, start it all again. If war began – I'd been very clear about this, in my last year at school – one would be tempted, the flood would seek to carry one with it; but only by intolerable betrayal of all those haggard men of the first war, I thought, only by turning one's back on Barbusse and Remarque and Sassoon, could one give in.

So as I made my leaden way to the Labour Exchange, I heard that voice within me, weeping for France, as the voice of disloyal temptation; and I registered as an objector. I was sent to the bottom of the buzzing room, alone, away from all the others; and it felt as though I were separating myself from the world . . .

■ From Edward Blishen, *A Cack-handed War*■

## C

Being among the nation's 18 million smokers, I have an obvious interest in keeping the non-smokers at bay. I certainly do not wish to encourage anyone else to smoke, and rather admire those who have given up. But if we all stopped smoking and lived an extra five years on average, the effects would be disastrous.

Not only would non-smokers have to produce the £5.5 million extra tax we pay - half the entire cost of the NHS hospital service - but the additional costs in care of the old - already out of hand - would be crippling.

All I beg young people is not to be stampeded into persecuting smokers. For the occasional whiff of tobacco, you are receiving a better health service, lower taxes and better care of the old.

■ Auberon Waugh in *Junior Guardian*■

**━━━━ D ━━━━**

# BACK CHAT

Sir, — I include some further topics for Auberon Waugh's brave and plain-speaking articles. Perhaps it's about time somebody did something along the lines of "The Ethiopian Famine: Money down the Drain?" Or "Aids: Twenty reasons to encourage it" and a long overdue exposé of the "Sunny side of nuclear war." Only Waugh has the guts for this.
Yours,
**M. Ounsley,**
Reading.

**━━━━ *Junior Guardian* (8–4–87) ━━━━**

2　Look again at these passages and consider how convincingly the point of view is argued in each case.

# 6.6 Debating

Another approach to presenting a point of view is to have a formal debate.

In a debate, the subject to be considered is called a 'motion'. A chairperson keeps order, calls on the particular speakers and ensures that no one speaks for too long. There are two speakers in favour of the motion (the proposer and a seconder), and two speakers against the motion (the opposer and a seconder).

The order of speaking is as follows:

1　The proposer (about four or five minutes).
2　The opposer (about four or five minutes).
3　The seconder for the motion (about three minutes).
4　The seconder against the motion (about three minutes).
5　Speakers from the floor (that is, the audience). Each contribution should be brief. Discussion might last for ten or fifteen minutes.
6　The opposer sums up (about three minutes).
7　The proposer sums up (about three minutes).

The four main speakers need to prepare their speeches. The two speakers on each side should get together to work out their strategy. There is no point in both saying the same thing. They must divide the subject between them and approach it from different angles. The seconder in each case has the opportunity to depart from a prepared speech to pick up points from the first speakers, answer them and comment on them. They have to be skilled in improvising.

This skill is also needed when it comes to the summing-up by the opposer and the proposer. They should prepare something to say, particularly a strong point to end on, but much of what they say will be based on what they have heard in the course of the debate – statements made by the other side that they can refute, supporting arguments that have come from the audience. This requires careful listening, quick note-making and the ability to marshal facts and arguments as you talk.

At the end, a vote can be taken to see whether the motion has been carried or defeated.

Choose one of the following as a motion for a debate:

1　This house believes that charity begins at home.
2　This house believes that woman's place is in the home.
3　This house believes that smoking should be banned from all public places.
4　This house believes that if you spare the rod, you spoil the child.
5　This house believes that beauty is in the eye of the beholder.

◀　　　*This could be used for oral assessment.*　　　▶

Time allowed: two hours and 45 minutes.

Answer all the questions in Section A and B and ONE question from Section C. Sections A and B are worth 40 marks each section. C is worth 20 marks.

# Section A

Read the short story below carefully and then answer the questions which follow.

## ■ THE POTATO GATHERERS ■

November frost had starched the flat country-side into silent rigidity. The 'rat-tat-tat' of the tractor's exhaust drilled into the clean, hard air but did not penetrate it; each staccato sound
5 broke off as if it had been nipped. Hunched over the driver's wheel sat Kelly, the owner, a rock of a man with a huge head and broken fingernails, and in the trailer behind were his four potato gatherers – two young men, permanent farm
10 hands, and the two boys he had hired for the day. At six o'clock in the morning, they were the only living things in that part of County Tyrone.

The boys chatted incessantly. They stood at the front of the trailer, legs apart, hands in their
15 pockets, their faces pressed forward into the icy rush of air, their senses edged for perception. Joe, the elder of the two – he was thirteen and had worked for Kelly on two previous occasions – might have been quieter, but his brother's
20 excitement was infectious. For this was Philly's first job, his first time to take a day off from school to earn money, his first opportunity to prove that he was a man at twelve years of age. His energy was a burden to him. Behind them,
25 on the floor of the trailer, the two farm hands lay sprawled in half sleep.

Twice the boys had to cheer. The first time was when they were passing Dicey O'Donnell's house, and Philly, who was in the same class as
30 Dicey, called across to the thatched, smokeless building, 'Remember me to all the boys, Dicey!' The second time was when they came to the school itself. It was then that Kelly turned to them and growled to them to shut up.

35 'Do you want the whole county to know you're taking the day off?' he said. 'Save your breath for your work.'

When Kelly faced back to the road ahead, Philly stuck his thumbs in his ears, put out his
40 tongue, and wriggled his fingers at the back of Kelly's head. Then, suddenly forgetting him, he said, 'Tell me, Joe, what are you going to buy?'

'Buy?'

'With the money we get today. I know what
45 I'm getting – a shotgun. Bang! Bang! Bang! Right there, mistah. Jist you put your two hands up above your head and I reckon you'll live a little longer.' He menaced Kelly's neck.

'Agh!' said Joe derisively.

50 'True as God, Joe. I can get it for seven shillings – an old one that's lying in Tom Tracy's father's barn. Tom told me he would sell it for seven shillings.'

'Who would sell it?'

55 'Tom.'

'Steal it, you mean. From his old fella.'

'His old fella has a new one. This one's not wanted.' He sighted along an imaginary barrel and picked out an unsuspecting sparrow in the
60 hedge. 'Bang! Never knew what hit you, did you? What are you going to buy, Joe?'

'I don't know. There won't be much to buy with. Maybe – naw, I don't know. Depends on what Ma gives us back.'

65 'A bicycle, Joe. What about a bike? Quinn would give his away for a packet of cigarettes. You up on the saddle, Joe, and me on the crossbar. Out to the millrace every evening. Me shooting all the rabbits along the way. Bang!
70 Bang! Bang! What about a bike, Joe?'

'I don't know. I don't know.'

'What did she give you back the last time?'

'I can't remember.'

'Ten shillings? More? What did you buy
75 then? A leather belt? A set of rabbit snares?'

'I don't think I got anything back. Maybe a shilling. I don't remember.'

'A shilling! One lousy shilling out of fourteen! Do you know what I'm going to buy?' He
80 hunched his shoulders and lowered his head between them. One eye closed in a huge wink. 'Tell no one? Promise?'

'What?'

'A gaff. See?'

85 'What about the gun?'

'It can wait until next year. But a gaff, Joe. See? Old Philly down there beside the Black Pool. A big salmon. A beaut. Flat on my belly, and – phwist! – there he is on the bank, the gaff
90 stuck in his guts.' He clasped his middle and writhed in agony, imitating the fish. Then his act switched suddenly back to cowboys and he drew from both holsters at a cat sneaking home along the hedge. 'Bang! Bang! That sure settled
95 you, boy. Where is this potato territory, mistah? Ah want to show you hombrés what work is. What's a-keeping this old tractor-buggy?'

'We're jist about there, Mistah Philly, sir,' said Joe. 'Ah reckon you'll show us, OK. You'll
100 show us.'

The field was a two-acre rectangle bordered

by a low hedge. The ridges of potatoes stretched lengthwise in straight, black lines. Kelly unfastened the trailer and hooked up the mechanical digger. The two labourers stood with their hands in their pockets and scowled around them, cigarettes hanging from their lips.

'You two take the far side,' Kelly told them. 'And Joe, you and –' He could not remember the name. 'You and the lad there, you two take this side. You show him what to do, Joe.' He climbed up on the tractor seat. 'And remember,' he called over his shoulder, 'if the school-attendance officer appears, it's up to you to run. I never seen you. I never heard of you.'

The tractor moved forward into the first ridges, throwing up a spray of brown earth behind it as it went.

'Right,' said Joe. 'What we do is this, Philly. When the digger passes, we gather the spuds into these buckets and then carry the buckets to the sacks and fill them. Then back again to fill the buckets. And back to the sacks. OK, mistah?'

'OK, mistah. Child's play. What does he want four of us for? I could do the whole field myself – one hand tied behind my back.'

Joe smiled at him. 'Come on, then. Let's see you.'

'Just you watch,' said Philly. He grabbed a bucket and ran stumbling across the broken ground. His small frame bent over the clay and his thin arms worked madly. Before Joe had begun gathering, Philly's voice called to him. 'Joe! Look! Full already! Not bad, eh?'

'Take your time,' Joe called back.

'And look, Joe! Look!' Philly held his hands out for his brother's inspection. They were coated with earth. 'How's that, Joe? They'll soon be as hard as Kelly's!'

Joe laughed. 'Take it easy, Philly. No rush.'

But Philly was already stooped again over his work, and when Joe was emptying his first bucket into the sack, Philly was emptying his third. He gave Joe the huge wink again and raced off.

Kelly turned at the bottom of the field and came back up. Philly was standing waiting for him.

'What you need is a double digger, Mr Kelly!' he called as the tractor passed. But Kelly's eyes never left the ridges in front of him. A flock of sea gulls swooped and dipped behind the tractor, fluttering down to catch worms in the newly turned earth. The boy raced off with his bucket.

'How's it going?' shouted Joe after another twenty minutes. Philly was too busy to answer.

A pale sun appeared about eight-thirty. It was not strong enough to soften the earth, but it loosened sounds – cars along the roads, birds in the naked trees, cattle let out for the day. The clay became damp under it but did not thaw. The tractor exulted in its new freedom and its splutterings filled the countryside.

'I've been thinking,' said Philly when he met Joe at a sack. 'Do you know what I'm going to get, Joe? A scout knife with one of those leather scabbards. Four shillings in Byrne's shop. Great for skinning a rabbit.' He held his hands out from his sides now, because they were raw in places. 'Yeah. A scout knife with a leather scabbard.'

'A scout knife,' Joe repeated.

'You always have to carry a scout knife in case your gun won't fire or your powder gets wet. And when you're swimming underwater, you can always carry a knife between your teeth.'

'We'll have near twenty ridges done before noon,' said Joe.

'He should have a double digger. I told him that. Too slow, mistah. Too doggone slow. Tell me, Joe, have you made up your mind yet?'

'What about?'

'What you're going to buy, stupid.'

'Aw, naw. Naw . . . I don't know yet.'

Philly turned to his work again and was about to begin, when the school bell rang. He dropped his bucket and danced back to his brother. 'Listen! Joe! Listen!' He caught fistfuls of his hair and tugged his head from side to side. 'Listen! Listen! Ha, ha, ha! Ho, ho, ho! Come on, you fat, silly, silly scholars and get to your lessons! Come on, come on, come on, come on! No dallying! Speed it up! Get a move on! Hurry! Hurry! Hurry! "And where are the O'Boyle brothers today? Eh? Where are they? Gathering potatoes? What's that I hear? What? What?"'

'Look out, lad!' roared Kelly.

The tractor passed within inches of Philly's legs. He jumped out of its way in time, but a fountain of clay fell on his head and shoulders. Joe ran to his side.

'Are you all right, Philly? Are you OK?'

'Tried to get me, that's what he did, the dirty cattle thief. Tried to get me.'

'You OK, mistah? Reckon you'll live?'

'Sure, mistah. Take more'n that ole coyote to scare me. Come on, mistah. We'll show him what men we really are.' He shook his jacket and hair and hitched up his trousers. 'Would you swap now, Joe?'

'Swap what?'

'Swap places with those poor eejits back there?' He jerked his thumb in the direction of the school.

'No sir,' said Joe. 'Not me.'

'Nor me neither, mistah. Meet you in the saloon.' He swaggered off, holding his hands as if they were delicate things, not part of him.

They broke for lunch at noon. By then, the sun was high and brave but still of little use. With the engine of the tractor cut off, for a brief time there was a self-conscious silence, which became relaxed and natural when the sparrows, now audible, began to chirp. The sea gulls squabbled over the latest turned earth and a cautious puff of wind stirred the branches of the tall trees. Kelly adjusted the digger while he ate. On the far side of the field, the two labourers stretched themselves on sacks and conversed in monosyllables. Joe and Philly sat on upturned buckets. For lunch they each had half a scone of homemade soda bread, cut into thick slices and skimmed with butter. They washed it down with mouthfuls of cold tea from a bottle. After they had eaten, Joe threw the crusts to the gulls, gathered up the newspapers in which the bread had been wrapped, emptied out the remains of the tea, and put the bottle and the papers into his jacket pocket. Then he stood up and stretched himself.

'My back's getting stiff,' he said.

Philly sat with his elbows on his knees and studied the palms of his hands.

'Sore?' asked Joe.

'What?'

'Your hands. Are they hurting you?'

'They're OK,' said Philly. 'Tough as leather. But the clay's sore. Gets right into every cut and away up your nails.' He held his arms out. 'They're shaking,' he said. 'Look.'

'That's the way they go,' said Joe. 'But they'll – Listen! Do you hear?'

'Hear what?'

'Lunchtime at school. They must be playing football in the playground.'

The sounds of high, delighted squealing came intermittently when the wind sighed. They listened to it with their heads uplifted, their faces broadening with memory.

'We'll get a hammering tomorrow,' said Joe. 'Six on each hand.'

'It's going to be a scout knife,' Philly said. 'I've decided on that.'

'She mightn't give us anything back. Depends on how much she needs herself.'

'She said she would. She promised. Have you decided yet?'

'I'm still thinking,' said Joe.

The tractor roared suddenly, scattering every other sound.

'Come on, mistah,' said the older one. 'Four more hours to go. Saddle up your horse.'

'Coming. Coming,' Philly replied. His voice was sharp with irritation.

The sun was a failure. It held its position in the sky and flooded the countryside with light but could not warm it. Even before it had begun to slip to the west, the damp ground had become glossy again, and before the afternoon was spent, patches of white frost were appearing on higher ground. Now the boys were working automatically, their minds acquiescing in what their bodies did. They no longer straightened up; the world was their feet and the hard clay and the potatoes and their hands and the buckets and the sacks. Their ears told them where the tractor was, at the bottom of the field, turning, approaching. Their muscles had become adjusted to their stooped position, and as long as the boys kept within the established pattern of movement their arms and hands and legs and shoulders seemed to float as if they were free of gravity. But if something new was expected from the limbs – a piece of glass to be thrown into the hedge, quick stepping back to avoid the digger – then their bodies shuddered with the pain and the tall trees reeled and the hedges rose to the sky.

Dicey O'Donnell gave them a shout from the road on his way home from school. 'Hi! Joe! Philly!'

They did not hear him. He waited until the tractor turned. 'Hi! Hi! Philly! Philly! Joe!'

'Hello,' Joe called back.

'Youse are for it the morrow. I'm telling youse. He knows where youse are. He says he's going to beat the scruff out of youse the morrow. Youse are in for it, all right. Blue murder! Bloody hell! True as God!'

'Get lost!' Joe called back.

'Aye, and he's going to report youse to the attendance officer, and your old fella'll be fined. Youse are ruined! Destroyed! Blue murder!'

'Will I put a bullet in him, mistah?' said Joe to Philly.

Philly did not answer. He thought he was going to fall, and his greatest fear was that he might fall in front of the tractor, because now the tractor's exhaust had only one sound, fixed forever in his head, and unless he saw the machine he could not tell whether it was near him or far away. The 'rat-tat-tat' was a finger tapping in his head, drumming at the back of his eyes.

'Vamoose, O'Donnell!' called Joe. 'You annoy us. Vamoose.'

O'Donnell said something more about the reception they could expect the next day, but he got tired of calling to two stooped backs and he went off home.

The last pair of ridges was turned when the sky had veiled itself for dusk. The two brothers and the two labourers worked on until they met in the middle. Now the field was all brown, all flat, except for the filled sacks that patterned it. Kelly was satisfied; his lips formed an O and he blew through them as if he were trying to whistle. He detached the digger and hooked up the trailer. 'All aboard!' he shouted, in an effort at levity.

On the way home, the labourers seemed to be fully awake, for the first time since morning. They stood in the trailer where the boys had stood at dawn, behind Kelly's head and facing the road before them. They chatted and guffawed and made plans for a dance that night. When they met people they knew along the way, they saluted extravagantly. At the crossroads,

350  they began to wrestle, and Kelly had to tell them
to watch out or they would fall over the side. But
he did not sound angry.

355  Joe sat on the floor, his legs straight out before
him, his back resting against the side of the
trailer. Philly lay flat out, his head cushioned on
his brother's lap. Above him, the sky spread
out, grey, motionless, enigmatic. The warmth
from Joe's body made him drowsy. He wished
the journey home to go on forever, the sound of
360  the tractor engine to anaesthetize his mind
forever. He knew that if the movement and the
sound were to cease, the pain of his body would
be unbearable.

'We're nearly there,' said Joe quietly. 'Are
365  you asleep?' Philly did not answer. 'Mistah! Are
you asleep, mistah?'

'No.'

Darkness came quickly, and when the last
trace of light disappeared the countryside
370  became taut with frost. The headlamps of the
tractor glowed yellow in the cold air.

'Philly? Are you awake, mistah?'

'What?'

'I've been thinking,' said Joe slowly. 'And do
375  you know what I think? I think I've made up my
mind now.'

One of the labourers burst into song.

'If I were a blackbird, I'd whistle and sing,
and I'd follow the ship that my true love sails in.'

380  His mate joined him at the second line and
their voices exploded in the stiff night.

'Do you know what I'm going to buy?' Joe
said, speaking more loudly. 'If she gives us
something back, that is. Mistah! Mistah Philly!
385  Are you listening? I'm going to buy a pair of red
silk socks.'

He waited for approval from Philly. When
none came, he shook his brother's head. 'Do you
hear, mistah? Red silk socks – the kind Jojo
390  Teague wears. What about that, eh? What do
you think?'

Philly stirred and half raised his head from his
brother's lap. 'I think you're daft,' he said in an
exhausted, sullen voice. 'Ma won't give us back
395  enough to buy anything much. No more than a
shilling. You knew it all the time.' He lay down
again and in a moment he was fast asleep.

Joe held his brother's head against the motion
of the trailer and repeated the words 'red silk
400  socks' to himself again and again, nodding each
time at the wisdom of his decision.

■■■■■■■ Brian Friel ■■■■■■■

## Questions

(The marks at the side of the page will give you a
guide to the amount of material required in your
answers.)

1  Show how the writer sets the scene for the story
and the situation in the opening paragraph.
(4 marks)

2  'His energy was a burden to him' (line 24).
Explain what this means and show how the writer
illustrates it.                                    (3 marks)

3  What difference is there between Joe and Philly
in their attitude towards the work – at least to
start with? How can you account for this difference?                                              (4 marks)

4  'His first opportunity to prove that he was a man
at twelve years of age (line 22). Does the way
Philly behaves during the morning suggest 'he
was a man', or do you think he is still a child?
(4 marks)

5  What are the reactions of the brothers to the
sound of the school bell (line 187)? Are their
reactions the same when they hear the lunch-time
squealing (line 253)?                              (3 marks)

6  How do the brothers respond to Dicey O'Donnell's taunting (lines 300–331)?       (2 marks)

7  Contrast the behaviour and attitude of the two
labourers on the journey home with what it had
been on the journey to work. Account for the
difference. Does it have any bearing on the
situation and feelings of Joe and Philly? (4 marks)

8  In what ways is Philly at the end of the story
different from the person he was at the beginning
of the story? Has Joe changed as well?   (5 marks)

9  Consider the appropriateness of 'The Loss of
Innocence' and 'Growing Pains' as alternative
titles for this story.                             (4 marks)

10  Imagine Philly writing about the day in his diary
that evening. Begin, 'It was going to be a great
day . . .' Write at least half a page.      (7 marks)

# Section B

Here are two reports of the same occasion when there
were delays in the flight home of holidaymakers from
Tenerife. The first report (I) is the transcript of a radio
news report; the second report (II) appeared in *The
Guardian*. The two reports follow the questions.

## Questions

(The marks will give you a guide to the amount of
material required in your answers.)

1  State the number of passengers on board the
Boeing 757 as it appears in each of the reports I
and II.                                            (2 marks)

2  Outline the number of attempts made to get the
passengers home and why each failed.   (4 marks)

3  Explain as fully as you can what was wrong with
the plane.                                         (5 marks)

4  'Nobody seemed to be taking a blind bit of
notice,' says Mrs Harvey in Report I. What explanation for this is given in Report II? (2 marks)

5  Quote the different words and descriptions used
for the way the oil was coming out of the engine.
Point out the differences in meaning between
them.                                              (4 marks)

6  What indications are there in the reports that the passengers were upset and worried?  (5 marks)

7  Which report, I or II, gives the more vivid account of what the passengers' feelings were? Give reasons for your answer.  (4 marks)

8  What evidence is there that Mrs Harvey's account is spoken English rather than written English?  (4 marks)

9  Which report, I or II, gives the more detailed account of what happened and what went wrong? Justify your answer.  (4 marks)

10  Describe how Air Europe tried to rectify the fault and how they handled the passengers. Do you think the airline did as much as they could in the circumstances?  (6 marks)

## I

It might be snowing here, but there are 300 people who are glad to be back from the sunny Canary Islands, no matter what the weather is like. These are the passengers of an Air Europe charter plane. Their return home was delayed by two days because of a faulty aircraft, but now they are all back safely. Here is Eric Walker with a report.

'The last of the stranded passengers arrived at Gatwick this afternoon. They were due to return two days ago after a fortnight's holiday in Tenerife. But there were problems. The trouble started after they had boarded the plane, a Boeing 757. One of the passengers noticed oil pouring out of one of the engines. This is how another of the passengers, Mrs Harvey, described it.'

'It was just pouring out. Like water from a tap. I was horrified when I saw it, really horrified. I didn't know what to think. And nobody seemed to be taking a blind bit of notice. None of the flight staff anyway. Well, we were all getting very upset about it. I was frightened out of my life. Someone must have reported it, because we were taken off.

'Then a couple of hours later, they said it was all right, and we got on board again. But there was still oil streaming out of one of the engines. We were all demanding to be taken off, and the flight was cancelled in the end. There was no way I was going to fly in that plane. And I wasn't the only one. We got up a petition saying we wanted another plane.

'We were put up overnight in a hotel, and then blow me next morning when we were getting ready for the flight, they rolled out the same plane. And there was *still* oil gushing out of it. I refused to get on it. So did everyone else. We weren't going to risk our lives in that thing. In the end, the airline agreed, and we were put up at the hotel for another night. And next morning they found another plane from somewhere, and here we are. I've never been so thankful in all my life.'

I can understand that. It certainly seems to have been quite an ordeal. A spokesman for Air Europe deeply regretted any inconvenience caused to passengers.

## II

# Passenger sees fault in jet ready for takeoff

By Gareth Perry

A group of passengers who refused to fly home from Tenerife in the Canary Islands after one of them spotted oil or fuel leaking from the engine of their Boeing 757 arrived back in Britain yesterday, two days late.

A petition from 140 of them to the charter airline, Air Europe, said that they had no confidence in the plane after a disturbing few hours on Friday when take-off was aborted twice.

Air Europe said last night that the Boeing was back in service on a different route after an overhaul during which an air governor had been replaced.

The trouble began when the plane indicated an engine fault as it approached Tenerife on Friday.

It was overhauled and was preparing to take off for Manchester with 321 people on board when a passenger saw the apparent leak as it taxied to the runway.

The passengers were put up overnight at an airport hotel as engineers flown in from Gatwick carried out further work, but the engine was still leaking when the plane taxied out on Saturday morning.

Mr Mark Robbins, aged 30, a steel salesman from Birmingham, said after the second aborted take-off that the pilot had said over the intercom that he would like to thank the passenger who had seen oil seeping out of a port engine.

The passenger, Mr Paul Bradley, a circulation representative at the Daily Telegraph, had noticed the fault as the plane revved up on the apron. He ran to the flight deck and insisted that the pilot let everybody off.

After another night in Tenerife at Air Europe's expense the passengers were returned to Britain yesterday on two flights.

Mr Robbins said: "The pilot said the only indication he would have had on the flight deck that anything was wrong would have been when the engines were at high revs, and he said that could have been serious."

Another passenger said the oil had been coming out with more force than from a hosepipe.

According to Mr Robbins, the engineers from Gatwick replaced 12 components: "They were overheard to say hydraulic seals had gone, the pump was clogged, and the plane constituted a risk."

Air Europe, founded in 1978 and owned by the International Leisure Group, the package holidays and hotels operation, has been named charter airline of the year for the past three years. Its flights are used by holiday firms within ILG such as Intasun, Select Holidays and Club 18–30.

*The Guardian*

# Section C

Write an essay on ONE of the following topics.

What you say and how you say it are more important than the length of your writing in itself. However, as a general guide, you should write at least one side.

1  In 'The Potato Gatherers', Philly regarded the job as 'his first opportunity to prove that he was a man'. Write about a time when you also felt you were facing this challenge – the chance to prove that you were grown-up.

2  Write about an occasion when you played truant or when you encountered a friend who was playing truant.

3  Write about an occasion which you were looking forward to excitedly that went wrong or turned sour.

4  Imagine you are about to start your first day at work. Write about your feelings of anticipation and/or anxiety.

(If you are not required to sit a written examination, this could be part of your coursework.)

# Unit Seven

# 7.1 Writing – describing an event

Describing an event requires many of the skills called for when describing a character or a scene. Revise what was said in sections 5.1 and 6.1.

Decide first of all on the form your writing is going to take. Is it going to be:

○ expressive (a piece of imaginative writing)
○ persuasive (presenting a point of view through your description)
○ expository (describing the event stage by stage as it actually happened)?

Get your facts and information together. These don't have to be 'exact'. You can invent, exaggerate, make more colourful, bring in contrasts and feelings that may not have existed, so long as your writing convinces the reader that you are describing an actual event.

Choose an approach. For instance, if you are describing a school sports day, you could:

○ use an impressionistic approach, concentrating on the sights and sounds (as Katherine Mansfield does in the extract from 'Bank Holiday' in section 6.1)

○ describe the event from a particular point of view, for example, a small child or a competitor or a doting parent
○ view the event as coloured by a particular feeling, for example, an expression of loathing for such events or amusement at its chaotic organisation.

● Here are two examples for you to study and compare. The first describes a train journey in rural Sardinia in about 1920. The second is a newspaper account of a boxing match in which one of the boxers died.

## A

The coach was fairly full of people, returning from market. On these railways the third-class coaches are not divided into compartments. They are left open, so that one sees everybody, as down a room... It is much nicest, on the whole, to travel third-class on the railway. There is space, there is air, and it is like being in a lively inn, everybody in good spirits.

At our end was plenty of room. Just across the gangway was an elderly couple, like two children, coming home very happily. He was fat, fat all over, with a white moustache and a little not unamiable frown. She was a tall, lean, brown woman, in a brown full-skirted dress and black apron, with a huge pocket. She wore no head covering, and her iron-grey hair was parted smoothly. They were rather pleased and excited being in the train. She took all her money out of her big pocket, and counted it and gave it to him: all the ten-lira notes, and the five-lira, and the two and the one, peering at the dirty scraps of pink-backed one-lira notes to see if they were good. Then she gave him her halfpennies. And he stowed them away in the trouser pocket, standing up to push them down his fat leg. And then one saw, to one's amazement, that the whole of his shirt-tail was left out behind, like a sort of apron worn backwards. Why – a mystery. He was one of those fat, good-natured, unheeding men with a little masterful frown, such as usually have tall, lean, hard-faced, obedient wives. . . .

So we ran on through the gold of the afternoon, across a wide, almost Celtic landscape of hills, our little train winding and puffing away very nimbly. Only the heath and scrub, breast-high, man-high, are too big and brigand-like for a Celtic land. The horns of black, wild-looking cattle show sometimes.

After a long pull, we come to a station after a stretch of loneliness. Each time it looks as if there were nothing beyond – no more habitations. And each time we come to a station.

Most of the people have left the train. And as with men driving in a gig, who get down at every public-house, so the passengers usually alight for an airing at each station. Our old fat friend stands up and tucks his shirt tail comfortably in his trousers, which trousers all the time make one hold one's breath, for they seem at each very moment to be just dropping right down: and he clambers out, followed by the long, brown stalk of a wife.

So the train sits comfortably for five or ten minutes, in the way the trains have. At last we hear whistles and horns, and our old fat friend running and clinging like a fat crab to the very end of the train as it sets off. At the same instant a loud shriek and a bunch of shouts from outside. We all jump up. There, down the line, is the long brown stalk of a wife. She had just walked back to a house some hundred yards off, for a few words, and has now seen the train moving.

Now behold her with her hands thrown to heaven, and hear the wild shriek 'Madonna!' through all the hubbub. But she picks up her two skirt-knees, and with her thin legs in grey stockings starts with a mad rush after the train. In vain. The train inexorably pursues its course. Prancing, she reaches one end of the platform as we leave the other end. Then she realises it is not going to stop for her. And then, oh horror, her long arms thrown out in wild supplication after the retreating train: then flung aloft to God: then brought down in absolute despair on her head. And this is the last sight we have of her, clutching her poor head in agony and doubling forward. She is left – she is abandoned.

The poor fat husband has been all the time on the little outside platform at the end of the carriage, holding out his hand to her and shouting frenzied scolding to her and frenzied yells for the train to stop. And the train has not stopped. And she is left – left on that God-forsaken station in the waning light.

So, his face all bright, his eyes round and bright as two stars, absolutely transfigured by dismay, chagrin, anger and distress, he comes and sits in his seat, ablaze, stiff, speechless. His face is almost beautiful in its blaze of conflicting emotions. For some time he is as if unconscious in the midst of his feelings. Then anger and resentment crop out of his consternation. He turns with a flash to the long-nosed, insidious, Phœnician-looking guard. Why couldn't they stop the train for her? And immediately as if someone had set fire to him, off flares the guard. Heh! – the train can't stop for every person's convenience! The train is a train – the time-table is a time-table. What did the old woman want to take her trips down the line for? Heh! She pays the penalty for her own inconsiderateness. Had *she* paid for the train – heh? And the fat man all the time firing off his unheeding and unheeded answers. One minute – only one minute – if he, the conductor, had told the driver! if he, the conductor, had shouted! A poor woman! Not another train! What was she going to do! Her ticket? And no money. A poor woman –

There was a train back to Cagliari that night, said the conductor, at which the fat man nearly burst out of his clothing like a bursting seed-pod. He bounced on his seat. What good was that? What good was a train back to Cagliari, when their home was in Snelli! Making matters worse –

So they bounced and jerked and argued at one another to their hearts' content. Then the conductor retired, smiling subtly, in a way they have. Our fat friend looked at us with hot, angry, ashamed, grieved eyes and said it was a shame. Yes, we chimed, it *was* a shame. Whereupon a self-important miss who said she came from some Collegio at Cagliari advanced and asked a number of impertinent questions in a tone of pert sympathy. After which our fat friend, left alone, covered his clouded face with his hand, turned his back on the world, and gloomed. . . .

Well, the journey lasted hours. We came to a station, and the conductor said we must get out: these coaches went no further. Only two coaches would proceed to Mandas. So we climbed out with our traps, and our fat friend with his saddle-bag, the picture of misery.

The one coach into which we clambered was rather crowded. The only other coach was most of it first-class. And the rest of the train was freight. We were two insignificant passenger wagons at the end of a long string of freight vans and trucks.

There was an empty seat, so we sat in it: only to realise after about five minutes that a thin old woman with two children – her grandchildren – was chuntering her head off because it was *her* seat – why she had left it she didn't say. And under my legs was her bundle of bread. She nearly went off her head. And over my head, on the little rack, was her *bercola*, her saddle-bag. Fat soldiers laughed at her good-naturedly, but she fluttered and flipped like a tart, featherless old hen. Since she had another seat and was quite comfortable, we smiled and let her chunter. So she clawed her bread bundle from under my legs, and, clutching it and a fat child, sat tense.

■■■ From D. H. Lawrence, *Sea and Sardinia* ■■■

1 Would you describe the writer as a participant or an observer? Justify your answer.
2 What does the writer appear to be particularly interested in?
3 How does the writer make his account interesting?
4 How successful would you say the writer is in giving an account of a train journey? What impression does he give?

━━━━━━ B ━━━━━━

# Steve, they said, is going to be fine

● Simon Brown on his bloody introduction to boxing

IT WAS a fight billed as "the showdown", a 10-round match, I was told, in which the needle between the two men stretched back to amateur clubs and teenage rivalries. In truth, I'd never heard of Rocky Kelly, nor of Steve Watt.

This was my first boxing match but, even before that horrific tenth and final round, when Watt, locked against the ropes just a few yards away, suffered a battering of blows that shut my eyes and turned my stomach, there was little to redeem the evening.

Both boxers had squared up with a look of concentration that never left their faces. Even in the final moments before the referee, Sid Nathan, stepped in to stop the fight, Steve Watt, his once jaunty crewcut plastered like cooking fat across his skull, was alert to Kelly's every move.

The seventh round had ended with Watt flat on his feet, each blow from Kelly sending a shower of sweat shimmering into the floodlights.

When the end came and Nathan intervened, Watt, led away, sank to his stool beneath a haze of bobbing heads. For perhaps a minute we had little idea that anything was wrong, as Kelly danced to each side of the ring with first aloft, his fans cheering.

But the melée went on in Watt's corner. Beneath the stooping bodies we could see the Scot stretched out on the blood-specked canvas. A second stuck his hand over the lens of a video camera, the press photographers stopped work; someone – later familiarised by the MC as Dr "Stevie" Johnson – was applying chest message to the helpless body.

As Steve Watt was stretchered from the ring and through the mob, the MC called for applause. There'd be a short break ... and of course they'd keep us all informed.

The men, talking into their pints of lager, their puffy eyes taking sidelong glances, had seen it all before. Exhaustion, said some; dehydration, said others. Their women, wearing heavyweight jewellery and lightweight smiles, said little. Money, stripped from rolls of notes, was changing hands. Ten minutes later, from the chandeliered boxing hall came the voice of the MC. Steve Watt, he boomed, had been taken to hospital, but all could be assured that he was going to be just fine.

The notes on the fight programme proved to be more accurate: "The way to the top is over the bodies of the top men."

5 In your opinion, how clear an account of the events does the writer give?
6 The writer doesn't describe the events in sequence. Why not? Does this make his account more or less effective?
7 How do the writer's feelings about the fight colour the way he describes it? Give examples.
8 Do you think this is a fair account of the fight or is it biased?

### 7.1.1 Describing an event – coursework
Write a description of one of the following:

1 The Cup Final
2 Bonfire night
3 Prize-giving
4 A school visit
5 A flower show
6 A jumble sale

# 7.2 Coursework – response to reading: the novel

There are obvious differences between a short story and a novel. Characters, setting, plot and theme, language and style are important in both. But in a novel, it is likely that there will be more characters, the settings will be more various, the plot will be more intricate and developed over a longer time-span, the theme more thoroughly or subtly explored, the language and style more varied and expansive. However, the kinds of questions you would consider when discussing or examining a novel are very similar to those you would apply to a short story. (Revise 'Writing narrative' (2.1) and 'Coursework – response to reading: the short story' (4.2).) Basically the questions are as follows:

*Characters* What kind of people are they? What part do they play in the plot? How do they react to and interact with each other? Are there similarities and differences in their attitudes? Do they develop in the course of the plot? From whose point of view are the events in the novel being seen? Do you think the writer shares this point of view?

*Plot and theme* What actually happens in the novel? Is there a kind of pattern in the events? How are things different at the end from what they were at the beginning? Is there any unifying idea behind the events and the characters? If so, how is it developed? What do you think the writer is trying to show by choosing to write about these events and these characters?

*Setting* Where is the novel mainly set? Are there any contrasts thrown up? Does the setting have any particular bearing on the characters and the plot?

*Language and style* What kind of language and tone does the writer use in the novel? Is it appropriate for the subject matter and the point of view? Are words used interestingly? Is the writing free of clichés? Does it move the plot along at an appropriate pace? What would you describe as the significant features of the style?

*Personal response* Did you enjoy reading the novel? Were there any aspects of it that you particularly enjoyed or found rather weak? Did the novel remind you of anything in your own life or experience? Did the novel extend your understanding of any area of life or humanity?

In your GCSE course, you are expected to read whole texts such as novels. You will probably have to provide evidence of this reading, possibly as part of your coursework. When writing about a novel, you can give an account of it as a piece of literature, using some of the questions above as a guide. You can say what the novel is about, what the main characters are like, what the writer seems to be saying in the novel, your own reactions to the novel. Alternatively, you could use some aspects of the novel to set you off on a piece of writing of your own or retell part of the novel in a different form.

● Here are some suggestions for you to choose from:

1 Write an account of a novel dealing with a character whose situation has aroused your sympathy and involvement.

2 'A good novel should have believable characters, an interesting story and something worthwhile to say.' Choose a novel you have read recently and say how far it meets these requirements.

3 If you have seen a film, television or stage version of a novel you have read, write about the similarities and differences you found and say what you think the novel gained and lost by being translated into a different medium.

4 Outline the theme of a novel you have read recently and describe how the author brings the theme out in the novel.

5 Have you read a novel which has been set in an area very similar to or very different from where you yourself live? Give an account of the novel and say how the setting contributed to your interest in it.

● Here are some suggestions for a freer response to a novel you have read:

6 Have any situations in a novel you have read recently reminded you of a similar situation that you were involved in yourself? Give an account of your own experience.

7 Choose an important episode in a novel. Imagine the letter one of the characters involved writes to a friend describing what has happened and what his or her feelings are. Or else write a letter to the character in which you sympathise or criticise.

8 Have you ever read a novel and wondered at the end what the main characters would be like in ten years' time? Write a story about these characters ten years' later, or describe a meeting between two of the characters that takes place after the events of the story. You could write this as a play.

9 If appropriate, write an account of an event in a novel as it might have been reported in a newspaper. Or else write a newspaper interview with one of the characters.

10 Imagine a character in a novel you have read keeps a diary. Write the entry he or she makes after an important episode in the novel.

## 7.2.1 Further reading

Here are some novels you may find interesting:

Achebe, Chinua, *Things Fall Apart*. Heinemann Educational Books.
Barstow, Stan, *Joby*. Heinemann New Windmill.
Cormier, Robert, *I am the Cheese*. Macmillan M Books.
Darke, Marjorie, *A Long Way to Go*. Puffin.
Desai, Anita, *The Village by the Sea*. Puffin/ Heinemann New Windmill.
Emecheta, Buchi, *Second Class Citizen*. Allison & Busby.
Golding, William, *Lord of the Flies*. Penguin Books.
Hines, Barry, *A Kestrel for a Knave*. Penguin Books.
Lee, Harper, *To Kill a Mockingbird*. Penguin Books/ Heinemann New Windmill.
Lee, Laurie, *Cider with Rosie*. Penguin Books.
Lingard, Joan, *The Twelfth Day of July*. Puffin.
Marshall, James Vance, *Walkabout*. Puffin/ Heinemann New Windmill.
Orwell, George, *Animal Farm*. Penguin Books/ Heinemann New Windmill.
————, *1984*. Penguin Books.
Paton, Alan, *Cry, the Beloved Country*. Penguin Books.
Sillitoe, Alan, *The Loneliness of the Long Distance Runner*. Pan Books.
Steinbeck, John, *Of Mice and Men*. Penguin Books/ Heinemann New Windmill.
Taylor, Mildred D., *Roll of Thunder, Hear my Cry*. Puffin/Heinemann New Windmill.
Waterhouse, Keith, *Billy Liar*. Penguin Books.
Wyndham, John, *The Chrysalids*. Penguin Books.

# 7.3 Writing – reformulating for a purpose

This exercise requires you to select the relevant information from a piece of writing and use that information in another form. For instance, given an article which deals with the difficulties and problems of old people, you may be asked to prepare a leaflet to be distributed to old people in your area giving them advice. Alternatively, you may be asked to change the point of view from which the facts or events in a piece of writing are seen. For instance, rewriting a story from the point of view of a different character.

You need to:

○ make sure you understand clearly the task set, that is the purpose given for the new piece of writing
○ select and make notes of material relevant to this task
○ have a clear picture of the audience you are writing for or the point of view you are writing from
○ rewrite the material in the way directed, using language and tone appropriate to this audience or point of view.

1 Read the following article about Mark Twain. Using only information given here, write the entry on Mark Twain that might appear in a biographical dictionary of authors.

# The adventures of Mark Twain

*America's Mark Twain had to cross the Atlantic to reach his peak. On the 150th anniversary of his birth James Munson recalls his career*

'VIR JUCUNDISSIME, lepidissime, facetissime.' – a man most pleasant, most humorous and most witty. With these words Oxford University's Public Orator greeted America's most famous writer, Mark Twain, in 1907. Amid the splendours of Oxford's Sheldonian Theatre the former printer, Mississippi river pilot, prospector and journalist was awarded an honorary Doctor of Letters degree.

It was the one honour which the man who had grown up along the banks of the 'mighty Mississippi' most desired; it became the one he most treasured. It was fitting because it was England which first recognised the true worth of Mark Twain's writings – the truth that lay beneath the humour and satire of his novels.

Samuel Clemens – he only began using the pen-name 'Mark Twain' in his late 20s – was born in 1835. He grew up in a small town called Hannibal in the state of Missouri. The townsfolk probably cared little for their connection with the famous commander of ancient Carthage. What did matter was the fact that Hannibal lay on the bank of 'the great Mississippi, the majestic, the magnificent Mississippi rolling its mile-wide tide along, shining in the sun, the dense forest away on the other side'.

A writer worth his salt must be the product of a society or culture which gives him an identity. But he must also have a native ability to detach himself from that culture, to look at it from outside. He must leave it, only to return.

Twain really began writing when he was left without work and turned to journalism. His subject was a territorial (later state) legislature; it was a field ripe for harvesting to a writer who combined a deep knowledge of and scant respect for human nature. Twain was naturally a 'humorous' writer. When he tried to be serious he became pompous.

His first fame came with a travel book called *The Innocents Abroad*, which described the hilarious exploits of the first real wave of American tourists bent on European culture-mongering. As with the petty politicians, Twain had the field all to himself. He followed the book with another on his days in the Wild West and a third, a political novel, *The Gilded Age*. This satirised the wholesale corruption which the triumphant Republicans brought after their defeat of the Confederacy in 1865.

It was not until 1876 that he returned to his childhood days, to write *The Adventures of Tom Sawyer*. In 1884 he published its sequel, *The Adventures of Huckleberry Finn*. Neither book was immediately a success, and *Huckleberry Finn* was denounced for its coarseness and vulgarity. Vulgar it was, and remains, because it describes a world – the western frontier of the American South – that *was* crude. But the books are funny, while at the same time touching on deep human feelings. They remain unique contributions to American literature, set in a time and space that only Mark Twain could have described.●

**2** Read the following advertisement for a holiday in Italy. Assume that all the information given here is correct. Imagine that you went on this holiday. Write a letter to a friend describing what it was like. Use only information given in the advertisement.

The beautiful Amalfi coast and the city of Rome, below, are two of the colourful places to visit on our Italian trip.

## Two holidays in one

# The best of Italy — from only £279

Lovely beaches, friendly hotels, spectacular excursions — all at a great value price. For your summer holiday next year why not sample the two-centre Italian holiday that so many *TVTimes* readers have already enjoyed?

This popular fortnight's break begins with a week in the little fishing village of Massalubrense, close to the famous town of Sorrento, then moves on for a second week to the attractive beach resort of Terracina, 50 miles south of Rome.

The price — including scheduled flights to and from Rome and half-board accommodation throughout — starts at just £279.

The quiet, unspoilt charm of Massalubrense will put you in a relaxed holiday mood right from Day One. Built on a hillside above the harbour, the village looks out across lemon groves to the bay of Naples and the Isle of Capri.

Your hotel is the family-run Hotel Maria, with magnificient views across the bay, a super swimming pool with sun terraces, and an excellent restaurant, bar and lounge. A local bus service, which stops at the hotel, will carry you to Sorrento — perfect for souvenir shopping — and optional excursions can take you to the lovely town of Amalfi on the Gulf of Salerno, or to the remains of the Roman city of Pompeii. You can also take trips to the active volcano of Mount Vesuvius, or across the bay to the Isle of Capri.

After the first week we take you north to the contrasting resort of Terracina. Apart from its fabulous sandy beaches, there are plenty of shops for browsing, wonderful fish restaurants, and a pretty harbour bustling with colourful craft.

Your hotel in Terracina is the Hotel Riva Gaia, close to the beach. You can be sure of a friendly welcome at this family-run hotel. There's a pleasant dining room, and, as with the Hotel Maria in Massalubrense, all rooms have their own private bath or shower and WC.

You can take optional excursions to Monte Cassino — site of the famous monastery which was destroyed during World War Two and has since been rebuilt — and to Rome for the day. The Vatican, the Trevi Fountain, the Colosseum and the Forum are just a few of the unforgettable sights of The Eternal City. Departures are between April and October.

PO Box 168, Leicester LE
two-centre holiday

**3** Read the following extract from the novel *A Question of Courage* by Marjorie Darke. It describes an attempt by suffragettes to disrupt a Liberal Party meeting at Caxton Hall. Using only these facts and information derived from the extract, write a report of the incident that might have appeared in a newspaper that supported the Liberal Party.

---

Afterwards she could never give a description of the Hall, except to say that it was big and filled to bursting with a mountain of flesh, which crowded in, a hostile threatening mass. She chose the centre of a row towards the back of the Hall where she would be fairly well protected by bodies from any official wanting to throw her out. People were already filing on to the platform, sitting on the respectable chairs; high collars, watch-chains and bald heads gleaming. A table stood before them, with a carafe of water and glasses. How she longed for a drink. Her throat was dry as a bone.

'Ladies and gentlemen . . .' The chairman was tapping on the table with his gavel. The murmurs quietened. Emily shrank. The meeting had hardly begun, but she felt exposed; sure that everyone must know her intention. In a minute they'd all be turning to stare, before she'd uttered one word. Frantically she scanned the sea of faces for the reassuring sight of Louise, and found her six rows away sitting straight and proud. If she can do it, Emily said inside herself, you can!

The chairman was working through an introductory speech, which seemed likely to last for six weeks at least. Louise was to stand up as soon as the principal speaker opened his mouth. Reginald McKenna, who had introduced that hated Cat and Mouse Act in Parliament! Emily watched him get to his feet. Smug bastard! Oh God, please let her stomach lie down. He was speaking now, but the thunder in her ears cut out the sound of his voice. She watched Louise get to her feet, unfurling the green, white and purple banner with VOTES FOR WOMEN printed on it. Listen . . . she must listen! The words of the speech she had read a hundred times were rolling from Louise's tongue, her resonant voice filling every corner of the Hall. No reaction; people stunned; even the man on the platform hesitated. A long, long moment.

'Suffragettes!' The cry was picked up in different parts of the Hall, then: 'Shame . . . throw her out!'

Four burly men were making their way down the aisle either side. The men and women seated beside Louise turned on her, snatching the banner. Officials closed in pushing along the row, treading on toes. There was no escape, but still she went on speaking: '. . . as the world looks on. It is the shame of England that half its population should be treated thus, denied the privilege as are convicts, and . . .' Her part was done. Half dragged, unresisting, the cloak torn from her shoulders, Louise was hurried into the aisle and ejected from the Hall.

But the speech was not over.

'Convicts and lunatics,' boomed a voice with the power of a foghorn. 'Is this the mark of a mature and well-tried civilization, or will in years to come the finger of scorn and derision be pointed at . . .'

Fury seething and wrestling with her unstable stomach, Emily watched the horsy woman roughly shoved from the body of the Hall. And still the speech was flowing. Another woman banished, trailing shreds of tulle and yelling. The fourth was Mary Grant, her deep voice compelling attention, conquering the noise of the angry crowd. Emily would be next.

'Give her a taste of the whip,' someone bellowed, but as Mary was grabbed and manhandled from her place, Emily caught another gentler comment from the woman next to her:

'Poor thing . . . it's not right to treat a woman so.'

The voice had gone, lost in her own trembling attempt to shout the words. Emily felt her whole body shaking as if she was suffering from a fever. Her heart was banging about, ready to leap out of her chest and the din in her head was past belief. She stared at the speech.

'. . . be pointed at . . . at Mr Asquith and his so-called Liberal Government. Yo may th . . . think their rule democratic, but . . . future generations will pronounce . . . it a tyranny, a dictatorship . . . a monstrous travesty of . . . justice. My friends, yo cannot sit here unmoved. We ask yo all . . .' The words on the paper were coming and going like a flock of sparrows against the sun, impossible to read, nothing like the practised confidence of the others, but keeping going. She was conscious of a little bound of proud happiness. However small and short-lived, she'd not failed.

And then came the blow, a painful crack on her spine which knocked her forward on to the shoulders of two men in front. The paper was torn from her hands and before she had time to recover her breath or attempt to go on speaking, the strong-arm men were on her. Well she'd not go without giving as good as she got. As the first man took a handful of her coat she clenched her fist, careful to keep thumb outside fingers, and lammed for all she was worth into his face. It was a foolish move, she knew it as soon as he let go and covered his face with his hands. Any sympathy there had been hedging her vanished as blood flowed from his nose. From behind, her hat was knocked off and her hair seized so painfully that she was forced to move in the direction she was being pulled. There were other blows, surreptitious kicks on shins and feet as she staggered over a forest of knees; inexorably dragged outside, where there seemed to be an army of policemen to deal with the handful of women.

Through tears of pain and fury, Emily glimpsed Louise in the grip of a burly policeman. For a moment their eyes met and without a word spoken Emily knew that the façade of cloak-and-dagger adventure had been swept away for ever. It was truth they faced together; the bare fact of physical weakness that seemed to control the destiny of women. She jerked ineffectually, trying to release her pinioned arms. Louise was being half carried, half dragged towards the street and the waiting police van. The doors moved constantly as more women were forced through. Uproar from the Hall came and went in bursts. Emily saw Vera swing her handbag at a policeman and close by Vic was struggling like a madman, shouting oaths that brought the ghost of a grin. His strength and ferocity brought a temporary diversion. The arm which held her like a band of steel relaxed ever so slightly. She didn't waste this heaven-sent chance, but swivelled to face the man, bringing her knee up sharply, seeing him fold with a cry that brought a strange mixture of satisfaction and horror. But she was free! The fighting that surrounded Vic was causing chaos. Several policemen were struggling in a confused tangle of arms and legs and rolling helmets. She looked round for Vera, but could not see her, and in the process of wriggling through the heaving crowd was elbowed in the eye. The blow acted like a spur, putting one thought in her head . . . to escape.

'Don't let that wild-cat get away, George,' someone shouted.

Emily did not stop to find out who George was, but sped along the pavement, past iron railings towards the main road and across with scarcely a look for traffic. There was the close rattle of wheels and a creaking of leather. The hot breath of a horse blew over her cheeks, with the blare of a motor horn and smell of petrol fumes.

'What the bloody 'ell are you up to . . . Tired of life, darlin'?'

Emily hardly saw or heard, racing blindly towards Victoria station and comparative safety.

■ From Marjorie Darke, *A Question of Courage* ■

# 7.4 Reading – bias

Words can reveal attitudes and can be used to influence readers. Look at the following words:
    slim      thin      skinny
    home    house   hovel.
'Slim' and 'home' produce a favourable impression; 'thin' and 'house' are neutral and objective; 'skinny' and 'hovel' are unfavourable.

In your own writing you have to be aware of the kinds of words you are using in order to produce the effect you want. In your reading, you have to be aware of the kinds of words the writer is using in order to detect the slant or bias behind the words.

Writers use 'biased' words legitimately to reveal character – to show how a particular character views a situation, for instance, or sees other characters.

1  Look at the following extract. Examine to what extent the words are neutral or biased and what that tells the reader about how the narrator sees the situation.

My first year there was terrible. The second wasn't all that good, either: but the first was murder. Landing up in a forest of fourth and fifth formers, giants all, with recently broken voices filling the air with foghorns, was like being born again into a very cold landscape. We clustered like visiting peasants near the gate, waiting for the whistle to say that we were doomed – and then it went, and they had us.

Those great echoing halls with the sounds of feet and teachers shouting commands: a different classroom for each subject, a different face, a different personality to get used to. Art saved me; and then English. I didn't mind those islands in a roaring sea. It was maths that killed me, day after day.

His name was Prentice, but we had other names for him. He was large and red-faced, and had a moustache that looked as if a squirrel had gone to sleep under his nose. He had huge hands and he wore the same shiny blue suit all the time I knew him. His voice was amazing in its range: it could whisper and wheedle and sing, and finally bellow. His eyes were like searchlights: they swivelled in his head, and he missed nothing – lighting up every mistake you made. He would bear down on you, waving your exercise book, slashed with corrections. As he did that last period, that Tuesday.

He stood over me (that ever-present smell of old pipe tobacco) and rammed his finger at a total.

'What is that?' he said.

■ From Christopher Leach, *The Lies of Boyo Butler* ■

Another kind of bias is that found in some newspapers where news is reported in a way that reflects the political slant or prejudice of the proprietors. Things to look out for are:

o  the bias of the language used
o  the size and wording of headlines
o  the one-sided selection of detail that supports the point of view being put forward
o  the importance given to the item in terms of its position and column inches
o  the political slant of the particular newspaper.

2  Consider the effect of the following headlines and consider where any bias lies:
   **a** Minister Misled Commons!/Minister Lied!
   **b** Agitators Arrested/Protesters Arrested
   **c** Religious Fanatic Given the Boot/Spiritual Leader Deported
   **d** Squatters Evicted/Homeless Forced Out
   **e** Youths Protest/Youths Go on Rampage

3  Compare two national newspapers, one 'popular', the other 'serious', published on the same day. For each, work out the five main stories for the day, taking into account position, size of headlines, column inches. What conclusions would you draw from the relative importance each newspaper gives to particular stories?

4  Compare a news bulletin on BBC TV with one on ITV for the same day. Note the order in which

items are presented in each case and the amount of time devoted to them. Note also how each item is treated – the use of film, interview, points of view expressed. What differences between the two news bulletins can you detect? Is there any evidence of bias in one or the other?

5  Find synonyms (words of similar meaning) for the following and indicate the particular bias of the different versions:

young  brave  fat  intelligent

stupid  news  to question.

6  Compare these two newspaper accounts of the same event. What elements of bias can you find? Which appears to give the fairer account?

━━━━━━━━━━ **A** ━━━━━━━━━━

*12-year-old Anne refused grant*

Holden Education Committee today refused to award 12-year-old Anne Faulkner a £1,200 grant so that she could enrol at Woodward Ballet School to continue her ballet training. Anne's mother said that she could not afford to pay for Anne's tuition. 'Anne is so talented. She has been attending the Royal Ballet Junior School, and they spoke highly of her. The committee's decision has come as a great blow.'

Councillor John Walker, leader of the opposition party on the Education Committee, deplored the decision. 'It's purely political,' he said. 'If Anne had been black and working class, the grant would have been awarded like a shot.'

━━━━━━━━━━ **B** ━━━━━━━━━━

*Grant refused*

Holden Education Committee today refused to award 12-year-old Anne Faulkner a £1,200 grant. Anne had been studying at the Royal Ballet Junior School but failed to gain a place in their Senior School. It was said that her physical development would result in her becoming too tall to have a future in ballet. The grant had been requested so that Anne could continue her studies at Woodward Ballet School.

Councillor Fred Lister, Chairman of the Education Committee, denied charges that Anne had been refused because she was white and middle-class. 'The race and class of the girl had no bearing on the decision,' he said. 'The girl was turned down by the Royal Ballet School, and there were no exceptional circumstances to justify a grant to another school.'

━━━━━━━━━━━━━━━━━━━━━

7  Write two brief accounts of one of the following. In one account use neutral words, and in the other use words that are favourable or unfavourable.

a  A hotel
b  A seaside resort
c  A house for sale
d  A school

# 7.5 Giving a talk

When giving a talk, think about the following:

○  choose a subject that you know about and feel enthusiastic about
○  provide examples and anecdotes from personal experience where possible
○  try to speak naturally and allow your enthusiasm to come through
○  speak the talk, don't read a prepared script
○  plan what you are going to say – how you are going to introduce the subject, the different aspects you are going to cover and how to lead from one to the next, how you are going to end
○  make notes you can refer to while speaking
○  use your voice and body to reinforce what you are saying
○  use visual aids
○  be prepared for any questions or comments that may be made.

Visual aids can take the form of diagrams, prepared slides, posters, models, maps, etc. Make sure you have them prepared beforehand. There is nothing worse for an audience than to be kept waiting while a speaker fumbles about trying to get visual aids in order. Use your visual aids to reinforce what you are saying, to direct your audience's attention to particular points, to help clarify something which may need explanation, and generally to hold your audience's attention. Don't use visual aids that will distract attention. For instance, it is not a good idea to hand round pictures or photographs while you are still speaking. Instead, wait until the end, or hold them up for the class to see, if they are large enough.

●  Prepare a talk on a subject of your own choice and give it to the class. It could be about a hobby or special interest, about a pet, or about a subject on which you have done research.

━━━━━◄ *This could be used for oral assessment.* ►━━━━━

# 8.1 Reading – different presentations of the same material

As was shown in 'Reading – bias' (7.3) and 'Reporting events' (earlier in this unit), it is possible for the same incidents to be reported differently and for the same material to be presented in different ways. This may come about because the events are seen from different angles. Witnesses to a road accident, for instance, often differ in their accounts because they did not all view it from the same spot, or because different things caught their attention.

But sometimes the disparity between one presentation and another can be the result of deliberate policy. If certain facts are left out of one account, it may be because they suggest a view of the subject which the writer wishes to conceal from the reader. In other words, the writer is presenting a biased view.

When comparing different presentations of the same material, you have to consider the following:

○ What has been included and what left out?
○ How is the material being presented? What is the approach of the writer to the material and what kind of tone is used?
○ What evidence or points of view are quoted? Are they all on one side? Is one side given more space and more prominence than another?

If the reports are in newspapers, consider the relative lengths of the reports, the size and wording of the headlines, the position in the newspaper, the nature of any pictures used.

● On the next page are three accounts of the same event for you to consider.

1 What conclusions would you draw from the positioning of these reports, the space devoted to each, the headlines, the use of pictures, the naming or otherwise of the writer?
2 Compare the statistics given.
3 Compare the way the composition of the demonstrators is presented.
4 Comment on the way the reasons for the demonstration are presented in each case.
5 Comment on how the views of the demonstrators and the police are presented.
6 Is it possible that one account gives a fairer view than another? Justify your answer.

**A** appeared on page 9 of *The Sunday Times*.
**B** appeared on page 1 of *The Sunday Telegraph*.
**C** appeared on page 2 of *The Observer*.

═══ **B** ═══

═══ **A** ═══

## Police besieged by marchers

ABOUT 1,000 demonstrators laid siege to the police station at Forest Gate, East London, for three hours yesterday after trouble broke during a march against race attacks. Black and Asian youths hurled stones and a policeman was taken to hospital with an eye injury. More than 20 people were arrested, mainly for public order offences. The marchers were demonstrating against what they said was lack of police action against race attacks. They stopped at the police station "to make a point."

## 33 arrested in race demo clashes

*Sunday Telegraph Reporter*

A TOTAL of 33 people were arrested yesterday during a protest march by 1,500 demonstrators in the East End of London.

Trouble on the march, organised by the Newham Seven Defence Campaign, began as the protesters passed Forest Gate police station.

Strips of wood, at least one bottle and other missiles were thrown, fighting broke out between the police and marchers, mostly Asian youths, who were demonstrating about racial attacks and what they see as lack of protection by police.

The Newham Seven are men due to appear at the Old Bailey on May 13 to face various charges, including affray and conspiracy.

A police spokesman said 19 people were arrested after Forest Gate violence yesterday and taken to West Ham police station where they were charged with public order offences. Marchers demanded the release of those arrested.

More fighting broke out two hours later as the police tried to remove the remaining 200 demonstrators. About three more people including one woman, were arrested.

Police were anxious not to lay the blame on the organisers of the march and said those responsible were unconnected with the main protest.

═══ **C** ═══

## Police in race protest siege

By Arlen Harris

MORE THAN 1,000 anti-racist demonstrators clashed with police yesterday during a protest march against racial attacks in East London.

Police arrested more than 30 people when black and Asian youths stopped outside Forest Gate police station midway through a four-mile march. They threw bottles and sticks at police. One youth was spreadeagled across the bonnet of a car surrounded by demonstrators.

Leaders of the march said last night that the trouble started when police snatch squads jumped over a barrier outside the police station and started arresting people. 'Nothing would have happened if they had not intervened,' said organiser, Mr Unmesh Desai.

The leaders tried to organise a sit-down protest outside the police station demanding the release of those arrested. Police cleared the demonstrators after three hours.

Eight marchers were released. Four have been charged and four released pending charges. The arrested demonstrators were taken to West Ham police station several miles away from Forest Gate.

A police spokesman said last night: 'The trouble was caused by an unruly element in the march who attacked the police.' Mr Desai said: 'Self defence against racial attacks should not be criminalised. We intend to defend ourselves if and when necessary.'

The demonstration comes at a time when the black and Asian communities are becoming increasingly militant in their response to race attacks.

Indeed the disturbance might itself have been more serious had a counter demonstration planned by the National Front in the same area gone ahead. In the event, the National Front march was postponed at the last minute.

In Waltham Forest, Asian self defence groups are patrolling the streets following a series of arson attacks on Asian families in Newham, the community is looking at strategies for self defence. In Greenwich, the black community is forming groups to strike back at organised attackers.

Mr Amarjit Uppal of Greenwich Action Committee said: 'There is no commitment on the part of the police to defend the community. When it comes down to the nitty gritty of life on the street we have to defend ourselves.'

This view is disputed by the police. Superintendent Raymond Tanner of Scotland Yard argues: 'The problem of race attacks has been made a priority by the Commissioner this year. We are extremely concerned by the serious erosion in the quality of life for Asians in particular in London.

'Every race attack is reported centrally and we are trying to find trends to facilitate detection.'

Despite an elaborate police system of follow-up visits and five pilot schemes to target racial attacks in London, the problem continues.

In Greenwich last month a young West Indian out walking his dog was attacked by a group of white youths wielding knives. They slashed his face and cut off the tail of his dog. In the same month an Asian was attacked by four hooded men with an iron bar.

In Walthamstow, an Asian man and his brother found burning paper stuffed through their letter box.

● Look at these weather forecasts which appeared in the afternoon editions of three different London newspapers for the same day.

1 What differences are there between them?
2 Which do you consider the most useful and most effectively laid out?

## A

WIND
MAX TEMP C

NOON TOMORROW

ROUGH

Tonight will be mainly dry and clear, though an occasional shower is still possible. It will still be windy. Temperatures will fall to 8C (46F).

**Outlook:** Tomorrow there will be a mixture of sunny spells and showers. It will feel much warmer than today. Winds will return to normal. Maximum temperature 15C (59F).

## B

Unsettled, heavy rain.
Outlook: Unsettled.

● 1, 2, 4, 5, 7, 8, 9, 10, 11, 12, 15: Sunny spells, showers developing, possibly with thunder. Max 14C (57F).
● 3, 6, 16: Rain, clearing to sunny spells and showers. Max 11C (52F).
● 13, 14, 20, 21, 22, 25, 26, 29: Frequent showers, possibly with hail, thunder and snow over the hills. Max 9C (48F).
● 17, 18, 19: Outbreaks of rain. Max 10C (50F).
● 23, 24, 27, 28: Bright spells, frequent showers. Max 10C (50F).
**Sun sets** 6.07 p.m., **rises** 7.25 a.m. tomorrow. **Moon sets** 4.24 p.m., **rises** 1 a.m. tomorrow. **High water at London Bridge:** 9.39 a.m. and 10.04 p.m. tomorrow.

### TEMPERATURES AROUND BRITAIN

| Birmingham | 10 | 50 | Jersey | 10 | 50 |
|---|---|---|---|---|---|
| Bristol | 11 | 52 | London | 11 | 52 |
| Cardiff | 11 | 52 | Manchester | 11 | 52 |
| Edinburgh | 8 | 46 | Newcastle | 9 | 48 |

WEATHER
ORKNEY IS. 27
SHETLAND, IS. 28
CHANNEL IS.

### WORLD TEMPS

| | | C | F |
|---|---|---|---|
| ATHENS | sun | 25 | 77 |
| BANGKOK | cloud | 33 | 91 |
| BARBADOS | cloud | 25 | 77 |
| BARCELONA | fair | 21 | 70 |
| BERLIN | sun | 17 | 63 |
| CORFU | sun | 23 | 73 |
| DUBLIN | cloud | 9 | 48 |
| FARO | fair | 22 | 72 |
| HONG KONG | cloud | 28 | 82 |
| HONOLULU | cloud | 32 | 89 |
| LAS PALMAS | sun | 24 | 75 |
| LISBON | cloud | 22 | 72 |
| LOS ANGELES | cloud | 22 | 72 |
| MADRID | cloud | 17 | 63 |
| MAJORCA | fair | 22 | 72 |
| MALAGA | sun | 22 | 72 |
| MALTA | fair | 27 | 81 |
| MIAMI | cloud | 28 | 83 |
| MOSCOW | sun | 10 | 50 |
| NEW YORK | clear | 16 | 61 |
| NICE | cloud | 21 | 70 |
| PARIS | rain | 15 | 59 |
| ROME | fair | 24 | 75 |
| SYDNEY | clear | 21 | 70 |
| TEL AVIV | fair | 26 | 79 |
| TENERIFE | sun | 25 | 77 |
| TOKYO | rain | 21 | 70 |
| TUNIS | sun | 29 | 84 |

## C

# Weather

JUST HOLD ON TIGHT

**FORECAST FOR THIS AFTERNOON AND TONIGHT:**
This morning's ferocious storms are on their way out now, trees have stopped coming down and dustbins will soon stop rolling around. But brollies are a no-no today unless you fancy doing a Mary Poppins. We should even get some sunny bits this afternoon, and by tonight the weather will almost be back to normal. 13°C (55°F) today, 6°C (43°F) tonight.

**OUTLOOK:**
Quite nice on Saturday with some sun and just the odd shower; more wet windy weather on Sunday, but no destructive gales this time.

EVENING NEWS RATING

SUNSHINE ☼☼
RAINFALL
COLDNESS ❄❄❄

### YESTERDAY – AROUND THE WORLD

IN THE CITIES

| Cities: | | C | F |
|---|---|---|---|
| Amsterdam | cloudy | 13 | 55 |
| Belfast | rain | 6 | 43 |
| Berlin | bright | 17 | 63 |
| Copenhagen | rain | 13 | 55 |
| Jerusalem | sunny | 25 | 77 |
| Los Angeles | sunny | 19 | 66 |
| Madrid | o'cast | 17 | 63 |
| Montreal | sunny | 15 | 59 |
| New York | sunny | 14 | 57 |
| Paris | rain | 15 | 59 |
| Rome | fair | 24 | 75 |
| Stockholm | cloudy | 10 | 50 |
| Sydney | sunny | 21 | 70 |
| Vienna | hazy | 26 | 79 |

AT THE SEASIDE

| Beaches: | | C | F |
|---|---|---|---|
| Algarve | cloudy | 22 | 72 |
| Corfu | sunny | 23 | 73 |
| Costa del Sol | bright | 22 | 72 |
| Crete | bright | 24 | 75 |
| Fr. Riviera | rain | 18 | 64 |
| Greek Islands | hazy | 25 | 77 |
| Ibiza | hazy | 23 | 73 |
| Italian Lakes | rain | 12 | 54 |
| Lanzarote | sunny | 25 | 77 |
| Madeira | fair | 25 | 77 |
| Majorca | cloudy | 22 | 72 |
| Miami | cloudy | 27 | 81 |
| Seychelles | fair | 30 | 86 |
| Tenerife | sunny | 25 | 77 |

HOT TRAVEL TIP: Grab a late-booking for the Canaries

# 8.2 Writing – reporting events

We expect reports in newspapers to be factual and impartial, but this is not always the case. How events are reported depends to a large extent on *why* they are being reported and the intended *audience*.

● Compare these reports of the same event.

## A

### Boy, aged 8 passes O level

EIGHT-year-old John Adams (above), of Asfordby, Leicestershire, yesterday became the youngest-ever school pupil to pass O-level Maths. He gained a grade B and is one year younger than Ruth Lawrence was when she passed the paper before going on to win a First in Maths at Oxford University, aged 13.

John said: "I've started doing A-level papers now and I hope to pass when I'm about 10. I just enjoy working things out and doing sums." He started reading at the age of two.

*The Guardian*

1 What facts are contained in B that are not in A? Do they give important additional information?
2 What part do puns and jokes play in B? Does this have any relevance?
3 How does the language of A compare with that used in B?
4 Can it be said that the photograph adds to the story above?
5 Compare the headlines and the sub-headings. What difference is there, and how do they contribute to the reports?
6 Compare the space devoted to the news item in A and B. Which do you think is more appropriate, given the importance (or lack of importance) of the event?
7 Do you think these accounts are aimed at different audiences? Justify your view.

## B

### John, 8 passes maths GCE

By Martin Stote

IT was sum celebration for eight-year-old John Adams yesterday.

He tabled a record by becoming the youngest pupil in history to pass O-level maths.

But the brilliant youngster, who'd like to be a professor when he grows up, wants no bookish rewards for his grade B triumph.

"I'm buying him a new pair of football boots," revealed his maths teacher dad Ken, 46.

"He loves sport, especially soccer, and supports Manchester United."

#### Confided

John sat the exam at a specially provided small desk and chair at the Melton Mowbray College of Further Education in Leicestershire — amongst candidates twice his age.

After getting the result yesterday he confided: "Some of the questions were very, very hard and some were very, very easy. I left the really hard ones!"

His success has snatched the record from genius Ruth Lawrence, who passed maths O-level at nine.

Ruth went on to take an Oxford University double first in maths and physics by 15.

John, of Klondyke Way, Asfordby, Leics. is heading the same way.

"I've started doing A-level papers and hope to pass when I'm ten," he grinned.

Dad Ken said "If a youngster is gifted enough it's possible to do maths at a very young age because it's based on logic."

*The Sun*

## 8.2.1 Reporting events – coursework

1 The school council has held a special meeting to discuss complaints about school dinners. Write a report of the meeting for the school magazine.
2 A pupil at your school has been selected to represent the county or the borough at a particular sport. Write an account of this that might appear in a local newspaper. It could include interviews.
3 'Open Day'. Write an account of an Open Day at your school. Decide whether your account is for the school magazine or the local newspaper.
4 The children's section of a Sunday colour supplement is offering a prize for 'the reporter of the year'. Write an article for submission. It could be about old people or teenage views, or drugs, or life on a local housing estate. Include 'original research' and interviews.
5 Imagine a local disaster. It could be flooding, or a fire, or a multiple car crash, or the collapse of a building. Write a report that might appear in a local newspaper. Consider especially the headlines and sub-headings.

# 8.3 Reading – sexist and racist language

○ Look at these two newspaper reports.

## ═══ A ═══

# No sexism, please, we're Bradford

STAFF of Bradford Metropolitan District Council have been instructed not to use the terms "average housewife," "lady doctor," "headmaster" or "dinner lady."

The council's sex equality advisory group has drawn up a list of words and phrases to be avoided because, it says, language has lagged behind social change.

Top of the banned list are "the working man" and "the average housewife" because they suggest that most men are breadwinners and most women full-time housewives. The preferred term for "housewife" would be "consumer" it says.

References to "manpower," "mankind" and "man-made" should be stopped, say the guidelines. In their place should be "workforce," "humanity" and "synthetic."

A report from the group said almost half of Britain's workers were women and two out of five of them were breadwinners. The guidelines were intended to ensure that the language of council officers and councillors reflected the reality of today.

But the councillors themselves caused a problem. It was agreed that the term "Councillors and their wives" should be dropped from official invitations but "partners" was rejected as an alternative.

Finally they opted for "councillors and their guests" which implied neither that a councillor was male nor married or living with someone.

## ═══ B ═══

# Blackmail charge 'insult to black defendants'

A black barrister yesterday objected to the word blackmail being used at the Old Bailey.

Mr Beriston Bryan told Judge Alan Lipfriend that the word "connotes a derogatory stigma."

He said: "If I were to say whitemail I am sure a lot of people would be up in arms. I am not seeking to say whitemail but I certainly don't accept blackmail."

Mr Bryan, one of three black barristers representing black defendants in an alleged blackmail case, made his remarks during an application to have the charge changed to demanding money with menaces. The application was refused.

He said: "As a black person myself, defending black clients, I do not accept blackmail – it connotes a derogatory stigma to our people.

It causes a tremendous amount of offence to black people."

Judge Lipfriend replied: "I do not want a speech about this matter. Neither do I want the court to be used as a vehicle for promoting certain views."

As he left the court Mr Bryan said: "Words containing black in them, I suggest, denote bad or evil. It is blatant racial prejudice to have black men on trial and call it blackmail.

"Words like black market, black spot, and black list are offensive to the black population. It's disgusting. Why should black people have to put up with such insults in everyday speech?"

The word blackmail is a hundred years old, and is thought to come from the name of protection money or goods paid by border farmers to freebooters, "mail" meaning tribute and "black" from the dirty appearance of copper coins or "black money," rather than "white money," which was silver.

1 How do you think the reports are presented? Are they sympathetic or sceptical, supportive or mocking? Look at the headlines, the manner in which the reports are written, the examples given, the tone in the first report, the inclusion of the origin of the word 'blackmail' in the second.

2 What do you think of the issues presented here?

You may feel that the people being reported are making a fuss about nothing. But there is a lot of truth in the view that the words people use can indicate their attitudes and that words can embody and reinforce prejudice. In your reading, be on the lookout for expressions that reveal a sexist or racist attitude, whether this is accidental or intentional. Avoid this in your own writing.

● Consider the following points:

1 Often masculine pronouns are used even when many of the people referred to must be women, for example, 'every writer has his own point of view'. How can examples like this be avoided?

2 Do you think 'Ms' is a useful alternative to 'Miss' and 'Mrs'?

3 What attitudes are suggested by sayings like 'it's a man's world', 'it's a man's job', 'what you need is a man about the house', 'man was made to work and woman to weep'?

4 What attitudes are suggested by words like 'Frog', 'Kraut,' 'Nip'? Are there any circumstances where such words are acceptable?

5 What attitudes are suggested by expressions like 'a black look', 'a black day', 'a black mark'? Can you think of any others like them? Do you think expressions like these should be avoided?

Sexist and racist attitudes are not restricted to words or expressions. They can run through whole books. A modern novel, for instance, in which women appear only in the roles of housewife, mother or girlfriend could be regarded as sexist. A novel in which black characters are looked down on and treated as inferior with the author's endorsement could be regarded as racist. Librarians and teachers have become much more aware in recent years of the need to scrutinise books in libraries and classrooms to make sure they are free from sexist and racist bias.

● Here are some guidelines on the selection of non-racist books and texts. Examine each of them in turn and see if you think they are reasonable.

# CRITERIA FOR SELECTING ▬ CLASSROOM MATERIALS ▬

▶ Select books which aim at a world view. Avoid books which equate the white man with 'civilization', those with patriarchal or white philanthropical approaches to other peoples, or which reduce all non-western societies to the exotic, the primitive or the quaint. These views may be evident in both what is said and what is *not* said: omissions can be equally damaging.

The rest of the criteria follow from this reassessment of viewpoint and attitude. Children need:

▶ Books that are factually accurate and up to date – the maps and illustrations as well as text.
▶ Books which present peoples with a variety of attributes, whether of personal characteristics or life-styles; not those where whole cultural groups or individuals are portrayed as stereotypes.
▶ Books which use language with care: do Africans live in homes or in huts; are they ruled by kings or by chiefs; do they gabble away, speak a language, or merely a dialect; are whole peoples ever described as 'childlike' or 'savage'?
▶ Books that give students information about a variety of cultures and societies, showing their effectiveness and achievements, whether historic or present-day.
▶ Books that could equally well be used 'in an all-black classroom and an all-white classroom', and those which 'would not give pain to even one black child'.
▶ Books which show children of different cultures and races carrying out the activities illustrated, be it in mathematics, design and technology, the sciences, music or movement, etc.

# CRITERIA FOR SELECTING FICTION AND OTHER PRIVATE ▬ READING MATERIAL ▬

Aim for a book stock which offers to children and young people:

▶ A balanced view of the world, seen from many different perspectives.
▶ Books which relate experiences common to children of all ethnic groups and in which they can all share.
▶ Books among which children from the variety of ethnic groups represented in Britain today can find characters which will confirm their own sense of self and enhance their self-esteem; in which ethnic minority characters have important social roles; where adults are seen to be supportive in family relationships and to hold positions of responsibility, doctors as well as orderlies; where ethnic minority children are seen to make their own decisions.
▶ Books which communicate vividly and perceptively how it feels to be a member of another ethnic or cultural group.
▶ Books in which ethnic minority characters do not have to justify their blackness to the white characters (or readers) by being unbelievably good, or brave, or strong.
▶ Books in which illustrations of ethnic minority characters are accurate and avoid caricature by using sensitive artists or photographs of real individuals.
▶ Books which accurately reflect the population of Britain – so that those with an urban setting show not just a 'token black' (prevalent in publications of the 1970s), but represent cities and towns as truly multicultural.
▶ Books in which language does not evoke stereotypes (avoid books in which 'savages' 'jabber and shriek' or the 'brown boy's eyes roll'); in which dialect is used appropriately – to extend expression and contribute to children's respect for one another's speech.

From Gillian Klein,
▬ *Resources for Multicultural Education* ▬

1 Discuss how far Gillian Klein's guidelines could be used for selecting non-sexist books.
2 In what way could each of the following statements be considered sexist? Rewrite them in a non-sexist form.
   a After fifteen years in the business, she is still the top girl in British tennis.
   b The government will have to appeal to the man in the street if it is to get support for its proposals.
   c Agatha Christie is a master of the detective novel.
   d Men have always striven hard to conquer disease.
   e Some textbooks still exist which depict the life and customs of the African in ways damaging to his dignity.
   f In the course of her studies, the student nurse gains considerable experience of clinical work.
   g Mrs Joan Little is chairman of the governors.
   h Marlene Sheldon, 26, vivacious, blonde and curvaceous, is to marry MP Ian Curry.
   i A new book has just been published by one of the country's leading women novelists.

#  8.4 Oral communication – scripted drama

A play depends for its effectiveness on speech. There may be stretches of silence or mime or wordless action, but essentially a play works through the words spoken by its characters.

Plays are normally either scripted or improvised. In scripted drama, the words are written down and you can only use the words given by the writer in the script. In improvised drama, there is no script as such. The actors make the words up as they go along in response to the situation and to what other actors say, though there would normally be discussion and agreement about the course the play is going to take and the kind of things the actors are going to say. The skills needed for these two kinds of drama therefore differ. (For 'Improvised drama', see section 9.6.)

In scripted drama, the skill lies in interpreting the words provided by the writer and in conveying their significance to the listener and/or spectator. In a good piece of dramatic writing, the words will be appropriate to the characters who speak them and reveal aspects of their personalities and attitudes. What you have to do is to say the words in a way that makes these things clear.

When you are preparing scripted drama, you have to consider many of the things you would consider when reading aloud a piece of prose or a poem – things like tone, emphasis, breathing, phrasing, volume, variety, dramatic effect, pace, interpretation. (See section 2.6.)

But scripted drama involves more than a straightforward reading by a single voice. As with group discussion, there is an interplay between one person and another, there is give and take of dialogue, there is action and reaction of speech as one character responds to what another says. It is a cooperative activity, and listening to what other characters say is as important as speaking the words of your own character well.

Scripted drama is not just about words. Even a radio play can make effective use of silences and sound effects and music. You may decide to give your play as a reading for a number of voices with or without effects such as these. On the other hand, you could act it out, using some or all of the additional aids that staged drama can provide – gesture, movement, make-up, costume, lighting, setting, props.

But however you present your play or extract, you must remember that you are not being judged on how well you can act or how well you can produce. What matters in this context is verbal communication, the ability to convey meaning through the spoken word, in this case words provided by a dramatist.

• Look at the following extract. It is the opening of a play written by Alan Bleasdale for BBC Schools Radio.

## LOVE IS A MANY ━ SPLENDOURED THING ━

*Scene:* **A classroom** [*The song* – Love is a Many Splendoured Thing – *plays by way of introduction. As the music fades, the sounds of a classroom can be heard. A lesson is going on.* **Mickey** *speaks directly to the audience*]

MICKEY Do you like songs and poetry? Do you? You'd like our English lessons then. I'm not kidding, we've got this English teacher, Mr Pitt, who thinks that there's nothing else in life but poems. Honest. He's the kind of bloke who'd like to see 'Coronation Street' done in rhyming couplets. Whatever it is we're doing, he drags poetry into it. Take this morning's lesson. We began this project on 'young love', didn't we? Well, I needn't tell you he was in his element, wasn't he? And do y'know what the first thing was that he did? He made us sit next to a girl. A girl! Urgh! That's about as bad as having a whole week of needlework lessons. And do you know who he made me sit next to? Dawn Darnell. Now, some of the others in the class might fancy that, 'cos she's supposed to be good-looking, but I'll tell you this now f'free – one big rope hanging around your neck, that's all a girl is. Once you're holding hands and going for walks in the park, you might as well kiss the world good-bye, 'cos your happy days are over and gone.

[*Towards the end of* **Mickey's** *introduction,* **Mr Pitt's** *voice can be heard reading an extract from* Twelfth Night]

MICKEY Listen, he's at it now. Mr Pitt, 'Cess' for short, the Poet Laureate of St Patrick's Comprehensive. . . .

MR PITT 'What is love? 'tis not hereafter;
      Present mirth hath present laughter;
      What's to come is still unsure:
      In delay there lies no plenty;
      Then come kiss me, sweet and twenty,
      Youth's a stuff will not endure.'

[*The* **Class** *fidgets, coughs and desk-moving can be heard*]

MR PITT Right, now then, Four Alpha, can any of you tell me something about that?

MICKEY Yes sir, me sir.

MR PITT Go on then, Murray.

MICKEY It was another poem.

[*There are a few sniggers*]

MICKEY It was, it rhymed: 'plenty' and 'twenty'.

MR PITT [*Without malice*] And in your case, Murray, it could so easily be 'empty'.

MICKEY I am a bit hungry, sir.

MR PITT [*Sighs*] You're incorrigible, aren't you, Murray?

MICKEY No, sir, I'm a Catholic.

[*Laughter from the rest of the* **Class**]

MR PITT All right, all right. Anybody else? Yes, Dawn?

DAWN Sir, the poem's about young love, and the poet's saying that you should enjoy it while it's here, because we don't know what the future holds for us, and one thing's certain, we won't be young for ever.

MR PITT Very good, Dawn. . . .

MICKEY [*Whisper*] Know it all. Teacher's pet. [*Makes sucking noises*] Creep, creep. . . .

DAWN Oh, go away. . . .

MR PITT And this afternoon we have also studied what 'young love' means – not just to the young, but to different generations. . . .

[*The bell goes and the* **Class** *immediately begins to shuffle.* **Mr Pitt** *calls above the noise*]

MR PITT Er, just hang on a moment, now for the homework tonight. . . .

[*The* **Class** *half-heartedly moans and mumbles*]

MR PITT . . . for the homework tonight, I want you to keep in the groupings you're in now, one boy and one girl, and I want you to work as a couple, like two reporters. . . .

[**Mickey** *groans*]

DAWN [*To* **Mickey**] It's worse for me – I've got to work with you.

MICKEY Very funny. Anyway, I'm going to the match tonight. Liverpool're at home.

MR PITT Murray, may I remind you of what happens in this school if homework isn't done on time?

MICKEY Oh, sir, but. . . .

MR PITT No 'buts', Murray. Detention. And I'm equally sure you need no reminding that *tomorrow* night the fourth-year football team have a very important. . . .

MICKEY [*Muttering*] I get the picture. . . .

MR PITT Now, all of you, I want you to talk to the people you know, your parents, your brothers and sisters, and I want you to find out what 'young love' means to them. Not what it used to mean once, but what it means *now*. Tomorrow we'll all present our findings. Okay, off you go, next lesson. . . .

[*The* **Class** *departs*]

MICKEY Can't we find out on our own, sir?

MR PITT No, Murray. That's one of the purposes of the exercise. I'm fed up with this class split right down the middle, with the boys on one side and the girls on the other.

MICKEY But I live miles and miles away from Dawn Darnell, sir. By the time I got to her house, it'd be time for me to go home again.

MR PITT Do I look soft, Murray?

MICKEY [*Pause*] No, sir.

MR PITT So it won't surprise you to know that I took the precaution of checking your addresses before the lesson, Murray. You're sitting next to Dawn because she happens to be the girl who lives nearest to you.

MICKEY [*Lying*] We moved house yesterday, sir.

MR PITT Go on, get to your next lesson, and grow up.

*Scene:* **A street** [*In the background the noise of traffic and pedestrians can be heard as* **Dawn** *and* **Mickey** *talk*]

MICKEY Look, Dawn, tell you what, you write yours and I'll write mine, and tomorrow morning we'll compare. What do you say?

DAWN No.

MICKEY Great. What do you mean 'no'?

DAWN I think Mr Pitt's right. The lads in our class act like babies. It's about time you lot realized we're human beings as well. And it's about time you grew up.

MICKEY Oh no, not you and all. He said that.

DAWN Well, it's true. Girls grow up quicker than boys.

MICKEY Rubbish.

DAWN It's not.

MICKEY Prove it.

DAWN Well, for a start, most girls in our class prefer talking to lads who are older than them – and that's because the boys their age are still messing about with train sets and push bikes. Even you, Mickey, you might think you're smart because you're the captain of the football team and you're the cross-country champion. . . .

MICKEY For the county. . . .

DAWN But you're still a kid. No one in their right mind would fall in love with you.

MICKEY Great. Suits me fine. But I'm no kid, Dawn, an' don't you go calling me one, or else. . . .

DAWN Or else what? You'll sulk? Run home to mummy?

MICKEY Get lost! [*Pause*] Ah, come on, Dawn, be a sport, don't be sly.

DAWN See, you're acting like a baby now.

MICKEY Right, you asked for it. I'll go around with you, I'll stand there while you ask all these soppy questions, I'll miss the match, but don't expect me to change, don't expect me to turn around and be David Essex or Robert Redford. I'm me, I'm Mickey Brown, I'm nearly fifteen, I like football, fishing, basketball and running; and I don't like girls. An' what's more, you're not coming to our house.

DAWN Do you practise making speeches? Do you stand in front of the mirror and rehearse?

MICKEY Oh, come on, let's get it over with. Where're we going first?

DAWN My grandad's flat's just around the corner. . . .

From Alan Bleasdale,
████ *Love is a Many Splendoured Thing* ████

1 What impression do you get of the characters in this extract?

2 Pick out some examples of how what they say and the way you think they would say it indicate their views and attitudes.

3 Say whether or not you feel the speech given to each of the characters is appropriate and justify your view.

4 What kinds of conflicts are there in this extract between characters and attitudes?

5 Consider the pace at which this extract should be performed. Are there some sections that would be more effective taken slowly or at a moderate pace and others that should be faster? Justify your answer.

6 What indications are there in this extract about the way the play is going to develop?

7 In groups, prepare a reading of this extract, with one of you acting as producer.

8 Choose an extract (lasting about five minutes) from a play. In groups, prepare and perform it. It could be read or staged.

9 Write your own play. It could be based on a news item, or an incident in something you have read, or an improvisation. Discuss the play in groups, and make alterations to the script that seem valid. Prepare and perform the play. It could be read or staged.

◄     *This could be used for oral assessment.*     ►

You may find a suitable extract from a play in one of the following books:

Bradley, Alfred (ed.), *Soundscene*. Blackie.

———, *Worth a Hearing*. Blackie.

———and Leake, Alison (eds), *Family Circles*. Longman.

Bennitt, Caroline (ed.), *Humour and Horror*. Longman.

Durband, Alan (ed.), *Playbill One*. Hutchinson.

———, *Playbill Two*. Hutchinson.

———, *Playbill Three*. Hutchinson.

Jones, Rhodri (ed.), *Living Together*. Heinemann Educational Books.

Marland, Michael (ed.), *Conflicting Generations*. Longman.

———, *Out of the Air*. Longman.

———, *The Pressures of Life*. Longman.

———, *Scene Scripts–1*. Longman.

Self, David and Speakman, Brian (eds), *Act One*. Hutchinson.

———, *Act Two*. Hutchinson.

———, *Act Three*. Hutchinson.

(See also the plays listed in 11.2.1.)

# Unit Nine

## 9.1 Writing – giving directions, explanations and instructions

Giving directions, explanations and instructions is a form of informative writing. The aim is to give facts or information as clearly as possible. It may be directions to a visiting speaker on how to get to your school, or an explanation of how an internal combustion engine works, or instructions on how to make a walnut cake. You need to think about the following:

o  state the facts clearly and logically

o  use language and sentence structure that is simple and appropriate
o  use non-technical language as far as possible
o  present facts in an orderly way so that the sequence of steps is clear
o  don't introduce irrelevant ideas
o  use visual material (diagrams, maps, tables) where appropriate
o  use the layout where possible to make the points clear, for example, use sub-headings, isolate points on separate lines, underline key words (or use bold type or italics), number the points.

•  Here is an extract from a leaflet about child benefit prepared by the Department of Health and Social Security. How successful do you think it is in getting the information across? Look at the language, the sentence structure and the layout.

Child Benefit is a tax-free benefit which is generally payable for all children, whatever your income. It is not means-tested. It is normally paid every 4 weeks in arrears. To find out the current rates of child benefit, get *Leaflet NI.196* from your local social security office.

---

### Could I get child benefit?

**You can** if you are responsible for a child who is:
► under age 16; *or*
► aged 16, 17 or 18, but still studying full time at school or college up to and including A-level or Ordinary National Diploma standard.

There is more about benefit for children over 16 in *leaflet CH.7* which you can get from your local social security office.

**You can't** get the benefit for a child who is:
► on an advanced course of education higher than A-level; *or*
► over age 16, has left school, and is in full-time gainful employment; *or*
► on a training course sponsored by an employer or the Manpower Services Commission; *or*
► getting non-contributory invalidity pension or severe disablement allowance; *or*
► getting supplementary benefit.

**You can't** get the benefit if:
► you (or your husband or wife, unless you are separated) have any earnings which are exempt from UK income tax because, for instance, you work for an overseas government or an international organisation in this country, or belong to foreign or Comonwealth armed forces. (If you have come from New Zealand, special arrangements may apply. Ask at your local social security office.)

If your tax-exempt earnings are low and you feel that child benefit would be of more value to you, you may be able to forgo the tax-exempt income. You should discuss this with your employer.

If you are not paying UK income tax and you are not sure whether this is because you are exempt or simply because your earnings after tax allowances are below the taxable level, ask at your local social security office.

**Also**, you may not be able to get child benefit if:
► your child is in the care of a local authority; *or*
► you are a foster parent to a child who is boarded out by a local authority or voluntary organisation (more about this in *leaflet CH.4A* from your local social security office); *or*
► you (or your husband or wife) or your child have not lived in Great Britain for more than 26 weeks in the past 52 weeks. But you may qualify under special rules which apply to people who are employed or self-employed, or who have come from Northern Ireland or certain other countries including EC countries (*see paragraph 9*).

---

### 9.1.1 Giving directions, explanations and instructions – coursework

Here are some assignments for you to choose from:

1 Your pen-pal who lives in a town two hundred miles away is planning to visit you. Write a letter giving directions on how to get to your home town and your house.

2 Write a dialogue in which you give a stranger directions on how to get from your school to the town hall or the local library or a local sports centre.

3 Your school is holding an open day with exhibitions and displays in subject rooms, labs, home economics rooms, etc. Write directions for the best route for parents to follow with brief descriptions of what is on show at each venue.

4 Write a recipe for a particular dish suitable for a cookery book entitled *The International Cook-Book*.

5 Write an account of how to use the subject catalogue in your school library, to be published in a handbook for new first-year pupils.

6 Imagine you are the secretary of a newly-formed sports or cultural activities club. Write out the aims and rules of this club.

7 Write an account of how to play a particular game or sport that would be suitable as an entry in a children's encyclopedia of games and sports.

# 9.2 Coursework – your own choice

Many of the assignments in this book specify what you should write about. Even when you are given a number of choices to select from, the range is still restricted. Here is an opportunity for you to choose your own subject and your own approach.

You may know straightaway what you want to write about. It may be some idea you have had at the back of your mind for ages but the right moment for writing about it has not presented itself. On the other hand, when given a free choice, your mind may become a complete blank. If so, think of some of the different kinds of writing you could do and see if that suggests an idea to you. Consider the following: narrative, a point of view, a letter, a response to something you have read or seen on television, a play, a description, an account of an event.

# 9.3 Writing – dialogue

Dialogue can give variety and interest to your writing, whether this is a story or an argument. But when you use dialogue, you must be conscious of why you are using it and what effect you hope to achieve by it. Simply having your characters say 'good morning' and talk about the weather just wastes words and holds up the movement of the story or argument.

Good dialogue is functional, that is, it fulfils a purpose. Dialogue can:

○ tell the reader about the character who is speaking
○ convey feelings and attitudes
○ give information and help move the story forward
○ bring out more effectively and dramatically a conflict or difference of opinion between characters.

● Examine the following extract and indicate to what extent the dialogue fulfils these requirements. The extract is the opening of Colin MacInnes' novel *City of Spades*, first published in 1957.

'It's all yours, Pew, from now,' he said, adding softly, 'thank God,' and waving round the office a mildly revolted hand.

'Yes, but what do I *do* with it all, dear boy?' I asked him. 'Why am I here?'

'Ah, as to that...' He heaved an indifferent sigh. 'You'll have to find out for yourself as you go along.'

He picked up his furled umbrella, but I clung to him just a bit longer.

'Couldn't you explain, please, my duties to me in more detail? After all, I'm new, I'm taking over from you, and I'd be very glad to know exactly *what*...'

Trim, chill, compact, he eyed me with aloof imperial calm. Clearly he was of the stuff of which proconsuls can even now be made.

'Oh, very well,' he said, grounding his umbrella. 'Not, I'm afraid, that anything I can tell you is likely to be of the slightest use....'

I thanked him and we sat. His eye a bored inquisitor's, he said: 'You know, at any rate, what you're *supposed* to be?'

Simply, I answered: 'I am the newly appointed Assistant Welfare Officer of the Colonial Department.'

He closed his eyes. 'I don't know – forgive me – how you got the job. But may I enquire if you know anything about our colonial peoples?'

'I once spent a most agreeable holiday in Malta....'

'Quite so. A heroic spot. But I mean Negroes. Do you happen to know anything about them?'

'Nothing.'

'Nothing whatever?'

'No.'

He emitted a thin smile. 'In that case, may I say I think you're going to have quite a lot of fun?'

'I sincerely hope so.... I have certain vague impressions about Negroes, of course. I rather admire their sleek, loose-limbed appearance....'

'Yes, yes. So very engaging.'

'And their elegant flamboyant style of dress is not without its charm....'

'Ah, that far, personally, I cannot follow you.'

'On the other hand, for their dismal spirituals and their idiotic calypso, I have the most marked distaste.'

'I'm with you there, Pew, I'm glad to say. The European passion for these sad and silly songs has always baffled me. Though their jazz, in so far as it is theirs, is perhaps another matter.'

He had risen once again. I saw he had made up his mind I was beyond hope.

'And what do I do with our coloured cousins?' I asked him, rising too.

'Yours is a wide assignment, limitless almost as the sea. You must be their unpaid lawyer, estate agent, wet-nurse and, in a word, their bloody guardian angel.'

The note of disdain, even though coming from a professional civil servant to an amateur, had become increasingly displeasing to me. I said with dignity: 'Nothing, I suppose, could be more delightful and meritorious.'

▬▬▬ From Colin MacInnes, *City of Spades* ▬▬▬

### 9.3.1 Dialogue – coursework

1 Write a dialogue that might take place at a bus-stop, on a park bench, on a train, on a bus, or in a queue.
2 Write a story in which dialogue is important. Some titles that could suggest ideas are: 'Caught in the Act', 'The Birthday Present', 'Good Neighbours'.
3 Write a playscript involving two or three characters. It could be about a family disagreement or a quarrel between friends or a surprise encounter.

# 9.4 Reading – evaluating information from a range of material

You may be presented with a range of material – a poem, a newspaper article, an extract from an autobiography, a set of statistics – relating in some way to the same subject. You may be asked to concentrate on one aspect of the subject and reach some conclusions about it, or to use the information in writing of another form.

The approach is similar to that in 'Reformulating for a purpose' (see 7.2) though clearly it is more complicated. As in that exercise though, two things are important – reading carefully, and keeping at the forefront of your mind the purpose for which you are reading.

Not all the pieces you read will necessarily be of equal relevance. Some may well contain more information which bears on the subject than others. You have to read all of them carefully and select the relevant points. Some pieces may require more 'interpretation' than others. Expressive writing (a poem or an extract from a novel, for instance) may not state facts or information in a direct way, so you may have to work out its relevance to the subject.

Read the material carefully. Write down in note form the relevant points. Check that nothing has been missed. Write the information up in the way requested, paying particular attention to language, tone and audience.

● Look at the following material, all of which deals with bullying or being bullied. Using only information or suggestions contained in this material, write an account of bullying which covers these two points: why bullies behave the way they do, and what methods can be used to combat bullying.

# A

So what should you do if you suspect your child of bullying?

**"First step** is to keep cool, says Sheila Miller. "Find out exactly what's happening." Asking around at school will help —approach the school and teachers as well as dinner ladies or other outsiders.

**Second step,** if it's not too serious, is to give things a while to sort themselves out. There are times when children are more prone to being aggressive—if they're under pressure with school work, for instance, or there's a new baby at home or problems between parents.

**Third step** if there is no obvious reason for your child's behaviour, is to spend time trying to get him or her to talk about it. If you can find out why it's happening you can help your child cope with the feelings.

**Lastly,** if you can't sort it out at home don't be afraid to seek help. You don't have to be referred by anyone to seek child guidance. The number is listed under your local education authority in the telephone directory, although as a result of cuts, there is often a waiting list for appointments.

According to Sheila Miller, many parents are too upset to seek help. "We are finding that teenagers sometimes come on their own. But in many areas, unless the parents do come, children under 16 may only be able to be seen alone once.

"Of course, it is hard to see anything relating to your child in a cool, detached way," she says, "especially if it's something so unpleasant. But if you are to be of any help, you have got to try."

# B
# Keeping an eye on bullies

AFTER READING your article on school bullies (Look! last week) I asked my eight-year-old son what he would do if he saw anyone being bullied at school. He hesitated a moment and then said, "Well, I wouldn't tell on them." "Why not?" "Because I'd be a tell-tale-tit."

Surely the habit of parents and teachers of more or less dismissing any unpleasant information given by a child with the reply, "Now run along and don't tell tales," is one of the chief reasons why bullying does reach such terrible proportions.

VIOLENCE: I was surprised that no mention was made in the article of the effect of TV violence. Day in and day out, goodies and baddies get their own way by violent means. Add to this the news reports in which we are spared no detail of killing and maiming. A society that condones brutality and admires toughness can hardly be surprised if its children emulate it.

NASTIES: After 27 years of teaching in primary schools, I feel that teachers are not always sufficiently watchful. They need to follow the children – yes – right into the lavatories: it is here that a lot of bullying starts. Here they will solve the smelly mystery of the culprits who urinate over each other (I never cease to feel wry amusement at the shocked mothers who have "never heard of such a thing"). Training colleges will probably not have told students about this kind of thing.

The odd glance under the table while supervising lunch often reveals the habitual shin-kicker, and a strategic vantage-point a few yards from the school gate will often catch the coat-snatcher, apple-thief or new-shoe-trampler. This is how bullying starts, and children have a right to be protected. Watch, follow, let these nasties see that they are observed.

THE STICK: As a teacher, I agree that physical assaults are increasing and that many teachers adopt a supine attitude. Most bullies are cowards and what they don't want is a humiliating thrashing. The stick must be made to hurt; it should whine as it comes through the air and raise welts, if not actually breaking skin. Modern humane thinking is against this approach. Punish a youth as I have described, and parents would be demanding – and getting – inquiries and apologies.

## C

### THE BULLY ASLEEP

One afternoon, when grassy
Scents through the classroom crept,
Bill Craddock laid his head
Down on his desk, and slept.

The children came round him:
Jimmy, Roger, and Jane;
They lifted his head timidly
And let it sink again.

'Look, he's gone sound asleep, Miss,'
Said Jimmy Adair;
'He stays up all the night, you see;
His mother doesn't care.'

'Stand away from him, children.'
Miss Andrews stooped to see.
'Yes, he's asleep; go on
With your writing, and let him be.'

'Now's a good chance!' whispered Jimmy;
And he snatched Bill's pen and hid it.
'Kick him under the desk, hard;
He won't know who did it.'

'Fill all his pockets with rubbish –
Paper, apple-cores, chalk.'
So they plotted, while Jane
Sat wide-eyed at their talk.

Not caring, not hearing,
Bill Craddock he slept on;
Lips parted, eyes closed –
Their cruelty gone.

'Stick him with pins!' muttered Roger
'Ink down his neck!' said Jim.
But Jane, tearful and foolish,
Wanted to comfort him.

John Walsh

## D

On 'Empire Day' we all had to salute the flag as we filed out after prayers, and it was accepted among the children, with no particular sense of outrage, that 'playtime' on that particular day should be a field-day for the bullies. A spirit of militant patriotism was in the air, and it was a kind of duty for the ruling caste of the school, to put everyone through hell. David White, the Führer, had an elder sister, Fanny, who by virtue of her size and strength was the supreme head of the school's physical aristocracy; she didn't, as a rule, go in for bullying – girls have other diversions – but on Empire Day she dropped everything else and put all her energies into terrorizing the lesser breeds. Her brother and his two henchmen, Dick Bones and Martin Barker, became, for this one morning, her minions; their job was to provide her with victims. As soon as one stepped out into the playground, one knew it was coming. This was one day when only the very fortunate would escape. The routine accusation was 'You didn't salute the flag!' No defence was allowed; as the words were spoken your arms were already being pinioned, and you were forthwith 'taken to Fanny White'. The interesting feature of this, for me, is that it opened yet another window on the adult world. When, in later years, I read accounts of, say, the 'Moscow trials', I understood perfectly what the mental atmosphere must have been like. It was that of Empire Day at this school. When David White and his gang accused you of not saluting the flag, they were using a purely ritual form of words; you had, of course, saluted the flag, just like everyone else, or you would have had the headmistress to reckon with, long before this. What the accusation meant was, 'You're for it. For motives of our own, we've decided to pick on you.' One never wasted one's breath in any protest that one *had* saluted the flag. This, of course, is one of the distinguishing marks of totalitarian rule everywhere.

I was learning faster out of school than in it. And the thing I was learning was what it always had been: that life was a perpetual effort to survive, to get by, to evade the vigilance of a bloodthirsty power in whose hand lay all the strength there ever had been or ever could be. One lived in a world dominated by an unshakeable tyranny, and all one's relationships were conditioned by the fact. Exactly as in German-occupied Europe, the subject peoples were a prey to divided loyalties, suspicions, fears, and envies. When someone else was 'getting it', one's attitude towards his sufferings was mixed. The chief feeling was relief, since it meant that the attention of the thugs was, for that length of time, distracted from oneself. But underneath, there was a nasty mess of contradictions. One pitied the victim; if he put up any kind of resistance, one felt a wild, half-formed, immediately stifled impulse to go and help him (the stifling of such impulses was a very easy matter); and mixed up in the general paste of feelings were little hard lumps of evil, for there is a part of one's nature that identifies, in such a situation, with the hunters against the hunted. On a tiny scale, we victims knew all the emotions that must have ravaged the inhabitants of occupied Europe a decade later.

An example: one of my schoolfellows was a boy called Michael, who lived very near me at home; we used to make the journey together. This brought us into a very close relationship though in fact we did not like each other much. Exactly as at a boarding school, a kind of blood-relationship, however unwelcome, existed between those who knew each other 'at home'. Well, one day the triumvirate were giving me the treatment. To get away from possible interference, they had taken me to a point where the lawn in front of the schoolhouse petered out in an elongated corner, shielded on one side by a steep rockery, on the other by a thick hedge. They had begun proceedings by tying my arms to my sides with a piece of string; this was more for effect than anything else, since they had nothing much to fear from my fists, even if I had had the guts to use them. But the fact that my arms were tied made it more necessary than ever to keep me from breaking away and running to where I might be seen by anyone in authority. So they sealed off the area with a human barrier, made up of some half-dozen children standing with spread arms and clasped hands. During a lull in the beating, I suddenly noticed that one of these children was Michael. I felt sickened. He had gone back on the sacred tie that bound us. At the same time I pitied him – the fear that drove him to submit to this without protest must have been great. *But it was no greater than my fear.* So much was clear, even in that instant. I knew that if it had been the other way round, I should have had only one thought – to get out of the way and stay unnoticed. But suppose I had been noticed, and dragged along to help prevent Michael's escape, should I have stood there mutely, like him? Neither at the time, nor afterwards, could I settle that question, or lay it to rest.

■■■ From John Wain, *Sprightly Running* ■■■

# 9.5 Reading – figurative language

Language can be used literally or figuratively. Another name for figurative language is metaphorical language. When we use words literally, we mean exactly what we say; the words are used in their actual literal sense. For example:

The boy caught the fish in his net:

The boy actually did have an object called a net and actually caught a fish in it.

When we use words figuratively or metaphorically, we do not use them with their basic literal meanings but as illustrations of what we want to say. They form pictures in our minds which help to make the idea clearer and more vivid. For example:

The fugitive knew that the net was closing in.

This can't really be taken literally. There was no actual physical net closing in on the fugitive. What is meant is that the fugitive's pursuers were getting closer, and he was surrounded and likely to be captured – just like a fish about to be scooped into a net. The writer could simply have said, 'The fugitive knew the pursuers were closing in' or 'The fugitive knew that capture was close', but the use of the image of the net creates a picture in the reader's mind. It calls forth other associations where a net might be used, and the reader connects these with the fugitive and his predicament. The fugitive's plight is made more vivid.

The two most common devices in figurative language are the simile and the metaphor. In a simile, we say that one thing is like another. For example:

The lawn was like a smooth green carpet.

In a metaphor, we say that one thing is another which it can't literally be, or is doing something which it can't literally do. For example:

The look he gave her would have fused the lights on a Christmas tree.

(For more information about these and other figures of speech, see Appendix F.)

We constantly use figurative language in everyday speech without noticing it. For example:

Why don't you shut your trap?
Let's get to the heart of the matter.
You're like a fish out of water.

● Can you recognise figurative language when it is being used? Look at the following sentences and say which are literal and which are figurative.

1   The church steeple was pointing to heaven.
2   It's difficult for some families to find the money when children grow out of their clothes so quickly.
3   Janet is like Tim: they both enjoy living in the country.
4   How can you say you like spinach when every time I serve it up you leave half of it on your plate?
5   The news that he had lost came like a body-blow.
6   The headteacher complained that her hands were tied, and there was nothing she could do to help.
7   The hostage complained that his hands were tied, but the kidnappers just ignored him.
8   The attack was so unexpected that she was lost for words.
9   Our team gave our opponents a good pounding in the chess tournament.
10  His head felt as though it was going to split in two.

Figurative language can be used to make a situation or a feeling more vivid. It can direct the reader to a more precise understanding of what the situation or feeling was like. It can also startle, surprise or shock the reader into seeing something familiar in a new and unexpected light.

In order to explain how effective an example of figurative language is, you have to decide why the writer is using it and what sort of effect is intended. Explore the image, analyse the comparison being made, consider whether the comparison is appropriate, explain how the image or comparison sheds light on the object described. For example:

The sky curved vast overhead as glorious as any cathedral vault.

The comparison is between the vast expanse of sky overhead and the arched roof of a cathedral. The comparison is appropriate because both sky and vault can be seen as different kinds of roof that have something in common. By comparing the sky curving over his or her head to a cathedral vault, the writer is trying to convey a sense of awe and majesty. The sky inspires the same kind of wonder and spiritual joy that one might get from gazing up at the grandeur and spaciousness of a cathedral vault. The image helps the reader to get closer to the writer's emotions as he or she looks at the sky.

● Look at the following examples of figurative language and comment on their effectiveness.

1   There is a tide in the affairs of men,
    Which, taken at the flood, leads on to fortune.
    (William Shakespeare, *Julius Caesar*)
2   Other women along the chain of resistance fighters who passed Sgt Miller along to safety remembered this disconcerting sadness, as if he carried his own little cloud like a black balloon on a string. (Nancy Banks-Smith, *The Guardian*)
3   A musty, dusty, leathery smell of boys, books and ink. Words drone and a family of flies stagger through the heavy air as if in pursuit of them. But they turn out to be Ancient History so the flies blunder moodily against the parlour window beyond which the June sun ripens tempting dinners at roadsides and down by the strong smelling beach; day after day after day. (Leon Garfield, *The Strange Affair of Adelaide Harris*)
4   Along the black
    leather strap
    of the night
    deserted road.                    (Herbert Read)
5   Walls have ears. (World War II slogan)
6   Childhood, it strikes me, is a little like being drunk. There is the same difficulty of knowing who people are, the same indistinct grasp of the geography of things. (Edward Blishen, *Sorry, Dad*)
7   My love is like a red red rose
    That's newly sprung in June.        (Robert Burns)
8   All car parts can be replaced with plastic. Apply for a Barclaycard now. (advertisement)
9   The beauty of the night made him want to shout. A half-moon, dusky gold, was sinking behind the black sycamore at the end of the garden, making the sky dull purple with its glow. Nearer, a dim white fence of lilies went across the garden, and the air all round seemed to stir with scent, as if it were alive. He went across the bed of pinks, whose keen perfume came sharply across the rocking, heavy scent of the lilies, and stood alongside the white barrier of flowers. They flagged all loose, as if they were panting. The scent made him drunk. He went down to the field to watch the moon sink under.

A corncrake in the hay-close called insistently. The moon slid quite quickly downwards, growing more flushed. Behind him the great flowers leaned as if they were calling. And then, like a shock, he caught another perfume, something raw and coarse. Hunting round, he found the purple iris, touched their fleshy throats, and their dark grasping hands. At any rate, he had found something. They stood stiff in the darkness. Their scent was brutal. The moon was melting down upon the crest of the hill. It was gone; all was dark. The corncrake called still.

(D. H. Lawrence, *Sons and Lovers*)

# ━━━━ YOU'RE ━━━━

10   Clown, happiest on your hands,
     Feet to the stars, and moon-skulled,
     Gilled like a fish. A common-sense
     Thumbs-down on the dodo's mode.
     Wrapped up in yourself like a spool,
     Trawling your dark as owls do.
     Mute as a turnip from the Fourth
     Of July to All Fools' Day,
     O high-riser, my little loaf.

     Vague as fog and looked for like mail.
     Farther off than Australia.
     Bent-backed Atlas, our travelled prawn.
     Snug as a bud and at home
     Like a sprat in a pickle jug.
     A creel of eels, all ripples.
     Jumpy as a Mexican bean.
     Right, like a well-done sum.
     A clean slate, with your own face on.

━━━ Sylvia Plath ━━━

# 9.6 Oral communication – improvised drama

In improvised drama, there is no written script. The actors develop the theme and find appropriate words for themselves as they go along, basing this on prior discussion. The group decide on how to portray a given theme, the setting, who the characters are and their attitudes, how to begin and end, what is to happen in each scene, and so on. Then the actors try out the improvisation and rehearse it, modifying and adding, altering and shaping.

Consider these points when working out your improvisation:

o  see if you can use conflict and/or contrast as a basis
o  avoid making your characters stereotypes and your situations hackneyed
o  keep it simple – avoid too many characters and too many different scenes
o  keep to the point – don't submerge the plot beneath a lot of irrelevant talk
o  choose situations you know about and use information and details you are familiar with.

Improvised drama is a cooperative activity. Each individual has a contribution to make. You have to:

o  assume a role and use your imagination to get inside the skin of your character
o  use speech that is appropriate in tone and language to your character
o  use speech that is dramatic (that is, indicating reactions and feelings and moving the action on)
o  respond to other characters convincingly
o  react quickly to what is going on and what is said
o  concentrate and know what you are doing, yet at the same time appear natural and spontaneous.

In oral assessment, the aim of improvised drama is not to see how well you can act but how well you can communicate orally. What counts is the effectiveness of the words you use and the way they are conveyed. Through speech, you have to show that you understand the role you are playing and can develop it convincingly and expressively.

●  Here are some suggestions for improvisations. Or you may choose your own. Your improvisation should be about five or six minutes long.

1  Your friend has been given a pet as a present. You would like one as well, but first of all you have to convince your mum and dad.
2  Injustice.
3  'The Examination Result'
Scene 1: At home on the evening after the exam – you and your family
Scene 2: The letter giving the result arrives
Scene 3: What you decide to do as a result of the letter.
4  You pluck up courage to ask a boy/girl for a date. The boy/girl agrees. You wait at the appointed place but the boy/girl doesn't turn up. Instead, another friend comes along and tells you the boy/girl had only accepted as a joke and had no intention of going out with you. Next day, you have it out with the boy/girl.
5  A group of people become trapped in a lift.
6  Would Gran be better off in a Home? The point has come (perhaps because of the death of Grandad) for the family to decide what would be best. But can they agree on a course of action? Will Gran accept it?

7  'I'm new here'. You could be new to an area, a school, a job. How do you feel? How do others react?
8  In the year AD 2084.

---

◄  *This could be used for oral assessment.*  ►

---

 # 9.7 Sustaining a discussion

When you are in groups, how do you keep a discussion going? You can say what your views are on the subject. You can counter the arguments made by someone else. But here are some other suggestions.

o  Ask questions. For example:

I don't understand what you mean. Could you explain please? What you say doesn't seem to make sense to me.

In this way, you can get someone to explain a point in other words or in some other way. You give the other person a chance to rephrase the argument.

o  Point to irrelevance. For example:

I don't see what the fact that your brother is a policeman has to do with nuclear disarmament.

In group discussion, people often bring up information which has nothing to do with the subject in hand. If they do this, point it out and keep the discussion on the right track.

o  Clarify the argument. For example:

First you say there's too much violence on television, and then you say you enjoy programmes like *Hill Street Blues* which is full of violence. You can't have it both ways. I think what you mean is that violence can be justified if it is a legitimate part of a quality programme.

Watch out for people contradicting themselves or getting into a confused state. If this happens, point it out and try to straighten out the argument.

o  Challenge bias, unsupported evidence, hearsay evidence, etc. For example:

A  I don't want to be a pen-pusher for the rest of my life.
B  Why d'you call them 'pen-pushers'? What's wrong with being a clerk? It's a perfectly decent job.

A All foreigners are stupid.

B How can you say that? Where's your evidence? How many foreigners do you know?

A That record's useless. Lofty said he wouldn't have it as a free gift.

B That doesn't prove a thing. Just because Lofty says he doesn't like it. He probably hasn't even heard it.

Different kinds of bias are discussed in section 7.3. If examples of these arise in discussion, point them out and make the person who uses them accept that they are defective or provide more acceptable evidence.

o Sum up an argument or a case so that you can move the discussion forward. For example:

What you are saying so far is that you disapprove of school uniform because it's a restriction of personal liberty and it causes rows between children and parents and pupils and teachers. But what about the uniform itself? I hate school uniform because it's so ugly and old-fashioned. I'm ashamed to be seen in it.

Use the ideas put forward by other speakers to bring in ideas of your own and take the discussion a step further.

o Explore the implications of an argument. For example:

You say you believe there should be no restrictions on free speech. I wonder if you really understand what you're saying. That means that people would be free to incite racial hatred and say any filth they like. Is that what you want?

People don't always think through fully what they say, so examine every statement made carefully. There may be implications in what is said that the speaker isn't aware of which can be used against the point of view being expressed.

o Compare points of view and weigh them against each other. For example:

Barry's been describing all the marvellous technological advances that space exploration is supposed to bring about. But I'm not convinced. Julie's pointed out the millions of dollars it's all costing. I think I agree with Julie. I think there are better uses for the money.

Use other people's ideas. Show that you have understood them by restating them in your own words. Use these ideas to argue where you yourself stand.

o Give a balanced summary of the views expressed. For example:

I think there are good arguments on both sides. Having advertisements on BBC TV would bring in extra money. As Danny said, the TV licence wouldn't have to keep going up. And that's important when you consider how many old people rely on television for company. But as Claire pointed out, it would mean the programmes would keep being interrupted, and there is some doubt as to whether there would be enough advertising to go round. That way, ITV could find itself running short of money. It's a difficult question.

By doing this, you show that you can hold in your mind the various views that have been expressed in the course of the discussion. You can gather them together and present them in a balanced way. A summary such as this could lead to further discussion or to some kind of conclusion.

1 In groups, discuss a subject like football hooliganism, or the commercialisation of Christmas, or sex education in schools.

2 If possible, record your discussion. Play it back and assess to what extent members of your group sustain the discussion effectively by using the methods described here.

◀ *This could be used for oral assessment.* ▶

# Test Paper 3

Time allowed: one and a half hours.

Answer BOTH questions.

You are advised to spend some time planning your answer in each case.

**1** Write on ONE of the following topics. You are advised to spend about an hour on this question.

(40 marks)

The quality of your writing is more important than its length, but as a general guide your work should cover 2 or 3 sides of the pages in your answer book.

**a** My brother or my sister.

**b** The joys or the miseries of cross-country running.

**c** The jumble sale

**d** Describe a crowded public square. As you watch, a thunderstorm breaks, and everyone hurries for shelter. Describe the events as they happen, ending by describing the deserted square.

**e** 'I never felt so relieved in all my life!' Write about a personal experience – perhaps losing something valuable and then finding it again, or thinking you were in trouble and discovering that you weren't – which ended with you feeling very relieved.

**f** Write imaginatively in response to ONE of the pictures A or B.

**g** A bit of bad luck.

**A**

**B**

**2** Read the following article and then answer both **a** *and* **b**.

### Hilton Herald, 21 October 1987
### Pupils on Rampage: Two Arrested

Hordes of pupils from Hilton High School went on the rampage on Tuesday in Hilton Shopping Centre. Fruit and vegetable stalls were overturned as a pitched battle developed between rival gangs. The police were called, and two youths were arrested, though it is understood that no charges are to be made.

Mr Alan Murphy, chairman of the Hilton Chamber of Commerce, described the incident as disgraceful. 'It was unbelievable. There was some kind of fight and a fruit stall was knocked over. Then all hell broke loose. There were apples and cabbages flying everywhere. Luckily someone phoned the police, and the hooligans just melted away. The police got two of them, and I hope they throw the book at them.'

Incidents like this have been going on for some time, Mr Murphy reported. 'There are always great masses of them after school, blocking the pavements, fighting with each other, using foul language. People are frightened to come here any more. They're driving all our customers away. It's time the school took action about it. Some shopkeepers have already banned pupils from the school from using their shops. I intend to write to the school about it and demand that something be done. It's costing us money.'

The Headmistress of Hilton High School, Mrs Angela Wilkes, said that she is investigating the incident and that the pupils involved would be severely punished.

Now answer **a** *and* **b**, basing your answers on the information given in the article.

**a** Write Mr Murphy's letter to Mrs Wilkes complaining about the behaviour of pupils of Hilton High School in the Shopping Centre. (10 marks)

**b** Write a letter from Mrs Wilkes to be sent to the parents of all pupils explaining what happened and making it clear that misbehaviour in the Shopping Centre will be severely dealt with. (10 marks)

◀ *If you are not required to sit a written examination, this could be part of your coursework.* ▶

# 10.1 Writing formal letters

Why do people write letters? Give as many reasons and instances as you can.

The degree of formality or informality of a letter depends on the person to whom you are writing and the purpose of the letter. Formal letters include applications for jobs, requests for information, letters of congratulation or complaint, business letters. Informal letters are between friends or members of a family. Letters to a newspaper may be formal or informal depending on the style favoured by the newspaper you are writing to.

In most cases, formal letters are written to people who are not known to you personally, or known only slightly. Usually, you want to make a good impression. You would be expected to use Standard English and to pay particular attention to the grammatical correctness of what you write. Formal letters need to be carefully planned with the points clearly presented in the most effective order.

● Look at these letters of application and the checklist. How effective are the letters and how helpful is the checklist?

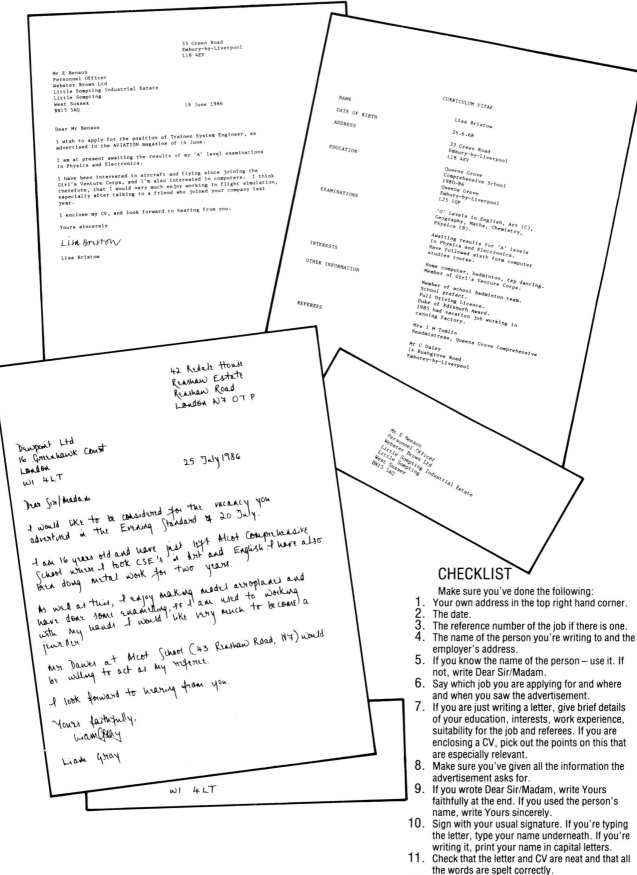

33 Green Road
Embury-by-Liverpool
L18 4EV

Mr E Benson
Personnel Officer
Webster Brown Ltd
Little Sompting Industrial Estate
Little Sompting
West Sussex
BN15 5AQ                          19 June 1986

Dear Mr Benson

I wish to apply for the position of Trainee System Engineer, as advertised in the AVIATION magazine of 14 June.

I am at present awaiting the results of my 'A' level examinations in Physics and Electronics.

I have been interested in aircraft and flying since joining the Girl's Venture Corps, and I'm also interested in computers. I think therefore, that I would very much enjoy working in flight simulation, especially after talking to a friend who joined your company last year.

I enclose my CV, and look forward to hearing from you.

Yours sincerely

Lisa Bristow

Lisa Bristow

---

NAME
DATE OF BIRTH
ADDRESS

EDUCATION

EXAMINATIONS

INTERESTS

OTHER INFORMATION

REFEREES

CURRICULUM VITAE

Lisa Bristow

26.6.68

33 Green Road
Embury-by-Liverpool
L18 4EV

Queens Grove
Comprehensive School
1980-86
Queens Grove
Embury-by-Liverpool
L25 1QP

'O' Levels in English, Art (C), Geography, Maths, Chemistry, Physics (B).

Awaiting results for 'A' levels in Physics and Electronics. Have followed sixth form computer studies course.

Home computer, badminton, tap dancing. Member of Girl's Venture Corps.

Member of school badminton team. School prefect. Full Driving Licence. Duke of Edinburgh Award. 1985 had vacation job working in canning factory.

Mrs I M Tomlin
Headmistress, Queens Grove Comprehensive

Mr C Daley
14 Rushgrove Road
Emburey-by-Liverpool

---

42 Redale House
Renshaw Estate
Renshaw Road
London N7 0TP

Dewpoint Ltd
16 Greenhawk Court
London                    25 July 1986
W1 4LT

Dear Sir/Madam

I would like to be considered for the vacancy you advertised in the Evening Standard of 20 July.

I am 16 years old and have just left Alcot Comprehensive School where I took CSE's in Art and English. I have also been doing metal work for two years.

As well as this, I enjoy making model aeroplanes and have done some enamelling, so I am used to working with my hands. I would like very much to become a jeweller.

Mrs Davies at Alcot School (43 Renshaw Road, N7) would be willing to act as my reference.

I look forward to hearing from you.

Yours faithfully,
Liam Gray
Liam Gray

W1 4LT

---

Mr E Benson
Personnel Officer
Webster Brown Ltd
Little Sompting Industrial Estate
Little Sompting
West Sussex
BN15 5AQ

---

## CHECKLIST

Make sure you've done the following:
1. Your own address in the top right hand corner.
2. The date.
3. The reference number of the job if there is one.
4. The name of the person you're writing to and the employer's address.
5. If you know the name of the person – use it. If not, write Dear Sir/Madam.
6. Say which job you are applying for and where and when you saw the advertisement.
7. If you are just writing a letter, give brief details of your education, interests, work experience, suitability for the job and referees. If you are enclosing a CV, pick out the points on this that are especially relevant.
8. Make sure you've given all the information the advertisement asks for.
9. If you wrote Dear Sir/Madam, write Yours faithfully at the end. If you used the person's name, write Yours sincerely.
10. Sign with your usual signature. If you're typing the letter, type your name underneath. If you're writing it, print your name in capital letters.
11. Check that the letter and CV are neat and that all the words are spelt correctly.
12. Check that you've addressed the envelope correctly.

- Here are two letters from residents of Maple Lane in response to a letter from the Council's Planning Department informing them of a proposal to build three houses in the field which runs down one side of Maple Lane.

━━━━━━ **A** ━━━━━━

Maple House,
Maple Lane,
Hilton,
Hertfordshire

10th August 1987

Ref. NO22346C
J. D. Banks, A.R.I.B.A.,
Controller of Development Services &
Deputy Director of Technical Services,
Town Hall,
Hilton,
Hertfordshire

Dear Mr Banks,

TOWN AND COUNTRY PLANNING ACTS, 1971–77
Location: R/o Maple House, Maple Lane, Hilton
Proposal: Three detached houses (outline)

I wish to object to this proposal.

Maple Lane is a small rural private road. Building three houses of the kind proposed would turn the road into an estate, and the character of the road would be completely altered.

It is likely that the proposed houses would be bought by families with at least two cars. The building of such houses would therefore result in considerably more traffic using the road which is un-made-up. The surface of the road would deteriorate and there would be increased danger to pedestrians. In addition, the building of these houses would remove parking space for those houses which already exist.

There would be even more damage to the surface of the road in the course of construction of the houses through the transit of heavy vehicles engaged in delivering supplies required for preparation of the plot and for building.

I understand that the Water Board has had problems in supplying water to the houses in Maple Lane, there has been flooding, and this has undermined the entire length of the road surface, something that the Water Board and the Borough are aware of and accept responsibility for. I wonder whether the water and sewage facilities are adequate to cope with the addition of three large houses.

Above all else, the land where it is proposed to build the houses is Metropolitan Green Belt, and I feel that such land should be preserved in its present state for its intended purpose.

If permission were to be given for the building of these three houses, there would be a major loss of amenity in terms of my house, Maple House. As you are aware, Maple House stands on the corner of Maple Lane and Hilton Road. At present, there is an uninterrupted view at the back of the house across open countryside to the British Telecom Tower, and this amenity was reflected in the purchase price. It would depend on the nature of the houses to be constructed, but if (as seems likely) they were to be two-storey houses with pitched roofs, then this view and my amenity would be completely obliterated.

There would also be the danger of the loss of privacy if windows were to be permitted in the north wall of the nearest house which would look immediately into the bedroom windows of Maple House.

I understand that previous applications to build on this land have been rejected. I presume that the objections then still apply.

Yours sincerely,

━━━━━━ **B** ━━━━━━

4 Maple Lane,
Hilton,
Hertfordshire

9th August 1987

Dear Mr Banks,

I have just received your letter telling me about the proposal to build three houses in the field opposite my home. I am appalled by this plan and I am protesting in no uncertain manner. This must not be allowed to happen.

I bought my house ten years ago, and it cost a lot then, I can tell you. One of the reasons why the house was expensive was because of the delightful views there were across open countryside. Now some speculator wants to come along, build his houses and spoil my view, all in the interests of making a quick buck and to hell with other people. Not only will my view be ruined but it will take thousands off the price of my house when I want to sell. I'm not having it.

That field is Green Belt land and it should stay like that. What kind of place would we have if every bit of open countryside was built on? It would just be a concrete jungle. You can't allow this to happen.

You may not know it, but Maple Lane is a private road. I'm sure I speak for other residents when I say that we will not allow contractors' lorries to come down the road with their supplies. The surface of the road is bad enough as it is. Heavy traffic like that will make it worse, not to mention the noise and the dust and the litter. I know what builders are like. They leave a mess everywhere. Life will be unbearable.

Well, I'm not going to let it happen. I'm quite prepared to sit in the road all day if need be to prevent it. That's how strongly I feel about it. Just let them dare try to run over me.

If you let them build those houses, then you have a fight on your hands.

Yours sincerely,

1 Comment on the degree of formality of each letter and which is more appropriate in the circumstances.

2 What arguments are used in the first letter? Are they presented in the best order?

3 What arguments are presented in the second letter? Are these arguments also presented in the first letter?

4 Which letter do you think is likely to carry more weight with the Planning Department?
(Note that neither of these letters is necessarily perfect.)

## 10.1.1 Formal letters – coursework

Choose one of the following:

1 As secretary of your youth club, write a letter to the headteacher of a local school requesting the use of the school gym one night a week. Explain why you want the use of the gym and give convincing guarantees of the good behaviour of the youth club members. Perhaps you could offer some kind of service in return as well.

2 Imagine your school is to be closed or reduced in size. Write a letter to your MP explaining why you are opposed to this move and asking for support to prevent it.

3 Write a letter to *Radio Times* or *TV Times* praising or criticising a particular television programme. Make it a formal letter and give plenty of reasons and references to the programme to support the view you are expressing.

4 You have bought an item (a radio, for instance, or a pair of trainers or a tennis racket) which is faulty or doesn't come up to expectations. Write a letter of complaint to the manufacturer.

5 Write a letter to the embassy of a foreign country asking for information for a project you are doing on the country. Be precise about the particular kind of information you require.

◀ *(For guidance on how to set out a letter, see Appendix G.)* ▶

# 10.2 Coursework – looking back

You are probably now more than halfway through your GCSE course. This is a good moment to look back at your file of coursework and to assess how far you have got and how far you still have to go.

If you have been working concientiously, you should have accumulated a considerable number of pieces of writing. Remember that for your final selection you have to choose your *best work*. How many of the pieces you have written so far would you consider to be your best work? If you are disappointed by your answer to that question, remember that you still have time to produce good work. In fact, it is quite likely that your writing will improve. As you develop, your writing could show a growing maturity. So this is no time for despair!

Check with your teacher how many marks are allocated to coursework in the syllabus you are following, and how many pieces of coursework are required. Examining boards differ. The proportion of marks for coursework varies from 20 per cent to 100 per cent. The number of pieces to be submitted varies from four to twelve.

Check what form the pieces of coursework submitted are required to take. Again examining boards differ. Generally, they specify that the pieces should demonstrate ability to write in a wide range of situations and styles, including expressive, persuasive and informative writing. Generally, they stipulate that one or more pieces should be in what may be called a 'closed' situation (for example, reporting, instructing, expressing opinion) and that one or more pieces must be in what may be called an 'open' situation (for example, narrative, personal writing). Some of the writing should demonstrate a response to reading undertaken during the course, including whole texts. There are also generally stipulations about the number and nature of pieces that should have been written in a controlled classroom situation.

Check also that you are aware of how your coursework is to be presented and that you are consistently fulfilling these requirements. Generally, on each piece of coursework you have to put your name, the date it was written or handed in, the nature of the assignment, the title and author of any text referred to, the time taken, the circumstances under which it was written.

Here is a checklist of questions to ask about your coursework:

○ What percentage of the final mark does coursework represent?

○ What specific kinds of writing should the coursework contain?

○ How many pieces of coursework are required?

o What requirements are there for 'response to reading' in the coursework?

o How many pieces of coursework have to be written in controlled classroom situations and what form do they have to take?

o What information must be written on each piece of coursework?

● Write a report on the coursework you have done so far. How many pieces have you written? How much could be considered your best work? Which kinds of writing are you most and least successful in? Have you covered the range of writing required by the syllabus you are following? What 'response to reading' is shown in your pieces? Does your coursework include writing done in a controlled classroom situation? Are you writing all the required information on each piece of coursework? What areas do you need to concentrate on in the future?

# 10.3 Writing – figurative language

Using figurative language in your writing can help to make what you are saying more vivid. It can give the reader a more interesting and clearer picture of what you are describing. Revise what was said in section 9.5.

Here is an example of figurative language:

The traction engine was a gross and greasy monster, and Jimbo was its master. (Edward Blishen, *A Cack-handed War*)

The writer might have said, 'Jimbo was in full control of the traction engine', but by using the image of 'monster' and 'master', the awkwardness of the machine and the degree of the skill and power Jimbo uses are much more sharply indicated.

Don't overdo the use of figurative language or other rhetorical devices. If every sentence contains a simile or a metaphor, the effect can be wearing and counter-productive. This is sometimes known as *purple prose*.

Avoid the following:

o Overloaded alliteration and exaggerated imagery. For example:

Striker Steve stalked the ball like a powerful panther after its prey.

o Inappropriate comparisons. For example:

Her cheeks were rosy as radishes.

o Clichés – that is, images that have been overused and are overfamiliar. For example:

He was as cool as a cucumber.

o Mixed metaphors – that is, where one image is combined too closely with another resulting in an illogical effect. For example:

He has a chip on his shoulder that could flare up at any moment.

o Ambiguous or ludicrous effect. For example:

The mayor was alight with joy at the fireworks display.

1 For each of the following write a descriptive sentence or a short paragraph using figurative language.

a a motorway     f a moonlit night
b a forest glade     g anger
c happiness     h heat
d a football crowd     i a tower block
e someone feeling sad     j thirst

2 In the following poem, written by a school pupil, an image or comparison is established and then extended and explored.

# ━━━ THE CLOUDS ━━━

They looked black, very dark
Like night-fighter planes in the sky
Searching for targets to strike,
Looming overhead, making ready,
Then striking again and again
With fire from the sky,
Forcing people to hide, search for shelter,
And then they move on
To another target.

━━━ Tongu Sait ━━━

Write your own 'image poem'. You may like to use one of the answers you gave in the previous question as a basis for this.

3 Find more interesting and original comparisons for the following:
a His answer came as quick as lightning.
b The news came like a bombshell.
c She felt as thought the ground was opening beneath her feet.
d The water was as cold as ice.
e His face went as red as a beetroot.
f When he knew he had passed his exam, he felt as happy as a sandboy.
g She was green with envy.
h She sent him off with his tail between his legs.
i She was so pleased at coming first, she was over the moon.
j He felt as strong as a horse.

◀ *(For more details on figures of speech and other rhetorical devices, see Appendix F.)* ▶

# 10.4 Reading – understanding, restating and challenging an argument

We are bombarded on all sides by opinions and arguments aimed at getting us to support different propositions and points of view.

Most arguments have two sides to them. Don't simply accept something because someone says so. Ask yourself questions. Is it true or false? Is it the whole truth or only part of the truth? Is it a generalisation with so many exceptions that it is meaningless? Are there any flaws in the argument? Are the views expressed logical? Are they based on bias or on assumptions? Are they based on opinion rather than fact? What evidence is there to support the view? Are facts that would undermine the argument carefully avoided?

It is through careful scrutiny such as this that you can begin to weigh up the value of an argument. You can then go on to think of examples and counter-arguments that challenge what has been stated.

● Look at the following views. They are all to varying degrees controversial. Some people believe them. You may believe them yourself. If so, say why and justify your belief. If not, point out any loopholes in the statements and say what arguments you would use to counter them. You could write an essay based on one of them.

1 Parents know what is best for their children.
2 All authority should be respected.
3 Communism is evil.
4 We live in a classless society.
5 It is because of nuclear weapons that we have had peace for forty years.
6 There is no excuse for anyone breaking the law.
7 Abolishing private education would be wrong because it would deprive parents of choice.
8 Selling off nationalised industries means giving the industries back to the people.
9 The only way to reduce the number of murders is to bring back the death penalty.
10 British is best.

● Here are three letters which challenge or support points of view expressed in newspapers.

1 In each case, explain the point of view being challenged or supported, outline the arguments being put forward in the letters and say how effective you think they are.
2 Write a letter in which you agree or disagree with one of these letter writers.

◀ *This could be part of your coursework.* ▶

## A

# You call housewives 'boring' at your peril

GRAHAM TURNER'S article on women in business really had me incensed. All the women interviewed have chosen this way of life, it would seem, to satisfy themselves, and little thought appears to have been given to the effect their way of life may have on their families in years to come.

This seems to me a very selfish attitude and sadly one that is increasingly shown by women today – they want the best of both worlds, wife and mother/career women reaping the honours and material benefits that come from being in business.

Perhaps this is one of the root causes of so many young people going off the rails today. Mother is not there when she is needed. Also I am sure the growing independence among women contributes to

the ever-increasing number of failed marriages.

I am one of those "boring housewives" whom Mrs Margaret Charrington seems to feel sorry for. However, I think my day, which starts at 6.15 am, is every bit as busy as some of these business-women. With a husband, daughter of 22 and son of 18 to get off to work in the morning, and a 10-year-old to get off to school, and then all the many jobs entailed in looking after five people, house and garden, plus helping where I can in the parish in which I live, I find I have little time to spare.

After 24 years of marriage I do not feel I have missed out on the material benefits that I might have had if I had returned to work. We have no care, few holidays and my annual clothes bill does not even

total the £80 that woman spends a month on shoes alone. It seems to me that we all have a mission while we are on this earth: a mother's surely is to see that her children have the right morals and standards of behaviour to enable them to live, work and play their part in present-day society.

Perhaps Graham Turner should now turn his attention to one or two of these "housewives" and see how they feel about women today. Also it might be interesting to hear the reactions of a few children, those who come home to an empty house and those who come home to Mum and are able to tell her the day's happenings and receive her comfort if things have gone wrong.

Maybe I am too easily pleased, but to me peace and contentment in the mind means peace in the home.

**B**  **C**

CONGRATULATIONS to Mary Kenny on her article "Hooliganism begins at home." She has made, I believe, the best analysis of present-day hooliganism I have ever read.

Family life as I knew it in my youth appears to have broken down completely since the last war – Mother is at the Bingo, Father is down the local and the kids are running wild, or alternatively parents are glued to the box: little wonder the youngsters look elsewhere for an outlet for their natural exuberance.

# Teaching more tiring than policing

I am writing about the letter from Elaine Walters (last week) in which she compared pay of teachers with that of the police.

I have taught for 12 years in an urban comprehensive and previously I was a PC in Scarborough and York. I hope I can make a useful comparison.

I am a better teacher than I was a policeman, yet I find teaching a far more tiring job. My father was a teacher before being a policeman and he was never as tired when policing as when teaching. And he spent many years as PC and sergeant in the middle of Liverpool; during the Second World War he worked 12-hour shifts.

The work of both groups has become increasingly difficult during the past two decades, often for similar reasons; we both have had reorganisations; we both have to deal with increasingly disturbed, desperate and recalcitrant people.

The essential difference is that while the police are provided with the resources, pay and recognition to cope, teachers are suffering a rapid decline in living standards, cutbacks in resources and constant criticism from employers which can only be calculated fundamentally to lower morale.

The justification is advanced that there was a shortage of police officers but there is a surplus of teachers. Personally, I find that argument – laws of the market/law of the jungle – primitive, nineteenth century and naïve.

Is education valued? Does society want an efficient and motivated work-force in schools, colleges and universities? The will is there amongst educators, given the encouragement, the recognition and the resources.

# 10.5 Reading – the effect of sentence structure

Writers use different kinds of sentence structure to achieve effects and to appeal to specific readers. This is true whether they use a series of short sentences, a series of long sentences, or a combination of the two. Revise what was said in section 5.3, and look at Appendix B.

The sentence structure should mirror the thoughts and intentions of the writer. It shouldn't become stuck in one mould that becomes monotonous or turgid. It should ensure that the reader is kept alert, responding to the varying rhythms and changes of mood.

● Analyse and comment on the effectiveness of the sentence structure in the following four passages. Consider the length of the sentences, the variety (or lack of it) of sentence structure, the audience aimed at, the writer's intention.

## A

## B

Work at the farm began early and ended late. Winter was a cruel time. Sometimes, as Tildy carried the forty great pails of water from the well in the road to the shippen, two for each cow, the child would pause, and pressing her numbed hands into her armpits, would look around her at the frozen hill-tops, and unknown desires would burst into bloom in her thin bosom, only to die as she heard her father's voice asking how much longer she was going to stand there 'gapin' at nowt'. The farmer far preferred sitting milking, with his head against the warm flanks of Bess or Beauty, to carrying the water in.

The dapper little farmer was proud of his daughter's capacity for work, and also of her sweet, clear voice. As soon as she was old enough, she went with him into the chapel choir, and even two or three nights a week to practise singing. The long walk to Starting Post and back home they reckoned as nothing; indeed, they never thought of it, or dreamed of putting off a practice, no matter how bad the weather. This was innocent joy. Meantime the mother would sit listening to the tock, tick-tock of the wall-clock, her eyes wide with fear, her ears alert for alien sound. But her life was set, planned for her by her husband, and she dared not deviate from his ways. He was a miser.

From Malachi Whitaker, *Frost in April*

# Clickety-click for a new firm

WINNING Sun Bingo changed the pattern of life for Caroline and Frank Wellborn.

They used the big win to start their own knitwear company in Leicester. And now they are clickety-clicking their way to another fortune.

The £20,000 prize was just what Frank needed to say goodbye to his £300-a-week job as a knitting technician.

Caroline also quit her job as a machinist overlooker in another Leicester knitting factory. Together they set up Wellborn Knitwear.

That was back in April. Now Frank and Caroline can boast a 1,250 sq ft factory, a bulging order book and a hard-working staff of four.

### Presents

Frank, 38, says: "We are our own bosses and past the hardest bit.

"We used only three-quarters of our Bingo win to get us started. We had enough left to spend £1,000 on new furniture and buy lots of presents."

**C**

Dear Sir,

I refer to your recent letter in which you submit a request for the provision of a bus passenger shelter in Lidgett Lane at the inward stopping place for Service 31 adjacent to Gledhow Primary School. The stated requirement for a shelter at this location has been noted, but as you may be aware shelter erection at all locations within West Yorkshire has been constrained in recent times as a result of instructions issued by the West Yorkshire Metropolitan County Council in the light of the Government's cuts in public expenditure and, although it seems likely that the Capital Budget for shelter provision will be enhanced in the forthcoming Financial Year, it is axiomatic that residual requests in respect of prospective shelter sites identified as having priority, notably those named in earlier programmes of shelter erection, will take precedence in any future shelter programme.

**D**

He stormed into the bedroom, righteous and indignant. What did she mean, taking their money like this? He bent over her. 'Nettie!' he shouted. 'Nettie, wake up!'

She did not stir. 'What've you done with my money!' he bellowed.

She stirred fitfully. The light from the street flushed over her beautiful cheeks.

There was something about her. His heart throbbed violently. His tongue dried. He shivered. His knees suddenly turned to water. He collapsed. 'Nettie, Nettie!' he cried. 'What've you done with my money!'

And then, the horrid thought. And then the terror and the loneliness engulfed him. And then the fever and disillusionment. For, without desiring to do so, he bent forward and yet forward again until his fevered ear was resting firmly and irrevocably upon her round pink bosom. 'Nettie!' he cried.

*Tick-tick-tick-tick-tick-tick-tick-tick-tick-tick-tick.*

■■■■ From Ray Bradbury, *Marionettes, Inc.* ■■■■

# 10.6 Interviews

Interviews can be of vital importance – interviews for a job, for instance, for social security, with a bank manager, with the police, with prospective parents-in-law. Some of these will be more formal than others. In some, the interviewer will be more sympathetic than others. But whatever the case, your role will be the same: to show yourself in the best possible light. In order to achieve this you need to do the following:

○ be alert and confident
○ be eager to talk about yourself and your knowledge
○ express yourself fluently and interestingly
○ take advantage of the questions asked and answer them fully by giving illustrations, examples, accounts of personal experience
○ make your arguments as persuasive as possible and give supporting evidence
○ use your voice and body effectively
○ prepare what you are going to say.

*Preparation* You may not know the precise questions you will be asked, but it is possible to organise your information beforehand so that you can refer to it in your mind quickly and adapt it to the questions that are actually asked. You can write down a list of facts you want to cover or make notes of answers to questions that you may be asked, and look through these just before the interview.

1 In groups, role play one of the situations suggested at the opening of this section. Take it in turns to be interviewed. As a group, assess which one of you would be most likely to succeed on the performance given and why.

2 Look at the following 'Job Interview Checklist'. How helpful do you think it is?

3 Prepare to be interviewed on one of the following subjects. If possible, choose a subject about which you have personal knowledge and can quote personal experience. Make sure that it is a subject about which you have a lot of information. The interview will last at least ten minutes.

  a A hobby, an interest or an activity in which you are involved.

  b A group or organisation to which you belong.

  c A team or an individual sports competitor, a pop group or an orchestra or an individual performer that you avidly follow and support.

  d A town or country that you have visited and know well.

◀ *This could be used for oral assessment.* ▶

1 Before the interview read any letters or leaflets sent to you by the prospective employers – and make sure you have done everything they ask you to do.

2 Find out as much as you can about the organisation from your parents, friends, teachers or local library.

3 Make a list in advance of questions you might want to ask the interviewers about the job itself, pay and conditions, and the organisation.

4 Think in advance about the questions the interviewers are likely to ask you – about your school career, special achievements, sports, hobbies, or responsibilities you have taken on – and plan the answers you will give.

5 Sort out the journey you have to make beforehand, find out how long it takes – and make sure you arrive with time to spare.

6 Dress smartly, be neat and tidy in appearance and well-groomed.

7 Be polite, friendly and as relaxed as possible. Aim to tell the interviewers as much as you can about yourself and why you think you could do the job.

8 Before going to the interview work out in your own mind what your strengths and abilities are – and be sure you try to get them across.

From Midland Bank, *Cheque in*

# Unit Eleven

 # 11.1 Writing informal letters

Informal letters are usually letters written to friends or family.

You have to bear in mind who you are writing to and why. This determines the tone of what you write and the content. Generally, with friends and family you are less formal, more personal, more gossipy and more natural. You write very much in the same kind of way that you speak. You can write in a colloquial or slangy style where appropriate, though it is still important to use punctuation correctly and paragraphs, so that your letter can be easily understood.

◄ *(See Appendix G for information about how to set out a letter.)* ►

● Read the following letters. The first (A) was one of the prize-winners in a competition organised by the Post Office in 1982. The subject was 'a letter to someone from another planet'. Kevin Pollard was 13 when he wrote it. The second letter (B) comes from the novel *Dear Comrade* by Frances Thomas which is written entirely in the form of letters between two sixthformers, Paul and Kate. In this letter, Kate has just returned to boarding school after the Christmas holidays.

### A

Dear Alien,

I write this letter in hope that you will acknowledge it and send aid to the remaining population of Earth. There is not much left on Earth. Several years ago, two great powers had a terrible war in which the lands were turned into barren deserts, and the seas to steam by the terrible heatwaves produced by the explosions.

However this was not the total cause of the terrible desolation.

It started many years before in an age when there was peace on Earth. In this time of peace industries started up and grew in city areas. This was all right at first on a small scale using fossil fuels which were burned, as it did not do too much damage to the natural environment.

But then there was a war, and at the end of it man discovered that tremendous amounts of energy could be produced by splitting microscopic elements called atoms. However, this new energy had many useless, as well as dangerous by-products. One of the most dangerous of these was radiation. I do not know much about radiation except that it is deadly to man, beast and plant. Radiation and its effects was one of the main things which led to the final disaster, and contamination of Earth. But it was not the only one.

With his new technology man became a danger to himself. Other fuels were discovered but these, when burned, gave off poisonous gases. Now man had more chemical waste to take care of than ever before. People started to ignore the scientists and turned technology to making money. Many a greedy business manager dumped harmful waste wherever was most convenient.

Pollution was a growing menace, and despite efforts to reduce it, streams and areas of land were chemically polluted. Even the sea became a fouled place, because of thoughtless ships-captains emptying oil into it. As this pollution got worse animals and plants began to die in vast numbers. Man had also hacked down miles of forest to make way for housing and factories. This meant that oxygen producing plants decreased greatly in number. Slowly and unnoticeably the amount of carbon dioxide in the air began to increase. So this planet was already half desert before the great war struck the final blow.

On the sixth of April Twenty-eighty four, one of the powers, Russia, declared war on America, for no apparent reason. At first conventional warfare took place, then Russia launched the dreaded horror of nuclear missiles against her enemies. Whole countries were laid waste by these weapons, and some of the smaller islands were ripped open, unable to stand the terrible convulsions which rent the Earth.

America finally hit back with laser weapons. This really was the end. Water was instantly turned to steam, metal melted, glass shattered and earth blasted open at the touch of these weapons.

Then, as abruptly as it had started, the war ceased. There were no weapons left and no armies to fire them. It was as had been predicted, 'from this war there would be no victor'.

The few survivors crawled out of shelters and holes to find themselves in the midst of a contaminated desert. Many died from sheer starvation and the lingering poisons of the war. But some such as my twenty companions and I are still living in shelters, with air filters and food supplies.

However food and water are running out, and I am compelled to write this letter in hope that somewhere intelligent beings will find it and send us aid, or rescue us from the wreckage. I have used the last of our fuel to blast this message into space, in a long range probe. We can only survive for another three months at the most. PLEASE HELP.

Yours hopefully,
Kevin Pollard

### B

Trebizon.
January 10th

God, isn't it awful how quickly you get back into the routines. I've had such a nice holiday, I was begining to feel like a different person, almost like a grown-up leading my own life. And then two minutes inside those doors, and there's the green baize notice board with pictures of last summer's holiday in Greece, cardboard boxes full of new exercise books waiting to be unpacked, Miss Mullard in a flap because Jane Cousins left all her hockey gear in her locker and it's been nicked, and the hall repainted yet another shade of vomit green. Within seconds, two teachers have asked me whether that's *eye make-up* I'm wearing (of course! What do they think it is, Marmite?) and isn't my skirt getting a fraction too short/long for regulations, dear? The Hon. Anne has said scathingly, 'I hope you had a good Christmas, Bannister,' and Emma Loughton has burst into the study and said, 'Gosh, there's so much work to do this term, I've got no *idea* how it's going to get done!' Van, of course, has not arrived. She will turn up several days late, suntanned, smiling and enigmatic.

I have unpacked my books and pinned up my large poster of Kark Marx scowling beautifully over my desk. (Just a gesture, really, but everybody loves it so!) Emma will unroll her posters (one of horses in a dewy meadow, the other saying, *Tomorrow Is The First Day Of The Rest of Your Life*). When Vanessa comes, her bit of wall will be covered by pictures of men; there's the large photograph that says *To Van, with love, Warren*. (She claims she went to bed with him once when she was fifteen, but I'm not sure that I believe her.) There's the nude male pin-up from some American Liberated Girls magazine – which she's collaged with a photo of a bunch of bananas stuck over the crucial bit. The staff aren't too keen on that one, but somehow no one seems to have come up with a reason to get her to take it down.

So here we all are again, and it's heads down for another term. Certainly it isn't the first day of the rest of my life. Still, I have our nice funny evening to think about. Oh, that dumb girl who kept getting the orders mixed up; it was two number twenty-fives and blue cheese salad for you, wasn't it? oh, I could have sworn you said blue cheese, oh no, maybe it was that guy over there, but you did ask for lager, didn't you? the garlic bread, oh sorry! And the punks at the next table – Well, he goes: listen, mate, you looking for trouble? And he goes: right, well, just you keep off my patch, right; and I goes: look here, mate, nobody goes telling me where I go, right? So of course I hit him, don't I? I also admire your not pointing out to me that they were a creation of a) the last Labour government, b) Lenin, c) free school milk.

In honour of you, I have just pinned up a double-page recruiting ad. from the *Sunday Times* colour supp. *Are you Man enough to be One of our Men*? it says. *Be an Officer in today's army*. Emma Loughton has just looked at it askance (she's very good at askance-looking, it's quite an art) and said, 'I don't think you ought to make fun of the army, Kate. I've got a cousin in the Guards.' I said that personally, some of my best friends were army officers, but I don't think she believed me.

I have been trying to work out why it is I like you, coming back in the car while Mummy was going on about whether she preferred the Sanderson chintz or the Liberty union for the drawing room curtains. I mean, there you are, a fearful reactionary, upholder of everything I despise; and here I am writing letters to you. I think it's because you make me laugh. Your one redeeming feature. When I'm talking to you, I quite forgot how much I ought to be disliking you.

I think that's intended to be a compliment.

Yours,

Kate

P.S. In case I haven't said so before, I really am serious about what I believe. I believe – no, it's stronger than that – I *know* that the only way we'll have social justice and equality in this country is by a serious commitment to socialism. And I do hate all the things I say I hate, especially the class structure. I'll give up the privilege and the Georgian crystal any day without a murmur.

I'm telling you this, because I think you think I'm a little flippant about my beliefs. I'm not.

■■■ From Frances Thomas, *Dear Comrade* ■■■

● Can it be said that one of these letters is more informal than the other?

## 11.1.1 Informal letters – coursework

Choose one of the following:

1 You have just come back from a holiday away from home. Write a letter to a friend describing what it was like. Perhaps you went with your family and this restricted your enjoyment, or perhaps one disaster happened after another.

2 Imagine an older brother or sister has moved away from home to study or work. Write a letter in which you bring him or her up to date with what has been happening at home. This could be real or imaginary.

3 Write a 'fan letter' to a sporting or entertainment personality you admire. Make it informal. You could even invent a personality to write to and play the part of an over-enthusiastic fan.

4 A friend has gone to boarding school. Write a letter in which you make plain your views about this move. Or write a letter from the friend regretting or defending the move.

5 Write the letter a visitor from another planet might write to a friend back home.

# 11.2. Coursework – response to reading – a play

When you study a play, the same considerations apply as when you examine a poem or a short story or a novel. You think about the characters, the setting, the plot and the theme, the language and style, the writer's purpose in writing the play. (See the Coursework sections 4.2, 6.2, 7.2.)

But, even more than in other forms of literature, a play is about conflict. This conflict may be between the view of one character and another or one group of characters and another. It may be a conflict of ideas or attitudes or interests.

In a play, characters are of paramount importance. There are events and actions as well, but on a stage there is a limit to the kind of events and actions that can be shown. It is easier on television where the use of film can extend the range of settings and involve more characters and include more action. But even there, much of what is revealed is revealed through the characters and what they say.

When it comes to the printed page, all you have to go on are the dialogue and the stage directions. Out of these you have to build an impression of the characters and what they feel and think.

Always keep in mind that a play is meant to be seen and heard rather than read. You have to try to visualise what it would be like on the stage or on television. Even when reading radio drama, you don't have the tone with which the actors read their lines or the sound effects. With stage and television drama, you also don't have the physical presence of the actors, their movements and actions, the settings, the costumes, the make-up, the lighting. You have to take all of these into account as you read.

Where possible, try to see a play in the theatre, or on television or hear it on radio. It can make a tremendous difference to your understanding and appreciation of the play.

As part of your GCSE course, you are expected to read some whole texts, and a play may be one of these. Writing about a play could form part of your coursework. You could write about a play as a piece of literature, or use it as a starting-point for your own writing, or rewrite some aspect of the play from a different angle.

● Here are some suggestions for a literary response:

1  Choose a crucial episode from a play and show how it contributes to the theme of the play.
2  Drama is conflict. Write an account of a play in which you bring out fully the conflicts that exist between the characters.
3  Write an introduction to a play that could appear in the programme on sale at a performance.
4  If you have read a play and also seen it performed on stage or on television, or heard it on radio, write about the differences between the two experiences and say what was lost and/or gained.
5  Describe a character in a play you have read or seen and explain how the writer and/or actor has made that character believable and 'alive'.

● Here are some suggestions for freer treatment:

6  Imagine a point in a play where the action stops and one of the characters steps forward and speaks directly to the audience, giving his or her thoughts and explaining his or her behaviour. Write what the character says.
7  Imagine you are able to interview a character in a play. Write an account of your interview. This could be in the form of a play or a newspaper article.
8  Have any of the plays you have read or seen reminded you of incidents in your own life or people you know? Write an account of your own experience or a description of the person the play has reminded you of.

9  At a crucial point in a play, perhaps at the end of an act, imagine a character writing a letter or writing in a diary, outlining what has happened and giving vent to his or her thoughts and feelings.
10 Look at the play from the pont of view of one of the minor characters. Imagine him or her telling a friend what has happened and describing his or her part in the events.

## 11.2.1 Suggested reading

Arden, John, *Sergeant Musgrave's Dance*. Methuen.
Bolt, Robert, *A Man for All Seasons*. Heinemann Hereford Plays.
Brighouse, Harold, *Hobson's Choice*. Heinemann Hereford Plays.
Delaney, Shelagh, *A Taste of Honey*. Methuen.
Hall, Willis, *The Long and the Short and the Tall*. Heinemann Hereford Plays.
Miller, Arthur, *The Crucible*. Heinemann Hereford Plays.
Priestley, J. B., *An Inspector Calls*. Heinemann Hereford Plays.
Shakespeare, William, *Henry V*.
———, *Julius Caesar*.
———, *Macbeth*.
———, *The Merchant of Venice*.
———, *A Midsummer Night's Dream*.
———, *Romeo and Juliet*.
———, *Twelfth Night*.
Shaw, George Bernard, *Androcles and the Lion*. Penguin Books.
———, *Pygmalion*. Penguin Books.
———, *Saint Joan*. Penguin Books.
Thomas, Dylan, *Under Milk Wood*. Dent.
Wesker, Arnold, *Roots*. Penguin Books.

# 11.3 Reading – recognising the author's standpoint

Usually authors have a clear idea of whether the characters they write about are good or bad, kind or cruel, likeable or unpleasant. In the course of a short story or a novel, the characters are displayed and the reader can gain an impression of what the author's feelings for the characters are and how the author wants the reader to feel about them. In other words, through careful reading, the author's standpoint emerges.

The author's standpoint does not just apply to characters. It applies to other things like social and moral issues, attitudes taken up towards incidents that occur in the story, the author's overall view of life.

Careful reading is important. An author is unlikely to tell you directly that this is a good character, or that war is evil. You have to pick up the clues and read between the lines. This, after all, is one of the pleasures of reading works of the imagination – sharing the authors' thoughts and feelings and exploring character and situation alongside them.

So what clues are there? An author can create an impression of a character by direct description, by what the character says and the way it is said, by what other characters say and how they react, by how the character responds to different situations. What you have to do is put all these different aspects together and make sense of them.

The same kind of approach applies to moral issues and attitudes. Does the author say anything directly? How do different characters react? Which characters seem to have the author's approval and which do not? What are the consequences for the characters and are we meant to see these as deserved or undeserved? Again, it is a case of collating the different impressions that emerge.

It is not always easy. Characters can be good *and* bad. Characters can develop and change. Sometimes authors can appear to be supporting something on the surface when in fact they are attacking it. You have to keep alert and try to get as close to the author's intention as possible. You have to search the words for meanings and implications.

Sometimes authors don't know what their attitude is or should be and they are uncertain. But this in itself is a standpoint which the reader ought to be able to identify.

● Consider the following poem. What is the poet's standpoint? How can you tell?

# ■■■ TO HANG A MAN ■■■

To hang a man:
To fit the cap,
And fix the rope,
And slide the bar,
And let him drop.
I know, I know:
What can you do!
You have no choice,
You're driven to;
You can't be soft –
A man like that;
But Oh it seems –
I don't know what –
To hang a man!

■■■ Ralph Hodgson ■■■

'To Hang a Man' is written in the first person, and it is probable that the poem represents the poet's own feelings. But in a short story or a novel written in the first person it is unlikely that the author is speaking in his or her own voice. Instead, it is a kind of impersonation, attempting to describe things from that person's point of view, a point of view that is not necessarily the same as that of the author. But sometimes the use of the first person can be a clue to the author's standpoint. Possibly the author feels so deeply about a character's situation that he or she wants to tell it as though it were happening to him or her. Do you think this is true of the following extract from Charlotte Brontë's *Jane Eyre*?

■■■■■■■■■■■■■■■■■■■■■

There was no possibility of taking a walk that day. We had been wandering, indeed, in the leafless shrubbery an hour in the morning; but since dinner (Mrs Reed, when there was no company, dined early) the cold winter wind had brought with it clouds so sombre and a rain so penetrating, that further outdoor exercise was now out of the question.

I was glad of it: I never liked long walks, especially on chilly afternoons: dreadful to me was the coming home in the raw twilight, with nipped fingers and toes, and a heart saddened by the chidings of Bessy, the nurse, and humbled by the consciousness of my physical inferiority to Eliza, John, and Georgiana Reed.

The said Eliza, John, and Georgiana were now clustered round their mamma in the drawing-room: she lay reclined on a sofa by the fireside, and with her darlings about her (for the time neither quarrelling nor crying) looked perfectly happy. Me, she had dispensed from joining the group; saying, 'She regretted to be under the necessity of keeping me at a distance; but that until she heard from Bessie and could discover by her own observation that I was endeavouring in good earnest to acquire a more sociable and child-like disposition, a more attractive and sprightly manner – something lighter, franker, more natural, as it were – she really must exclude me from privileges intended only for contented, happy little children.'

'What does Bessie say I have done?' I asked.

'Jane, I don't like cavillers or questioners; besides, there is something truly forbidding in a child taking up her elders in that manner. Be seated somewhere; and until you can speak pleasantly, remain silent.'

A small breakfast-room adjoined the drawing-room; I slipped in there. It contained a book-case: I soon possessed myself of a volume, taking care that it should be one stored with pictures. I mounted into the window-seat: gathering up my feet, I sat cross-legged, like a Turk; and, having drawn the red moreen curtain nearly close, I was shrined in double retirement.

Folds of scarlet drapery shut in my view to the right hand; to the left were the clear panes of glass protecting, but not separating me from the drear November day. At intervals, while turning over the leaves of my book, I studied the aspect of that winter afternoon. Afar, it offered a pale blank of mist and cloud; near, a scene of wet lawn and storm-beat shrub, with ceaseless rain sweeping away wildly before a long and lamentable blast.

● ● ● ● ●

I was then happy: happy at least in my way. I feared nothing but interruption, and that came too soon. The breakfast-room door opened.

'Boh! Madam Mope!' cried the voice of John Reed; then he paused: he found the room apparently empty.

'Where the dickens is she?' he continued. 'Lizzy! Georgy!' (calling to his sisters) 'Jane is not here: tell mamma she is run out into the rain – bad animal!'

'It is well I drew the curtain,' thought I; and I wished fervently he might not discover my hiding-place. Nor would John Reed have found it out himself; he was not quick either of vision or conception; but Eliza just put her head in at the door, and said at once: –

'She is in the window-seat, to be sure, Jack.'

And I came out immediately, for I trembled at the idea of being dragged forth by the said Jack.

'What do you want?' I asked, with awkward diffidence.

'Say, "What do you want, Master Reed,"' was the answer. 'I want you to come here;' and seating himself in an arm-chair, he intimated by a gesture that I was to approach and stand before him.

John Reed was a schoolboy of fourteen years old; four years older than I, for I was but ten; large and stout for his age, with a dingy and unwholesome skin; thick lineaments in a spacious visage, heavy limbs and large extremities. He gorged himself habitually at table, which made him bilious, and gave him a dim and bleared eye and flabby cheeks. He ought now to have been at school; but his mamma had taken him home for a month or two, 'on account of his delicate health'. Mr Miles, the master, affirmed that he would do very well if he had fewer cakes and sweetmeats sent him from home; but the mother's heart turned from an opinion so harsh, and inclined rather to the more refined idea that John's sallowness was owing to over-application and, perhaps, to pining after home.

John had not much affection for his mother and sisters, and an antipathy for me. He bullied and punished me; not two or three times in the week, nor once or twice in a day, but continually. Every nerve I had feared him, and every morsel of flesh on my bones shrank when he came near. There were moments when I was bewildered by the terror he inspired, because I had no appeal whatever against either his menaces or his inflictions. The servants did not like to offend their young master by taking my part against him, and Mrs Reed was blind and deaf on the subject: she never saw him strike or heard him abuse me though he did both now and then in her very presence; more frequently, however, behind her back.

Habitually obedient to John, I came up to his chair. He spent some three minutes in thrusting out his tongue at me as far as he could without damaging the roots. I knew he would soon strike, and while dreading the blow, I mused on the disgusting and ugly appearance of him who would presently deal it. I

wonder if he read that notion in my face; for all at once, without speaking, he struck suddenly and strongly. I tottered, and on regaining my equilibrium retired back a step or two from his chair.

'That is for your impudence in answering mamma awhile since,' said he, 'and for your sneaking way of getting behind curtains, and for the look you had in your eyes two minutes since, you rat!'

Accustomed to John Reed's abuse, I never had an idea of replying to it; my care was how to endure the blow which would certainly follow the insult.

'What were you doing behind the curtain?' he asked.

'I was reading.'

'Show the book.'

I returned to the window and fetched it thence.

'You have no business to take our books; you are a dependent, mamma says; you have no money; your father left you none; you ought to beg, and not to live here with gentlemen's children like us, and eat the same meals we do, and wear clothes at our mamma's expense. Now, I'll teach you to rummage my book-shelves: for they *are* mine; all the house belongs to me, or will do in a few years. Go and stand by the door, out of the way of the mirror and the windows.'

I did so, not at first aware what was his intention; but when I saw him lift and poise the book and stand in act to hurl it, I instinctively started aside with a cry of alarm: not soon enough, however; the volume was flung, it hit me, and I fell, striking my head against the door and cutting it. The cut bled, the pain was sharp: my terror had passed its climax: other feelings succeeded.

'Wicked and cruel boy!' I said. 'You are like a murderer – you are like a slave-driver – you are like the Roman emperors!'

I had read Goldsmith's *History of Rome*, and had formed my opinion of Nero, Caligula, etc. Also I had drawn parallels in silence, which I never thought thus to have declared aloud.

'What! what!' he cried. 'Did she say that to me? Did you hear her, Eliza and Georgiana? Won't I tell mamma? but first –'

He ran headlong at me: I felt him grasp my hair and my shoulder: he had closed with a desperate thing. I really saw in him a tyrant, a murderer. I felt a drop or two of blood from my head trickle down my neck, and was sensible of somewhat pungent suffering: these sensations for the time predominated over fear, and I received him in frantic sort. I don't very well know what I did with my hands, but he called me 'Rat! rat!' and bellowed out aloud. Aid was near him: Eliza and Georgiana had run for Mrs Reed, who was gone upstairs; she now came upon the scene, followed by Bessie and her maid Abbot. We were parted: I heard the words, –

'Dear! dear! What a fury, to fly at Master John!'

'Did ever anybody see such a picture of passion!'

Then Mrs Reed subjoined, 'Take her away to the red-room, and lock her in there.' Four hands were immediately laid upon me, and I was borne upstairs.

■■■ From Charlotte Brontë, *Jane Eyre* ■■■

● Look at this extract again. What do you think the author's standpoint is towards the characters and the situation? How can you tell? To help you, consider the following questions:

1 Do you think the description of the weather is significant?
2 What do you think of Mrs Reed's attitude in keeping Jane 'at a distance'? How does this affect your feelings towards Jane?
3 Do you think Mrs Reed is right to resent Jane's questioning?
4 What does the author want you to feel about Jane sitting on the window-seat, reading?
5 Do you think Jane's description of John Reed is factually correct or is she giving a prejudiced account?
6 What impression do you get of John Reed and his treatment of Jane. How does that make you feel towards Jane?
7 What do you learn from John Reed's complaints about Jane's situation in the house? Is this information meant to make you feel sympathy for Jane or to make you approve of John Reed's attitude?
8 Jane accuses John Reed of being 'wicked and cruel'. Do you think that is a fair statement?
9 Whom does Mrs Reed blame for the fight? How does that make you feel towards Jane?
10 'Four hands were immediately laid upon me, and I was borne upstairs.' How are you meant to feel about Jane's fate from this description of what happens?

● Look at some of the other poems and passages used in this book and examine the author's standpoint. Suitable examples would be:

'The Shave' by Ray Bradbury (3.4)
'But does he get by without his rabbit pie?' by Peter Bradshaw (4.1)
'A Read is a Read is a . . .' by Keith Waterhouse (5.2)
'Is Work Good?' by Andre Drucker (5.4)
'Mr Bleaney' by Philip Larkin (6.2)
'Steve, they said, is going to be fine' by Simon Brown (7.1)
The extract from *A Question of Courage* by Marjorie Darke (7.3)
'Anthem for Doomed Youth' by Wilfred Owen (12.3)
'Executive' by John Betjeman (12.4)
'Putting Poodles Before People' (12.5)
'The Lemon Orchard' by Alex La Guma (13.1)
'The Normal Fifth' by Michael Frayn (15.5)

# 11.4 Reading – the effect of paragraphing

Reading material is divided into paragraphs or sections which help the reader to follow the different points being made. When the writer starts a new paragraph, the reader knows that something slightly different is being written about. Paragraphs also break up the page for easier reading.

A paragraph should deal with one aspect of the subject or the action. There should be a unity about it. If the writer moves on to another aspect of the subject or the next stage of the action, there should be a new paragraph. Grouping related ideas together in the same paragraph can help the reader to see the connection. Starting a new paragraph implies a change in the thought or a move in the action.

As with short sentences, short paragraphs can move the action or the argument on quickly. The eye hurries from one paragraph to another and what the reader takes in is similarly moved along step by step. Short paragraphs can isolate and set out instructions or important facts in a way that gives each of them greater emphasis. The reader has time to digest each before moving on to the next.

Longer paragraphs allow the writer – and the reader – to explore points or describe things at a more leisurely pace. They can provide more details, examples and illustrations, and give a more developed account.

A sequence of short or long paragraphs may be effective, depending on the purpose of the writing, but there is a danger of monotony setting in on the one hand, or of exhaustion on the other.

Variety of paragraphing has its advantages. For instance, if several long paragraphs are followed by a short paragraph, the point being made in that short paragraph is given greater emphasis by contrast. A number of short paragraphs followed by a long paragraph allows for a change of pace.

When examining the paragraphing in a particular piece of writing, bear in mind what the writer's intention is, the audience, the content of the writing, and the kind of writing it is.

● Examine the following pieces and comment on the effect of the paragraphing.

# It only takes a minute to prove which motoring organisation is best.

One minute is all the time it takes for the AA to answer 4.7 breakdown calls.

That's one breakdown every 13 seconds, or so.

Of course, these figures are only averages.

Some days, we're even busier.

But, however you work it out, it means that the AA handles a million more breakdowns a year than our nearest competitors.

And not just because we have more Patrols. A staggering 3,200 of them together.

It's knowing how to deploy them that really counts.

This is where our computers come into action.

For many years we've been keeping a record of every single breakdown we handle.

The date, location and how quickly we deal with the problem.

So now, at the press of a button we can actually pin point where we're most likely to be needed.

(To the nearest ten sq. kilometres right across the country, in any given week.)

So we're usually somewhere in the locality when you're in a spot.

It might sound simple but, surprisingly, no other motoring organisation can do it.

Naturally, we couldn't rely on computers to deliver our service.

That's why we place so much importance on training our Patrols.

And, this is another unique aspect of the AA.

At a place called Widmerpool Hall, outside Nottingham, we have the very biggest training centre of its kind. And it's certainly no holiday camp.

Our recruits have to attend lecture after lecture, day after day.

Then, there's a gruelling series of highly technical examinations for them to pass.

And it's no good just writing down what they've learned. We demand to see their new found skills put into practice, too.

It's tough. But it has to be.

Because when they finally make the grade, more quickly, wherever you are.

our Patrols have our reputation to maintain. More experienced help,

There are lots of other reasons for choosing the AA.

To join, call in at the local AA Centre now or where you see one of our 'Join Here' signs.

Alternatively, you can phone us on 0272 276294 anytime for further details.

It could prove to be vital of any day."

## B

The ride to Stone Court, which Fred and Rosamond took the next morning, lay through a pretty bit of Midland landscape, almost all meadows and pastures, with hedgerows still allowed to grow in bush beauty and to spread out coral fruit for the birds. Little details gave each field a particular physiognomy, dear to the eyes that have looked on them from childhood: the pool in the corner where the grasses were dank and trees leaned whisperingly; the great oak shadowing a bare place in mid-pasture; the high bank where the ash-trees grew; the sudden slope of the old marl-pit making a red background for the burdock; the huddled roofs and ricks of the homestead without a traceable way of approach; the grey gate and fences against the depths of the bordering wood; and the stray hovel, its old, old thatch full of mossy hills and valleys with wondrous modulations of light and shadow such as we travel far to see in later life, and see larger, but not more beautiful. These are the things that make the gamut of joy in landscape to Midland-bred souls – the things they toddled among, or perhaps learned by heart standing between their father's knees while he drove leisurely.

But the road, even the byroad, was excellent; for Lowick, as we have seen, was not a parish of muddy lanes and poor tenants; and it was into Lowick parish that Fred and Rosamond entered after a couple of miles' riding. Another mile would bring them to Stone Court, and at the end of the first half, the house was already visible, looking as if it had been arrested in its growth toward a stone mansion by an unexpected budding of farm-buildings on its left flank, which had hindered it from becoming anything more than the substantial dwelling of a gentleman farmer. It was not the less agreeable an object in the distance for the cluster of pinnacled corn-ricks which balanced the fine row of walnuts on the right.

Presently it was possible to discern something that might be a gig on the circular drive before the front door.

'Dear me,' said Rosamond, 'I hope none of my uncle's horrible relations are there.'

From George Eliot, *Middlemarch*

## C

One noon, Susie and little Drew giggled and played with the scythe while their father lunched in the kitchen. He heard them. He came out and took it away from them. He didn't yell at them. He just looked very concerned and locked the scythe up after that, when it wasn't being used.

He never missed a day, scything.

Up. Down. Up, down, and across. Back up and down and across. Cutting. Up. Down.

Up.

Think about the old man and the wheat in his hands when he died.

Down.

Think about this dead land, with wheat living on it.

Up.

Think about the crazy patterns of ripe and green wheat, the way it grows!

Down.

Think about . . .

The wheat whirled in a full yellow tide at his ankles. The sky blackened. Drew Erickson dropped the scythe and bent over to hold his stomach, his eyes running blindly. The world reeled.

From Ray Bradbury, *The Scythe*

## D

# Michelle names the day!

By KEVIN O'SULLIVAN

EASTENDERS sweethearts Lofty and Michelle have named the day.

The couple will walk down the aisle on September 27.

And BBC bosses are predicting there will be MORE people watching than the 22million who tuned into last month's royal wedding.

## Dressing

Yesterday, scruffy Lofty, alias actor Tom Watt, 30, said "I'm really looking forward to dressing up for once."

But Tom and Susan Tully, 18, who plays gymslip mum Michelle, wouldn't say whether Lofty will be jilted at the altar, as The Sun predicted.

# 11.5 Oral communication – giving instructions

Section 9.1 discusses how to give written directions, explanations and instructions. Revise what was said there.

There are clear differences between written and spoken instructions. Think about how a recipe of a particular dish might appear on the printed page and how a cook on television might tell you how to make it. What differences would there be in manner, presentation and effect? Which would be more useful if you wanted to do it yourself?

Written instructions are likely to be formal and impersonal. Speakers can adapt what they say to their audience. The visual aspect of spoken instructions is important. Written instructions may have a picture or an annotated diagram, but speakers can often show the object itself and point to specific features of it in the course of their instructions. This may make the instructions easier to follow. But if the instructions are complicated, you may have to refer to a written version if you want to do it yourself. Written instructions form a permanent record which you can refer to

as required; spoken instructions are normally given only once, so they have to be very precise, and speakers may repeat and recapitulate as they go along so that listeners have a chance to consolidate the information.

So, as well as the points made in Unit 9, keep the following in mind:

○ adapt what you say to your audience
○ use visual material, for example, the object you are talking about, diagrams, maps, drawings on the blackboard
○ choose a subject that is not too complicated
○ repeat and recapitulate where necessary.

● Give instructions on one of the following:
1  How to cook a particular dish
2  How to knit or make a particular piece of clothing or a piece of furniture
3  How to care for a particular pet
4  How to play a particular sport or game
5  How to make a particular repair on a bicycle or car
6  How to tour and see the sights of a particular town
7  How to take a pleasant country walk in your area.

Someone could be delegated to make notes and give a resumé of the instructions and say how easy – or otherwise – they were to follow.

◄       *This could be used for oral assessment.*       ►

# Unit Twelve

# 12.1 Writing – making a report

Making a report involves gathering information about a subject, collating it, summarising it where necessary, and presenting it in a form that can be easily understood. Generally speaking, a report consists of three parts:

○ an introduction
○ the body of the report
○ conclusions and/or recommendations.

It is useful for the body of the report to be arranged under various sub-headings. These help the writer in planning and writing the report, and they present the reader with a guide to follow. Illustrative material – diagrams, lists, statistics, tables, charts – may be appropriate and could help to clarify points being made. The conclusions and/or recommendations should arise naturally out of the body of the report.

For instance, a headteacher's annual report to the governors of a school could consist of the following items:

o Introduction – a general survey of the year
o Developments in the curriculum
o Examination results (including tables and statistics)
o Funding for books and equipment
o Discipline
o School buildings
o Sporting successes
o School events
o Out-of-school activities
o School Fund
o Parent-Teachers' Association
o Conclusion – recommendations for the year to come.

In making a report, you need to

o gather the material and information required
o arrange it under different headings
o decide on the most effective order
o keep your language simple
o keep in mind the audience you are writing for
o use only material that is relevant to the subject of the report.

### 12.1.1 Making a report – coursework

Choose one of the following:

1 Write a report on evening television (that is, from 6pm onwards) using the issues of *Radio Times* and *TV Times* for one particular week. Things to consider are the variety of programmes, the balance of programmes, the differences (if any) between the channels, the way minority groups, young people and people with special interests are catered for, the use of old films, the use of imported American series, and so on.

2 Imagine you are the secretary of a school society or a youth club group and have to draw up a report of the previous year's activities. Use sub-headings as appropriate, such as membership, range of activities, finances, innovations, fund-raising, successes, failures, visits, and so on.

3 Imagine you are the class representative on the school council. You are asked to prepare a report for the school council on your class's view of the school. You may be able to use some of the same sub-headings suggested above for the headteacher's report. It may also help if you canvass opinions among your fellow pupils.

4 Write a report on some aspect of teenage opinion or behaviour. To get information for this report, make a survey of the class and base your report on this survey. Suitable subjects could be teenagers and television, teenagers and money, teenagers' fears and hopes for the future. Make sure the questions you ask in your survey explore your chosen subject fully.

5 Collect as many advertisements as you can for cars, or holidays, or cosmetics and perfume. Write a report on them in which you consider the techniques they use, the design, the language, the appeal they make, their effectiveness, and so on. Sunday colour supplements are good sources for such advertisements.

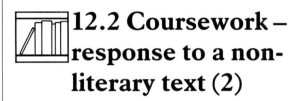

# 12.2 Coursework – response to a non-literary text (2)

It is likely that you will have to include at least one piece of writing in your coursework showing an understanding of and a response to a non-literary text. (You may already have tackled the example given in 5.2. But if you are to be in a position to present specimens of your best work for coursework, then you need to attempt writing about more than one non-literary text.)

Non-literary texts take many forms, including advertisements, newspaper and magazine articles, reports, information leaflets, political manifestos, recipes, guide books, record sleeves. Response to them could be in the form of a comprehension exercise, a summary of the points being made, using the information given in another form, supporting or attacking the point of view being expressed, a personal reaction to the piece of writing, and so on.

In some instances, the text may be discussed beforehand in groups or as a class, and this is something that should be stated on your paper. In others, you may be asked simply to read the text and present your response.

● Read the following article, and then write about it in controlled classroom conditions. In your writing, you should give an outline of the views expressed in the article, consider how effectively the writer presents her views, and say what your own reactions are about the subject. You should take about an hour over the writing. You should write about 400 or 500 words. There are many other non-literary texts in this book that you could write about in a similar way.

# We are not a sub species...

THE WORST thing about being a teenager is the word "teenager." Being a teenager doesn't feel any different to being a normal person. I don't seem to be undergoing any emotional traumas, or identity crises – I must be letting somebody down. The word teenager prevents some people from treating adolescents as young adults; in their eyes we become a kind of sub-species.

My sixth form used to be regularly visited by various speakers. One week the local insurance man came. In an unfortunate effort to obtain group participation and yet remain in control of the talk, he treated 200 intelligent 18-year-olds like a load of morons. Smiling benignly, he said: "Now what do we find under roads?" The answers he received – worms, moles, and dead insurance men – were not what he was looking for. Actually it was pipelines. Ask a stupid question! The point is, that man would not have spoken to adults in the same way, so why to teenagers? If you treat people like idiots, they act like idiots.

There might not be that much difference between a 34-year-old and an 38-year-old, but there's a hell of a lot of difference between a 14-year-old and an 18-year-old. When I was 13, I thought being in the fifth year was the ultimate in maturity: I could wear a navy jumper instead of the putrid regulation royal blue. Now at the worldly age of 18, 16 seems a mere nothing.

The word teenager is misleading because it leads to generalisations and it is so derogatory. For many adults there is no such thing as a teenager who doesn't like discos – if you happen not, as many teenagers don't – they label you as an awkward, antisocial adolescent. For a short time I was a waitress in a restaurant. The average age of the staff was 19, that of the clientele about 40. We, the staff, used to watch amused and slightly disgusted as overweight middle-aged swingers, who in the light of day would claim that discos were a load of nonsense, jerked violently around to the latest hits – as they say. (They were either dancing or having heart attacks – I couldn't quite tell.) If, in the eyes of adults,

"teenage culture" is such a contemptible thing, why, given the opportunity, do they throw themselves into it with so much enthusiasm and a lot less style?

I may be cynical, but I think it is partly due to jealousy. Some adults patronise teenagers because they are envious of their youth and because the respect they don't get from their peers they demand from their juniors. Even on the lofty level of our local tennis club, this type of jealousy rears its head, or rather, swings its racket. If we were to put forward our strongest women's team, it would consist entirely of teenage girls. Of course, this never happens. The elder women play by virtue of their age, not skill. After all, teenage girls don't count as women.

It always seems like sour grapes to me, when I say something predictable like 'I won't get married," and adults smile knowingly and say equally as predictably 'you'll soon change." Whether they believe I'll change or not, doesn't matter, what they don't like is that I'm indirectly criticising their way of life. Also I'm enjoying a freedom of opinion and expression which they never had. What their "you'll soon change" actually means is: "shut up you stupid girl, you don't know what you're talking about. We know best." I don't think you would find such narrow mindedness in an adolescent.

If there is such a thing as a teenager, it refers to a state of mind and not a particular age range. At 20, you don't automatically become an adult because you've dropped the "teen" in your age. Unfortunately "teenager" has come to connote things like selfishness, irresponsibility, and arrogance. This means there are a lot of adults around who are still teenage. Equally, if maturity is measured by attributes such as compassion and tolerance, and not merely the number of years you've totted up, then there are a lot of adult teenagers around.

I would like the word "teenager" to be banned, but I suppose that will never happen, as a lot of people would stop making a lot of money.

Lois McNay

# 12.3 Writing – planning, drafting and redrafting

If you are doing a piece of writing during an examination or in a controlled classroom situation, then you may have to work hard simply to get some words down on paper. However, most people are likely to be able to use some of the prescribed time to plan what they are going to write and to revise it afterwards.

Even so, writing in such circumstances with tight time restraints is to some extent an artificial exercise. Most people who write professionally are not tied down in this way. Some novelists, for instance, take two or three years over one novel and produce many versions before they are satisfied.

It is probably best to think of writing as being of two kinds – one where you are concerned with getting a coherent and reasonably accurate account down on paper, and the other where you can spend time on more detailed planning and revision.

Here are some suggestions about planning:

o think about the idea for a long time before you write about it
o read round the subject or research how other writers have approached it
o jot down ideas and/or sentences and phrases that you might use
o work out the best way to begin and end and the best sequence for your ideas.

After writing your first draft, look at it critically and ask yourself questions like these:

o are the approach, tone and point of view right?
o could some sections be cut and others expanded with more informative detail?
o are there instances where you could use more interesting and expressive words?
o do your sentence structure and paragraphing help your meaning?
o would reported speech be more dramatic as dialogue?
o would sentences in the passive be more effective if put into the active?
o have you started and ended at the best places?

You are then in a position to write your second draft, incorporating your changes. After that, it would be a good idea to leave the piece of writing on one side for two or three weeks if you can. This allows time for the writing to mature as it were. You can return to it with fresh eyes and perhaps new ideas. You can look at it more objectively and make any further amendments.

Ideas don't always come all at once when you need them. When you are preparing a piece of writing, it can be helpful to have a couple of clear pages in a notebook where you can jot down your first thoughts and add other ideas as they arise. When writing your first draft, leave a very wide margin where you can put any revisions you make in the text or, better still, write on a right-hand page and have the left-hand page available for alterations and additions.

1   Here is the first draft (A) and the final version (B) of the opening pages of the novel *Getting It Wrong*. Compare these versions. Comment on the nature of the revisions and their effectiveness or otherwise.

## A

Half-term and nothing to do.

Donovan roamed moodily around his bedroom. He had exams coming up, and he ought to do some studying, but he didn't feel like it.

He sat down at his drum kit and beat out a rhythm. But it was half-hearted. What was the point of beating out a rhythm when there was only you there? He could practise of course, but what was the point of that when there was nothing to practise for? Anyway, Mum wouldn't like it.

He beat another roll just for the sake of it, and sure enough, Mum's voice came calling, 'Ain't you got not'in' better to do?'

'I was just practisin'', Donovan called back.

'Well, practise some other time,' Mum said. 'I got a 'eadache already. I don' want you makin' it no worse.'

She was probably doing the ironing, and that always made her bad-tempered.

Donovan got up and wandered round the room again. He couldn't go round to Sandra's. She wouldn't be there. She was working. So what else was there to do? He picked up one of his school books. But no, this wasn't the moment. He felt very restless. He just couldn't put his mind to it.

He let out a stream of air. Of exasperation. Of boredom. He opened the door and went into the kitchen.

Sure enough, Mum was ironing. She looked up as he came in and gave him a beady stare.

'What you moochin' round fo'?' she asked. 'Can' you find somet'in' useful to do?'

'Like what?' Donovan asked in return.

'I don' know, do I? Perhaps you could do some studyin'. That'd make a change.'

'I ain't in the mood.'

'You never is. I wish I'd never bought you that drum kit.'

Mum glowered at him for a moment and then went back to her ironing. She thumped the iron down on the shirt she was doing as though she was stamping out devils.

## B

Half-term and nothing to do.

Donovan roamed moodily round his bedroom. It was the year of his exams. There would be the mocks in January, in just over two months, and then the real exams in June. He ought to be doing some studying, but he didn't feel like it.

He sat down at his drum kit and beat out a rhythm. But it was half-hearted. What was the point of beating out a rhythm when there was only you there?

Anyway, it didn't sound right. He knew all black men were supposed to have rhythm, but it sounded nothing. It really needed a guitar or a keyboard to provide a melody. Then he could really get going with a bass and a rhythm. You couldn't play a tune on the drums. Well, you could actually, but it came out a bit monotonous.

He could practise, of course, but what was the point of that when there was nothing to practise for? Anyway, Mum wouldn't like it.

He tried another roll just for the sake of it, and sure enough, Mum's voice came calling: 'Ain't you got not'in' better to do?'

'I were just practisin',' Donovan yelled back.

'Well, practise some other time,' Mum cried. 'I got a 'eadache already. I don' want you makin' it no worse.'

She was probably doing the ironing, and that always made her bad-tempered. She was a cleaner at the hospital, but she was on the late shift this week. She wouldn't be going out until after one o'clock.

Donovan got up and wandered about the room again. He couldn't go round to Sandra's. She wouldn't be there. She was working. He wouldn't be able to see her until the evening. The thought made him feel more discontented. He was longing to see her again. To be with her. The evening seemed so far away.

So what else was there to do? He picked up one of his school books and thought about that again. But no, this wasn't the moment. He just couldn't put his mind to it.

He filled his lungs and let out a long slow stream of air. Of exasperation. Of boredom. He opened the door and went into the kitchen.

Sure enough, Mum was ironing. She looked up as he came in and gave him a beady stare.

'What you moochin' round fo'?' she asked. 'Can' you find somet'in' useful to do?'

'Like what?' Donovan asked in return.

'I don' know, do I? Perhaps you could do some studyin'. That'd make a change.'

'I ain't in the mood.'

'When is you?' She glared at him for a moment and added darkly, 'I wish I'd never bought you that drum kit.'

Then she went back to her ironing. She thumped the iron down violently on the shirt she was doing as though she was stamping out devils.

From Rhodri Jones, *Getting It Wrong*

2   Here is an early version (A) and the final version (B) of a poem by Wilfred Owen. Compare the two and comment on the effect of the alterations made.

**━━━━ A ━━━━**

### ANTHEM FOR DEAD YOUTH

What passing-bells for you who die in herds?
  – Only the monstrous anger of the guns!
  – Only the stuttering rifles' rattled words
Can patter out your hasty orisons.
No chants for you, nor balms, nor wreaths, nor bells,
  Nor any voice of mourning, save the choirs,
And long-drawn sighs of wailing shells;
  And bugles calling for you from sad shires.

What candles may we hold to speed you all?
  Not in the hands of boys, but in their eyes
Shall shine [the] holy lights of our goodbyes.
  The pallor of girls' brows must be your pall.
Your flowers, the tenderness of comrades' minds,
And each slow dusk, a drawing-down of blinds.

**━━━━ B ━━━━**

### ANTHEM FOR DOOMED YOUTH

What passing-bells for these who die as cattle?
  Only the monstrous anger of the guns.
  Only the stuttering rifles' rapid rattle
Can patter out their hasty orisons.
No mockeries now for them; no prayers nor bells,
  Nor any voice of mourning save the choirs, –
The shrill, demented choirs of wailing shells;
  And bugles calling for them from sad shires.

What candles may be held to speed them all?
  Not in the hands of boys, but in their eyes
Shall shine the holy glimmers of good-byes.
  The pallor of girls' brows shall be their pall;
Their flowers the tenderness of patient minds,
And each slow dusk a drawing-down of blinds.

**━━━━ Wilfred Owen ━━━━**

3   Look back at the pieces of writing in your file. Choose a piece that you think could be improved. Write another draft of it. Explain in writing or in discussion with your teacher or in discussion with the class what alterations and adjustments you have made and why.

4   Choose a subject for a story. You could choose your own subject or select one of the assignments in this book. Write the story, showing your first notes and ideas, your plan, the various drafts you write and your final version. Take at least three weeks to complete the whole process. Keep thinking about the project during this time and work on it as time allows. Don't leave it all until the last minute.

◄   *This could be part of your coursework.*   ▶

# 12.4 Reading – understanding how a character's motives and attitudes are indicated

One of the wonders of expressive writing is the way that characters can 'come alive' simply from the words on the printed page. We can picture them in our minds; we can understand how they feel and why they behave the way they do; we care about them and want to know what happens to them.

There are a number of ways in which writers help us to 'know' their characters and understand what the characters' motives and attitudes are:

o   They can tell us directly and comment on the characters.
o   They can explain by giving a detailed psychological exploration of the characters' minds and background and experiences.
o   They can show characters acting in a way that reveals their motives and attitudes.
o   They can indicate characters' motives and attitudes by the way the characters respond to moral issues and moral situations.
o   They can indicate characters' motives and attitudes by what the characters say and think, and how they react to other characters, and by contrast with other characters.
o   They can show what other characters say and think about them, and how other characters respond to them (though you have to take into account whether these other characters are being honest or show bias or are to be trusted).
o   They can use language to influence the way readers see the characters through the use of emotive words, for instance, or figurative language or irony.

Usually, writers do not depend on a single method. In the course of a story, a novel or a play, they are likely to employ a combination of approaches, and it is through the accumulation of information and impressions that readers build up their picture of the characters. In a sense, readers are active participants in the process. They have to see the significance of an event, making deductions and reading between the lines. They have to compare one reaction with another, one character with another. They have to be able to hold impressions in their minds, refer back mentally to what has happened before, and speculate about what is to come.

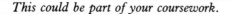

Usually too, characters do not remain static. They develop and change. Their motives and attitudes are influenced and modified by what they go through and the other characters they come in contact with. Just as in life, characters can learn by experience.

In order to indicate changes and developments like these, writers need to have room to expand and give enough information and detail so as to make such changes and developments realistic and convincing. That is one of the reasons why it is important to read and study whole texts. Looking at an extract from a novel or a play, you may be able to gain an impression of one side of a character's personality. But that may not be the complete story. The whole point of a novel may be to show how a character's attitudes alter, and that is not something that can usually be revealed in an extract.

● Read the following three extracts. In each case, say what impression you get of the motives and attitudes of the characters. Analyse how these motives and attitudes are indicated.

## A

Horace descended to join his family at dinner. They sat at one end of the family board, and occupied four chairs out of the two dozen that surrounded it. There were occasions when all came into use, but as these involved the building of the fire, the unearthing of stores of china and plate, and the revival and even the rehearsal of formalities fallen into disuse, they tended to be rare. Horace believed that the austerities of his home were unknown, and that periodical hospitality disposed of doubt, an opinion that showed how far the wish can be father to the thought. . . .

'Six cutlets would have been enough,' said Horace. 'They know we do not eat seven. One cold cutlet does not serve any purpose. It means that one of the servants will eat it for supper.'

'And is that quite a useless end for it?' said Mortimer.

'Of course it is, when other things are provided. It will be eaten as an extra, and that is pure waste.'

'Not quite pure is it?' said Emilia, smiling.

'I suppose Cook thought Emilia or I might take a second cutlet,' said Charlotte. 'It was not such an unnatural line of thought.'

'I wish they would not think,' said Horace, who tended to take both this view and the opposite. 'Their thinking can be done for them.'

'And other things cannot,' said Emilia. 'That is the strength of their position.'

'I will have the cutlet,' said Charlotte, 'and prevent the end that is feared for it.'

'But it will establish the custom of having one too many,' said Horace.

'It is not so easy to mould the future. One cutlet will hardly do so much. They will only think we don't usually have quite enough to eat, and I dare say they already think that.'

'They cannot,' said Horace, sharply. 'We are not large eaters, and why should we supply the table simply for show?'

George entered to remove the plates, and cast his eyes over the empty dish.

'George had counted on the cutlet,' said Horace, with grim comprehension.

'Do not expose the tragedies underlying daily life,' said Charlotte. 'We do not want George to come back and find me in tears. Though of course he would not know I was weeping for him.'

'You are childish at times, Charlotte. You know that George is well fed.'

'I know nothing about it. I somehow feel he is not. I cannot ask him if he has the same feeling.'

'The housekeeping is not your province.'

'No, it is a dark undercurrent that I do not dare to sound. That may be why I like to refer to it. Speaking of things robs them of half their terrors.'

From Ivy Compton-Burnett, *Manservant and Maidservant*

## B

EXECUTIVE

I am a young executive. No cuffs than mine are cleaner;
I have a Slimline briefcase and I use the firm's Cortina.
In every roadside hostelry from here to Burgess Hill
The *maîtres d'hôtel* all know me well and let me sign the bill.

You ask me what it is I do. Well, actually, you know,
I'm partly a liaison man and partly P.R.O.
Essentially I integrate the current export drive
And basically I'm viable from ten o'clock till five.

For vital off-the-record work – that's talking transport-wise –
I've a scarlet Aston-Martin – and does she go? She flies!
Pedestrians and dogs and cats – we mark them down for slaughter.
I also own a speed-boat which has never touched the water.

She's built of fibre-glass, of course. I call her 'Mandy Jane'
After a bird I used to know – No soda, please, just plain –
And how did I acquire her? Well to tell you about that
And to put you in the picture I must wear my other hat.

I do some mild developing. The sort of place I need
Is a quiet country market town that's rather run to
  seed.
A luncheon and a drink or two, a little *savoir faire* –
I fix the Planning Officer, the Town Clerk and the
  Mayor.

And if some preservationist attempts to interfere
A 'dangerous structure' notice from the Borough
  Engineer
Will settle any buildings that are standing in our way –
The modern style, sir, with respect, has really come to
  stay.

■■■■■ John Betjeman ■■■■■

■■■■■■ C ■■■■■■

INSPECTOR: Mr Birling?

BIRLING: Yes. Sit down, Inspector.

INSPECTOR (*sitting*): Thank you, sir.

BIRLING: Have a glass of port – or a little whisky?

INSPECTOR: No, thank you, Mr Birling. I'm on duty.

BIRLING: You're new, aren't you?

INSPECTOR: Yes, sir. Only recently transferred.

BIRLING: I thought you must be. I was an alderman for years – and Lord Mayor two years ago – and I'm still on the Bench – so I know the Brumley police officers pretty well – and I thought I'd never seen you before.

INSPECTOR: Quite so.

BIRLING: Well, what can I do for you? Some trouble about a warrant?

INSPECTOR: No, Mr Birling.

BIRLING (*after a pause, with a touch of impatience*): Well, what is it then?

INSPECTOR: I'd like some information, if you don't mind, Mr Birling. Two hours ago a young woman died in the Infirmary. She'd been taken there this afternoon because she'd swallowed a lot of strong disinfectant. Burnt her inside out, of course.

ERIC (*involuntarily*): My God!

INSPECTOR: Yes, she was in great agony. They did everything they could for her at the Infirmary, but she died. Suicide, of course.

BIRLING (*rather impatiently*): Yes, yes. Horrible business. But I don't understand why you should come here, Inspector –

INSPECTOR (*cutting through, massively*): I've been round to the room she had, and she'd left a letter there and a sort of diary. Like a lot of these young women who get into various kinds of trouble, she'd used more than one name. But her original name – her real name – was Eva Smith.

BIRLING (*thoughtfully*): Eva Smith?

INSPECTOR: Do you remember her, Mr Birling?

BIRLING (*slowly*): No – I seem to remember hearing that name – Eva Smith – somewhere. But it doesn't convey anything to me. And I don't see where I come into this.

INSPECTOR: She was employed in your works at one time.

BIRLING: Oh – that's it, is it? Well, we've several hundred young women there, y'know, and they keep changing.

INSPECTOR: This young woman, Eva Smith, was a bit out of the ordinary. I found a photograph of her in her lodgings. Perhaps you'd remember her from that.

INSPECTOR *takes a photograph, about postcard size, out of his pocket and goes to* BIRLING. *Both* GERALD *and* ERIC *rise to have a look at the photograph, but the* INSPECTOR *interposes himself between them and the photograph. They are surprised and rather annoyed.* BIRLING *stares hard, and with recognition, at the photograph, which the* INSPECTOR *then replaces in his pocket.*

GERALD (*showing annoyance*): Any particular reason why I shouldn't see this girl's photograph, Inspector?

INSPECTOR (*coolly, looking hard at him*): There might be.

ERIC: And the same applies to me, I suppose?

INSPECTOR: Yes.

GERALD: I can't imagine what it could be.

ERIC: Neither can I.

BIRLING: And I must say, I agree with them, Inspector.

INSPECTOR: It's the way I like to go to work. One person and one line of inquiry at a time. Otherwise, there's a muddle.

BIRLING: I see. Sensible really. (*Moves restlessly, then turns.*) You've had enough of that port, Eric.

*The* INSPECTOR *is watching* BIRLING *and now* BIRLING *notices him.*

INSPECTOR: I think you remember Eva Smith now, don't you, Mr Birling?

BIRLING: Yes, I do. She was one of my employees and then I discharged her.

ERIC: Is that why she committed suicide? When was this, Father?

BIRLING: Just keep quiet, Eric, and don't get excited. This girl left us nearly two years ago. Let me see – it must have been in the early autumn of nineteen-ten.

INSPECTOR: Yes. End of September, nineteen-ten.

BIRLING: That's right.

GERALD: Look here, sir. Wouldn't you rather I was out of this?

BIRLING: I don't mind your being here, Gerald. And I'm sure you've no objection, have you, Inspector? Perhaps I ought to explain first that this is Mr Gerald Croft – the son of Sir George Croft – you know, Crofts Limited.

INSPECTOR: Mr Gerald Croft, eh?

BIRLING: Yes. Incidentally we've been modestly celebrating his engagement to my daughter, Sheila.

INSPECTOR: I see. Mr Croft is going to marry Miss Sheila Birling?

GERALD (*smiling*): I hope so.

INSPECTOR (*gravely*): Then I'd prefer you to stay.

GERALD: (*surprised*): Oh – all right.

BIRLING (*somewhat impatiently*): Look – there's nothing mysterious – or scandalous – about this business – at least not so far as I'm concerned. It's a perfectly straightforward case, and as it happened more than eighteen months ago – nearly two years ago – obviously it has nothing whatever to do with the wretched girl's suicide. Eh, Inspector?

INSPECTOR: No, sir. I can't agree with you there.

BIRLING: Why not?

INSPECTOR: Because what happened to her then may have determined what happened to her afterwards, and what happened to her afterwards may have driven her to suicide. A chain of events.

BIRLING: Oh well – put like that, there's something in what you say. Still, I can't accept any responsibility. If we were all responsible for everything that happened to everybody we'd had anything to do with, it would be very awkward, wouldn't it?

INSPECTOR: Very awkward.

BIRLING: We'd all be in an impossible position, wouldn't we?

ERIC: By Jove, yes. And as you were saying, Dad, a man has to look after himself –

BIRLING: Yes, well, we needn't go into all that.

INSPECTOR: Go into what?

BIRLING: Oh – just before you came – I'd been giving these young men a little good advice. Now – about this girl, Eva Smith. I remember her quite well now. She was a lively good-looking girl – country-bred, I fancy – and she'd been working in one of our machine shops for over a year. A good worker too. In fact, the foreman there told me he was ready to promote her into what we call a leading operator – head of a small group of girls. But after they came back from their holidays that August, they were all rather restless, and they suddenly decided to ask for more money. They were averaging about twenty-two and six, which was neither more nor less than is paid generally in our industry. They wanted the rates raised so that they could average about twenty-five shillings a week. I refused, of course.

INSPECTOR: Why?

BIRLING (surprised): Did you say 'Why?'?

INSPECTOR: Yes. Why did you refuse?

BIRLING: Well, Inspector, I don't see that it's any concern of yours how I choose to run my business. Is it now?

INSPECTOR: It might be, you know.

BIRLING: I don't like that tone.

INSPECTOR: I'm sorry. But you asked me a question.

BIRLING: And you asked me a question before that, a quite unnecessary question too.

INSPECTOR: It's my duty to ask questions.

BIRLING: Well, it's my duty to keep labour costs down, and if I'd agreed to this demand for a new rate we'd have added about twelve per cent to our labour costs. Does that satisfy you? So I refused. Said I couldn't consider it. We were paying the usual rates and if they didn't like those rates, they could go and work somewhere else. It's a free country, I told them.

ERIC: It isn't if you can't go and work somewhere else.

INSPECTOR: Quite so.

BIRLING (to ERIC): Look – just you keep out of this.

You hadn't even started in the works when this happened. So they went on strike. That didn't last long, of course.

GERALD: Not if it was just after the holidays. They'd be all broke – if I know them.

BIRLING: Right, Gerald. They mostly were. And so was the strike, after a week or two. Pitiful affair. Well, we let them all come back – at the old rates – except the four or five ringleaders, who'd started the trouble. I went down myself and told them to clear out. And this girl, Eva Smith, was one of them. She'd had a lot to say – far too much – so she had to go.

GERALD: You couldn't have done anything else.

ERIC: He could. He could have kept her on instead of throwing her out. I call it tough luck.

BIRLING: Rubbish! If you don't come down sharply on some of these people, they'd soon be asking for the earth.

GERALD: I should say so!

INSPECTOR: They might. But after all it's better to ask for the earth than to take it.

■■■ From J. B. Priestley, *An Inspector Calls* ■■■

# 12.5 Reading – a sense of audience

Many poets and novelists say that they write primarily for themselves and that publication and other readers come second. What matters to them is the process of working out their thoughts and battling with words to get it right. Other writers gauge their readership carefully and write accordingly. Writers of 'romances', for instance, have to stick to certain 'rules' about what to write about and what not to write about – for instance, the degree to which they can be explicit about sex.

Writers for teenagers and children too have to be aware of their audience and make sure that what they write about is of interest to the particular age-group and is presented in a way and style that will appeal.

When it comes to expository and persuasive writing, it is even more important for writers to have a clear image of their audience, and this is reflected in the way material is presented. For instance, what difference do you think there would be in material and presentation between:

o   *The Sun* and *The Times*
o   magazines like *Woman* and *Gardening from Which?*
o   an advertisement for toys and an advertisement for soap powders
o   welfare leaflets aimed at old people about keeping warm in winter and those aimed at children about road safety
o   holiday brochures for Club 18–30 and for Saga Holidays (catering for the over 60s)?

● Look at the following editorial from *The Guardian* which is regarded as one of the 'serious' newspapers.

# Putting poodles before people

Compared with the vast sums denied to the Treasury each year from the black economy as a whole, the annual £1 million shortfall attributable to non-enforcement of the dog licensing laws is . . . er . . . small dog biscuits. Only about half of the nation's dog owners now bother to shell out the 37p for a licence. As a result, the cost of the licence system is four times the total of the revenue obtained from it. Faced with a choice of whether to increase the licence fee (a rise in line with inflation would mean a fee of about £8.50) or to tighten its collection methods, the Government has not shirked the brave course. It has decided to cut its losses and to abolish the licence altogether.

There will be some Tories on the ultra-libertarian loony right who will see this decision as a great victory for market forces over the nanny state. For these people, dog licences are only the beginning. Which taxed pleasure will be next to be freed? Take car licences, for example. Only this week, the Comptroller and Auditor General has reported that 1.1 million vehicles are evading taxation, at a cost to the Exchequer of £100 million a year. Or take the television licence. Every year, 1.6 million people try to dodge the TV licence, losing £80 million in revenue. There are, of course, plenty of people who either can't or won't pay for these licences. Yet, in the real world, in spite of occasional bouts of wishful thinking to the contrary, most of us accept both the principle that such goods can be taxed and the reality that the tax should increase from time to time also. When they try to evade, they know they run the risk of legal action – some 305,000 cases involving cars last year and a further 108,000 TV cars last year and a further 108,000 TV licence dodging prosecutions. With cars and televisions, we have sensible fees enforced. Why not with dogs too?

The answer, allegedly, is that no government wishes to offend the dog-loving voters. Suggest raising the dog licence to a suitable sum and you are told that the electorate won't stand for it. Conversely, it is the hope that abolition will bring political dividends that explains the timing of the announcement in the week of the local elections. But it really is a pathetic argument. It is a fair bet that far more voters see themselves as car-lovers or TV-lovers than as dog-lovers. Yet governments are perfectly prepared to go on licensing cars and TVs, and rightly so. That's why we suspect that this great deference to dog-owners is really pretty bogus. The real problem about the dog licence is that the Government does not have a dog policy. If it wanted to, a government could do something really effective about stray dogs in town and country. That would please a lot of people, including the farmers. If it really wanted to, a government could ban dogs from public parks and could clamp down on dangerous and unsupervised dogs more generally. That would please everyone who values the parks, the pavements and their own safety. If the best way to pay for that sort of control is a higher dog licence, then fine. Some political party ought to try being anti-dog for a change. What was that about "putting people first"?

1 What do you think the use of the word 'poodles' in the title implies about the writer's attitude towards the government's decision? Is it simply there for the alliteration?

2 'The Government has not shirked the brave course.' Is the writer being ironic? How can you tell? Are there any other examples of irony?

3 What argument is the writer putting forward in the second paragraph?

4 What reasons are given for the government abolishing dog licences?

5 Why does the writer consider 'it really is a pathetic argument'?

6 What does the writer consider 'a dog policy'?

7 Comment on the paragraphing.

8 Comment on the sentence structure.

9 Comment on the kind of language and tone used.

10 What kind of reader do you think this editorial is being written for?

The editorial is critical of a government decision. It uses irony and ridicule, statistical facts and argument to make its point. It outlines what the government should have done and why in some detail. From this, you could deduce that the reader is someone who is interested in keeping an eye on what the government is up to, able to understand irony and to appreciate it, prepared to read and follow fairly lengthy marshalling of facts and arguments. It would suggest someone with a reasonable intelligence and education, and someone interested in current affairs. The editorial ends with a topical reference that would test the reader's awareness. 'Putting people first' was the title of a document produced by the opposition party a few weeks previously. A reader could feel pleased at getting the reference and the joke.

The length of the paragraphs and some of the sentences suggest someone with a reasonable degree of literacy. They require the reader to carry quite a lot in his or her mind as the arguments unfold. The choice of language shows a mixture of slang and formal language. There are expressions like 'shell out', 'cut its losses', 'loony', 'nanny state', 'pathetic'. But there are also phrase like 'shortfall attributable to non-enforcement', 'the total of the revenue obtained', 'tighten its collection methods', 'a great victory for market forces'. This mixture mirrors the tone which is half jokey, half serious.

All of this would again suggest that an intelligent educated reader is being catered for, someone younger rather than older, someone who uses slang in his or her speech at least at times instead of Standard English, someone who tries to be 'with it' rather than someone who is staid and old-fashioned.

From this analysis, it can be seen that writers provide a lot of clues about the audience they are writing for. You have to look at the following:

o subject matter
o language, sentence structure and paragraphing
o tone and approach of the writer
o length and degree of complexity of the argument or description
o references and details used.

● Look at the following examples. What impressions of the audience do you get from the way each of them is written?

**A**

## Oompah ace Rory drums up a record

ONE-MAN band Rory Blackwell crashed into the record books yesterday.

He walked 15 noisy miles playing 26 instruments—including drums, a trumpet, kazoo, and a cow bell.

The 54-year-old holiday camp entertainer smashed the old record of five instruments for ten miles—set exactly 20 years ago.

### Claim

Doctors told Rory he was carrying a hundredweight—and his feat was the equal to a 100-mile run.

He said: "Not bad for an old 'un, eh?"

The madcap musician raised around £1,000 for children's charity in his hike between Torquay, Devon, and Brixham.

Rory, of Kenton, Devon, already holds two instrument-playing records.

## Bill loses hooter at domi-nose

DOMINOES player Bill Smith had his nose bitten off—in a pub row over a 10p bet.

Factory worker Bill, 37, had popped into his local for a pint when a stranger challenged him to a game.

The two men played for half an hour before Bill won the game and the 10p stake.

But then his opponent followed him into the gents, wrestled him to the ground and bit half an inch off the end of his nose.

Bill, a father of two, of Bilston, West Midlands, was found in agony outside the Newmarket pub in Wolverhampton.

His wife June, 36, said: "Bill often plays dominoes with his friends but there's never been trouble before."

Police are hunting a white man in his early 30s with dark wavy hair.

**B**

One day, Pete was walking down the road with no one but his shadow, when he found a stick. It wasn't an ordinary kind of stick that anyone might find. It was almost a tree. It had branches growing from it, with green leaves on them, and it was very, very big.

Pete bent down to pick it up. His shadow bent down too.

'Silly,' thought Pete, noticing his shadow. 'There's no stick for you.' But Pete was wrong. There *was* a stick for his shadow, and the shadow picked it up when Pete picked up *his* stick. Now they each had one.

Leila Berg, *Little Pete Stories*

## C

The time is now. You're young, independent and looking for excitement. You know what you want, and you want to get it before it's too late. You want to see and be seen. You are the scene.

You're not alone. All over the country there are people like you making the most of their freedom, determined to live life to the limit before they get trapped within the system. They too want to get away from their everyday surroundings, to spend their hard earned holidays not stuck in some boring British seaside town watching the rain, but basking on a sun-kissed beach, sharing the days and nights with new friends who speak their language.

It's an exclusive Club and you're a member. It meets every summer in resorts all over the Mediterranean. It's for you to share and it's the time of your life for you to have the time of your life.

Don't let it pass you by.

From Club 18-30 holiday brochure

## D

As you get older your body may need some extra help to keep you warm. Exercise will help your circulation. Avoid sitting down for long periods of time and be prepared to get up and walk around the room every now and again. Your local library will know of keep fit classes if you want to take up more strenuous exercise.

Eating and drinking can also help to keep you warm. Don't be tempted to skip meals or live on snacks. Start the day with a warming breakfast such as hot milk with your breakfast cereal. Prepare a simple hot meal at midday or if you have difficulties doing that, your local lunch club or meals on wheels may be able to help. Contact your Social Services department for details. At teatime have a lighter meal such as soup with bread or savoury biscuits or sandwiches and a cup of tea.

It is important to have plenty of hot drinks, particularly between meals, and do have a warming nightcap before you go to bed. Keep a hot drink in a flask by your bed, so that it's handy if you wake up in the night feeling cold.

Try to keep a well-stocked store cupboard so that you always have something to eat and drink even on those days when you can't get out to the shops.

Duvets, underblankets, hot water bottles and electric blankets all help to keep you warm in bed. But remember, always switch off your electric blanket before you get into bed, unless it is a special overblanket. Thermal underwear, woollens, scarves and woolly hats will all help to keep you warm. Several lighter layers of clothing are more effective than a few thick ones, and don't worry about how you look, just concentrate on keeping warm!

Bend Down Touch Your Toes

Don't forget plenty of exercise and at least one hot meal a day

use your Hot water bottles and flasks

Wear your Winter Woollies

# 12.6 Role-playing

Role-playing is thinking yourself into the mind of someone else and speaking the words that person might speak and reacting to others as that person might in a particular situation. The same skills are required as in improvised drama. Revise what was said in Unit 9 (9.6).

Role-playing could take the form of:

○ an interior monologue – the thoughts going on in someone's head which are articulated
○ a dramatic situation with an imagined audience
○ someone else's view of a subject you know well.

Give your role-playing a shape – for example:

○ establish quickly but not too obviously who you are and what your situation is
○ make sure there is a point to your role-playing, something you are trying to show
○ have a conclusive ending.

Props and visual aids can be useful in providing you with something to use or refer to in the role-play. It also helps if you think about the physical shape or posture or facial expression of your character. But remember that the important thing is not how cleverly you can impersonate this character, but how effectively you can use speech to reveal what your character is like.

Role-playing in pairs requires cooperation. There must be interplay between the two characters and reaction of one to the other. Both characters must have a chance to have their say. Choose a subject where there is some possibility of conflict or contrast. Think of a setting where such an encounter could take place naturally. It might be at a bus-stop, on a park bench, in a doctor's waiting-room.

● Here are some suggestions for role-playing. Or you could choose your own. Try to make the role-play about three minutes long.

1 'Thinking Aloud'. Imagine you are a character in a doctor's waiting-room. Speak the thoughts that run through this person's head.

2 Choose a subject you know something about. It could be a hobby or a project you have studied. Give another person's view of the subject – someone who disapproves or doesn't really know about it.

3 'The Interview'. Play the part of someone being interviewed. It could be for a job or by the headteacher or by a policeman. You have to imagine that the interviewer is present, leaving pauses for questions and reacting to what the interviewer is supposed to be saying and doing

4 'Things aren't what they used to be'. Express the views of an old man or woman looking askance at the younger generation.

5 Role-play someone who is experiencing one of the following: grief, excited anticipation, disappointment, envy, jealousy.

6 Role-play someone who disapproves of Christmas or noisy children playing in the street or television.

● Here are some suggestions for role-playing in pairs:

7 A pupil is waiting outside the headteacher's office. Another pupil arrives to wait as well. Why are they there? Is it for misbehaviour or to receive praise? Or don't they know? Imagine the conversation between them.

8 Two people are waiting at a bus-stop. Imagine their reactions as they wait and wait and no bus arrives, or else buses which are already full speed past without stopping. Do they both react in the same way?

9 Your boyfriend/girlfriend is late for a date. It is not the first time. Imagine the scene when he/she finally turns up.

10 Imagine a situation in which a customer complains to a shop assistant about something unsatisfactory or defective he or she has bought.

11 Imagine a telephone conversation between two people which begins in a friendly way but ends in anger.

12 Someone 'respectable' is sitting on a park bench. A tramp or a bag woman comes and sits down next to him or her. Develop the conversation between them.

◀ *This could be used for oral assessment.* ▶

# Test Paper 4

## Part I

Time allowed: 15 minutes.

Read the following two pasages (**A**) and (**B**). Both give accounts of children in school. As you read, you should consider the following:

- The reactions of the pupils to what is happening and their feelings
- The attitudes of the teachers to the pupils and the situations
- The way in which things are described.

You will be asked questions on these points in Part II.

You have fifteen minutes' reading time. You may make notes on details of the passages in your answer book.

After fifteen minutes you will be given Part II. This will give you the questions to answer on the passages.

### Passage A

'Now listen to the answers,' said Miss Paton. 'Number one: thirty-five minutes. Number two, forty-seven thousand and eighty-one. Number three . . .'

My eyes followed my figures in anguish. They were wrong as usual.

'Hands up those who have eight sums right.'

A hand went up here and there.

'Hands up those who have seven right.'

More hands up.

'Six right. Five right. Four right . . .'

It was narrowing down, narrowing down. She would soon come to me. My heart thumped against the edge of the desk.

'Three sums.'

I looked at her. Her pinched smile was beginning, the smile that she smiled when she was going to say something clever. Fury seized me. She shouldn't say it.

'Two sums.'

I took the plunge. I put my hand up.

There was silence.

'I said two sums right,' said Miss Paton, clearly and coldly.

My hand remained in the air.

'Have *you* two sums right?'

'Yes,' I said, blushing violently.

Miss Paton leaned forward on her desk and looked piercingly at me.

'But this is a world-shaking event,' she said.

My eyes fell from hers.

'Which are they?'

I bent over my book. This was worse, far worse than admitting to none.

'One and two,' I said at random.

'Ah – one and two,' said Miss Paton. 'More extraordinary than ever. Wonders will never cease. Girls, I beg you to notice that on the sixth of June our genius staggered us by the announcement that she had two sums right.'

I was conscious that they all turned to look at me and that Miss Paton went on talking. But I didn't know what she said.

'So I am to enter two marks for you this morning, am I?' I found her saying later, her pen poised over the register like that of a recording angel.

I nodded.

The bell rang. She gathered up her books and left the room.

But her going brought me no relief. I knew I should be found out. I knew I had done for myself. In the cat and mouse game, she had won.

Lesson succeeded lesson, the morning dragged on.

The last bell rang. We put our books into our desks and stood beside them waiting for the signal to file out of the room, across the hall, downstairs to the cloakroom. Once there, I could fly home.

Perhaps I was going to escape after all. The signal was given. I plunged forward, banging against the desks in my haste to get out.

Outside the classroom stretched the shining floor of the great hall. Once let me get across that . . . I saw, with a leap of the heart, that the headmistress was standing at the door of her room, with dignity and folded hands. I hurried in the file, jostling the girl in front of me. Let me get past . . . only let me get past and I would run all the way home and never come back.

But my name was called out. I left the file and walked across to her room.

'Close the door,' she said.

I closed myself in with her. On her desk my exercise book lay open with the sums exposed. Somebody must have taken it from my desk during break.

'This is your exercise book, is it not?' I nodded.

'You must not nod at me,' she said, in the same level voice.

I knew, but could do nothing else. My throat was too tight. I stood with bent head, my eyes on the fatal exercise book.

'This morning in the arithmetic lesson you said you had two sums right, but you had no sums right and you knew it, didn't you?'

I nodded.

'So you are a cheat?' said the headmistress.

I nodded again. I was a cheat. I submitted to the shame as a dog submits to the tying of the dead hen round his neck.

'You will have to be watched,' said the headmistress, who was no doubt annoyed by my silence. 'And if I have any further complaint, it will be serious. You have been warned.'

I nodded in acceptance.

'You may go,' she said.

I went.

After that day Miss Paton never called me to the platform again. She ignored me. She let me muddle through as best I could.

But at the next lesson she announced that in future we should not be allowed to correct our own books, but must exchange them one with another, and I knew she was taking precautions against me. She let me understand that I was now outside the pale.

■ From Dorothy Whipple, *The Other Day* ■

# ■ Passage B ■

[Father Dolan, the prefect of studies (that is, the teacher in charge of discipline), has gone into Father Arnall's class. He has just beaten Fleming six times on each hand.]

Fleming knelt down, squeezing his hands under his armpits, his face contorted with pain; but Stephen knew how hard his hands were because Fleming was always rubbing rosin into them. But perhaps he was in great pain for the noise of the pandybat was terrible. Stephen's heart was beating and fluttering.

– At your work, all of you! shouted the prefect of studies. We want no lazy idle loafers here, lazy idle little schemers. At your work, I tell you. Father Dolan will be in to see you every day. Father Dolan will be in tomorrow.

He poked one of the boys in the side with his pandybat, saying:

– You, boy! When will Father Dolan be in again?

– Tomorrow, sir, said Tom Furlong's voice.

– Tomorrow and tomorrow and tomorrow, said the prefect of studies. Make up your minds for that. Every day Father Dolan. Write away. You, boy, who are you?

Stephen's heart jumped suddenly.

– Dedalus, sir.

– Why are you not writing like the others?

– I . . . my . . .

He could not speak with fright.

– Why is he not writing, Father Arnall?

– He broke his glasses, said Father Arnall, and I exempted him from work.

– Broke? What is this I hear? What is this your name is! said the prefect of studies.

– Dedalus, sir.

– Out here, Dedalus. Lazy little schemer. I see schemer in your face. Where did you break your glasses?

Stephen stumbled into the middle of the class, blinded by fear and haste.

– Where did you break your glasses? repeated the prefect of studies.

– The cinder-path, sir.

– Hoho! The cinder-path! cried the prefect of studies. I know that trick.

Stephen lifted his eyes in wonder and saw for a moment Father Dolan's white-grey not young face, his baldy white-grey head with fluff at the sides of it, the steel rims of his spectacles and his no-coloured eyes looking through the glasses. Why did he say he knew that trick?

– Lazy idle little loafer! cried the prefect of studies. Broke my glasses! An old schoolboy trick! Out with your hand this moment!

Stephen closed his eyes and held out in the air his trembling hand with the palm upwards. He felt the prefect of studies touch it for a moment at the fingers to straighten it and then the swish of the sleeve of the soutane as the pandybat was lifted to strike. A hot burning stinging tingling blow like the loud crack of a broken stick made his trembling hand crumple together like a leaf in the fire: and at the sound and the pain scalding tears were driven into his eyes. His whole body was shaking with fright, his arm was shaking and his crumpled burning livid hand shook like a loose leaf in the air. A cry sprang to his lips, a prayer to be let off. But though the tears scalded his eyes and his limbs quivered with pain and fright he held back the hot tears and the cry that scalded his throat.

– Other hand! shouted the prefect of studies.

Stephen drew back his maimed and quivering right arm and held out his left hand. The soutane sleeve swished again as the pandybat was lifted and a loud crashing sound and a fierce maddening tingling burning pain made his hand shrink together with the palms and fingers in a livid quivering mass. The scalding water burst forth from his eyes and, burning with shame and agony and fear, he drew back his shaking arm in terror and burst out into a whine of pain. His body shook with a palsy of fright and in shame and rage he felt the scalding cry come from his throat and the scalding tears falling out of his eyes and down his flaming cheeks.

– Kneel down, cried the prefect of studies.

Stephen knelt down quickly pressing his beaten hands to his side. To think of them beaten and swollen with pain all in a moment made him feel so sorry for them as if they were not his own but someone else's that he felt sorry for. And as he knelt, calming the last sobs in his throat and feeling the burning tingling pain pressed into his sides, he thought of the hands which he had held out in the air with the palms up and of the firm touch of the prefect of studies when he had steadied the shaking fingers and of the beaten swollen reddened mass of palm and fingers that shook helplessly in the air.

– Get at your work, all of you, cried the prefect of studies from the door. Father Dolan will be in every day to see if any boy, any lazy idle loafer wants flogging. Every day. Every day.

The door closed behind him.

The hushed class continued to copy out the themes. Father Arnall rose from his seat and went among them, helping the boys with gentle words and telling them the mistakes they had made. His voice was very gentle and soft. Then he returned to his seat and said to Fleming and Stephen:

– You may return to your places, you two.

Fleming and Stephen rose and, walking to their seats, sat down. Stephen, scarlet with shame, opened a book quickly with one weak hand and bent down upon it, his face close to the page.

From James Joyce, *A Portrait of the Artist as a Young Man*

# Part II

Time allowed: one hour and 45 minutes.

The questions which follow are based on the passages given to you in Part I. Using only the information you have gained from reading these passages, *answer questions 1–5*. The five questions carry equal marks.

You may make any further notes to help you in your answer book. Cross out all your notes when you have answered all the questions.

You are reminded of the importance of clear English and orderly presentation in your answers.

## Passage A

1 Describe the different emotions that go through the pupil (Dorothy) in this passage.
2 Imagine that Dorothy keeps a diary. Write her diary entry for the day on which this lesson took place.

## Passage B

3 Describe the different emotions that go through Stephen Dedalus in this passage.
4 How does the writer make the beating of Stephen (beginning at 'Stephen closed his eyes and held out in the air his trembling hand . . .') vivid and effective? What impression do you think the writer wants to leave in the reader's mind?

## Both passages

5 Describe the attitudes of the teachers in these passages – Miss Paton, the headmistress, Father Dolan and Father Arnall – towards their pupils. To what extent do you approve or disapprove of the methods they use? Give reasons for your answer.

(If you are not required to sit a written examination, this could be part of your coursework.)

# 13.1 Directed writing

Directed writing is the name given to an exercise in which you are given selected reading material and directed to use the information in it in a piece of writing of your own. See also 'Reformulating for a purpose' (7.2) and 'Evaluating information from a range of material' (9.4).

The purpose of the exercise is partly to see whether you can understand the information supplied and select the points relevant to the task set; partly to test whether you can use the information in the way required, changing the perspective or the point of view as directed; and partly to find out whether you can present the information in an orderly and interesting way, with the tone or emphasis laid down in the instructions.

1   Read the following account of shopping in the *souq* at Marrakech. Then in your own words write an account of a visit to the *souq*, using the first person and using only facts and information contained in this article.

North of the square are the narrow, covered alleyways of the *souq*. People who have never been in one of these crowded bazaars tend to be amazed when they enter the labyrinth: it is a world so totally different from their own that it seems almost unreal – like an elaborate Hollywood film set created by a producer who is hooked on *Arabian Nights*. Sights, smells and sounds assault the senses.

There are hundreds of little shops, booths and stalls selling a wide range of merchandise – gleaming brass kettles, pottery, carpets, embroidered caftans, sandals and *babouches*, belts and handbags, silver bracelets, ribbons, bird-cages, baskets, plants, woodwork, antiques, olives and much else. They stopped holding slave auctions in 1912, and many of the shops now welcome American Express credit cards, but the overwhelming impression, as you drift along in a moving stream of humanity, is that you have been transported back into another century.

At the entrance to the *souq*, young boys wait for enthusiastic but bewildered tourists, offering their services as guides. 'I am student,' said one to me. 'I go with you to practise my English, no money.' I politely declined, but he refused to be shaken off. 'You need me,' he explained with irrefutable logic, 'to keep the others away.'

His real purpose, I soon discovered, was to steer me towards the shop of his 'uncle', where, he assured me, I would find incredible bargains. All the unofficial guides, it seems, have 'uncles' who are eager to offer you irresistible deals.

Haggling in *souqs* is a form of commercial combat, a battle of wits which the seller invariably wins. You may pride yourself on your skill in business matters, but few Westerners are a match for these shrewd students of human nature. They are great actors and almost always gracious hosts: you may expect that within minutes of entering a shop you will be offered coffee or mint tea and asked if you know the shopkeeper's cousin, who once worked in New York (or Paris, or London, or Rome).

'You are my first customer today,' they will tell you, 'so I must sell you *something*, even if it means a big sacrifice. It brings good luck.' Some pretend not to understand your language, which gives them a useful edge: your scope for debate is restricted, and they can overhear your comments to a companion, which provide valuable clues to your thinking.

The biggest burden on the bargain hunter is simply desiring the object for which he or she is bargaining. The first axiom of bargaining is that the more you long for an object, the more you are likely to pay for it; the less anxious you are the better the price you will get. The inevitable conclusion is that you will get real bargains only on objects you don't want. The proof lies in numerous attics around the world.

The most obvious ploy is to look horrified when he gives you a price and start to walk away with great determination. If he asks what you are willing to pay, offer one third of the asking price. He may turn his back on you in disgust, but if he starts haggling you know that your offer wasn't far wrong.

If you are with a companion, try saying in a loud voice: 'If only we could get a better price here we could go back to the hotel and tell the other TWO HUNDRED members of our tour what a great shop this is.'

It may get you a better deal, but make no mistake: the merchant always makes a handsome profit.

Having made his sale, he will almost certainly insist on introducing you to *his* 'uncle', who happens to have a shop in the next lane and who will provide merchandise at particularly low prices, indeed at a loss, for such fine new-found friends. How will you get all this stuff to New York? No problems; he will post it to you. Credit cards? They will do nicely.

So you end up back home, a week or two later, wondering where on earth you are going to put that huge brass pot, that camel saddle-bag, that incense-burner and that bright red rug.

From William Davies,
━━ *The pleasures of Morocco* ━━

2 Read the following short story. Using your own words, retell the story from the point of view of the coloured man. Use only facts and information contained in the story.

## ━━ THE LEMON ORCHARD ━━

The men came down between two long, regular rows of trees. The winter had not passed completely and there was a chill in the air; and the moon was hidden behind long, high parallels of cloud which hung like suspended streamers of dirty cotton-wool in the sky. All of the men but one wore thick clothes against the coolness of the night. The night and earth were cold and damp, and the shoes of the men sank into the soil and left exact, ridged foot prints, but they could not be seen in the dark.

One of the men walked ahead holding a small cycle lantern that worked from a battery, leading the way down the avenue of trees while the others came behind in the dark. The night close around was quiet now that the crickets had stopped their small noises, but far out others that did not feel the presence of the men continued the monotonous creek-creek-creek. Somewhere, even further, a dog started barking in short high yaps, and then stopped abruptly. The men were walking through an orchard of lemons and the sharp, bitter-sweet citrus smell hung gently on the night air.

'Do not go so fast,' the man who brought up the rear of the party called to the man with the lantern. 'It's as dark as a kaffir's soul here at the back.'

He called softly, as if the darkness demanded silence. He was a big man and wore khaki trousers and laced-up riding boots, and an old shooting jacket with leather patches on the right breast and the elbows.

The shotgun was loaded. In the dark this man's face was invisible except for a blur of shadowed hollows and lighter crags. Although he walked in the rear he was the leader of the party. The lantern-bearer slowed down for the rest to catch up with him.

'It's cold, too, Oom,' another man said.

'Cold?' the man with the shotgun asked, speaking with sarcasm. 'Are you colder than this verdomte hotnot, here?' And he gestured in the dark with the muzzle of the gun at the man who stumbled along in their midst and who was the only one not warmly dressed.

This man wore trousers and a raincoat which they had allowed him to pull on over his pyjamas when they had taken him from his lodgings, and he shivered now with chill, clenching his teeth to prevent them from chattering. He had not been given time to tie his shoes and the metal-covered ends of the laces clicked as he moved.

'Are you cold, hotnot?' the man with the light jeered.

The coloured man did not reply. He was afraid, but his fear was mixed with a stubbornness which forbade him to answer them.

'He is not cold,' the fifth man in the party said. 'He is shivering with fear. Is it not so, hotnot?'

The coloured man said nothing, but stared ahead of himself into the half-light made by the small lantern. He could see the silhouette of the man who carried the light, but he did not want to look at the two who flanked him, the one who had complained of the cold, and the one who had spoken of his fear. They each carried a sjambok and every now and then one of them slapped a corduroyed leg with his.

'He is dumb also,' the one who had spoken last chuckled.

'No, Andries. Wait a minute,' the leader who carried the shot-gun said, and they all stopped between the rows of trees. The man with the lantern turned and put the light on the rest of the party.

'What is it?' he asked.

'Wag'n oomblikkie. Wait a moment,' the leader said, speaking with forced casualness. 'He is not dumb. He is a slim hotnot; one of those educated bushmen. Listen, hotnot,' he addressed the coloured man, speaking angrily now. 'When a baas speaks to you, you answer him. Do you hear?' The coloured man's wrists were tied behind him with a riem and the leader brought the muzzle of the shotgun down, pressing it hard into the small of the man's back above where the wrists met. 'Do you hear, hotnot? Answer me or I will shoot a hole through your spine.'

The bound man felt the hard round metal of the gun muzzle through the loose raincoat and clenched his teeth. He was cold and tried to prevent himself from shivering in case it should be mistaken for cowardice. He heard the small metallic noise as the man with the gun thumbed back the hammer of the shotgun. In spite of the cold, little drops of sweat began to form on his upper lip under the overnight stubble.

'For God's sake, don't shoot him,' the man with the light said, laughing a little nervously. 'We don't want to be involved in any murder.'

'What are you saying, man?' the leader asked. Now with the beam of the battery-lamp on his face the shadows in it were washed away to reveal the mass of tiny wrinkles and deep creases which covered the red-clay complexion of his face like the myriad lines which indicate rivers, streams, roads and railways on a map. They wound around the ridges of his chin and climbed the sharp range of his nose and the peaks of his chin and cheekbones, and his eyes were hard and blue like two frozen lakes.

'This is mos a slim hotnot,' he said again. 'A teacher in a school for which we pay. He lives off our sweat, and he has the audacity to be cheeky and uncivilized towards a minister of our church and no hotnot will be cheeky to a white man while I live.'

'Ja, man,' the lantern-bearer agreed. 'But we are going to deal with him. There is no necessity to shoot him. We don't want that kind of trouble.'

'I will shoot whatever hotnot or kaffir I desire, and see me get into trouble over it. I demand respect from these donders. Let them answer when they're spoken to.'

He jabbed the muzzle suddenly into the coloured man's back so that he stumbled struggling to keep his balance. 'Do you hear, jong? Did I not speak to you?' The man who had jeered about the prisoner's fear stepped up then, and hit him in the face, striking him on a cheekbone with the clenched fist which still held the sjambok. He was angry over the delay and wanted the man to submit so that they could proceed. 'Listen you hotnot bastard,' he said loudly. 'Why don't you answer?'

The man stumbled, caught himself and stood in the rambling shadow of one of the lemon trees. The lantern-light swung on him and he looked away from the centre of the beam. He was afraid the leader would shoot him in anger and he had no wish to die. He straightened up and looked away from them.

'Well?' demanded the man who had struck him.

'Yes, baas,' the bound man said, speaking with a mixture of dignity and contempt which was missed by those who surrounded him.

'Yes there,' the man with the light said. 'You could save yourself trouble. Next time you will remember. Now let us go on.' The lantern swung forward again and he walked ahead. The leader shoved their prisoner on with the muzzle of the shotgun, and he stumbled after the bobbing lantern with the other men on each side of him.

'The amazing thing about it is that this bliksem should have taken the principal, and the meester of the church before the magistrate and demand payment for the hiding they gave him for being cheeky to them,' the leader said to all in general. 'This verdomte hotnot. I have never heard of such a thing in all my born days.'

'Well, we will give him a better hiding,' the man, Andries, said. 'This time we will teach him a lesson, Oom. He won't demand damages from anybody when we're done with him.'

'And afterwards he won't be seen around here again. He will pack his things and go and live in the city where they're not so particular about the dignity of the volk. Do you hear, hotnot?' This time they were not concerned about receiving a reply but the leader went on, saying, 'We don't want any educated hotten-tots in our town.'

'Neither black Englishmen,' added one of the others.

The dog started barking again at the farm house which was invisible on the dark hillside at the other end of the little valley. 'It's that Jagter,' the man with the lantern said. 'I wonder what bothers him. He is a good watch-dog. I offered Meneer Marais five pounds for the dog, but he won't sell. I would like to have a dog like that. I would take great care of such a dog.'

The blackness of the night crouched over the

orchard and the leaves rustled with a harsh whispering that was inconsistent with the pleasant scent of the lemons. The chill in the air had increased, and far-off the creek-creek-creek of the crickets blended into solid strips of high-pitched sound. Then the moon came from behind the banks of cloud and its white light touched the leaves with wet silver, and the perfume of lemons seemed to grow stronger, as if the juice was being crushed from them.

They walked a little way further in the moonlight and the man with the lantern said, 'This is as good a place as any, Oom.'

They had come into a wide gap in the orchard, a small amphitheatre surrounded by fragrant growth, and they all stopped within it. The moonlight clung for a while to the leaves and the angled branches, so that along their tips and edges the moisture gleamed with the quivering shine of scattered quicksilver.

━━━━━━━━ Alex La Guma ━━━━━━━━

◄    *This could be part of your coursework.*    ►

# 13.2 Coursework – extended writing

Coursework can provide the opportunity for extended writing. Some pieces of coursework have to be written in a controlled classroom situation with a fixed time limit, but others can be worked on at your own pace and can be whatever length you like. Part of your coursework might be a short novel or a report (maybe of a piece of research) or a project. You may not be able to submit the whole work for assessment, but a section of it may be suitable.

For work like this on a larger scale, planning is vital. Don't rush into it. Spend time thinking about it, making notes about it, reading and researching, collecting suitable material. Think how the work is to be organised. Will it be a story with several chapters? Will you use headings and sub-headings? Will you use illustrative material and diagrams?

Revise the advice given in 'Making a report' (12.1) and 'Planning, drafting and redrafting' (12.3).

● Here are some suggestions for extended writing.

1 Write a short novel containing five or six chapters. It could be about someone who has to undertake a journey, or about someone moving to a new area and a new school, or about someone having to face a crisis of some kind.

2 Write a number of stories about one character, or a number of stories about a group of friends or a family with each story being seen from a different point of view. You could base the stories on personal experience.

3 Write a number of pieces suitable for an anthology on the subject of the seasons, or growing up, or town and country. The pieces could be of different kinds – poems, stories, descriptions, reports, plays, interviews. This could be a group activity.

4 Write a report on an item of national or local importance. You could use newspaper accounts, television and radio reports, interviews as part of your material.

5 Write a monograph on a subject that interests you. It could be a hobby or an activity or a special interest. It could be a subject that you have prepared for oral assessment.

6 Undertake some research on a subject such as the state of employment in your area, or how old people are treated in your area, or how your school is organised and run. Write a report on it. You could include interviews, statistics, references to books and leaflets.

# 13.3 Writing – a sense of audience

Just as the person to whom you are speaking affects the way you speak, so the audience for whom you are writing should affect the way you write. You would probably speak differently to a headteacher, a magistrate, your parents, friends. Similarly, you would write differently if you were writing a letter of application for a job, a letter to a friend, a report of a meeting, a story, or a poster for a disco.

It is important to identify the audience you are writing for and shape your writing to match that audience. Factors you need to take into account are:

Subject matter and how it should be treated

○ Language and sentence structure
○ Approach and emphasis
○ Length and degree of complexity of your writing
○ References and details you use
○ Layout and use of illustrations and examples.

Revise what was said on 'Reading – a sense of audience' (12.5).

1 The following is a news item as it appeared in a 'serious' newspaper. Rewrite it as it might have appeared on the front page of a 'popular' newspaper. Use headlines and sub-headings. For a model, see 'Michelle names the day!' in Section 11.5.

# Police escort plan for ferry fans

**By David Rose**

Sealink ferries will refuse to carry football supporters without a police guard at ports and on board after a series of measures announced yesterday in response to the fight last Friday aboard a vessel bound for Holland between supporters of West Ham and Manchester United.

The organisers of the "friendly" tournament in Amsterdam where Manchester United fans were responsible for several violent incidents at the weekend said that they would not be inviting British clubs for the foreseeable future.

Sealink announced that after the fight on the MV Konningen Beatrix, in which three people were stabbed, many injured and glass cases ripped from walls, the company was "no longer willing to put their passengers and property at risk."

It would refuse to carry football supporters without a police guard at ports and on board ships, and reserved the right to confiscate passports for the duration of a voyage. Those making block bookings of fans may be required to provide a security deposit, from which the cost of any damage would be deducted.

Sealink said that under maritime law ships' masters could refuse passengers access to a vessel, while bars and duty free shops could be closed. The company called on the Government to take action to prevent further violence of this kind.

2 Write a paragraph or two which would be appropriate for each of the following. Pay particular attention to the audience for which you are writing.

  **a** Copy for an advertisement for a new model of bicycle intended for the teenage market.

  **b** A 'serious' newspaper article on conservation.

  **c** A 'teenage' magazine article on clothes.

  **d** A public information leaflet on safety in the home aimed at children.

  **e** Part of a story suitable for reading to children aged four to seven.

# 13.4 Reading – following directions, explanations and instructions

Being able to understand and follow directions, explanations and instructions can be important – for example, filling in an income tax form, or follow up the instructions in a car manual, or fitting together self-assembly furniture, or finding your local social security office, or preparing food for a baby, or knowing how to grow tomatoes.

In real life, your ability to follow instructions of this kind is usually indicated by an end-product which is successful or otherwise. Below are some exercises for you to practise on. In reading of this kind, you have to get clear in your mind the various steps of the process being described. In some ways it is like picking out the main points (see 1.4, 2.3) or reformulating information for a purpose (see 7.2).

Some explanations or instructions are clearer and easier to follow than others. Factors which determine this are the kind of language used, the sentence structure, the orderliness with which each step is described in sequence, the use of visual aids such as diagrams and maps, the layout and presentation of the information. Ask yourself if the language is simple or too technical. Are the sentences short and straightforward or long and confusing? Is the information outlined logically? Do illustrations help you to follow what is being described? Does the setting out of the information aid understanding?

● Read the following advice on how to feed birds in winter.

# ▬ BIRD TABLE TREATS ▬

Birds have a tough time finding food in winter. Here's how you can help.

Now that we look set for a cold, hard winter, don't forget the birds in your garden.

'During cold, icy weather, many birds rely for their survival on what you can spare from the kitchen,' said Pat Hope, of the Royal Society for the Protection of Birds. 'You can give them most scraps – but avoid salted peanuts: too much salt can be fatal for birds. White bread is not too good for them either, but they adore wholemeal.'

Birds only feed during daylight hours, and as their feeding time is so short in winter, it's best to put out their food early in the morning. Anything with a high fat content is good – bacon rinds chopped up small, shredded suet – these all give the birds energy.

Pat Hope has a recipe for a tasty bird pudding, which will keep them chirpy through zero temperatures. Mix together brown breadcrumbs, porridge oats and chopped unsalted peanuts. Work these into lard or dripping until you have a hard, solid mass. Pack this mixture into half a coconut and hang it on a tree. You'll find the birds will flock round to enjoy this treat. If buying peanuts specially, do get cheap ones – those labelled 'unfit for human consumption' – from petshops.

Cooked potato chopped up small, left-over crumbled cake, cheese, rotten apples, all these will be quickly gobbled up when thrown on to the lawn. No peel or uncooked vegetables, though – the birds can't cope with these.

They will enjoy pecking at a bone with scraps of meat left on. All crust should be cut up very small, otherwise pigeons, seagulls and starlings will swoop down and take the lot, leaving nothing for the tiny birds.

'It is most important to put food out every day,' Pat Hope said. 'They do come to rely on particular gardens. And do put out water – in icy conditions, it's almost impossible for them to find their own.'

A variety of foodstuffs will attract a wide variety of birds to the garden. You may even have the thrill of recognising ones you have never seen before. The Great and Lesser Spotted Woodpeckers, for example, will visit garden bird tables when food is scarce in their native woodland. And even shy birds such as the magpie and jay will be lured by daily food supplies.

You can feed birds from now until March, but only until then. When the new growth comes in spring, it's better for the birds to find their own food from natural sources.

▬ Liz Hodgkinson ▬

1  How clearly do you think the information is presented in this article? Look particularly at the order in which the information is set out.
2  Using only relevant information from this article, write an entry, suitable for a book about birds, on feeding birds in winter. Use about 130 words.

● Read the following advice from the Department of Trade and Industry on how to run a firework display safely.

# HOW TO RUN A FIREWORK ▬ DISPLAY SAFELY ▬

Public firework displays are becoming more popular because they encourage safety and can offer good value for money. But they are only as safe as organisers make them.

This leaflet sets out guidelines and safety points for running a display. Most of these will apply only to organisers of large functions, but some of the advice is relevant to everyone.

## BEFORE THE DISPLAY
*Organisation*
Most groups now set up a small organising committee with one member given full-time reponsibility for safety arrangements before, during and after the display. Try to include the help of at least one person with experience of firework displays. Clearly define the duty of each member of the committee and make sure that each understands his or her responsibilities. It is important that each member has a copy of this leaflet and studies it thoroughly.

*Where?*
Give yourself as much space as possible – at least half the size of a football pitch (55 m × 45 m – 60 yds × 50 yds). Site the display area so that spectators stand with their backs to the prevailing wind. An area roughly the same size at the back of the display area should be kept clear of spectators to act as a dropping zone for spent fireworks. The area from which the fireworks are let off must be kept clear during the display. Use an adequate and strong barrier.

Keep well clear of buildings, trees and hazards like overhead electricity and telephone cables. Clear any undergrowth or long grass. Choose a site with as many entrances and exits as possible, particularly if a large crowd is expected. Make sure these are well lit, clearly marked and kept free from obstructions.

If you are providing car parking facilities do not forget that fireworks – particularly falling rockets – can cause damage. Make sure that the parking area is well away from and upwind of the display ground. No parking should be allowed outside the area. It should be clearly signposted and access to it should be separate from the pedestrian access to the site. Metal litter bins should be provided and arrangements made for emptying them afterwards.

*Advance precautions*
Well in advance, inform the fire brigade, police and first aid organisations about the display and keep in close contact with them. Check with them that your arrangements are adequate. Fire extinguishers and

supplies of sand, buckets of water, etc., should be handy. Check that all these are in good working order before the night and that two or three stewards are taught how to use them. Don't forget to set up first aid points manned by qualified people. These should be clearly signposted. Fireworks will probably be delivered in advance. You should check with your local authority regarding storage. Bulk storage may require a licence.

## AT THE DISPLAY
*Looking after the fireworks*
Restrict the number of people actually involved with the fireworks: *the fewer, the safer*. If possible, choose helpers who have had previous experience of firework displays. On the night they will need electric torches. Make sure they read the manufacturers' general instructions well before the display.

Never smoke when handling the fireworks or at any time during the display. Unpack fireworks carefully, away from open fires and flammable materials, and keep them separate from their packaging. Remember that they can easily break or tear. Keep them in a metal or wooden box, which *must* be kept closed.

*Lighting the fireworks*

*Read the instructions on each firework carefully.*
Always light them at arm's length. Make sure that all aerial fireworks, such as rockets, are angled away from spectators. They should never be fired over the heads of spectators. Fireworks for re-loading must be kept in a box which must be kept closed after each firework is taken out.

For lighting display fireworks a device called a portfire is usually provided by the manufacturer – only this should be used. Do not carry your portfires in your pocket; keep them in a metal or wooden box.

If a firework fails to go off don't in any circumstances go back to it; it may still be live and could go off unexpectedly in your face.

Bear in mind that a sudden change of wind could cause sparks and dead rockets to fall among spectators and smoke to blot out the display. In very windy weather it might be better to put off the display altogether.

*Looking after the spectators*

Good arrangements for crowd control are essential. Arrange for a number of stewards to be responsible solely for crowd control – at least two for every 500 spectators. They should be easily identifiable – for example, they might wear fluorescent jackets – and should be on constant watch for emergencies. It is essential that they remain at the end of the display to keep spectators off the site and ensure that it is made safe.

Make sure that all the organising staff know what they have to do if it should become necessary to clear the site. Work out a drill for calling the police, fire or ambulance service. Lay on some form of public

address system, even if it is only a loud hailer, so that you can talk to the crowd. Locate the nearest telephone boxes.

Particular attention should be given to keeping spectators out of the display area. Be careful not to allow any overcrowding. Should spectators break through the barrier into the display area, stop the display immediately.

No spectators should be admitted to the display with their own fireworks, and proper notice of this should be published in advance and at all entrances.

*Bonfires need particular care*

Bonfires can be a hazard and may detract from the firework display. If you decide to have one, make sure it is built well away from the display. Under no circumstances should a bonfire be lit before the firework display, as stray sparks may fall in the firework area and the light spoils the firework effects. Never put fireworks on the bonfire, even if they are dud.

Make one person responsible for the bonfire. Don't use flammable liquids such as paraffin or petrol to light the fire. Don't burn dangerous rubbish such as foam-filled furniture, aerosols, tins of paint and bottles. Make sure these are taken right away from the area. Before lighting the bonfire, check the construction to make absolutely sure that there is no child or animal inside.

## AFTER THE DISPLAY
Wearing leather gloves, carefully collect all the firework cases with tongs, or some other implement. If there are any that appear not to have functioned, douse them in a bucket of water and seek the advice of the fire brigade. If you decide to burn the spent cases, this should be done with the utmost care after the spectators have gone. Aerial shells in particular must be doused in a bucket of water and then removed and buried. Empty the litter bins. Make sure that the bonfire has been put out completely.

■■■ Department of Trade and Industry ■■■

1 Comment on how clearly this advice is presented. Look particularly at the language, the sentence structure and the layout.
2 Draw up a check-list of final arrangements based on the information given here. You ought to be able to list eight items. You could work on these in groups.
3 Draw up a list of dos and don'ts to remember on the night based on the information given here. You ought to be able to list ten points. You could work on these in groups.

(The check-list and the list of dos and don'ts supplied by the Department of Trade and Industry is given at the end of this unit. See how closely your lists match them.)

● Read the following directions for a walk from Piccadilly to Soho Square.

# PICCADILLY
# ━━━ TO SOHO SQUARE ━━━

Pause at the subway entrance nearest to the Bank and note the statue of Eros, the focal point of the Circus. The statue was erected to the memory of Lord Shaftesbury, nineteenth-century social reformer and champion of the anti-slavery cause.

Go down the subway and walk around the Underground concourse with its shops, world clock and all information on London Transport services. Leave the concourse by the Shaftesbury Avenue exit and proceed nort-east along Shaftesbury Avenue, passing the former Trocadero (now renamed Tiffanys). It was also about here that the old Shaftesbury Theatre stood, where the 'Belle of New York' was staged in 1908 and the 'Arcadians' in 1909.

Continue along the Avenue, and turn left into Rupert Street. On your left again, you will pass Archer Street, where musicians come to arrange for bookings. Walk through the street market, cross Brewer Street and enter Walker's Court. On the right-hand corner stands Isow's Restaurant, universally known for its Jewish cuisine and theatrical clientele. Pass through the Court to the junction of Berwick Street and Peter Street. This point commands a good view of Berwick Market with its old shops on one side and typical new building development on the other. Turn right into Peter Street and proceed across Wardour Street (where the offices of most of the film companies and distributors are situated) and enter Meard Street.

In Meard Street stands a terrace of Georgian houses built in 1732: some have small shops on the ground floor, the most interesting being H. Peen, Boot, Shoe and Tree Last Maker, next to Le Macabre Expresso Bar, where coffee is served on 'coffins' and skulls and bones decorate the sinister interior.

On leaving Meard Street, turn right into Dean Street and then left into Old Compton Street, the very heart of Soho, with its many restaurants and delicatessen. Continue along Old Compton Street and turn left into Frith Street, a typical Soho street of restaurants and wineshops, etc. At No. 6 Frith Street, a Georgian house on the right-hand side, the English essayist William Hazlitt died in 1830 at the age of 52.

Frith Street leads into Soho Square which has two rather unusual churches: St Patrick's R.C. Parish Church on the east side, and the French Protestant Church on the north side. In the centre of the Square is a most attractive garden with a statue of Charles II, sculptured by Caius Gabriel Kibber in 1681. Unfortunately, the small Tudor style building in the centre is only a modern innovation and exists merely to conceal an air vent for London's Underground. The Square's great treasure, however, is the House of St Barnabas, on the corner of Greek Street (No. 1), built in 1745. The interiors by Isaac Ware are the finest examples of mid-Georgian décor in London. The house has wood and plaster carved ceilings, walls and fireplaces, and an elegant wrought-iron staircase. In 1754 it became the home of a wealthy Member of Parliament and City Alderman, Richard Beckford. In 1862, it was opened as a House of Charity by Dr Henry Munro, and the Victorian Gothic chapel was added in 1863. He and other members of the religious Oxford Movement, which included William Gladstone, used to meet here. Charles Dickens, the novelist, also came to the house, and it is thought to be the setting for scenes from two of his books, 'A Tale of Two Cities' and 'Nicholas Nickleby'.

This marks the end of the walk; but, if time permits, visit the G.P.O. Tower, which commands a panoramic view of London, and within a few minutes' walking distance from Soho Street via Charlotte Street.

━━ From *Ten 15-minute Walks from Piccadilly* ━━

1  Comment on how easy you think it would be to follow these directions. Look particularly at the language, the sentence structure and the map.
2  Draw an enlarged version of the route as shown in the map. Mark and annotate on it all the places of interest mentioned.

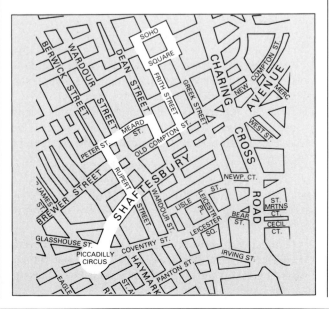

# 13.5 Oral communication – the language of persuasion

Listen carefully to what people say – in the classroom, at home, on television and radio, at public meetings, on the doorstep. All around you there are people trying to influence you and persuade you by what they say. Not everything that people say can be taken at its face value.

One situation where you have to listen carefully to what someone is saying is when a salesman appears unexpectedly on your doorstep.

● Here is the advice given by the Office of Fair Trading.

## HOW TO COPE WITH ── DOORSTEP SALESMEN ──

Most doorstep salesmen are reputable and you may find their service helpful and convenient, particularly if you live a long way from a big shopping centre, or find it difficult to get about because of illness or old age.

But some are rogues and their activities can cause misery for people who don't know how to recognise or cope with them ... Could you? Read on and find out.

**'Good evening ... I'm doing some market research on how people spend their spare time ...'**

A well-known opening to gain your confidence, get inside the door and see what sort of home you've got. Seeing how you live can tell a salesman (or saleswoman) a lot about you – and help them to decide which type of sales patter you are likely to fall for. At some point, as if by magic, the chat will switch from research to selling.

**'I'm carrying out educational research ...'**

Nothing like talking about your children for putting you off guard. How are they getting on at school? What do they want to do when they leave? And so on. And then, suddenly, you're talking about ... BOOKS! Whether it's encyclopaedias, or other educational books, the aim is to play on your natural desire to help your children. The books may be very tempting, but you may not be told the full cost and you could be involved in high interest charges over a long period. There may even be an offer to leave 'free' books with you, but watch out – the catch is that you would be paying a high price for what might be called an 'information service for life'; you'd be supplied with 'question vouchers' to send up whenever you couldn't find an answer in the encyclopaedia. Lucky you!

**'I happened to be passing, and I noticed you have a tile loose ...'**

If you're not as agile as you need to be, or you live alone, you're wide open for this approach, because you're hardly likely to shin up a ladder to check. He's banking on doing a quick, very expensive and possibly unnecessary job, and he's almost certain to ask for cash on the spot which you may be tempted to pay to avoid an accident. Look out, too, for a similar approach about 'woodworm in your rafters'.

Don't panic, there are plenty of firms who will be glad to check your house and give you written estimates. And never pay cash in advance for this type of job.

**'I'm a consultant on back ailments/rheumatism ...' etc.**

This one will try to impress, and maybe frighten you with his medical knowledge and sales talk which could be about special beds, massage equipment or some other 'medical' product. Few things concern us more than our health, and if you have a problem he'll urge you to act before it gets worse.

If it's all that serious, perhaps you should be talking to your doctor, not a salesman.

**'Congratulations! My company has picked your house to be the showhouse for the area ...'**

Naturally, you'd feel flattered. The next step is to offer you a product or a service 'at a *very* special price' – it's usually double glazing or central heating, but could be anything for the house. Be sure to compare this 'bargain' with the price other firms are charging for the same goods. (Don't for a minute imagine that yours would be the *only* 'showhouse' for the area.)

**'I'm selling for the blind/disabled/old age pensioners ...' etc.**

He could be selling for himself and making a big profit on goods – often 'seconds' – which you may feel duty-bound to buy; things like all-purpose cloths, felt-tipped pens and oven gloves which, if they have any connection with the old or disabled, are most likely to have been packed by them for very low wages.

If you want to buy, ask for proof of identity.

**'I've been sent by the council/housing/social security/education department, or the gas/electricity board ...' etc, etc.**

A surefire way to rivet you to the doorstep. Who'd blame you for thinking this caller's business was 'official'? Some salesmen have even been known to suggest that you may be eligible for a local council grant.

Ask for proof of identity. Check it carefully.

He's probably done his homework, too, and knows yours is the type of house that's plagued by draughts. He's called to give you the benefit of his 'free' advice on double glazing or central heating – but this advice could prove very expensive in the end.

For major installations like these, you should always get and compare estimates from other firms; and for central heating, find out about the running costs.

**'I'm a student working to win a travel scholarship . . .'**

Don't be surprised if this one's got hold of your name and says that he, or she, needs points to win a scholarship which they will get simply by talking to you. 'Lack of understanding in the world today' is a popular subject. There'll be a questionnaire, too, on books that would interest you and before you can say 'doorstep salesman' you may find yourself committed to a subscription for books and magazines, which could prove expensive reading – if they ever arrive!

**'I'm an adviser on security (or fire) precautions . . .'**

Here's that 'official' tone again, and this time it's meant to frighten you. You're likely to hear that your home is at risk without a special type of lock on the doors, or a fire extinguisher; you will probably see the word 'SECURITY' in big letters on the card he flashes quickly in front of you.

If you're not sure what protection you need, you can get free advice from your local crime or fire prevention officer.

*These are just some of the more common 'disguises' – there are many more. And some 'rogue' salesmen try to play on your better nature or use flattery to put you off your guard.*

■■■■■■■ Office of Fair Trading ■■■■■■■

1 Like advertisers, doorstep salesmen often use appeals to different kinds of emotions. What different kinds of appeal are illustrated here?
2 What advice is given about what to do if confronted by a doorstep salesman and the 'offers' made?
3 In pairs, role-play one of the following situations. Pay particular attention to the language of persuasion and the use of dubious arguments.

   a A policeman interviewing a suspect
   b A salesman and a householder
   c A car salesman and a prospective buyer
   d A pupil in trouble being interviewed by a teacher
   e A customer asking a shopkeeper for a particular brand and finding it is no longer stocked
   f A teenager trying to persuade a parent to let him or her go to an all-night party
   g A political canvasser trying to gain the support and the vote of a householder
   h A stall-owner trying to persuade a customer to buy the last tomatoes on the stall

4 Study the following speech from *Julius Caesar*. Antony is speaking over the body of Caesar who has been assassinated by Brutus and his fellow conspirators because they considered he was becoming too ambitious. Analyse the way Antony uses language to appeal to his audience and to attack Brutus who was held by the Romans to be an honourable man.

■■■■■■■■■■■■■■■■■■■

ANTONY:
Friends, Romans, countrymen, lend me your ears;
I come to bury Caesar, not to praise him.
The evil that men do lives after them;
The good is oft interred with their bones;
So let it be with Caesar. The noble Brutus
Hath told you Caesar was ambitious:
If it were so, it was a grievous fault;
And grievously hath Caesar answer'd it.
Here, under leave of Brutus and the rest, –
For Brutus is an honourable man;
So are they all, all honourable men, –
Come I to speak in Caesar's funeral.
He was my friend, faithful and just to me:
But Brutus says he was ambitious;
And Brutus is an honourable man.
He hath brought many captives home to Rome,
Whose ransoms did the general coffers fill:
Did this in Caesar seem ambitious?
When that the poor have cried, Caesar hath wept:
Ambition should be made of sterner stuff;
Yet Brutus says he was ambitious;
And Brutus is an honourable man.
You all did see that on the Lupercal
I thrice presented him a kingly crown,
Which he did thrice refuse: was this ambition?
Yet Brutus says he was ambitious;
And, sure, he is an honourable man.
I speak not to disprove what Brutus spoke,
But here I am to speak what I do know.
You all did love him once, – not without cause:
What cause withholds you, then, to mourn for him?
O judgment, thou art fled to brutish beasts,
And men have lost their reason! – Bear with me;
My heart is in the coffin there with Caesar,
And I must pause till it come back to me.

■■■■ From William Shakespeare, *Julius Caesar* ■■■■

◄ *This could be used for oral assessment.* ►

● Here is the Department of Trade and Industry check-list of dos and don'ts on 'How to run a firework display safely' to compare with your own lists in answer to questions 2 and 3 on page 142.

CHECK YOUR FINAL ARRANGEMENTS AGAINST THIS LIST

1  Have you told the fire brigade, police and a local first aid organisation early enough about the date and time of display? Have you prepared a drill for calling the emergency services? ☐

2  Have you made sure you have plenty of space, at least 55 m × 45 m (60 yds × 50 yds), within which the fireworks will be let off? Will spectators be kept at least 30 m (32 yds) from the fireworks and have you used a rope or a strong barrier to mark the area? ☐

3  Have you made sure you have plenty of stewards who can be easily identified and that entrances and exits are clearly marked and free from obstruction? ☐

4  Have you made it clear in advance that people are not to bring their own fireworks, and posted notices to this effect at all entrances? ☐

5  Have you provided fire extinguishers, buckets of water, sand and metal litter bins? ☐

6  Have you sited any bonfire well away from the fireworks and fenced it off for the safety of spectators? ☐

7  Have you made sure that people who are lighting fireworks will read in advance and follow carefully both the manufacturers' instructions and this leaflet? ☐

8  Have you made sure that fireworks will be kept in a closed metal or wooden box while other fireworks are burning? ☐

ON THE NIGHT, REMEMBER

1   To light fireworks at arm's length.
2   Never to smoke while handling fireworks.
3   Not to have more than three or four people lighting fireworks.
4   Not to fire rockets or other aerial fireworks over the heads of spectators.
5   Not to allow people to bring their own fireworks.
6   Not to touch a dud firework for at least half an hour, and then hold it well away from your face.
7   Never to use petrol or paraffin to light the bonfire.
8   Not to let children collect spent firework cases when the display has finished.
9   Not to let anybody into the firing display area either before or after the display except those people responsible for lighting the fireworks.
10  To make certain that the bonfire is put out completely and litter bins are emptied.

# Unit Fourteen

# 14.1 Writing – exploring feelings and reactions

Writing which explores feelings and reactions is a form of personal writing in which you can work out where you stand on a particular issue, and which can help you to straighten out your own feelings. Aspects you could consider are:

- ○ how the subject first came to your attention
- ○ whether your feelings about the subject have changed
- ○ how you feel when you encounter someone who holds different views
- ○ whether you have any doubts about the way you feel
- ○ incidents that have strengthened or undermined your attitude.

Try not to write in the abstract. Enliven your writing with examples and evidence, and personal reactions and experiences that have helped to form your views.

● Here is a piece by a 15-year-old pupil in which she works out her feelings about free speech.

# ▬ SPEAKING FREELY ▬

I have often marched out my lungs in demonstrations on behalf of Soviet Jewry. On one particular march, I remember coming to the end and overhearing the latter part of someone's querulous complaint to a policeman. 'Oh well,' he replied tolerantly, 'the kids enjoy it.' Utter deflation: there was I supposedly exercising my power of free speech on behalf of those denied it, but the arm of the law, the ones who were supposed to be so impressed and so agitated as to immediately bash down the Iron Curtain with their truncheons – they simply regarded it as a pleasant afternoon's entertainment for the kids.

That experience made me a bit wary of shouting defiantly about free speech. If you want to know why I march in demonstrations now, it is because I enjoy them.

And yet, suddenly a party has emerged that is not marching out of enjoyment, but out of hate and vindictiveness; a party with the ghost of that German moustache shadowing its face – a menacing face, and therefore more necessary to confront rather than ignore in the hope that it will go away just like that nasty little man eventually did.

The memory of a lone National Front leader marching through a city, surrounded by what may as well have been a halo of policemen, exploiting a democracy that is very precious to me, is part of the reason for this essay.

The rest of the reason is a slightly unmathematical equation. It seems to take an enormous amount of free speech to achieve anything towards the progress of world democracy, but the denial of only the very last little bit of it sends democracy slipping back a long, long almost irretrievable way.

That realisation came to me shortly before I had to admit to myself that I would like to deny the National Front free speech. This essay is about the resultant conflict.

At home I can talk about whatever I want – but there are certain topics that a nice Jewish girl does not discuss at the table. In my family this would include sex and any coarse reference to death, except on a halachic (i.e. in relation to Jewish law) plane. Religion is completely un-taboo, which is a relief as there are many questions that I would not ask outside my home, but which I want to discuss with a group.

I do not mind that others have rejected these values, but I am scared and disturbed by their violation of my guiding principle:

There is only one race: the human race – and we are all in this mess together.

Ultimately, race is the one issue that forced me to define how far I think free speech should go.

It was in school, where free speech seems to be virtually against the rules, that I first had to wrestle with myself over what the limits of free speech should be. When I came into conflict with authority they punished me for being rude. In the background could be heard my protests that my rights of free speech were being abused.

I had to work out whether in fighting to express my views I was extending democracy, or whether habitual argument simply causes a breakdown of society. I could not see anything very democratic about wreaking havoc in my placid secondary school.

But if anyone did want to challenge the system...? Recently a report was published which stated that if children were taught about politics, they might pick up enough information to throw the education establishment into chaos. Therefore, the report concluded, politics should not be on school curriculums.

My instinctual reaction to that was that it would be very beneficial for the ... autocrats to have their ... system challenged. (Free thought's O.K. but when I want to write down what I have thought, I am constrained to use a series of cryptic dashes.) This led me on to wonder why schooling is the one area of life that has not undergone a revolution. Oh I know, teachers are using revolutionary methods (so-called) but there has not been a revolution by the eternally grey student. Furthermore, I thought, it would not be at all a bad thing if – having learnt to invoke the names of Marxism, socialism and occasionally (Young) Conservatism – the school system was disrupted by the students. Visions of a dictatorship of the pupils by the pupils began to fill my mind, but fear not: having once taught me the odd Marxist doctrine, they also made sure that I knew Marx's system never had worked.

Still, a girl can dream...

What exactly would happen if I ever said exactly what I think of the way I am being educated? For a start my teachers would be hurt and insulted. They would call me arrogant, and would in future be greatly on the defensive: in effect, I would achieve nothing. (End of dream). But if, possibly and improbably, they did change their methods because of my dissent, then I would believe that something which was wrong had been put right. I would believe that, not only because their methods had changed, but because SOMEONE HAD BEEN ALLOWED TO SPEAK UP.

However, and this is where I had to struggle with myself, was it still right to speak up even if it would only cause damage? In other words, should free speech be employed in every circumstance, just for its own sake, and because it is so valuable a right? Is it always healthier to allow dissent, simply because by disallowing it the right of free speech is being abused?

What happens in my school is not really important. One day, I shall realise that they were right all the time. But, I am using my school experience as a comparison with the emergence of the National Front, and the dilemma it confronted me with.

Here was the sudden growth of a party, declaring racial enmity at a time when I was, at least in my personal life, completely unaware of such hatred. As the popular appeal of Mrs. Thatcher's remarks on immigration show, the NF have stirred up some perverted form of nationalism in Britain which may one day harm my people and other non-Anglo Saxons. Not only that, but the NF have already hit at my contemporaries and infiltrated schools. It scared me to see the NF youth spokesman, aged 16, speaking on television. His eyes were glazed and his face immobile. If his expression was a result of appearing before cameras, his vicious words could only have been a result of persistent indoctrination. How many more schoolchildren will look like this in 10 years' time?

So, do I want the NF marching through my life?

### NO

But they too are entitled to free speech, even if with that they also become entitled to stir up hatred and corrupt the youth. Why? Because if free speech is denied to them, then who is to say to whom it may not be denied? Who will be the final judge? Who will compose the law that will ban racist groups – and when the law is written, who is to say that it may not be used by the NF, should they or their like ever get into power, against fighters for democracy? What politician will be anxious to pass such a law? Who is to ensure that race does not become just another election issue?

No, the NF must have free speech, even if it is only so that we can always be assured of being able to fight back. Free speech must be allowed at all times for its own sake. That way, there is no possibility that the good guys will be trampled in the rush to beat down the enemy.

**■■■■ Dina Rabinovitch ■■■■**

1  Trace the course that the writer's feelings about free speech take.
2  Comment on the relevance and effectiveness of some of the personal experiences the writer uses in her account.
3  Do you agree with her conclusions?

A piece of writing that explores feelings and reactions can also take the form of a narrative or a dramatisation with action and dialogue. Feelings and reactions are often revealed by what people do and say.

● Here is an account of the feelings of someone at the death of her parents. It was written by a 13-year-old pupil. There is no way of telling whether the piece of writing is based on personal experience or not, but the writer uses the first person and imagines how someone would feel and react in that situation.

# ■■■ AFTER THE FUNERAL ■■■

The beach had always been my favourite place. Perhaps that's why I couldn't go back there for so long afterwards. I didn't want to do any of the things that I had enjoyed doing before the accident. I suppose I was afraid that they might make me happy and I couldn't have coped with that. I couldn't have coped with the guilty aftermath even a momentary ray of happiness might bring.

During all the wretched business, it was the funeral that made the most impression on me. It still revolts me to think of those people, calling themselves my relations, dressed in black and peering at me across the coffins. They were shocked that I didn't cry. If only they'd known the nights I'd spent clutching the sheets, desperately trying to cry, to feel grief. I couldn't. I felt so angry. I hated them, my parents, and the guilt of admitting to that feeling strangled all my other emotions.

Aunt June took me in. She lived in Cornwall. I met her for the first time at the funeral. She wore a black coat, but had on a blue skirt underneath. I liked her for doing that, wearing that skirt.

She wasn't being so piously false as my other 'relations'. God only knows how they would have coped with me if they had had to look after me. I was a real drag. I just drooped around and I seemed to go out of my way to hurt Aunt June. I think, actually, she understood how much I needed to hurt someone. She lost her temper once though and gained my respect in doing so. Later she asked me if I wanted to go back to the house. I said no. She said 'Alex – you'll have to face up to it sometime.' Face what, I asked myself. Me? Or the memory of my parents? I don't know why but after a few days I told her that I did, after all, want to visit the house.

Well, that's how I ended up on the beach. The house was cold and the furniture was covered with sheets. The only room that had remained untouched was mother's studio. She was an artist. She said she was a part-time artist and not a very good one. She taught occupational therapy to people in hospital and she was a very good artist. When I was nine she made me a pen and ink sketch of a seagull. It was very beautiful and I treasured it, but after the funeral I locked it in a drawer and wouldn't look at it.

Aunt June had been assigned to clear the studio and she had set up two camp-beds in there for us to spend the night. We were to sort things out that evening. I was dreading it. I didn't want to have to remember the good times – the memories would hurt too much.

Aunt June was making lunch when I went to the beach. She came out with a hamper and walked towards me. I was annoyed – I had wanted to be alone.

'Thought we'd have a picnic out here. It's a lovely day. Cold, but beautiful.'

I smiled sourly and we unloaded the hamper in silence. I was eating my third sandwich when she said,

'It is better to have loved and lost, than never to have loved at all.'

I choked on my sandwich and looked at her furiously.

'How could they leave me like this? I need them.'

'I know.'

'You don't. No one understands.'

'Oh come on, Alex, I wouldn't have thought you were the type for dramatic scenes.'

I was too livid to find a suitably crushing remark, but I couldn't have said it if I'd found one, for she said gently,

'Who do you hate, Alex, them or yourself?'

'Both,' I replied miserably.

She waited.

'I was partly responsible you know. If I hadn't insisted on going to that stupid party, they wouldn't have had to pick me up and then it wouldn't have happened.'

Aunt June remained silent for a minute. She seemed to be weighing something up in her mind. Eventually she said,

'Dear Alex, don't you think you want to feel responsible for their deaths?'

I looked at her sharply.

'I mean that it is a fact that human beings need to be needed. I think that since your parents' death you've realised just how much you really needed them and you want to feel that they needed you as much, but you have a suspicion that maybe they didn't. So, to compensate, you make yourself feel responsible for their deaths, to make yourself feel that you influenced them and that they needed you.'

She stopped speaking for a minute and looked at me but I made no comment. To be quite honest, I was rather shattered that someone should be doing such a quick job of psychoanalysing me. Perhaps because she was not involved in my life, she could take a clear unbiased look at me.

She carried on. 'You see, Alex, you can't reverse the inbuilt roles of parent and child, or at least, not until you yourself become a parent. As a child your need for your parents was the basis of your love for them. Now you're older and you start to question their love for you, but you've been comparing it on the same scale as your love for them. Well, I'm afraid you can't do that. There are so many different kinds of love, but they do love you, because you are you and also a part of them. You've also got to accept that most human beings have a good degree of independence in them. A child could not survive without its mother, whereas it would be very dangerous for there to be that degree of need in adult relationship.'

I couldn't help seeing her point, but I wasn't giving in so easily.

'I'm still partly responsible though.'

Her answer surprised me.

'Yes you are. People do a lot of things they wouldn't do if it weren't for other people. You do have to learn to take the responsibility of having an influence on other people, but you cannot and must not take full responsibility for a person's actions. That would diminish their own ability to make decisions for themselves, which would, in the long run, harm their personality.'

She looked at me and laughed.

'I'm confusing you. Let me tell you a true story. When your mother was seventeen and I was sixteen we had a holiday in Greece. We all thought it was lovely but your mother was especially impressed. Some time after the holiday a friend wanted to go on holiday abroad, but she didn't know where to go. Your mother immediately suggested that part of Greece. The friend went and, to cut a long story short, was killed there, diving. Your mother spent weeks in a depressed state for the girl's death. Now do you see?'

I did.

'You mean,' I said, 'that although it was mum's influence that made the friend go to Greece, mum wasn't actually responsible for her death.'

'Yes, that's exactly it.'

I felt as though a light had been switched on in front of my eyes and although I was rather dazzled at first, I saw a lot of things that had previously been hidden in the shadows.

Later that evening I came upon a box with some books belonging to my father, and one of my mother's paintings, of the beach in winter. I stared at them for a long time and then, painfully at first, I began to cry.

■■■■■■■■ Frances Jennifer Tyler ■■■■■

4  Describe the mixture of feelings that Alex experiences at the funeral.
5  How does Aunt Jane 'explain' Alex's feelings and help her to come to terms with them? Do you find this convincing?
6  What part do places – the beach, the house – play in this account?
7  'I began to cry.' What does this action tell you about Alex's feelings?

## 14.1.1 Exploring feelings and reactions – coursework

Explore your feelings and reactions about one of the following subjects:

1  An occasion or occasions when you felt happy
2  An occasion or occasions when you felt left out of things
3  Yourself when you were in the first year of your secondary school
4  'My brother and I' or 'My sister and I'
5  Religion and religious experience
6  Old people and growing old
7  The future for yourself and for society
8  'Everyone has the right to work'.

# 14.2 Writing – using language to achieve effects

Words can be plain and factual, or they can be powerful and evocative. The purpose of your writing and your audience will determine which kind of word you choose and how you put these words together. Sometimes simple words and a direct statement will be effective. At other times richer words and more complex sentence structures will be effective.

Think about how you use the following:

*Adjectives* These can give precision and interest to what you are describing. For example:

the dark **gloomy** house

*Adverbs* These can help to define an action or a mood more clearly. For example:

He walked away **despondently**.

*Verbs* Choosing the right verb can give a greater vitality and precision to an action. Compare:

He **went** into the room.
He **burst** into the room.
He **sidled** into the room.

*Active and passive* Using a passive verb tends to be more formal and stilted. For example:

All candidates **are required** to sign their names.
Jack **was punched** in the face by Tom.

Using an active verb tends to be more immediate and less formal. For example:

All candidates **should sign** their names.
Tom **punched** Jack in the face.

*Figurative language* See section 10.3 and Appendix F.

*Sentence structure* See section 5.3 and 10.5 and Appendix B.

A part of sentence structure is the *sentence pattern*:

○ Repeating the same pattern of sentence can give emphasis and greater impact. For example:

You need to study your spelling. You need to study your punctuation. You need to study your sentence structure.

○ A question in the middle of a series of statements can jolt the reader into thought. For example:

This is a bad policy. Who in his right mind would vote for it? It is bound to fail.

○ A sentence carefully balanced in two halves could make two points or a contrast clearer. For example:

Some people feel that reducing inflation is the first priority while others regard reducing unemployment as the most important thing.

○ Holding back the most important point in your sentence until the end can give it emphasis. For example:

Everyone knows that this is what we must do – reduce unemployment.

○ An introductory statement can prepare the reader for the ideas that follow. For example:

There are three things that need to be done: unemployment must be reduced, inflation must be kept under control, and Britain must regain its rightful place in the world again.

1 Consider the following four passages. What effect is each trying to achieve? How does the way language is used help to achieve that effect?

## A

We shall defend our Island, whatever the cost may be. We shall fight on the beaches, we shall fight on the landing-grounds, we shall fight in the fields and in the streets, we shall fight in the hills; we shall never surrender.

Winston Churchill, in a radio broadcast during the Second World War

## B

Doolittle, a dustman, has discovered that his daughter is living in the same house as two gentlemen. He suspects the worst, but is quite happy to accept the situation in return for a reasonable payment. (Please note that Shaw's original punctuation has been retained in this passage.)

DOOLITTLE: What am I, Governors both? I ask you, what am I? I'm one of the undeserving poor: thats what I am. Think of what that means to a man. It means that he's up agen middle class morality all the time. If theres anything going, and I put in for a bit of it, it's always the same story: 'Youre undeserving; so you cant have it.' But my needs is as great as the most deserving widow's that ever got money out of six different charities in one week for the death of the same husband. I dont need less than a deserving man: I need more. I dont eat less hearty than him; and I drink a lot more. I want a bit of amusement, cause I'm a thinking man. I want cheerfulness and a song and a band when I feel low. Well, they charge me just the same for everything as they charge the deserving. What is middle class morality? Just an excuse for never giving me anything. Therefore I ask you, as two gentlemen, not to play that game on me. I'm playing straight with you. I aint pretending to be deserving. I'm undeserving; and I mean to go on being undeserving. I like it; and thats the truth. Will you take advantage of a man's nature to do him out of the price of his own daughter what he's brought up and fed and clothed by the sweat of his brow until she's growed big enough to be interesting to you two gentlemen? Is five pounds unreasonable? I put it to you; and I leave it to you.

■ From George Bernard Shaw, *Pygmalion* ■

**C**

Yes, the newspapers were right: snow was general all over Ireland. It was falling on every part of the dark central plain, on the treeless hills, falling softly upon the Bog of Allen and, farther westward, softly falling into the dark mutinous Shannon waves. It was falling, too, upon every part of the lonely churchyard on the hill where Michael Fury lay buried. It lay thickly drifted on the crooked crosses and headstones, on the spears of the little gate, on the barren thorns. His soul swooned slowly as he heard the snow falling faintly through the universe and faintly falling, like the descent of their last end, upon all the living and the dead.

■ From James Joyce, *Dubliners* ■

**D**

There are no frowns or scowls or sudden rages in the colour supplements. Everyone is perpetually smiling. Smiling lips disclose smiling teeth; all the exquisite, flimsy lingerie, one feels, enfolds a tender, loving smile. A smiling, smiling world. Old age only exists in the lined and seasoned faces of peasants in national costume; death loses its sting on the way through a lens. Colour supplement frost does not chill, nor colour supplement sun scorch. Colour supplement wars are far, far away; in Vietnam or the borders of Tibet.

From Malcolm Muggeridge, *Life in a Colour Supplement*

2  Write a short paragraph in which adjectives play an important part in achieving the effect you want.
3  Write some sentences in which adverbs are used effectively.
4  Write two short paragraphs, one using passive verbs, and the other using active verbs. Comment on the difference in effect between them.
5  Look at the following sentences:
   a She went home.
   b He spoke.
   c She looked at him.
   For each of them, give as many different versions as you can that use more interesting and precise verbs.
6  Write down five sentences each of which is constructed in a different way. Explain the effect of the construction in each case.

# 14.3 Reading – identifying, illustrating and commenting on significant features of a text.

The many examples of writing included in this book illustrate the tremendous variety of forms that written English can take. The differences between them depend on the attitude, approach and style of the individual writers, the purpose of the writing, and the intended audience. By now, you ought to be able to distinguish between one kind of writing and another, and be able to identify, illustrate and comment on the significant features of a text. In doing this you can assess whether the writer has something worthwhile to say and whether it is being said effectively.

● Read the following extract.

It was a cold white day in High Street, and nothing to stop the wind slicing up from the docks, for where the squat and tall shops had shielded the town from the sea lay their blitzed flat graves marbled with snow and headstoned with fences. Dogs, delicate as cats on water, as though they had gloves on their paws, padded over the vanished buildings. Boys romped, calling high and clear, on top of a levelled chemist's and a shoe-shop, and a little girl, wearing a man's cap, threw a snowball in a chill deserted garden that had once been the Jug and Bottle of the Prince of Wales. The wind cut up the street with a soft sea-noise hanging on its arm, like a hooter in a muffler. I could see the swathed hill stepping up out of the town, which you never could see properly before, and the powdered fields of the roofs of Milton Terrace and Watkin Street and Fullers Row. Fish-frailed, net-bagged, umbrella'd, pixie-capped, fur-shoed, blue-nosed, puce-lipped, blinkered like drayhorses, scarved, mittened, galoshed, wearing everything but the cat's blanket, crushes of shopping-women crunched in the little Lapland of the once grey drab street, blew and queued and yearned for hot tea, as I began my search through Swansea town cold and early on that wicked February morning. I went into the hotel. 'Good morning.'

The hall-porter did not answer. I was just another snowman to him. He did not know that I was looking for someone after fourteen years, and he did not care. He stood and shuddered, staring through the glass of the hotel door at the snowflakes sailing down the sky, like Siberian confetti.

■ From Dylan Thomas, *Return Journey* ■

1 Look at the way the writer uses adjectives and the effect they have.
2 Look at the way the writer uses hyphenated words. What effect do they have?
3 Pick out some of the examples of figurative language and comment on their effectiveness.
4 Pick out some instances where the writer treats non-human things as though they were human. Why do you think he does this?
5 Pick out some examples of descriptive detail that you think are particularly apt or striking or amusing.
6 Compare the sentence structure of the first paragraph with that of the second. Can you account for the difference? What is the writer trying to do in the first paragraph compared with the second paragraph?
7 What kind of mood is the writer trying to create?
8 Identify the main features of this piece of writing. Illustrate them. Comment on how effective they are in helping the writer to say what he wants to say.

That is the kind of process you go through when you are studying a piece of writing. You examine things like:

○ the language
○ the sentence structure
○ the paragraphing
○ the tone
○ the purpose
○ the audience.

Significant features of the extract from 'Return Journey' are the use of figurative language and adjectives. Sometimes adjectives are piled on top of each other to create a rich and comic profusion. A feature of the first paragraph is the use of long sentences which allow the writer to add detail to detail to fill out his description as he turns from one aspect of the scene to another. In the second paragraph, the sentences are shorter. The writer has moved into action, and the short sentences help to illustrate this change and dramatise it.

The main purpose of the writing is descriptive, to create a picture of the scene in the reader's mind. This is achieved by the writer's use of exuberant language – the adjectives, the hyphenated words one after another, the descriptive phrases, the metaphors and similes. The use of 'active' words adds to the vitality of the scene, bringing it to life – words like 'slicing', 'padded', 'romped', 'threw', 'cut up', etc. – as well as the way the writer personifies the wind and the hills. The scene is enlivened by the way dogs, boys, a little girl, shopping-women are picked out and described with telling detail and amusing or striking comparisons. The whole piece gives the impression that the writer enjoys using words, playing with them, using the sound of them to make effects, getting the right ones, creating unexpected impressions with them, surprising and amusing the reader.

● Identify, illustrate and comment on the significant features of the following:

## A

I guess looking at it, now, my old man was cut out for a fat guy, one of those regular little roly fat guys you see around, but he sure never got that way, except a little toward the last, and then it wasn't his fault, he was riding over the jumps only and he could afford to carry plenty of weight then. I remember the way he'd pull on a rubber shirt over a couple of jerseys and a big sweat shirt over that, and get me to run with him in the forenoon in the hot sun. He'd have, maybe, taken a trial trip with one of Razzo's skins early in the morning after just getting in from Torino at four o'clock in the morning and beating it out to the stables in a cab and then with the dew all over everything and the sun just starting to get going, I'd help him pull off his boots and he'd get into a pair of sneakers and all these sweaters and we'd start out.

'Come on, kid,' he'd say, stepping up and down on his toes in front of the jocks' dressing-room, 'let's get moving.'

■ From Ernest Hemingway, *My Old Man* ■

## B

The season of strikes seemed to have run itself to a standstill. Almost every trade and industry and calling in which a dislocation could possibly be engineered had indulged in that luxury. The last and least successful convulsion had been the strike of the World's Union of Zoological Garden attendants, who, pending the settlement of certain demands, refused to minister further to the wants of the animals committed to their charge or to allow any other keepers to take their place. In this case the threat of the Zoological Gardens authorities that if the men 'came out' the animals should come out also had intensified and precipitated the crisis. This imminent prospect of the larger carnivores, to say nothing of rhinoceroses and bull bison, roaming at large and unfed in the heart of London, was not one which permitted of prolonged conferences. The Government of the day, which from its tendency to be a few hours behind the course of events had been nicknamed the Government of the afternoon, was obliged to intervene with promptitude and decision. A strong force of Blue-jackets was despatched to Regent's Park to take over the temporarily abandoned duties of the strikers. Blue-jackets were chosen in preference to land forces, partly on account of the traditional readiness of the British Navy to go anywhere and do anything, partly by reason of the familiarity of the average sailor with monkeys, parrots, and other tropical fauna, but chiefly at the urgent request of the First Lord of the Admiralty, who was keenly desirous of an opportunity for performing some personal act of unobtrusive public service within the province of his department.

■ From Saki, *The Unkindest Blow* ■

## C

### SHE POPS HOME

She pops home just long enough

> to overload the washing machine
> to spend a couple of hours on the phone
> to spray the bathroom mirror with lacquer
> to kick the stair-carpet out of line
> to say 'that's new – can I borrow it?'

She pops home just long enough

> to dust the aspidistra with her elbow
> to squeak her hand down the bannister
> to use the last of the toilet roll
> to leave her bite in the last apple

She pops home just long enough

> to raid her mother's drawer for tights
> to stock up with next month's pill
> to hug a tenner out of Dad

She pops home just long enough

> to horrify them with her irresponsibility
> to leave them sweating till next time.

She pops home just long enough

> to light their pond like a kingfisher

She pops home just long enough

Cal Clothier

## D

THE TELEVISION EQUIPMENT (herein referred to as the Equipment) shall remain the sole and absolute property of the Owners and the Renter shall not sell, assign, pledge, underlet, lend or otherwise deal with or part with possession of the Equipment and shall not without the Owners' consent remove the Equipment from the installation address set out overleaf or from such other address as the Owners may from time to time consent to and will protect the Equipment against distress, execution, poinding, landlord's sequestration and any manner of seizure and indemnify the Owners against all losses, costs, charges, damages and expenses incurred by the Owners by reason of or in respect thereof.

## E

# Princess soaks up the sun in Spain

From HARRY ARNOLD in Majorca

CAREFREE Princess Di grabs her chance to soak up the sunshine after arriving on holiday in Majorca with her family.

The swimsuit Princess relaxed yesterday during a peaceful cruise around Palm Bay on a yacht belonging to King Juan Carlos of Spain.

She chatted and laughed with two royal pals—the King's wife Queen Sophia and Princess Irene of Greece. Diana joined the yacht with Prince Charles and their young sons William and Harry soon after flying into Palma yesterday morning.

### RULE

The four royals all travelled on the same plane for the first time to cut costs—sparking off a safety row.

Their journey broke the rule that direct heirs to the throne should not fly together.

*If the Hawker Siddeley 146 had crashed or been shot down, the three next in line to the throne could have been killed.*

Prince Andrew and new bride Fergie would then have been next in line to be King and Queen.

Royalty expert Harold Brooks-Baker slammed it as "unbelievably imprudent."

*The Sun*

# 14.4 Reading – audience appeal and advertising

An area where success or failure depends on getting the sense of audience right is advertising. A good advertising campaign can make all the difference to the sale of a product.

Not everyone approves of advertising. Here are some questions to think about:

1 Is it fair to say that advertising persuades people to buy things they don't need?
2 Does advertising create a sense of envy and deprivation in people who can't afford to buy the products advertised?
3 Is it 'immoral' that millions of pounds should be spent on advertising while millions of people starve?
4 Can advertising be described as 'opinions and assertive statements masquerading as facts'?
5 Is it true that most advertisements appeal to 'unadmirable' aspects of human emotions such as greed, snobbery, envy, fear, insecurity, sex, pride, 'keeping up with the Joneses', being one of the 'in-group', showing off? Can you give examples of all of these?
6 Can you give examples that appeal to a sense of humour?
7 Is it true that the consumer has to pay for advertising?
8 What points can you find in favour of advertising?
9 Have you ever been persuaded to buy something by an advertisement?

When considering an advertisement, you have to look at the following:

o Design, layout and visual appeal (How does it catch your interest?)
o Use of headlines (Do they capture the attention through a dramatic statement or a play on words or humour or paradox?)
o The language and tone used (Is it formal or informal? Why? What effect is intended?)
o Content (How much hard information about the product is given? Are claims supported by evidence?)
o Emotional appeal (Is an indirect, or underhand, appeal being made to greed, envy, snobbery, fear, insecurity, sex, pride, 'keeping up with the Joneses', being one of the 'in-group', showing off?).

1 How effective do you think the following headlines and slogans are?

a A flock of flights. A pride of staff. No herds. (Air France)

b No room for passengers. (RAF Officer)

c Now, a shower with real power. (British Gas)

d Everything is compact except the sound. (Ferguson)

e You'll leave Spain far richer than when you arrived. (Spanish Tourist Board)

f It costs more to get to Mauritius than any other tropical paradise. (Thank goodness.) (Mauritius Tourist Board)

g Stripped, rubbed down and ready for anything. (Black and Decker)

h It's a pussycat until you step on it. (Peugeot 205 GTI)

i When villains start working 9 to 5, so will we. (Metropolitan Police)

j The new Toyota Supra. Even stationary it has the power to move you. (Toyota)

**2** Compare these two advertisements for car phones. Would you say that one is 'better' or 'more successful' than the other, or are they appealing to different sections of the public? Consider headlines, language and tone, content, design, appeal.

**━━━━━ A ━━━━━**

TO: SECURICOR COMMUNICATIONS, AMBASSADOR HOUSE, BRIGSTOCK ROAD, THORNTON HEATH, SURREY CR4 8YL.

NAME_____

ADDRESS_____

_____

POST CODE_____ TEL No_____

MORE INFORMATION ☐

FREE DEMONSTRATION ☐

APPROVED for connection to telecommunication systems specified in the instructions for use subject to the conditions set out in them

DM 7/86

# IF YOU WANT A CAR PHONE FROM A COMPANY YOU CAN TRUST, CUT OUT THE COWBOY.

These days all sorts of people want to sell you a car phone. On the cheap. No questions asked. But when you buy mobile communications from Securicor you're buying more than just a product. You're buying a service. You're buying experience. You're buying something that's tried and trusted. Ask one of our security officers. His mobile radio isn't there for show.

That's why at Securicor we have to know what we're doing. We've been handling mobile communications for over 20 years (that's 20 years more than most) and we have one of the largest mobile radio networks in Europe.

We also have the facilities to match it. An extensive range of cellular equipment (car phones, portables and transportables), experts to install them and a nationwide servicing network of over 50 workshops.

So before you choose a mobile phone, imagine yourself in a 999 situation. Then ask yourself which one you'd trust when it matters. For further information clip the coupon or call London 01-627 2052, Birmingham 021-525 1771, Manchester 061-834 9640.

**SECURICOR** COMMUNICATIONS

**EVERY DAY WE TRUST OUR SAFETY TO MOBILE COMMUNICATIONS.**

**B**

# Have you ever thought the man in the next car could be stealing your business?

You know how it is when you see someone on the phone in a car.

Who is he talking to? What is he talking about?

You can bet your shirt he's not passing the time of day chatting up his mother-in-law.

Nor is he sitting there boasting he's got one of those swanky new Cellphones.

No, the odds are he's stealing

a march on one of his competitors. That frustrated fellow after the same piece of business as he is, also stuck in a traffic jam not getting anywhere fast. You, perhaps?

There is only one way out of this unfortunate situation, and that is to get a Cellphone yourself.

Then you'll be too busy pulling off your own deals to worry what the chap in the next car's up to.

Buying, or leasing, a British Telecom Cellphone is particularly painless.

Prices start at £899* (leasing, from around 75p a day*). Not much compared to the immediate advantage of being able to carry on business from the car.

The system works just like an ordinary telephone, which means you can call almost anywhere in the world without having to go through an operator.

You can even 'store' up to thirty long international numbers for quick, safe two-digit dialling.

It has been calculated that a businessman travelling 25,000 miles a year spends on average five hundred hours in the car.**

That is the equivalent of sixty-two and a half eight hour days, or, put it another way, no less than twelve and a half forty hour working weeks.

No wonder so many are fitting and using a British Telecom Cellphone.

How much longer can you afford to be without one?

To discover more of the business advantages of Cellnet and the wide range of British Telecom car, portable and pocket-size Cellphones, call us on 01-730 0899. Or send the coupon.

**British Telecom Cellphones get business moving.**

To British Telecom Mobile Communications, FREEPOST, London NW1 7YS. I would like more information about the British Telecom range of Cellphones.

Name_____

Position_____

Business_____

Address_____

_____ Postcode_____

Telephone_____

*List price and approximate daily cost based on 5 year lease. (Excludes installation charges, standing charge for Cellnet system, call charges and V.A.T.)  **At overall average speed of 50 mph.

3   Analyse the following two advertisements.

**━━━━━━━━━━━━━━━━ A ━━━━━━━━━━━━━━━━**

# If men had a taste of what most women do, they'd soon be looking into a Creda.

Eric Bristow is more used to rolling out the barrel than hanging out the washing.

So, if he had to do his own shirts he'd certainly be looking for all the help he could get.

Like the Creda Supertron; a washing machine that's so smart, handwashing becomes a thing of the past (despite what it says on his garment labels).

It also has an exceptionally fast spin speed which results in clothes coming out that much drier.

However, in order to avoid having to wait for the weather to finish drying his washing, what he needs is a Creda Tumble Dryer.

The ingenious action of the Reversair, for instance, will not only get his clothes airing cupboard fresh, it will actually help with the ironing by reducing creasing.

Every Creda machine comes with a full five year parts guarantee and is British made to the highest possible design standards.

He'll even discover a special switch on the Supertron, that allows him to take care of the washing while he's.....well......playing darts.

It's hardly any wonder they call him the Crafty Cockney.

**Creda**
Science for womankind.

BUY A CREDA MODEL AT AGRI, APOLLO, COMET, CO-OPS, CURRYS, JOHN LEWIS, MILLER BROTHERS, POWER CITY, RUMBELOWS, TIGER, VALLANCES.   TI CREDA LTD, PR (OM/2), BLYTHE BRIDGE, STOKE ON TRENT, STAFFORDSHIRE ST11 9LJ

**B**

# Spend an evening with us.
# (It won't kill you.)

We joke about playing soldiers and all that rot. But the fact is, we're a lethal bunch. We need to be.

In the event of things getting sticky on the international front, the Territorial Army would form at least a third of the Army's strength. Apart from being an important contribution to the country's security, we have a hell of a lot of fun.

Every year we go off together for a two week camp, which could be abroad. We also meet annually for a course on the firing range.

Between times we do six weekends a year out in the field training. On top of this we put in a few evenings a month preparing.

The pay isn't breathtaking. It starts at £850 pa and goes up with your rank and the amount of extra time you spend with us.

You'll notice we're variously dressed and equipped. But the picture represents the tip of the iceberg.

There are twenty eight regiments in the London T.A. Between them they cover just about every job in the Army.

If you'd like to get the whole picture, send the coupon for an illustrated booklet. And then take up our invitation and pop along to your local T.A. for an evening to get the feel first hand.

You'll find us at fifty seven locations around London. So you won't have a route march to get there.

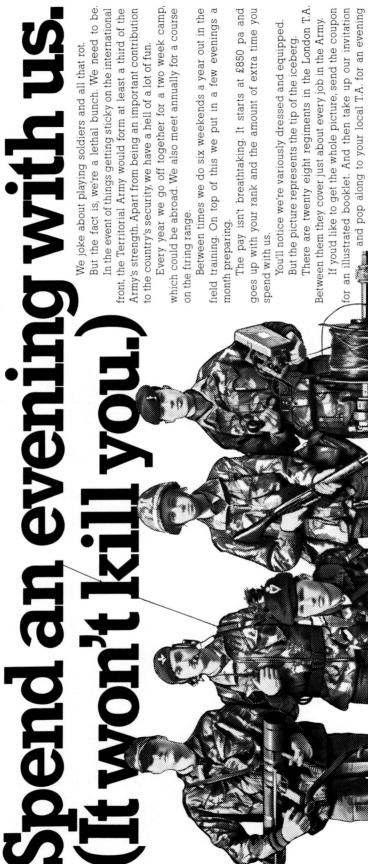

For further details of London's T.A. complete the coupon and post it to Major Charles Knight. Duke Of York's HQ Kings Rd. Chelsea, London SW3 4RY. ring 01-730 8138 any time day or night or contact your nearest Army Careers Information Office (in the telephone book under 'Army').

Name

Address

Tel.                              Age

State Regiment/Corps preferred (if known)

## London's Territorial Army.

# 14.5 Oral communication – describing an event or a process

Clearly the description of an event could be more personal than the description of a process. When describing an event, you are trying to get over to your listeners what it was like to be there and to experience. You could describe the atmosphere and your own feelings. You could use more vivid language and descriptive detail to get over your impressions.

A description of a process would probably be more factual. You would be more concerned with getting the details correct and making the process clear to your listeners than with giving an exciting and vivid account. There would be less opportunity for personal involvement. This could have an effect on the kind of tone and language you use. A description of a process is likely to be more formal.

● Study the following description of an earthquake in Peru given on radio by Marian Cook.

We were on a 62,000 mile world trip. We set out in a Landrover and we were now in South America, hitchhiking round the place. And we are both very fond of mountains. We were going into the mountains, north of Lima in Peru, to see the beautiful scenery there, and to see the Indian villagers (these are the descendants of the Incas) and they are a fascinating people. They are a charming people. And we wanted to spend about a week walking round the countryside there.

So it was a beautiful peaceful day, and we'd hitchhiked right up in a very high valley. We were driving along this valley now in a collective taxi . . . and with about sixteen Indians in the taxi . . . and Robin White and myself, the only two Europeans. It was a perfectly peaceful day . . . the birds were singing . . . we were passing through little green fields of maize, and little villages with Spanish red tiles on the roofs. And then just suddenly, out of the blue, with no warning, 3.25 p.m. it was, and somebody exclaimed, and we looked across the valley – we were in this very steep gorge – we looked across the other side of the river, and we saw rocks falling down the wall. But then something caught my eye, and I looked behind and I saw rocks pouring down our side, as well. And then everybody yelled: 'Terremoto, terremoto!' And it was an earthquake.

The driver didn't panic, he was very good. He stopped the car, and you, suddenly, you know, you couldn't see a thing. It was just a thick cloud of yellow dust and the whole of the world was just obliterated, you couldn't see anything. There was a tremendous roaring sound, a fantastic roar – it sort of filled your ears – and rocks came crashing down everywhere, you could just hear it you know. And so I covered my head with my handbag, and the Indians were all crossing themselves, and calling on the saints, and wailing, and rocks kept striking the roof. And we thought – I thought – my number was up. I thought that the road would simply slip hundreds of feet down to the river, and that we would just tumble over and over with it. But the earthquake itself only lasted about a minute, but it must have taken about five minutes for the actual rock fall to abate sufficiently for us to get out and look around. And it was incredible. We were so lucky. It was just a miracle that we're alive to tell the tale. Immediately behind where we'd gone round a sharp bend in the gorge and over a waterfall, the whole wall was completely broken, and it had gone straight down to the river. You couldn't see the road. Just the little bit in between was all right.

We were going on to Huaraz, and we thought, well there's been this earthquake, we didn't realize the full extent of it, we didn't know then it extended for hundreds of miles, and it was the biggest natural disaster in the whole of South American history. We decided that the best thing to do was to go north to Huaraz, as we had intended, because it was very much bigger than the previous little village. So we started walking towards Huaraz: we were about seven miles south of it. There was a road, sometimes it was blocked for maybe fifty yards or more. We'd have to climb over great falls of rock and earth, and dust and great chunks of broken fleshy cactus, and things like this. Whole trees had fallen down, we'd be climbing over everything, and the wind was blowing stones and dirt down still. You had to watch and wait, you know, and go across when it was safe. And then people would run across.

But when it got to nightfall, which came very early there, about six, we decided it would be too risky and foolhardy to try to continue over these obstacles to Huaraz in the dark. It would just invite disaster, you know. So we stayed in a little shop in a tiny village, a little hamlet, just a few houses. We spent the night there, and then we thought well, supposing Huaraz is badly damaged – everybody said it was damaged, they said: 'Huaraz no hay: Pampa no más.'(It doesn't exist any more, you know, it's flattened.) We couldn't believe this, because 55,000 people lived there, and how could a place that size be non-existent just like that, you know, in a minute?

When we got there, it looked as though an atom bomb had struck it. It was just as they said.

Marion Cook, talk on 'Speak',
BBC Schools Radio

1 What things would you point to to show that this is spoken language? What effect does this have on 'the feel' of the piece?
2 Is the first section of this account, up to 'little villages with Spanish red tiles on the roofs', irrelevant or does it serve a purpose?

3 Pick out some of the details the speaker gives which help to make her account more vivid.
4 How much do personal feelings and reactions play in this description of an event? Are personal feelings and reactions appropriate in this case?

● The following is a description of how coal was mined in the 1930s. It is an extract from the book *The Road to Wigan Pier* by George Orwell.

When you have been down two or three pits you begin to get some grasp of the processes that are going on underground. (I ought to say, by the way, that I know nothing whatever about the technical side of mining: I am merely describing what I have seen.) Coal lies in thin seams between enormous layers of rock, so that essentially the process of getting it out is like scooping the central layer from a Neapolitan ice. In the old days the miners used to cut straight into the coal with pick and crowbar – a very slow job because coal, when lying in its virgin state, is almost as hard as rock. Nowadays the preliminary work is done by an electrically-driven coal-cutter, which in principle is an immensely tough and powerful band-saw, running horizontally instead of vertically, with teeth a couple of inches long and half an inch or an inch thick. It can move backwards or forwards on its own power, and the men operating it can rotate it this way and that. Incidentally it makes one of the most awful noises I have ever heard, and sends forth clouds of coal dust which make it impossible to see more than two or three feet and almost impossible to breathe. The machine travels along the coal face cutting into the base of the coal and undermining it to the depth of five feet or five feet and a half; after this it is comparatively easy to extract the coal to the depth to which it has been undermined. Where it is 'difficult getting', however, it has also to be loosened with explosives. A man with an electric drill, like a rather smaller version of the drills used in street-mending, bores holes at intervals in the coal, inserts blasting powder, plugs it with clay, goes round the corner if there is one handy (he is supposed to retire to twenty-five yards distance) and touches off the charge with an electric current. This is not intended to bring the coal out, only to loosen it. Occasionally, of course, the charge is too powerful, and then it not only brings the coal out but brings the roof down as well.

After the blasting has been done the 'fillers' can tumble the coal out, break it up and shovel it on to the conveyor belt. It comes out at first in monstrous boulders which may weigh anything up to twenty tons. The conveyor belt shoots it on to tubs, and the tubs are shoved into the main road and hitched on to an endlessly revolving steel cable which drags them to the cage. Then they are hoisted, and at the surface the coal is sorted by being run over screens, and if necessary is washed as well. As far as possible the 'dirt' – the shale, that is – is used for making the roads below. All that cannot be used is sent to the surface and dumped; hence the monstrous 'dirt-heaps', like hideous grey mountains, which are the characteristic

scenery of the coal areas. When the coal has been extracted to the depth to which the machine has cut, the coal face has advanced by five feet. Fresh props are put in to hold up the newly exposed roof, and during the next shift the conveyor belt is taken to pieces, moved five feet forward and re-assembled. As far as possible the three operations of cutting, blasting and extraction are done in three separate shifts, the cutting in the afternoon, the blasting at night (there is a law, not always kept, that forbids its being done when there are other men working near by), and the 'filling' in the morning shift, which lasts from six in the morning until half past one.

Even when you watch the process of coal-extraction you probably only watch it for a short time, and it is not until you begin making a few calculations that you realise what a stupendous task the 'fillers' are performing. Normally each man has to clear a space four or five yards wide. The cutter has undermined the coal to the depth of five feet, so that if the seam of coal is three or four feet high, each man has to cut out, break up and load on to the belt something between seven and twelve cubic yards of coal. This is to say, taking a cubic yard as weighing twenty-seven hundredweight, that each man is shifting coal at a speed approaching two tons an hour. I have just enough experience of pick and shovel work to be able to grasp what this means. When I am digging trenches in my garden, if I shift two tons of earth during the afternoon, I feel that I have earned my tea. But earth is tractable stuff compared with coal, and I don't have to work kneeling down, a thousand feet underground, in suffocating heat and swallowing coal dust with every breath I take; nor do I have to walk a mile bent double before I begin. The miner's job would be as much beyond my power as it would be to perform on the flying trapeze or to win the Grand National. I am not a manual labourer and please God I never shall be one, but there are some kinds of manual work that I could do if I had to. At a pitch I could be a tolerable road-sweeper or an inefficient gardener or even a tenth-rate farm hand. But by no conceivable amount of effort or training could I become a coal-miner; the work would kill me in a few weeks.

■ From George Orwell, *The Road to Wigan Pier* ■

5 Describe the tone and language used here.
6 Do you think this account could be effectively spoken, or would it have to be modified?
7 Comment on some of the comparisons Orwell uses to make his description clearer.
8 To what extent is this account factual and to what extent is it personal?
9 Point out where Orwell brings in his own feelings and experience. Do they add to the description of what mining coal was like?
10 How easy would it be to extract the basic facts about the way coal was mined from this account? Try to do it and compare your version with Orwell's. What is gained and/or lost?

● Here are some suggestions for describing an event:

1  An outing. It could be with family, school or friends.
2  A historic day. Describe an event of national significance such as a royal occasion, an election or a demonstration.
3  Bad weather. Describe an occasion when bad weather has seriously affected where you live. You may have been flooded or snowed up.
4  A school event. It could be a speech day or a school match or a school fête.
5  A red-letter day.

● Here are some suggestions for describing a process:

6  How to use a machine, for instance a sewing machine or a pocket calculator or a motorbike.
7  How something is manufactured or produced. It could be beer or cars or newspapers.
8  Give an account of a piece of music or a play from first rehearsals to final performance.
9  Give an account of a scientific experiment.
10  Give an account of how democracy works. You could limit yourself to your school or your local authority or the parliamentary system.

◄   *This could be used for oral assessment.*   ►

# 15.1 Writing about actual and imagined experience

Throughout this course you have had many opportunities for writing in a wide variety of styles and situations – personal experience, stories, expressing points of view, writing formal and informal letters, and so on. It is not expected that every pupil will be equally proficient in all these kinds of writing. By now, you should have gained some impression of where your strengths as a writer lie and which kinds of writing you can handle best.

Look back at the writing you have done over the past eighteen months or so. Divide it into different kinds of writing. Which kinds are you best at?

One area where you are required to show competence is in writing about real and imagined experience. The categories themselves are clear enough. Real experience consists of things that have actually happened. They may be things that have happened to you or things you have observed or been involved in. With imagined experience, you invent a situation or a series of events, or you put yourself in the place of a particular character and try to think, feel and act like that character.

In a sense, whether you are writing about actual or imagined experience, you are trying to achieve the same effect. In writing about actual experience, you are trying to recreate something that happened, to make it as fresh as it was to you at the time. In writing about imagined experience, you want the reader to accept what you invent as though it were real.

● Look at these three pieces of writing about fights. Is there any way you can tell which is describing actual experience and which is describing imagined experience?

## A

Johnny, for the first time, hoped that the hour ending school would take a long time to come. He could slip away on the way home, but he knew that he must stand by the boy who had stood up for him. There was no escape from having to watch these three fellows pounding each other's faces. He hoped that someone would come forward and make peace; or, that somehow, Slogan would hear of it, and prevent the fight. Too soon he saw the head boy of each class collecting the books, and knew that the school for that day was nearly done. The boys brought the books up to an assistant teacher who piled them back in the press, and shut and locked the door. He saw the boys returning to their places to sit down or stand up, waiting tensely for the word of dismissal. He saw the sun shining on the bald part of Slogan's head as he bent over a book, made a mark, shut it with a sharp movement, and put it aside. He saw him stand up, and give the signal for the parting prayer. There was a shuffling noise as the boys went down on their knees. Johnny heard Slogan tell some boy to fold his hands and close his eyes, and then the prayer came booming over the quiet school, asking that all done that day might sink deeply into the young innocent hearts gathered together, and bring forth fruit to the boys' good and the glory of God's holy name, Amen.

There was a loud shuffle of feet as the boys hurriedly rose from their knees and streamed impatiently out of the school. As Johnny moved out in the crowd, he felt a hand catching his arm, and looking up, saw the flushed and anxious face of Middleton looking down at him.

– You'll hold my coat for me, sonny, he said, and watch me turning the faces of two bowseys into chunks of bleeding beef.

Johnny smiled wanly up at him and murmured, You knock hell outa the two of them, Georgie.

– You wait, he answered, you just wait.

A group of boys walked round Massey and Ecret, telling them how best Middleton was to be bayed, harried, and, finally, tired out, so that when it was plain that he had weakened enough, they could sail in and finish him off in their own good time.

– For Jasus' sake, don't let him get one home on either of you, or else you're done; fence him off, and fight cute; dodge round him just outa reach till he puffs, then dart in under his guard and give it to him fair on the solar plexus.

In Brady's Lane, a narrow gutway running between the backs of a row of little houses and a railway bank, all halted and got ready. The backyards of the houses, with the group favouring Massey and Ecret, stretched across the north end; and the railway bank, with the group favouring Middleton, stretched across the south end of the gutway, forming an oblong in which the fight was to take place. Middleton slowly and firmly removed his coat and handed it to Johnny, who slung it over his shoulder. Then Middleton unbuttoned his braces at the front, and tied them as a belt round his middle, rolled up the sleeves of his shirt, showing his grimy and knotty arms, and waited, venomous and nervous, for the fight to begin. Two big boys, one from Massey's group and one from Middleton's, took charge of the affair, to see that everything was done on the square, and to watch for fouls. Middleton's second took a step forward, and announced to the other group that Middleton was ready. Massey and Ecret were trying to settle with their second as to which of them should first tackle Middleton.

– Best for Ecret to go in first, argued Massey, 'cause he's lighter than me, an' take the puff outa him.

– I say you're the best, retorted Ecret. You're heavier than me, an' if you can only manage to give him a few homers in the higher bit of his belly, I'll dance in then and put the tin hat on him.

– Eh, you there, said Middleton's second, settle who's to go in first, will you, and don't keep Middleton waitin' here till he's groggy with age.

– Here, if you can't agree, said the other second impatiently, toss for the one that's to go in first; tails for Ecret, heads for Massey; and he deftly spun a well-worn halfpenny in the air. The coin fell and showed a head. First turn for you, Massey, said the second. Massey peeled off his coat deliberately, rolled up his shirt sleeves, and rubbed his arms briskly, while Johnny prayed that the battle would go against the two boys, and that Georgie would prevail.

From Sean O'Casey, *I Knock at the Door*

## B

I was standing at the end of the lower playground and annoying Mr Samuels, who lived in the house just below the high railings. Mr Samuels complained once a week that boys from the school threw apples and stones and balls through his bedroom window. He sat in a deck chair in a small square of trim garden and tried to read the newspaper. I was only a few yards from him. I was staring him out. He pretended not to notice me, but I knew he knew I was standing there rudely and quietly. Every now and then he peeped at me from behind his newspaper, saw me still and serious and alone, with my eyes on his. As soon as he lost his temper I was going to go home. Already I was late for dinner. I had almost beaten him, the newspaper was trembling, he was breathing heavily, when a strange boy, whom I had not heard approach, pushed me down the bank.

I threw a stone at his face. He took off his spectacles, put them in his coat pocket, took off his coat, hung it neatly on the railings, and attacked. Turning round as we wrestled on the top of the bank, I saw that Mr Samuels had folded his newspaper on the deck chair and was standing up to watch us. It was a mistake to turn round. The strange boy rabbit-punched me twice. Mr Samuels hopped with excitement as I fell against the railings. I was down in the dust, hot and scratched and biting, then up and dancing, and I butted the boy in the belly and we tumbled in a heap. I saw through a closing eye that his nose was bleeding. I hit his nose. He tore at my collar and spun me round by the hair.

'Come on!' I heard Mr Samuels cry.

We both turned towards him. He was shaking his fists and dodging about in the garden. He stopped then, and coughed, and set his panama straight, and avoided our eyes, and turned his back and walked slowly to the deck chair.

We both threw gravel at him.

'I'll give him "Come on!"' the boy said, as we ran along the playground away from the shouts of Mr Samuels and down the steps on to the hill.

We walked home together. I admired his bloody nose. He said that my eye was like a poached egg, only black.

'I've never seen such a lot of blood,' I said.

He said I had the best black eye in Wales, perhaps it was the best black eye in Europe; he bet Tunney never had a black eye like that.

'And there's blood all over your shirt.'

'Sometimes I bleed in dollops,' he said.

On Walter's Road we passed a group of high school girls and I cocked my cap and hoped my eye was as big as a bluebag[1] and he walked with his coat flung open to show the bloodstains.

I was a hooligan all during dinner, and a bully, and as bad as a boy from the Sandbanks, and I should have more respect, and I sat silently, like Tunney, over the sago pudding. That afternoon I went to school with an eye-shade on. If I had had a black silk sling I would have been as gay and desperate as the wounded captain in the book that my sister used to read, and that I read under the bed-clothes at night, secretly with a flashlamp.

[1]barrister's brief bag.

From Dylan Thomas
**■■■** *Portrait of the Artist as a Young Dog* **■■■**

**■■■■■■■■ C ■■■■■■■■**

The whole school knew about the fight next morning. I was a bit frightened in case any of the teachers got to know about it, but proud in a way because I was so famous. All day me and Raymond Garnett kept out of each other's way. I thought I could beat him with one hand tied behind my back, but as the day wore on I started getting like a sinking feeling and wanting to go to the lavatory all the time. I didn't want to go back to school after dinner and I wished I could break my leg. But I knew I would have to go, and on the way back to school Ted shouted after me. 'Have you made your will out?'

Anyway, that afternoon while we were having geography I was balancing my inkwell on the edge of my desk and it went and tipped up and spilt ink all over the floor. Old Ma Bates was taking us that afternoon and she was in a bad temper. She went: 'You clumsy article! Now you stay in after four o'clock and wipe it up!' I felt as though a lead weight had been lifted out of my stomach and I breathed in heavily. Next to me Ted whispered: 'Needn't think you're getting away with it, cos you're not!' But there was a chance, though. For all I knew Old Ma Bates would keep me in till half-past four.

The bell went for going-home time and Old Ma Bates said everyone could go. I thought for a minute she was going to forget about keeping me in, but she didn't. 'You get to and clean that mess!' she said. Ted whispered: 'We'll be waiting for you, so don't try to get away.'

I started mopping at the floor with bits of old blotting paper, soaking the ink in as slowly as I could. Old Ma Bates sat at her desk marking exercise books. Once I looked up and saw Ted and Little Rayner peering in through the French windows. Ted was pretending to slit his throat with his finger. Soon they went away. I finished cleaning up the ink off the floor and sat at my desk with my arms folded, hoping Old Ma Bates wouldn't look up.

It must have been about quarter-past four when she closed her exercise books and said: 'You can go now, and don't let me catch you touching those inkwells again!' I walked slowly out of the class room, down the corridor and out of the main entrance with 'BOYS' printed up over it in stone, through the half-closed trellis gates and into the playground. At first it looked as though the others had gone but then I saw them all standing up near the railings – Ted, Little Rayner, Mono and Raymond Garnett.

'Thought he wouldn't come out!' said Little Rayner.

'Has he got his coffin with him?' said Ted.

We walked out of the playground and round by Parkside towards the fighting field. We walked without saying anything. The only one who spoke was Ted who said: 'Got any chewy?' to Little Rayner, and that was the only thing that was said.

I was frightened when we got down onto the field, not by Raymond Garnett but by this big crowd of kids who had waited to see the fight. At the same time I was happy because they were waiting to see me and Raymond Garnett and nobody else.

There was a big ring of kids round the grey patch that was worn in the grass, where the fights were always held. They parted to let us through, and looking round I saw hundreds of other kids teeming on to the field after us, some of them running. Little Rayner shoved his way to the front, singing: 'Whipsey-diddle-de-dandy-dee,' this stupid song we had to learn at school.

I had never had a fight before. I felt important and pleased at the crowds who were round us, none of them touching us but leaving it to us to have our fight.

'Back a bit,' I said, and I was right pleased when they moved back. I took off my coat and handed it to a kid I did not know. He took it and held it carefully over his arm, and this pleased me too.

Raymond Garnett took off his coat and his glasses. I had never seen him without his glasses before, except that time when we were playing in Clarkson's woods with Marion. He had a white mark over his nose where he had taken them off and it gave me the feeling that I could bash him easy. He gave them to a kid to look after and as the crowd started pushing the kid went: 'Mi-ind his glasses!'

We both stepped forward to meet each other and put our fists up. We stood staring at each other and dancing round a bit like they do on the pictures, then I shot out my right hand to Garnett's chin but it missed and caught his shoulder. The next thing I knew was that his fist had caught me a stinging clout over the forehead. I was surprised and worried at the size of the blow and I began to notice, in a far-off sort of way, that he was a lot bigger than me and that his arms were thicker and longer.

■ From Keith Waterhouse, *There is a Happy Land* ■

Extract **A** is from Sean O'Casey's autobiography *I Knock at the Door*. But instead of writing in the first person as one would expect, he writes from the point of view of Johnnie (the English version of his name.) Extract **B** is from one of a series of autobiographical stories by Dylan Thomas. Extract **C** is from the novel *There is a Happy Land* by Keith Waterhouse. It is written in the first person, but the 'I' is not the author. He is the character through whose eyes the writer is telling the story.

Extracts **A** and **B** are real experience, though probably much embroidered and with much invented detail. Extract **C** is imagined experience, though it is possibly based on details remembered from the writer's childhood. But all three writers use the same skills. They use language and emotional involvement and tension to heighten the experience. They also (in the complete versions) give the experience a shape and unity.

Sometimes the tone when writing about actual experience can be more formal and analytical. For instance, the way John Wain describes his experience of being bullied in the extract from *Sprightly Running* (see section 9.4). Which do you think is the more effective? Or are the writers trying to do different things?

When you write about actual experience, you are likely to write in the first person, and you write about yourself as you are now or as you were when younger. Imagined experience could be in the first or third person and could be about anyone of any age or either sex.

Writing about actual experience could also take the form of a description of an event at which you were present, or a sketch of someone you know, or an account of your feelings about a particular subject. Writing about imagined experience could include an informal letter, or a description of an invented scene, or a report of a fictitious event.

### 15.1.1 Writing about actual and imagined experience – coursework

Choose two of the following to write about, one about actual experience, and the other about imagined experience. It may help if first of all you discuss different ideas for how each title could be approached and developed.

1  The protest march
2  At the circus
3  Lost in time
4  No regrets
5  After the bomb
6  A special place
7  The truth will out
8  You should have seen the mess.

# 15.2 Coursework – organising your file

Check the requirements laid down for coursework in the syllabus you are following. How many pieces of work should you submit? What kinds of writing should be included? Should some of the writing show a response to reading? How many pieces and of what kind should have been written in controlled classroom conditions?

Check the requirements for the presentation of coursework too. You will probably have to indicate the date each piece was written or handed in, the title and type of assignment, the author and title of texts referred to, the conditions under which each was produced, the time taken for each piece. You will have to enter this information on the front or cover sheet.

You will have to sign a declaration that the work was produced without external assistance. Any acceptable assistance (such as preliminary discussion) will have to be indicated. Your teacher will also have to sign a declaration stating that the work presented is your own unaided work.

Each piece of coursework submitted must be the version handed to your teacher for marking and must bear evidence of your teacher's assessment. Work which has been rewritten after your teacher has marked it is not acceptable unless the original version is also included.

Your work should be handwritten; typed material other than photocopies of extracts from a text should not be submitted.

The selection of pieces for assessment will normally be made by you with the guidance of your teacher. The pieces chosen should represent your best work within the various categories of writing specified. By now you should have written many more pieces than the number required for your coursework. In that way, you have a basis from which to select. If you are unable to provide the number of pieces required, or if your pieces do not cover the range specified, you will not be able to get so many marks.

Coursework gives you the opportunity to show the best that you are capable of without worries about a written examination or nerves or feeling under the weather on the day. Take advantage of this opportunity.

# 15.3 Writing – a final revision

● Read the following article. It is based on the report produced by one of the GCE examining boards on the English Language examination in 1979. The examination and the year are both different now, but the points being made are certainly still valid. Be warned that you may find the tone the writer uses unappealing, possibly even offensive.

1  How would you describe the tone in which this article is written?
2  Point out some of the instances where the writer deliberately imitates the errors that he is describing.
3  What audience do you think this article is intended to appeal to?
4  Leaving aside the writer's attitude, do you think this article is helpful or unhelpful? Does it pinpoint any of the weaknesses in your own writing?

# English as she tends to be writ

Bob Doe

Those avid historians of juvenile fashion, culture and the monumental howler, the English language examiners, have declared 1979 the year of "to hassle" and "no way", the year of remarkable levels of sex and violence in pupils' scripts and yet another year when the misused apostrophe reigned supreme.

The University of Cambridge Local Examinations Syndicate has just issued its examiners' report on the summer of that year. Bad spelling was the most obvious though not necessarily the most serious fault, it says. Punctuation was careless and haphazard with little distinction being drawn between full stops and commas by some candidates.

When asked to write essays about such apparently dull pursuits as "looking after your small brother or sister" or "weekend shopping" there was a rash of kidnappings, fires, accidental deaths, bank robberies, terrorism and murders.

For the title "They cancelled the wedding" many of the answers had their "origins in teenage magazines where the sparkling blue eyes inevitably brim with tears."

Cancellation was variously attributed to death in World War One, incurable disease, murder, unwanted pregnancy or the bride fancying the best man.

"The leak" was taken to refer to leaks of information, gas, liquid and radiation. "Uncertainty about spelling led several candidates to extol the virtues of a prize vegetable," say the examiners.

Under the heading "ambiguous constructions", the traditional repository of light relief in examiners'

reports, were "a rapid wash in the sink and a bowl of cornflakes and it was time to leave"; "she shook her head slightly and put it through the post-box slot"; and "thatched cottages, small quaint homes one sees driving through the countryside on a summers day."

The fashionable phrases and words in 1979 were "hassle, no way, no chance, meaningful, great, hectic, ace, magic and entertainment-wise." "More sophisticated vogue words not always happily sited in the context" included "motivates, syndromes, pressures (of modern life), peer group and socially unacceptable."

Candidates invented "authentiveness, discluding, in particularly, neglectance" and "debation." People had "sedimentary" jobs and violence was on the "uptake", which is perhaps not surprising in the present "economical" position of Britain.

"The inability to spell commonly used words was still a major problem for many candidates." Where, were, and wear; are and our; off and of and too and to were all confused. Sutfisticated, ackstravigent, illeagle and biscet are auquadly spelt nower days of cause.

Words were incorrectly joined together: "nextime, alot of, just incase, nightime" and improperly put asunder "a go, a way, and fan fare". Words were misheard: "hang-bag, people do their upmost, as gooder place as any", and the "confinds of home".

"All the characters in this assay are fact and not fiction, in other words my village is a phycologists parade," was an example of spelling combined with other errors. So was "large fir coats

with their collers up." and "a loverly lady with bags of personality."

Tenses continued to cause difficulties. "A few started in the present tense, failed to maintain it and became lost in confusion."

One candidate wrote; "I had just began to understand the use of the French subjunctive ..."but not, the examiners quip, the English pluperfect.

Colloquialisms in inappropriate contexts and clichés cause examiners some concern at this moment in time. Trains "grind to a halt", bangs and explosions are always almighty and stomachs inevitably turn, churn or harbour butterflies. "Far between" followed every "few" and the examiners complain of "spoken rather than written language" being used.

"As I said before," "like I said" and "seeing as how" all caused offence.

In one school many pupils produced the same patches of purple prose, presumably learnt or remembered from their reading. Leaves were always tiger-striped by the sun, determination was always pink-faced, spectacles made expressionless marbles out of eyes, things were as brittle as coral and "wind nipped our finger tips with the viciousness of slamming doors."

In another school the majority of candidates used the word "alway's".

Repetitious phrasing, clumsy sentences and contradictions were present in many average and below average answers. One of those cited clearly knew how to back a winner, however, "It was no use putting violence against violence because violence will always win."

Here is a list of the points the writer and the examiners refer to:

o spelling
o punctuation
o sentence structure
o the content of writing
o ambiguity
o the use of fashionable and vogue words
o invented words
o mixed tenses
o inappropriate use of colloquialisms
o clichés
o purple prose
o repetitious phrasing
o clumsy sentences
o contradictions.

Make sure you understand what all these are about.

● Look at some of your recent writing. Which, if any, of the weaknesses commented on in the examiners' report does your writing suffer from?

Get a second opinion on your writing. Ask your teacher or a friend to comment on the coursework in your file.

# 15.4 Reading – recognising the overall structure and thematic development of a text

When considering the structure of a piece of writing – the way it has been built up and organised – you should try to look at it as a whole. Try to get a clear picture of the pattern.

Here are some approaches to think about:

o Try to see the writing laid out in the same way as a landscape is when you look down on it from a hill.
o Try to see it as a shape like a graph – rising from a quiet beginning to a climax, rising and falling alternately, starting at a high point and gradually falling away.
o Consider the pace. Is it uniformly slow or fast? Are there deliberate alternations between the two?
o See if contrast plays a part in the structure, for example, between one character and another, between one point of view and another, between one idea and another.

Having gained an idea of how a piece of writing has been structured, consider how appropriate and effective the structure is. Think about these questions:

o Why has the writer shaped the material this way?
o What does it contribute to the overall impact of the piece?
o Does it help to reinforce the points being made or the purpose of the writing?
o Would it have been better if the writer had organised the ideas in a different way?

The theme of a piece of writing is the basic idea the writing is about. The theme of most novels and plays, for instance, can be stated in very basic terms. Jane Austen's *Mansfield Park* could be described as showing the relationship between money and marriage. Shakespeare's *Macbeth* can be seen as a study of how ambition corrupts. Characters, events and ideas all contribute to an exploration of the themes and their development.

You have to ask yourself:

o What is the writer trying to say?
o What is the point of the writing?
o How do the characters or events or ideas contribute to this point and illustrate it?

● Outline and comment on the structure and thematic development of the following three pieces.

═══════ A ═══════

THE PARACHUTIST

The hurricane came down from Capricorn, and for two days and a night it rained.

In the darkness of the second night, softening away to dawn, there was silence. There was only the gurgle and drip of the wet world, and the creatures that lived on the earth began to appear, freed from the tyranny of the elements.

The hawk, ruffled in misery, brooding in ferocity, came forth in hunger and hate. It struck off into the abyss of space, scouring the earth for some booty of the storm – the sheep lying like a heap of wet kapok in the sodden paddocks, the bullock like a dark bladder carried down on the swollen stream and washing against a tree on the river flats, the rabbit, driven from its flooded warren and squeezed dead against a log.

With practised eye it scrutinised the floating islands of rubble and the wracks of twigs lying askew on the banks for sign of lizard or snake, dead or alive. But there was nothing. Once, in the time before, there had been a rooster, draggled, forlorn, derelict, riding a raft of flotsam: too weak to fight and too sick to care about dying or the way it died.

The hawk rested on a crag of the gorge and conned the terrain with a fierce and frowning eye. The lice worried its body with the sting of nettles. Savagely it plucked with its beak under the fold of its wings, first on one side, then on the other. It rasped its bill on the jagged stone, and dropped over the lip. It climbed in a gliding circle, widening its field of vision.

The earth was yellow and green. On the flats were chains of lagoons as if the sky had broken and fallen in sheets of blue glass. The sun was hot and the air heavy and humid.

Swinging south, the hawk dropped over a vast graveyard of dead timber. The hurricane had ravaged the gaunt trees, splitting them, felling them, tearing off their naked arms and strewing the ground with pieces, like a battlefield of bones, grey with exposure and decay.

A rabbit sprang twenty yards like a bobbing wheel, and the sight drew the hawk like a plummet, but the rabbit vanished in a hollow log, and stayed there, and there was no other life.

Desperate, weak, the hawk alighted on a bleak limb and glared in hate. The sun was a fire on its famished body. Logs smoked with steam and the brightness of water on the earth reflected like mirrors. The telescopic eye inched over the ground – crawled infallibly over the ground, and stopped. And then suddenly the hawk swooped to the ground and tore at the body of a dead field mouse – its belly bloated and a thin vapour drifting from the grey, plastered pelt.

The hawk did not sup as it supped on the hot running blood of the rabbit in the trap – squealing in eyeless terror; it did not feast in stealthy leisure as it did on the sheep paralysed in the drought, tearing out bit by bit its steaming entrails. Voraciously it ripped at the mouse, swallowing fast and finishing the meal in a few seconds.

But the food was only a tantalisation, serving to make the hawk's appetite more fierce, more lusty. It flew into a tree, rapaciously scanning the countryside. It swerved into space and climbed higher and higher in a vigilant circle, searching the vast expanse below, even to its uttermost limits.

Hard to the west something moved on the earth, a speck; and the hawk watched it: and the speck came up to a walnut, and up to a plum, and up to a ball striped with white and grey.

The hawk did not strike at once. Obedient to instinct, it continued to circle, peering down at the farmhouse and the outbuildings, suspicious; seeing the draught horses in the yard and the fowls in the hen coop, the pigs in the sty, and the windmill twirling, and watching for human life in their precincts.

Away from them all, a hundred yards or more, down on the margin of the fallowed field, the kitten played, leaping and running and tumbling, pawing at a feather and rolling on its back biting at the feather between its forepaws.

Frenzied with hunger, yet ever cautious, the hawk came down in a spiral, set itself, and swooped. The kitten propped and froze with its head cocked on one side, unaware of danger but startled by this new and untried sport. It was no more than if a piece of paper had blown past it in a giant brustle of sound. But in the next moment the hawk fastened its talons in the fur and the fat belly of the kitten, and the kitten spat and twisted, struggling against the power that was lifting it.

Its great wings beating, paddling with the rhythm of oars, the hawk went up a slope of space with its cargo, and the kitten, airborne for the first time in its life, the earth running under it in a blur, wailed in shrill terror. It squirmed frantically as the world fell away in the distance, but the hawk's talons were like the grabs of an iceman.

The air poured like water into the kitten's eyes and broke against its triangular face, streaming back against its rippling furry sides. It howled in infinite fear, and gave a sudden desperate twist, so that the hawk was jolted in its course and dropped to another level, a few feet below the first.

Riding higher and higher on the wind, the hawk went west by the dam like a button of silver far below. The kitten cried now with a new note. Its stomach was rumbling. The air gushing into its mouth and nostrils set up a humming in its ears and an aching dizziness in its head. As the hawk turned on its soundless orbit, the sun blazed like flame in the kitten's eyes, leaving its sight to emerge from a blinding greyness.

The kitten knew that it had no place here in the heart of space, and its terrified instincts told it that its only contact with solidity and safety was the thing that held it.

Then the hawk was ready to drop its prey. It was well practised. Down had gone the rabbit, a whistle in space, to crash in a quiver of death on the ruthless earth. And the hawk had followed to its gluttonous repast.

Now there at two thousand feet the bird hovered. The kitten was alarmingly aware of the change, blinking at the pulsations of beaten air as the wings flapped, hearing only that sound. Unexpectedly, it stopped, and the wings were still – outstretched, but rigid, tilting slightly with the poised body, only the fanned tail lifting and lowering with the flow of the currents.

The kitten felt the talons relax slightly, and that was its warning. The talons opened, but in the first flashing shock of the movement the kitten completed its twist and slashed at the hawk's legs and buried its claws in the flesh like fish-hooks. In the next fraction of a second the kitten had consolidated its position, securing its hold, jabbing in every claw except those on one foot which thrust out in space, pushing against insupportable air. And then the claws on this foot were dug in the breast of the hawk.

With a cry of pain and alarm the bird swooped crazily, losing a hundred feet like a dropping stone. And then it righted itself, flying in a drunken sway that diminished as it circled.

Blood from its breast beaded and trickled down the paw of the kitten and spilled into one eye. The kitten blinked, but the blood came and congealed, warm and sticky. The kitten could not turn its head. It was frightened to risk a change of position. The blood slowly built over its eye a blinding pellicle.

The hawk felt a spasm of weakness, and out of it came an accentuation of its hunger and a lust to kill at all costs the victim it had claimed and carried to this place of execution. Lent an access of power by its ferocity, it started to climb again, desperately trying to dislodge the kitten. But the weight was too much and it could not ascend. A great tiredness came in its dragging body; an ache all along the frames of its wings. The kitten clung tenaciously, staring down at the winding earth and mewling in terror.

For ten minutes the hawk gyrated on a level, defeated and bewildered. All it wanted to do now was to get rid of the burden fastened to its legs and body. It craved respite, a spell on the tallest trees, but it only flew high over these trees, knowing it was unable to perch. Its beak gaped under the harsh ruptures of its breath. It descended three hundred feet. The kitten, with the wisdom of instinct, never altered its position, but rode down like some fantastic parachutist.

In one mighty burst the hawk with striking beak and a terrible flapping of its wings tried finally to cast off its passenger – and nearly succeeded. The kitten miauled in a frenzy of fear at the violence of the sound and the agitation. Its back legs dangled in space, treading air, and like that it went around on the curves of the flight for two minutes. Then it secured a foothold again, even firmer than the first.

In an hysterical rage, the hawk tried once more to lift itself, and almost instantly began to sweep down in great, slow, gliding eddies that became narrower and narrower.

The kitten was the pilot now and the hawk no longer the assassin of the void, the lord of the sky and the master of the wind. The ache coiled and throbbed in its breast. It fought against the erratic disposition of its wings and the terror of its waning strength. Its heart bursting with the strain, its eyes dilated wild and yellow, it came down until the earth skimmed under it; and the kitten cried at the silver glare of the roofs not far off, and the expanding earth, and the brush of the grass.

The hawk lobbed and flung over, and the kitten rolled with it. And the hawk lay spraddled in exhaustion, its eyes fiercely, cravenly aware of the danger of its forced and alien position.

The kitten staggered giddily, unhurt, towards the silver roofs, wailing loudly as if in answer to the voice of a child.

D'Arcy Niland

## B

As the music intensifies, the boxers fly at each other with animalistic ferocity – legs, arms, elbows and thighs attack the opponents' most vulnerable points. Thai-boxing, known as *Muay-Thai* in Thailand, is unlike any other martial art. It bears no similarity to the international-style boxing except in the shape of the ring.

The opponents chase each other round the ring, their gloved hands held high, huge against their lightly-built bodies; they stalk like sleek tigers ready to pounce. With a brisk jerk, one swings his foot and slams it hard into the other's belly; the crowd calls out enthusiastically and the match is on.

Until recently, this ferocious battle continued until blood was drawn, now the game is confined to five rounds of three minutes' duration with a two-minute break. Unlike international boxing where defensive fighting gains points, the referee in *Muay-Thai* keeps track of the fighter's offensive hits. There are no rules in Thai-boxing except that a fighter cannot kick his opponent while he is down and biting is forbidden.

*Muay-Thai* developed as a battle technique in medieval times when warriors, trained in hand-to-hand combat, used *Muay-Thai* as an effective strategy for close combat where spears and swords were ineffective. In AD1560, King Naresuen of Siam, ancient Thailand, brought the boxing notoriety and popularity. Captured by the Burmese, he challenged his captors to a hand-to-hand match in exchange for his freedom. Victorious, Naresuen returned to Siam, and from that time this ritualised sport gained national popularity.

Gradually *Muay-Thai* was abandoned as a form of combat and became organised into competition matches. With few rules, the sport was decidedly dangerous. Regulations determined that the battle was over when one fighter fell to the mat – sometimes fatally.

Around the 1900s, *Muay-Thai* was introduced into schools. However, because of the dangers, it was eventually banned. It was only in the '30s that *Muay-Thai* took on the regulations which were to transform it into a sport rather than a dangerous combat.

The boxers enter the ring, their bodies wrapped in brightly coloured robes, their crowns encircled by a *mongkon*, a mis-shapen, sacred cord which is kept on during the rituals preceding the fight. Their slight, muscled bodies, without a gram of excess fat, look fragile. Though they rarely weigh heavier than light or bantam-weight in their class, appearances are deceptive: intensive training has finely-honed their physique to a high level of finesse and strength.

During the first minutes of each match a number of time-honoured rituals, unique to Thai-boxing, are performed. Prayers and dances, that appear out-of-place to those familiar with international-style boxing, offer a stylised display of the boxer's talent. First, they bow to their teachers in respect. Each man then turns in the direction of his birthplace, kneels and raises his heavily-gloved fists to his forehead for a few moments of prayer. Finally, touching his head to the canvas, he prostrates himself three times in an act of humility.

The boxing-dance which follows is the final act of this pre-fight theatre: the boxers contort their bodies in a dance, knees bent, toes pointing at right angles to their bodies; stylistic, deliberate movements resembling Siamese dancing are performed. The dance differs from each fighter and tells boxing enthusiasts which region the boxer hails from; they respond with hoots of support for a local contender or for a particularly imaginative choreography.

The preliminaries over, the umpire calls the boxers to touch gloves. The bell clangs and the confrontation begins. With a shrill, the *Pi Chawa*, an out-of-shape wind instrument, pierces above the sound of cymbals and the beat of a hand-drum. A haunting rhythm rises and falls with the action in the ring, an accompaniment inextricably part of Thai-boxing. For the Western observer, the presence of a four-piece band is a little disconcerting. The musicians, reacting almost instinctively to the changing intensity of the action, mount the tempo at the appropriate moments.

The fighters tack each other, drawing energy from the melodious music; an air of concentration in their step. For the first two rounds the crowd looks on. Suddenly, the fighters fly into a fierce display, legs and elbows crush painfully into thighs and groin. The music crescendos to a squeal and the crowd cries out 'kom, kom!', urging their favourite to knee his opponent.

Fiery betting ensues, which spurs the spectators' enthusiasm as the fight takes a vicious, aggressive turn. In a flurry of hand-signs and deafening shouts, unofficial bets are laid with the odds changing by the second.

The bell sounds, the fighters withdraw, sweating, to their corners. In the two-minute pause trainers rush in to massage and towel the fighters down and pour forth spirited instructions for the next offensive. The three-minute rounds of high-tension fury keep the spectators impassioned.

Clang! It's on again. The men parry at first, then advance, striking out violently with their feet at any vulnerable spot in the defence. Change of tactics and fists come into play.

Blows from feet, knees and elbows, legal manoeuvres in Thai-boxing, give a more potent delivery than fists – often crippling in their effect. The flexibility needed to drive through effectively comes from stringent training and the contortions involved add drama to the scene. Blows are more varied than those used in international boxing, while the aggressive, high-speed, straight-limbed leg kicks whap stingingly into the opponent's body.

Training is rigorous. Most boxers begin to train at 13 or 14, though a few may start much younger. By the time they are 16 the apprentices are ready to turn professional. Fighters rarely combat more than once a month in the boxing stadiums as the trials of Thai-boxing are exhausting on the body. By the age of 18 or 19, some fighters are at their peak in a short-spanned career where retirement often comes at 29 or 30.

Two sessions a day, one and a half hours in the morning and two hours in the cool of the afternoon, is the usual training routine. A jogging session begins the day, followed by a session on a punch bag which is used to practise both leg kicks and punches and this is followed by flexibility exercises. Finally, they enter the ring with their trainers to practise defence and offence moves. As the agile use of legs and elbows is an important facet of Thai-boxing, considerable time is devoted to building up the force and aim of kicks as a high-level of endurance, flexibility and strength is needed to ram through leg-kicks continually.

The popularity of *Muay-Thai* in Thailand is uncontested and is a regular feature of entertainment in Bangkok. Every day of the week except Sunday combats are held in Bangkok's two stadiums – Lumpini and Rajdamnern. Bouts are occasionally held in out-door stadiums which attract large crowds. Heads protected under sheets of newspaper or umbrellas from the sweltering heat of the Thai sun, the crowd banters, rails or cheers as the bout swings for or against their favourite. Fists waving in anger or encouragement, the spectators follow the highs and lows with ever-changing humour.

The live music stirring up the adrenalin and inciting both fighters and spectators to a frenzy, the ritualistic dance at the beginning of each fight, the non-stop yelling and betting of Thai spectators and the murderous ferocity of the fighters make a contest of *Muay-Thai* an unforgettable one.

■ Margaret O'Loan, *High Life* ■

# C

## TO AUTUMN

Season of mists and mellow fruitfulness!
　　Close bosom-friend of the maturing sun;
Conspiring with him how to load and bless
　　With fruit the vines that round the thatch-eaves run;
To bend with apples the mossed cottage-trees,
　　And fill all fruit with ripeness to the core;
　　　　To swell the gourd, and plump the hazel shells
With a sweet kernel; to set budding more,
And still more, later flowers for the bees,
Until they think warm days will never cease,
　　　　For Summer has o'er-brimm'd their clammy cells.

Who hath not seen thee oft amid thy store?
　　Sometimes whoever seeks abroad may find
Thee sitting careless on a granary floor,
　　Thy hair soft-lifted by the winnowing wind;
Or on a half-reaped furrow sound asleep,
　　Drowsed with the fume of poppies, while thy hook
　　　　Spares the next swath and all its twined flowers;
And sometimes like a gleaner thou dost keep
　　Steady thy laden head across a brook;
　　Or by a cider-press, with patient look,
　　　　Thou watchest the last oozings, hours by hours.

Where are the songs of Spring? Ay, where are they?
　　Think not of them, thou hast thy music too,
While barréd clouds bloom the soft-dying day,
　　And touch the stubble-plains with rosy hue;
Then in a wailful choir, the small gnats mourn
　　Among the river sallows, borne aloft
　　　　Or sinking as the light wind lives or dies;
And full-grown lambs loud bleat from hilly bourn;
　　Hedge-crickets sing; and now with treble soft
The redbreast whistles from a garden-croft,
　　And gathering swallows twitter in the skies.

■ John Keats ■

# 15.5 Reading – making you think

Writers usually express themselves in straightforward statements. They may not tell readers directly what they mean, but usually they lay the facts squarely on the page so that readers can make their own deductions. For instance, if a writer makes a character say, 'Men are better than women', it doesn't take much imagination on the part of the reader to deduce that this character is prejudiced and sexist. The writer doesn't actually say so, but the conclusion is obvious.

But sometimes, writers feel it is more effective to put things in an indirect way and make their readers work at the meaning intended in the hope that that approach will have a greater impact. This can be true of the use of figurative language, paradox and irony.

*Figurative language* This has already been discussed in sections 9.5 and 10.3. Many images are comparatively straightforward – for example, 'The kitten was like a fluffy ball of wool'. But others can demand greater thought to understand. In one of his poems, T. S. Eliot wrote, 'I have measured out my life with coffee spoons.' The reader is forced to make an imaginative leap in order to share the poet's thoughts. The idea of 'coffee spoons' brings to mind endless cups of coffee, hours spent uselessly sitting in cafés, time going by with nothing achieved. It becomes a kind of symbol for the futility the poet feels. By having to work out the meaning, the reader gains a richer experience from the words.

*Paradox* In paradox the words on the surface appear to be nonsensical or contradictory, but on closer examination can be seen to be stating something quite profound. For instance, G. K. Chesterton said, 'If a thing is worth doing, it is worth doing badly.' The statement brings the reader up with a jolt. How can that be true? But then the reader begins to think about it. Perhaps what Chesterton is suggesting is that if something is worth doing (such as painting a picture or running a race or writing a story) it is worth doing for its own sake regardless of whether the end-product is successful or not. By using a paradox, Chesterton forces the reader to puzzle out the meaning. And because the reader has had to make an effort to get the meaning, the writer's point comes over more forcefully.

*Irony* In irony, the writer says one thing on the surface when in fact his real meaning is something quite different. For instance, Jonathan Swift in his pamphlet *A Modest Proposal for Preventing the Children of Ireland being a Burden to their Parents or Country* wrote:

I have been assured by a very knowing American of my acquaintance in London, that a young healthy child well nursed is at a year old a most delicious, nourishing, and wholesome food, whether stewed, roasted, baked, or boiled, and I make no doubt that it will equally serve in a fricassee, or a ragout.

He can't mean it, can he? The proposition is so far-fetched, absurd and horrific that we can't take it at its face value. We begin to examine it more closely. The suggestion being made is nauseating, and yet the writer appears to be making it seriously. He extends the horror by providing so much detail, so many different ways the children could be cooked. He is overdoing it. We begin to suspect that he has his tongue in his cheek. He is leading us on. He means something different. He is saying that what has been suggested as a means of dealing with the growing population of Ireland at the time is absurd, just as far-fetched as the method he himself is proposing. The title of the pamphlet provides a clue to this meaning. It is called a *modest* proposal, yet the action suggested is far from modest.

By putting forward this idea, by revolting us with it, by forcing us to reject it, Swift influences us into thinking that the alternative idea is equally revolting and unthinkable. By saying something different from what he means, he makes us think in order to get his real meaning. And again, because of the effort involved, the point the writer is really making has a greater impact.

1   Here are some more images of T. S. Eliot's for you to discuss and explore.
   a The yellow fog that rubs its back upon the window-panes.
   b When the evening is spread out against the sky
      Like a patient etherised upon a table.
   c I should have been a pair of ragged claws
      Scuttling across the floors of silent seas.
   d And I have seen the eternal Footman hold my coat, and snicker.
   e I grow old . . . I grow old . . .
      I shall wear the bottoms of my trousers rolled.

2   What do you think is the meaning of the following paradoxes?
   a 'A man cannot be too careful in the choice of his enemies.' (Oscar Wilde)
   b 'How wonderful opera would be if there were no singers.' (Gioacchino Rossini)
   c 'When my love swears that she is made of truth
      I do believe her, though I know she lies.' (William Shakespeare)
   d 'In married life three is company and two none.' (Oscar Wilde)
   e 'To give an accurate and exhaustive account of that period would need a far less brilliant pen than mine.' (Max Beerbohm)
   f 'Wha man dohn know is good to know.' (Caribbean proverb)
   g 'Wagner's music is better than it sounds.' (Bill Nye)

3 Study the following article. How can you tell that it is meant to be ironic? How does the use of irony help to put the writer's point of view across more forcefully?

# THE NORMAL FIFTH

The normal home contains a pet, and the normal pet is a cat or a budgerigar, according to the statistics in the Official Handbook published by the Central Office of Information. The normal man, it apears, spends the normal evening at home with his cat or his budgerigar in front of his television set.

The leader-writer in the *Daily Mail* is appalled by the picture the figures conjure up. 'What a miserable collection of stick-in-the muds we are!' he writes. 'Why don't we go out and enjoy ourselves? Why don't we throng the streets, talk to our neighbours, or sit about in cafés just looking at people?'

Sit about in cafés just looking at people? Sit about in which cafés, just looking at what people? In the Nell Gwynne Tea Shoppe in the High Street? Looking at old Mrs Poorly and her friend Ida Know eating buttered scones?

And throng which streets, pray? Throng Delamere Gardens, N.W.12? Throng Jubilee Road, Screwe? There are some streets which in my experience are really pretty well unthrongable.

Anyway, whatever the pleasures of street-thronging, it's 'splendidly normal people' that the National Children Adoption Association are looking out for to become adoptive parents, according to the secretary in *The Times*. What seems splendidly normal to the N.C.A.A. turns out to be remarkably similar to what seems normal to the Central Office of Information, except that the N.C.A.A.'s standards of normality are so searching that only one in five of their applicants turns out to be splendidly normal enough to qualify.

The ideal couple, says the secretary, probably live in the outer suburbs, and have a middle-sized detached or semi-detached house with a garden. 'They are splendidly normal people, in good health and completely without neuroses now or in the past. He probably goes up to the City every day and she has no ambitions outside her home and her family. They usually have a pet – a cat or a budgerigar, and they don't have a lot of outside interests. But this doesn't mean to say they need to be exactly dull.'

Of course, when one hears about all the splendidly normal people like this, one cannot help worrying once again about the abnormal ones, and what can be done to help them. Because, lets face it, there *are* abnormal people around; we can't just shrug the problem off and pretend they don't exist.

Some of them have only mild abnormalities, such as living in large houses, or keeping dogs, which might disqualify them from adopting children, but which need not otherwise prevent them leading decent and useful lives.

But a few of them do suffer from gross abnormalities, like not working in the City. Progel, in 'The Abnormal Englishman', identifies this condition as dysmetropolia, and attributes it to the absence or inadequacy of the patient's uncle-figures during adolescence. He sees working in other parts of the country as a subconscious evasion of reality – a symptom of neurosis allied to, and often co-present with, neurotic manifestations such as dropping aitches, doing manual work and playing out masochistic guilt-fantasies by refusing to earn a normal middle-sized salary.

Hergstrom takes a more radical view. He believes that everyone, however disturbed, *knows* somewhere inside him that he works in the City and lives in a middle-sized suburban house with a budgerigar, and that delusions to the contrary are merely hysterical.

McStride and Leastways, in their classic study 'Behaviour Patterns of Budgerigarlessness', put more emphasis on learned reflexes. One of their most grossly disturbed patients presented an extraordinary range of symptoms. He lived in a *terraced house* in Sheffield, worked in a *factory*, and confessed that he often *went out in the evening*.

McStride and Leastways achieved a partial cure by attaching electrodes to the patient, and administering painful electric shocks when he went to work, when he came home, and when he went out again at night. After prolonged treatment the patient moved to Nottingham, which was at any rate 37 miles along the road to recovery from his dysmetropolia. (When last heard of he was undergoing further conditioning therapy to overcome his irrational dread of electricity.)

The abnormality symptoms presented by women can sometimes be even more serious. In his survey of married women arrested for reading in Beckenham Public Library, Didbold estimates that there may be as many as 200 or even 300 married women in this country suffering from ambitions outside the home and family.

According to Meany, outside ambitions in women are the result of emotional deprivation in infancy, possibly aggravated by over-intense educational experience. He wants the Government to launch a crash programme for the early detection of unnatural ambition, and warns that if nothing is done the country may in a year or two's time face a full-scale epidemic.

In both men and women, ambitions and interests outside the home tend to be the most dangerous abnormalities, if allowed to go unchecked. Strabolgi, for instance, has demonstrated a definite correlation between extra-domiciliary interests and certain forms of criminal behaviour. In his sample of 317 men and women in the Barnet area, *not one* committed burglary, simony, or robbery with violence while sitting at home watching the television.

It's true that 14 were later convicted of tax offences, six of wounding their wives, and one of strangling his budgerigar.

But that's normal.

━━━━━ Michael Frayn ━━━━━

#  15.6 Group oral test

It is possible that a group oral test will play an important part in assessing your final grade for Oral Communication. Check with your teacher. (Even if it doesn't, it can be a useful exercise.)

The group oral test takes the form of discussions which develop from short talks given by each member of the group in turn. Each group consists of five or six pupils, and the test lasts forty-five minutes.

Pupils should prepare a talk on a subject that interests them. It should be a subject of their own choice which is submitted to the teacher beforehand. Each pupil is expected to talk for about three minutes. It should be a talk and not a reading from a prepared script. Notes may be used and appropriate visual and other aids. Each talk is followed by a group discussion lasting about five minutes. All members of the group should take part in these discussions as their contributions are taken into account in the final grading.

The assessment is made by two teachers. One teacher conducts the session, taking part where necessary to encourage contributions and make sure everyone has a chance. The other teacher makes detailed notes on the performances of each member of the group. At the end of the session, the two teachers discuss the marks each of them has given and agree a final assessment.

In preparing for your group oral test, it could be helpful to revise the following sections:

○   Oral assessment (1.6)
○   Group discussion (1.7)
○   Giving a talk (7.4)
○   Sustaining a discussion (9.7)

●   Prepare a talk for a group oral test. Give it to your group and assess with your group its success or otherwise.

◄   *This could be used for oral assessment.*   ►

Time allowed: one and a half hours.

You are advised to spend 45 minutes on Section A and 45 minutes on Section B.

Answer ALL questions in Section A and ONE question in Section B.

Read the following poem and then answer the questions below.

## ■■ THE READING LESSON ■■

Fourteen years old, learning the alphabet,
He finds letters harder to catch than hares
Without a greyhound. Can't I give him a dog
To track them down, or put them in a cage?
He's caught in a trap, until I let him go,
Pinioned by 'Don't you want to learn to read?'
'I'll be the same man whatever I do.'

He looks at a page as a mule balks at a gap
From which a goat may hobble out and bleat.
His eyes jink from a sentence like flushed snipe
Escaping shot. A sharp word, and he'll mooch
Back to his piebald mare and bantam cock.
Our purpose is as tricky to retrieve
As mercury from a smashed thermometer.

'I'll not read any more.' Should I give up?
His hands, long-fingered as a Celtic scribe's,
Will grow callous, gathering sticks or scrap;
Exploring pockets of the horny drunk
Loiterers at the fairs, giving them lice.
A neighbour chuckles. 'You can never tame
The wild-duck: when his wings grow, he'll fly off.'

If books resembled roads, he'd quickly read:
But they're small farms to him, fenced by the page,
Ploughed into lines with letters drilled like oats:
A field of tasks he'll always be outside.
If words were bank-notes, he would filch a wad;
If they were pheasants, they'd be in his pot
For breakfast, or if wrens he'd make them king.

■■ Richard Murphy ■■

# Section A

Answer ALL the following questions.

1  What do you learn about the narrator, the boy and their situation from the first verse? (4)
2  'He finds letters harder to catch than hares.' Why is that an appropriate image? (4)
3  Explain what is meant by

    Our purpose is as tricky to retrieve
    As mercury from a smashed thermometer.  (4)

4  What is the narrator's attitude towards the boy and the task he is undertaking? Give reasons for your answer. (4)
5  In what ways does verse four look at the situation from a different angle? (4)
6  Does the poem gain from being written in the present tense (as if it is happening now)? Refer to the poem in your answer. (2)
7  What impression do you get of the boy and his future from the poem? (6)

(total 30 marks)

# Section B

Choose ONE of the following.

You may write in playscript, poetry or prose. If you write in playscript, just put the speaker's name in the left margin, and then the words spoken. Remember that credit will be given for your ability to describe scenes, people, thoughts and feelings, and for your choice of words.

You should write between 200–250 words.

1  Imagine a conversation about the boy between the narrator and the neighbour referred to in the poem.
   OR
2  Put yourself in the place of the boy having his reading lesson. Write down the thoughts that run through his head. Use the first person.(30 marks)

(If you are not required to sit a written examination, this could be part of your coursework.)

# Appendices

# A   Spelling

1   When adding -ed, -ing, -able to a word consisting of one syllable containing one vowel followed by one consonant, this consonant is doubled, for example:

*stop* becomes *stopped*
*star* becomes *starring*
*bid* becomes *biddable*
*stoop* (two vowels) becomes *stooped*
*sort* (two consonants) becomes *sorting*
*account* (two vowels, two consonants) becomes *accountable*.

Similarly with words of more than one syllable if the stress is on the last syllable, for example:

*occur* becomes *occurred*
*fulfil* becomes *fulfilled*
*propel* becomes *propellable*
*prohibit* (accent *not* on the last syllable) becomes *prohibited*
*contain* (two vowels) becomes *containing*
*inhabit* (accent *not* on the last syllable) becomes *inhabitable*.

Note A: Words like *infer* and *prefer* have varying stress and spelling, thus: *infer, inferred, inference, inferable; refer, referred, referring, reference, referable; prefer, preferred, preference, preferable*.

Note B: Words ending in a vowel + a single *l* double the *l* before adding the suffix, whether the final syllable is stressed or not, for example, *quarrel, quarrelled; travel, travelling; signal, signalled.*

Note C: There are a few exceptions: *kidnap, kidnapped; worship, worshipped; handicap, handicapped; parallel, paralleled.*

2   In words of two or more syllables, a long vowel is followed by a single consonant, and a short stressed vowel is followed by a double consonant.

Compare:

| | |
|---|---|
| later, latter | confused, concussed |
| fury, furry | staring, starring |
| Mary, marry | shining, shinning |
| diner, dinner | holy, holly |
| referred, referee | |

But note words ending in *l* mentioned in rule 1.

3   In compounds, a silent final *e* is kept before a consonant but dropped before a vowel (unless it is preceded by a soft *c* or *g*), for example:

| | | |
|---|---|---|
| hopeful | writing | manageable |
| lively | likable | noticeable |
| likeness | lovable | changeable |
| advertisement | sensible | (*e* retained to |
| minutely | admirable | keep *c* or *g* soft |
| immediately | | before *a*, *o* and |
| homeless | | *u*). |

Note A: Before -*ment* the final *e* is dropped in the following words: *abridgment, acknowledgment, argument, judgment,* (however, the spellings *abridgement, acknowledgement* and *judgement* are also possible).

Note B: The *e* is sometimes retained in the following words: *hireable, likeable, rateable, saleable, sizeable, tameable, unshakeable.*

Note C: The final *e* is dropped when adding -*ing* and -*ish*, except *ageing, cueing, lungeing, routeing* ('sending by a route'), *syringeing, singeing, swingeing, twingeing blueish.* The *e* is retained in words ending in *oe*, for example, *canoeing, hoeing, shoeing.*

Note D: The final *e* is sometimes retained when adding *y*, for example, *bluey, cagey, clayey, gluey.* Most other common words drop the *e*, for example, *chancy, gamy, horsy, mousy, nervy, noisy, nosy.*

Note E: The final *e* is retained when adding -*ly*, for example, *immediately, immensely, fortunately, vaguely.* Exceptions: *duly, truly, wholly.*

Note F: *Acreage* and *mileage* retain the *e.*

**4** When adding to a word ending in *y*, the *y* is kept if the preceding letter is a vowel; if the preceding letter is a consonant, the *y* is changed to *i*, for example:

| | |
|---|---|
| dainty, daintily | lovely, lovelier |
| merry, merriment | carry, carried |
| ready, readiness | study, studious |
| lady, ladies | pity, pitiful |
| joy, joyful | boy, boys |
| employ, employment | coy, coyly |
| grey, greyness | pray, prayed |

Note A: Before *-ing* the *y* is retained, e.g. *carrying, tidying, worrying*. This is to prevent two *i*'s coming together. Similarly with words like *babyish, dryish*.

Note B: *Dry* becomes *drier, driest, drily* (or *dryly*), *dryish, dryness; gay* becomes *gayer, gayest, gaily, gaiety; shy* becomes *shyer, shyest, shyly, shyness; sly* becomes *slyer, slyest, slyly, slyness; wry* becomes *wryer* or *wrier, wryly, wryness*.

Note C: *Busy* becomes *business* ('job'), *busily*; but *busyness* ('the state of being busy'), *busybody*.

**5** Double *l* becomes single in compounds, for example:

joy + full = joyful
un + till = until
spoon + full = spoonful
full + fill = fulfil
well + come = welcome
will + full = wilful
all + ready = already
all + ways = always
all + together = altogether
all + though = although
all + most = almost
skill + full = skilful
all + mighty = almighty

Note, however, *stillness, wellbeing, chockfull, illness*.

**6** *i* before *e* except after *c* when the sound is *ee*, for example:

| | | |
|---|---|---|
| brief | ceiling | beige |
| fierce | conceit | feint |
| grief | conceive | heir |
| mischief | deceive | reign |
| pier | perceive | rein |
| shriek | receipt | reveille |
| yield | receive | skein |

Exceptions: *seize, seizure, weir, weird*. Note also: *counterfeit, foreign, surfeit, forfeit, plebeian, leisure*.

**7** In cases other than those already mentioned, when you add a prefix or a suffix do not drop or add a letter to the root, for example:

dis + appear = disappear
dis + satisfy = dissatisfy
dis + appoint = disappoint
mean + ness = meanness
usual + ly = usually
ad + dress = adress
il + legible = illegible
im + mature = immature
col + lect = collect
cor + respond = correspond
un + necessary = unnecessary

## Forming plurals

**1** Most nouns form the plural by adding *-s* to the singular, for example, *cats, cats; boy, boys*.

**2** Nouns ending in *-ch, -s, -sh, -ss, -x* form the plural by adding *-es*, for example, *church, churches; gas, gases; dish, dishes; pass, passes; box, boxes*.

**3** A few nouns ending in *-f*, or *-fe* change this to *-ves* in the plural. They are: *calves, halves, knives, lives, loaves, selves (ourselves, etc.), sheaves, shelves, thieves, wives, wolves*. The plural of *hoof* can be *hoofs* or *hooves; scarf* can be *scarfs* or *scarves; wharf* can be *wharfs* or *wharves;* staff *can be* staffs *or* staves (depending on the sense). All other nouns ending in *-f* or *-fe* just add *s*, for example, *cliffs, dwarfs, roofs*.

**4** Nouns ending in *-y* preceded by a consonant change the *y* to *ies* in the plural, *baby, babies; family, families; lady, ladies*. Nouns ending in *-y* preceded by a vowel form the plural by adding *s*, for example *donkeys, monkeys, valleys*.

**5** A number of nouns form the plural by changing the vowel sound, for example, *foot, feet; goose, geese; louse, lice; man, men; mouse, mice; tooth, teeth; woman, women*. These are survivals of older ways of forming the plural, as are the following: *brother, brethren; child, children; cow, kine; die, dice; ox, oxen; penny, pence; sow, swine*. **Brethren** and *kine* are now used only in Biblical language; the more regular plurals are *brothers* and *cows*. *Sows* is also more common than *swine*.

**6** Nouns ending in *-o* preceded by a vowel form the plural by adding *s*, for example, *cameos, cuckoos, curios, radios*. Nouns ending in *-o* preceded by a consonant tend to form the plural by adding *-es*, for example, *cargoes, echoes, heroes, tomatoes, volcanoes*. But there are many exceptions, such as *cantos, dynamos, grottos, photos, pianos, provisos, solos, stilettos*. The plural of *tempo* is *tempi*.

**7** Most compound nouns form the plural by changing or adding to the most important word, for example, *brothers-in-law, girl-guides, goings-on, good-for-nothings, lookers-on*. When *man* or *woman* is the first element of the compound, both elements take the plural form, for example, *menservants, women writers* (compare *girlfriends* and *maid-servants*). Words like *basketful* add *s* at the end, thus *basketfuls, handfuls, mouthfuls, spoonfuls*.

**8** Some nouns have the same form in the singular and the plural, for example, *deer, sheep, salmon*.

**9** Some nouns are almost always used in the plural, for example, *billiards, draughts, spectacles, trousers*.

Note: The apostrophe (') should only be used to form a plural in the case of letters, for example, Dot your i's and cross your t's.

Pronouns can also be singular or plural. Some pronouns are singular only for example, *each*; some are plural only, for example, *both*; some have the same form in the singular and the plural, for example, *who*; and some have separate forms for singular and plural:

I – we; he, she, it – they;
myself – ourself, etc;
this – these; that – those.

# Words commonly misspelled

abridgment (or abridgement)
abysmal
abyss
accelerate
accidentally
accommodate
acknowledgment (or
    acknowledgement)
acquaintance
acquire
acquit
adjacent
advantageous
ageing (or aging)
amiable
appalling
assassin
awkward

bachelor
bailiff
behaviour
benefit
bicycle

cannibal
capital (= main town)
caricature
catarrh
caterpillar
cellar
cemetery
centenary
clamour
commemorate
committee
conscience

definite
democracy
develop
development
different
disappear
discreet
disease
dissatisfy

eerie
embarrass
endeavour
exaggerate
exceed
except
excite
exercise
exhilarating
extravagant
extreme

favour
favourite
feasible
February
fervour
fictitious
flavour
foreign
forfeit

gawky
glamour
glamorous
government
grammar
grievous

handkerchief
harass
hindrance
humour
hypocrisy
hypocrite

idiosyncrasy
independence
inflammable
innocent
intelligent
intrigue
intriguing
irrelevant

jewellery
judgment (though 'judgement' is
    found in legal contexts)

khaki

laboratory
leisure
lieutenant
lightning
likable (though 'likeable' is
    becoming common)
listener
livelihood
loneliness

manoeuvre
mantelpiece
mattress
medicine
Mediterranean
miniature
minute
mischievous

necessary
neighbour

obscene
occurrence
outrageous

pastime
Piccadilly
pigeon
piteous
Portuguese
possess
possession
precede
prejudice
pretension
privilege
proceed
professor
pursue

quarrel
queue

rarefy
recommend
relevant
resistance
restaurant
rhyme
rhythm
rigorous
rigour

safety
satellite
scandal
seize
seizure
separate
sergeant
sheriff
siege
silhouette
skilful
slander
solemn
splendour
sprightly
squalor
squawk
stomach
stubborn
stubbornness
succeed
success
surprise

tendency
terrible
tragedy
treachery

twelfth
tyranny

vapour
veterinary
vigorous
vigour
visitor

Wednesday
weird
wilful
withhold
woollen

yacht
yield

## The possessive case

The possessive case indicates the possessor or owner of something, for example:

the *boy's* book
the *girl's* hat.

In these examples, *boy* and *girl* are possessing something, *book* and *hat* respectively, and to indicate this the *'s* is added.

The possessive case is formed thus:

1   If the possessor is singular, add *'s*, for example, *the man's coat, the sun's heat.*

Note: Some proper names ending in *s* add only *'*, e.g. *Mars' Hill, Achilles' heel.* Other examples of this are: *for goodness' sake, for peace' sake.*

2   If the possessor is plural, add *'*, for example, *ladies' hats, books' covers.*

Note: If the plural possessor does not end in *s*, then the possessive case is formed by adding *'s*, for example, *men's coats, children's games.*

The possessive case is also used in such phrases as: *out of harm's way, two hours' work, five days' time, today's dinner.*

The possessive case of personal pronouns is formed without an apostrophe, thus:

That book is *theirs.*
Ours is better than *yours.*

# B   Sentence structure

A sentence is a group of words that can stand by itself and make sense. Strictly speaking, a sentence should have a subject and a predicate, that is contain a finite verb (a verb that forms a tense and has a subject). For example:

| Subject | Predicate |
|---|---|
| The man in the white suit | was sitting on the park bench. |
| She | smiled. |
| The ship | was a long way from the shore. |

'Was sitting', 'smiled' and 'was' are finite verbs.

However, there are many instances of perfectly acceptable sentences which do not contain finite verbs. For example:

About time.
No entry.
No flowers by request.
Yes.

The important thing is that the group of words should make sense in its context.

Sentences begin with capital letters and end with full stops.

Sentences can be of varying types depending on how they are constructed.

| Type | Description | Example |
|---|---|---|
| simple | consisting of one clause only (a clause being a group of words containing one finite verb) | The sun was shining brightly. |
| compound | consisting of two or more main clauses | The sun was shining brightly, and the breeze was beginning to die down. |
| complex | consisting of one main clause and one or more subordinate clauses | When we reached the top of the hill, the sun was shining brightly. |
| compound-complex | consisting of two or more main clauses and one or more subordinate clauses | When we reached the top of the hill, the sun was shining brightly, and the breeze was beginning to die down. |

# C   Punctuation

The purpose of punctuation marks is to make sure that the meaning of a piece of writing is clear to the reader. The following punctuation marks are used:

| Punctuation mark | Description | Example |
|---|---|---|
| full stop | 1 used to show the end of a sentence | The snow was falling fast. |
| | 2 used to show an abbreviation | Esq., i.e., B.A. |
| comma | 1 used to separate different statements in a sentence | When you have finished your homework, you may watch television. |
| | 2 used to separate the different items of a list | We shall need eggs, cheese, butter and tea. |
| | 3 used before and after words or phrases added to a sentence | There is, however, no need to panic. |
| exclamation mark | used to indicate strong feeling | Help! I'm drowning! |
| question mark | used to indicate a question | Why are you late? |

| Punctuation mark | Description | Example |
|---|---|---|
| semi-colon | 1 used between statements that are related to each other | Long avenues of trees stretched down to the river; they provided a dappled shade that kept off the fierceness of the sun. |
| | 2 used instead of commas for lengthy items in a list | The gardens were extensive with long, smooth lawns; ornamental archways smothered with honeysuckle; well-stocked ponds where goldfish glinted. |
| colon | 1 used to indicate the balancing of one phrase or idea against another. | Man proposes: God disposes. |
| | 2 used to introduce an illustration or a quotation or a conclusion instead of an expression like 'namely' | There was only one thing we could do: surrender. |
| | 3 used to introduce a list | The house consisted of the following: a lounge; a kitchen; two bedrooms; a bathroom. |
| dash | 1 used to cut off an afterthought or an added example or explanation from the rest of the sentence | The window – the one that leaked – was finally replaced. |
| | 2 used to link a series of disconnected phrases | There was glass everywhere – pieces of furniture – boxes – slabs of plaster. |
| brackets | used (like dashes) to cut off an afterthought or an added example or explanation from the rest of the sentence | The dress in the window (a shocking pink) caught her eye. |

## Punctuating speech

**1** Actual words spoken are enclosed by quotation marks. Quotation marks (or inverted commas as they are also called) can be single or double. It doesn't matter which you use, so long as you are consistent, for example:

'What are you doing here?' Tom asked. OR
"What are you doing here?" Tom asked.

'What are you doing here?' are the actual words Tom spoke, and they are therefore enclosed in quotation marks.

**2** The first spoken word has a capital letter, even if it comes in the middle of a sentence, for example:

Mary said, 'My feet are aching.'

Note that when a spoken sentence is interrupted by a verb of saying, the continuation of the sentence does not begin with a capital letter, for example;

'I have been walking all day,' she said, 'going from store to store.'

**3** A comma (or some other punctuation mark) is required before a verb of saying and after a verb of saying if the quoted words continue, for example:

'You are very late,' she said.
'There were no buses,' he replied, 'and I had to get a taxi.'

**4** Punctuation marks connected with the quoted words are placed inside the quotation marks, for example:

'What a long time you have been!' she exclaimed.
'I was as quick as I could be,' he replied.

**5** It is usual to begin a new paragraph every time there is a new speaker, for example:

'Your dinner is ready,' she said.
'Very well,' he replied. 'I shall just wash my face and change. Then I'll be ready.'
'Don't take too long,' she warned.

**6** If words are quoted within the spoken words, these are enclosed in double quotation marks if single ones are normally used, or in single quotation marks if double ones are normally used, for example:

'He said, "Hurry up",' she informed him. OR
"He said, 'Hurry up'," she informed him.

**7** If a quoted speech continues for more than one paragraph, quotation marks appear at the beginning of each paragraph but not at the end except for the final one, for example:

'The store was absolutely crowded,' she said, 'There were people everywhere. It didn't seem worthwhile trying to get anywhere near the counter. So I left and went to Oxford Street.

'Things were much better there. For some reason or other, there were not so many shoppers.'

# D  Paragraphing

Any extended piece of writing should be divided into paragraphs, that is, sections into which the subject can be broken up, each dealing with a separate aspect. Each paragraph should have a certain unity within itself, that is, it should deal with *one* aspect of the subject.

The first line of a paragraph is normally indented, though there is a tendency now simply to separate paragraphs by a space.

Often, one sentence within a paragraph will indicate what aspect of the subject the paragraph is dealing with. This is called the topic sentence. For example, in the following paragraph, the opening sentence is the topic sentence.

> The weather that day was disappointing. At first there were only a few intermittent showers between which the sun was able to break through for a few moments. But the clouds grew thicker and heavier, and the rain became more persistent. All that could be heard was the sound of the rain beating against the windows. When darkness fell, it was still raining.

# E  Parts of speech

The name given to the various groups into which words can be divided according to the way they are used grammatically: noun, pronoun, adjective, adverb, verb, preposition, conjunction and interjection. Often, a word can be more than one part of speech depending on how it is used in a sentence. For example, the word 'round' can be used as follows:

He had to rise early for his paper-round. (noun)
He tried to round the corner at high speed. (verb)
It was five minutes before the boxer came round. (adverb)
They collided going round the corner. (preposition)
I prefer the round shape. (adjective)

**Noun** The *name* of anything. For example:
The *table* stood in front of the *window*.
*Fear* made his *hands* tremble.

**Pronoun** The name given to a word which can be used in place of a noun. For example:
Hilary was late. *She* reached school after the bell had gone.
*This* is better than *that*.
The books *which* filled the shelves were not in any particular order.

**Adjective** The name given to a describing word which gives more information about a noun or pronoun and helps to define the noun or pronoun more clearly. For example:

The *last* train had just left.
The *driving* wind made him shiver.
*Which* book do you want?

**Adverb** The name given to a word that modifies (or gives more information about) a verb or an adjective or another adverb. For example:
He spoke *slowly*.
I feel *too* hot.
Stop walking *so* slowly.

**Verb** The name given to a word which tells what action someone or something is performing, what state he, she or it is in, or what process of change he, she or it is going through. For example:
She *ran* down the street.
He *felt* ill.
He *grew* more miserly each year.

A *finite verb* is a verb which forms a tense and has a subject. For example:
He *talked* to himself.
'Talked' refers to past time. 'He' is the subject of 'talked'. 'Talked' is a finite part of the verb 'to talk'.

**Participles** are non-finite parts of the verb. The present participle, always ends in *-ing*, for example, 'running', 'thinking', 'being'. The past participle usually ends in *-ed*, for example 'hoped', 'walked', 'looked'. But there are many exceptions, for example, 'woven', 'made', 'struck'.
Participles can form a tense with the help of an auxiliary verb, for example:
She *was talking* about the latest scandal.
I *am telling* you the truth.
She *has broken* my new vase.
They *have left* the district.
Participles can also introduce phrases, for example:
He thought he would have the advantage by *striking* the first blow.
*Lost* in thought, she didn't notice the fog descend.
Participles can also act as adjectives, for example:
The *running* stream has a pleasant sound.
I require *written* permission before I can allow you to go.

**Preposition** The name given to a word which shows the relationship between one word and another. For example:
She gave her brother the basket *of* fruit.
He jumped *over* the wall.
It was early *in* the morning.

**Conjunction** The name given to a connecting word. For example:
Janice *and* Anne were friends.
He was unable to attend *because* he was ill.
*When* the train arrived, there was a rush to get on.

**Interjection** The name given to an exclamation, usually unconnected grammatically with the rest of the sentence. For example:
*Oh*, what a shame!
*Ah*, I see what you mean.

# F  Figures of speech and other rhetorical devices

**Alliteration** The repetition of the same letter or sound to produce a particular effect. For example:
Puccini's opera *Tosca* has been called 'a *sh*abby little *sh*ocker'.

**Anticlimax** (or **Bathos**) The spoiling of the effect of a climax by a final item which is inferior or less dignified than those preceding it. For example:
I feasted like a king, like four kings, like a boy in the fourth form.

**Antithesis** The arrangement of words so as to emphasise contrast. Words or phrases are usually balanced against each other. For example:
Better to reign in Hell, than serve in Heaven.

**Apostrophe** An exclamatory address, often, though not necessarily, to someone absent or dead. For example:
Milton! Thou shouldst be living at this hour.

**Assonance** The repetition of a particular vowel sound within the space of a few words in order to produce a particular effect. For example:
Music that gentler on the spirit l*ie*s,
Than *ti*red *eye*lids upon *ti*red *eye*s.

**Circumlocution** (or **Periphrasis**) The use of a large number of words where a few would do. For example:
The answer is in the negative.

**Climax** The effect of adding one word or phrase to another with increasing importance or impressiveness. For example:
Some books are to be tasted, others to be swallowed, and some few to be chewed and digested.

**Euphemism** A figure of speech by which a harsh or unpleasant fact is given a milder or more gentle expression, or is expressed in a more roundabout way. For example:
He has passed away.

**Hyperbole** The use of exaggeration for the sake of emphasis but without any intention of deceiving. For example:
A thousand thousand thanks for your assistance.

**Irony** This is a device whereby we say the opposite of what we mean, or something different from what we mean, in order to make our real meaning more emphatic. For example:
What a clever girl you are!

**Metaphor** This is a compressed simile. A simile is a comparison in which we say that one thing is *like* another; a metaphor is a comparison in which we say that one thing *is* something else, which in literal fact it cannot be. For example:
Life's but a walking shadow, a poor player,
That struts and frets his hour upon the stage,
And then is heard no more.

**Onomatopoeia** The stylistic device whereby the sound of a word or words echoes the sense. For example:
The bare black cliff clang'd round him, as he based
His feet on juts of slippery crag that rang
Sharp-smitten with the dint of armed heels.
Some words are onomatopoeic in origin, for example, crash, sizzle, cuckoo.

**Paradox** A statement which on the surface seems to be nonsensical or self-contradictory, but which on further inspection proves to say something of sense and even wisdom. For example:
The child is father of the man.

**Personification** A kind of metaphor in which an inanimate object or an animal or an emotion is regarded as having the qualities of a human being. For example:
Famine stalked the streets of the village that bleak winter.

**Pun** A play on words where two words have a similar sound but different meanings, usually for comic effect. For example:
When I am dead, I hope it may be said:
'His sins were scarlet, but his books were read.'
(Hilaire Belloc)

**Rhetorical question** A question asked for effect only and not seeking an answer. For example:
Are we down-hearted? (No.)

**Sarcasm** The use of mocking or contemptuous language in order to wound or hurt. For example:
You ought to live in a pig-sty. Your manners would be perfect there.
Sarcasm sometimes involves the use of irony. For example:
What a fine fellow you are!

**Simile** A figure of speech in which two objects are compared with respect to some quality which they have in common. For example:
The snowflakes were as light as feathers.
The autumn leaves under the trees were like piles of golden coins.

# G   Setting out letters

## The writer's address

All letters should begin with the address of the person writing. This is placed in the top right-hand corner of the page. It may be indented and punctuated as follows:

> 4, Mill Road,
> Hilton,
> Hertfordshire.
> EN2 8HH

Note that the comma after the house number is optional. There is a full stop after the county. The postcode is not indented; it appears immediately below the county name and is unpunctuated.

Alternatively, the address can be written without punctuation and as a block as follows:

> 4 Mill Road
> Hilton
> Hertfordshire
> EN2 3HH

(Similar styles may be used when addressing the envelope. Begin the address about halfway down the envelope, well clear of the stamps and any possible postmark. It should be written towards the left-hand side of the envelope, but there should still be a wide margin on the left.)

## The date

Always date your letters. The date is normally placed immediately below your address on the right-hand side of the page as follows:

> 1 October 1987

Note that there is no punctuation and no abbreviations.

Other forms of the date are possible, for example: 1st October 1987 or 1st October, 1987 or 1st Oct. 87.

## Salutations

For formal business letters, you would put the name and the address of the person to whom your are writing on the left-hand side of the page lower than your own address, making sure you leave a generous margin. You would then begin with 'Dear Sir,' or 'Dear Mr Elliot,' on the next line and on a line by itself. The first line of your actual letter begins on the following line and is indented from the margin. For example:

> 4 Mill Road
> Hilton
> Hertfordshire
> EN2 3HH
>
> 1 October 1987

Mr J L Elliott
Firestone Building
Hilton Road
Hilton
Hertfordshire
EN2 6JK

Dear Mr Elliott,
   I am writing to you in the hope that . . .

Note that 'Dear Sir,' and 'Dear Madam' are very formal. You would use them in business letters to someone you have not met. 'Sir' and 'Madam' have capital letters. 'Mr', 'Mrs', 'Miss' and 'Ms' are never followed by full stops.

For informal letters, to friends or members of the family, there is no need to use the name and address of the person you are writing to. You begin straightaway with the salutation. For example:

Dear Jane,
   Thank you so much for sending me the book I asked you for . . .

## Endings

Formal letters end with 'Yours faithfully' or 'Yours sincerely' followed by a comma. This is placed centrally on the page on a line by itself and is followed by your signature on the next line below it. For example:

> I look forward to receiving the information I have requested.
>
>       Yours faithfully,
>       James Hamilton

Note that 'Yours' always has a capital letter and 'faithfully' and 'sincerely' do not. If you begin your letter with 'Dear Sir' or 'Dear Madam', you should end it 'Yours faithfully'. This is more formal that 'Yours sincerely' which you would use if you begin 'Dear Mr Thompson' or 'Dear Ms Grant'.

Informal letters can be ended in a number of ways depending on your relationship to the person to whom your are writing. For example:

> With best wishes
> Love from
> Your affectionate nephew
> Yours ever

Note that these are placed centrally and the first word beings with a capital letter. You would normally sign letters of this kind with your first name on the following line.

# H   Solecisms

A solecism is the name given to something which offends against grammatical rules or correct usage. Here are some of the more common examples.

**Amount/number** You should avoid expressions like 'a large amount of people'. The word to use in cases like this is 'number'. 'Amount' is used in referring to an object considered as one mass (butter, sea, grass); 'number' is used in referring to a collection of individual objects (people, houses, books). For example:
> He spread a vast amount of butter on his bread.
> A large number of people gathered to hear the preacher.

**Best known** 'Best known' is the correct form, not 'most well known.' For example:
> The actor was best known for his performances at the National Theatre.

**Both ... and** In sentences containing 'both ... and', each word should be followed by identically shaped phrases. For example:
> He was renowned both as a conductor and as a composer.

**Between you and me** This is the correct form of the expression, *not* 'between you and I'.

**Can/may** 'Can' means 'know how to', 'have the ability to'; 'may' means 'have permission to'. For example:
> Can you lift this table?
> May I leave the room?

**Centre on/centre round** 'Centre on' is the correct form. For example:
> The argument centred on who was telling the truth.

**Different** 'Different' is normally followed by 'from', not 'to' or 'than'. For example:
> The book was different from what I expected.

**Done** The past tense of the verb 'to do' is 'did', not 'done'. For example:
> I *did* the best I could.

**Double negative** Two negatives in a statement cancel each other out. Instead of
> He had not done no work

say
> He had not done any work.

**Due to** 'Due' is an adjective and should therefore refer to a noun or a pronoun. There must be something (a noun or pronoun) which is 'due' to something else. For example:
> The warm weather was due to an area of high pressure.

**Fewer/less** 'Fewer' is used with objects considered as a collection of individual items; 'less' is used with abstract nouns and objects considered as a mass. Compare 'amount' and 'number' above. For example:
> There is less space in our new house.
> There are fewer houses for sale in this area.

**Hanged/hung** Both of these are the past tense and past participle of the verb 'to hang'. 'Hanged' is the form used when referring to capital punishment or to suicide by hanging. 'Hung' is used in all other cases. For example:
> He hanged himself from a beam in the ceiling.
> He hung desperately from the narrow ledge.
> He hung the picture above the fireplace.

**Lay/lie** The verb 'lay' (as in 'lay the table' or 'lay an egg') has the present participle 'laying' and past tense and past participle 'laid'. For example:
> He laid the table for supper.
> The hen has laid an egg.
'Lie' (meaning 'to be in a horizontal position') has present participle 'lying', past tense 'lay' and past participle 'lain'. For example:
> She lay on the sofa.
> The wounded man had lain on the floor for three hours.

**Like/as** 'Like' should not be used as a conjunction. Use 'as' instead. For example:
> You should have gone straight home as I said.

**Of/have** Beware of using the word 'of' for 'have' in cases where the pronunciation of the two words is similar. For example:
> I could have murdered him.

**The reason why ... because** 'The reason why' should be followed by 'that', not 'because'. 'Because' merely repeats the idea already expressed in 'the reason why'. For example:
> The reason why he went to the police was that he was afraid.
> He went to the police because he was afraid.

**So as/so that** 'So as' is followed by the infinitive; 'so that' is followed by a clause. For example:
> She got up early so as to be on time for the train.
> She got up early so that she could be sure of catching the train.

**Try and/try to** The form 'try to' followed by a verb is preferable to 'try and'. For example:
> Try to be on time.

**Which/who** Use 'who' when referring to people, not 'which'. For example:
> People who drive when drunk should be prosecuted.

**Who/whom** The form 'who' is used when it is the subject. The object form is 'whom'. For example:
Look who is standing over there.
There is the girl whom I saw in the street.
I don't care to whom you speak.

**Than** 'Than' is a conjunction, not a preposition. When it links two pronouns, these should both be in the same case. For example:
He is taller than I.

# I   Confused words

There are a large number of words in the English language which are often confused or used incorrectly. Confusion may arise either because the words are similar in sound or meaning or have some uses in common but not others, or because of a misunderstanding of the true meanings. Here are some examples:

adapt, adept
advice, advise
affect, effect
afflict, inflict
agnostic, atheist
all together, altogether
alley, ally
allusion, illusion
alternately, alternatively
amend, emend
amoral, immoral
angel, angle
appreciable, appreciative
astrology, astronomy
aural, oral
authoritarian, authoritative
avenge, revenge

barbaric, barbarous
bath, bathe
beside, besides
biannual, biennial
breath, breathe

canal, channel
cancel, postpone
capital punishment, corporal punishment
carefree, careless
ceremonial, ceremonious
childish, childlike
cloth, clothe
collaborate, corroborate
coma, comma
comic, comical
complacent, complaisant
complement, compliment

comprise, include, compose
contagious, contiguous
contemptible, contemptuous
continual, continuous
council, counsel
councillor, counsellor
credible, credulous

defective, deficient
definite, definitive
delusion, illusion
deprecate, depreciate
derisive, derisory
detract, distract
device, devise
dialogue, duologue
discover, invent
disinterested, uninterested
distinct, distinctive
dully, duly

earthen, earthly, earthy
economic, economical
effective, effectual, efficacious, efficient
elemental, elementary
elicit, illicit
emigrate, immigrate
eminent, imminent
employee, employer
enormity, enormousness
entomology, etymology
envelop, envelope
exceedingly, excessively
exhausting, exhaustive
explicit, implicit
exterior, external
extravert, introvert

famous, infamous, notorious
fatal, fateful
flaunt, flout
flotsam, jetsam
flounder, founder
forego, forgo

gorilla, guerrilla
gourmand, gourmet

historic, historical
human, humane

idle, idol, idyll
imaginary, imaginative
imbue, infuse
imperative, imperious
imply, infer
inedible, uneatable
informant, informer
ingenious, ingenuous
instantaneous, simultaneous
intelligent, intellectual
interior, internal

judicial, judicious

later, latter
laudable, laudatory
learn, teach
libel, slander
liqueur, liquor
loose, lose
luxuriant, luxurious

marital, martial, marshal
masterly, masterful
meretricious, meritorious
misogamy, misogyny
momentarily, momently
moral, morale
mythical, mythological

nationalise, naturalise
negligent, negligible
new, novel

observance, observation
official, officious
ordinance, ordnance
ostensible, ostentatious
overlay, overlie
overlook, oversee

parricide, patricide
pennant, pennon
persecute, prosecute
personal, personnel
perspicacity, perspicuity
popular, populous
practicable, practical
precede, proceed
precipitate, precipitous
presumptive, presumptuous
prologue, epilogue
proof, prove
psychiatrist, psychoanalyst, psychologist

re-enforce, reinforce
resin, rosin
respectable, respectful, respective
restive, restless

salvage, selvage
seasonable, seasonal
sensual, sensuous
sociable, social
stalactite, stalagmite
stentorian, stertorous
stimulant, stimulus
subconscious, unconscious
supernatural, unnatural

temporal, temporary
terminal, terminus
thrash, thresh
titillate, titivate
tortuous, torturous

translucent, transparent
triumphal, triumphant

vacation, vocation
venal, venial
veracious, voracious
visible, visual

# J  Ambiguity

When a statement is open to two interpretations, it is said to be ambigious. For example:

Coming round the corner the library came into view. Here are some particular cases where there is a danger of ambiguity.

**Antecedent** Make sure that the relative pronoun (who, which, whom, whose, that) comes after the word if qualifies (that is, its antecedent). This sentence is ambiguous:

I was in real trouble when my mother discovered the vase on the shelf which was broken.

**Because** Take care when using 'because' after a negative statement. This sentence is ambiguous:

She did not like him because he was tall.

**Hyphen** Make sure you use a hyphen to join words that are related. This sentence is ambiguous:

Three year-old cars need M.O.T.s.

**Figurative language** Sometimes it is not clear whether what is being said is figurative or literal. This sentence is ambiguous:

The scientist exploded when his experiment went wrong.

**Misrelated participles** Participles should be related to the subjects they describe. This sentence is ambigious:

Hurrying up the street a broken piece of paving caught his foot.

**Only** Make sure the word 'only' is placed as near as possible to the word it modifies. This sentence is ambiguous:

Only dogs on a leash are admitted to this park.

**Personal pronouns** Sometimes personal pronouns are used when a noun should be used in order to avoid ambiguity. This sentence is ambiguous:

Peter asked his father if he could get him a newspaper when he was out.

**Titles** If titles are not properly punctuated with quotation marks, there can sometimes be ambiguity. This sentence is ambiguous:

Jane Eyre is my favourite.

# Index of Authors and Titles

# Acknowledgements

The authors and publishers would like to thank the following for permission to reproduce copyright material:

The Controller of Her Majesty's Stationery Office for the leaflets *How to Run a Firework Display Safely* and *How to Claim Child Benefit* Crown Copyright; Olwyn Hughes for the poem 'You're' by Sylvia Plath from *Collected Poems* by Sylvia Plath, published by Faber & Faber, London, © Ted Hughes 1965 & 1981; Faber and Faber for the poem 'Mr Bleaney' from *Whitsun Weddings* by Philip Larkin; Curtis Brown Ltd for the story 'The Potato Gatherers' by Brian Friel © Brian Friel, the extract from 'Sprightly Running' by John Wain CBE © 1962 John Wain, and the extract from *Manservant and Maidservant* by Ivy Compton Burnett © the Estate of Ivy Compton Burnett 1947; Curtis Brown (Aust) Ltd for the story 'The Parachutist' by D'Arcy Niland © Kemalde Pty Ltd c/o Curtis Brown (Aust) Pty Ltd, Sydney; Carcanet Press for the extract from 'Frost in April' from *The Crystal Fountain and Other Stories* by Malachi Whitaker © Michael Whitaker, 1984, Carcanet Press, 1984; *The Radio Times* for the articles 'Earth in Peril' by Geoffrey Lean, 11–17 December 1982 and 'The adventures of Mark Twain' by James Munson, 30 November–6 December 1985, the extract from Film Guide, 14–20 March 1987, the Letters 'Boring Sport, Disaster and Insights', 7–13 March 1987 and 'The Philadelphia Story', 14–20 March 1987; William Collins for the extract from *Majorca* by Christopher Sidgwick © Christopher Sidgwick; William Heinemann Ltd for the extract from *The Village by the Sea* by Anita Desai and 'The Twins' by Aidan Chambers; John Murray (Publishers) Ltd for the poem 'Executive' from *Collected Poems* by John Betjeman; The Society of Authors on behalf of the Bernard Shaw Estate for the extract from *Pygmalion* by George Bernard Shaw; A.M. Heath on behalf of the late Sonia Brownell Orwell and Secker and Warburg Ltd for the extract from *The Road to Wigan Pier* by George Orwell; Jonathan Cape Ltd on behalf of the executors of the Ernest Hemingway Estate for the extract from 'My Old Man' from *The First Forty-Nine Stories* by Ernest Hemingway and on behalf of the executors of the James Joyce Estate for the extracts from *A Portrait of the Artist as a Young Man* and *The Dubliners*; Mrs A.M. Walsh for 'The Bully Asleep' by John Walsh from *Poets in Hand* published by Puffin; Fontana for the extract from 'The Normal Fifth' from *At Bay in Gear Street* by Michael Frayn © The Observer 1965; Macmillan, London and Basingstoke for the poem 'To Hang a Man' from *Collected Poems* by Ralph Hodgson, the extract from *I Knock at the Door* by Sean O'Casey and the extract from 'The Lies of Boye Butler' by Christopher Leach; Wayland (Publishers) Ltd for the extract from *Freedom from Work* by Barrie Sherman; The Bodley Head for the extracts from *Dear Comrade* by Frances Thomas and from *Children of the Dust* by Louise Lawrence; Deborah Rogers Ltd for the extract from *A Question of Courage* by Marjorie Darke © Marjorie Darke 1975; Midland Bank plc for the extract from the booklet *Cheque-In Careers* and *Ten 15-minute Walks from Piccadilly*; Methuen Children's Books Ltd for the extract from *Little Pete Stories* by Leila Berg; Hamish Hamilton Ltd for the extract from *A Cack-handed War* by Edward Blishen © Edward Blishen 1983; Barnabas J. Ramon-Fortuné for the extract from 'The Devil Dealer'; Club 18–13 Holidays for their advertisement; Solid Fuel Advisory Service for their advertisement; Weidenfeld & Nicolson Ltd for the extract from 'Today there are no Gentlemen' by Nik Cohn; J.M. Dent & Sons Ltd for the extract from *Portrait of the Artist as a Young Dog* and *Quite Early One Morning* by Dylan Thomas; Office of Fair Trading for the booklet *How to Cope with Doorstep Salesmen* Crown copyright; Hamish Hamilton Children's Books for the extract from 'I Know What You Did Last Summer' by Lois Duncan; *Woman* for the article from *Woman Talk* entitled 'Could your child be the school bully?' 6 September 1986; W.H. Smith Children's Literary Competition (now known as the W.H. Smith Young Writers' Competition) for 'Me' by David Dekon, 'After the Funeral' by Frances Jennifer Tyler and 'Speaking Freely' by Dina Rabinovitch from *Children as Writers 20th Year*; London's Territorial Army for the advertisement 'Spend an evening with us'; *The Daily Express* for 'Brake faults on death bus'; *The Daily Telegraph* for the article 'No sexism, please,' 20 October 1985, and *The Sunday Telegraph* for the article '33 arrested in race demo clashes' 28 April 1985 and *The Sunday Telegraph Magazine* for 'But does he get by without his rabbit pie?' by Peter Bradshaw, 24 October 1982, 'Is Work Good' by André Drucker, 22 November 1987; *The Guardian* for the articles 'Boy, aged 8 passes O level' of 22 August 1986, 'Putting poodles before people', 8 May 1986, 'Police escort plan for ferry fans', 13 August 1986, 'We are not a sub-species', 22 September 1981, 'Passenger sees fault in jet ready for takeoff', 12 January 1987 and 'Blackmail charge insult to black defendants', 27 June 1985, the extract from Auberon Waugh in Junior Guardian, 8 April 1987 and the Letter from Junior Guardian, 8 April 1987; Automobile Association for the advertisement 'Stopwatch'; TI Creda Ltd for the advertisement for Creda Supertron; Securicor Communications for the advertisement for Securicor Car Phones; *The Sun* for the articles 'Oompah ace Ray drums up a record', 'Bill loses hooter at demi-nose' of 28 August 1987, 'It's so jolly in jail', 8 August 1986, 'O Boy' John, 8, passes Maths GCE' by Martin Stote, 'Michelle names the day', 8 August 1986, 'Clickety-click for a new firm', 8 August 1986, and 'Princess Di soaks up the Sun in Spain'; *The TV Times* for the 'TV Times Travel' offer, Issue 42, 1985; Phillip Adams for the extract from 'The Unspeakable Adams'; British Telecom Mobile Phone Division for the advertisement for the British Telecom Cellphones; Olympus Optical Co (UK) Ltd for the advertisement for the Olympus AF-1 Camera; Michael Joseph for the extracts from *There is a Happy Land* and *Waterhouse at Large* by Keith Waterhouse; Help the Aged for the leaflet 'Keep Warm This Winter'; Heinemann Educational Books for the story 'The Lemon Orchard' from *A Walk In The Night And Other Stories* by Alex La Guma; William Heinemann for the extract from *An Inspector Calls* by J.B. Priestley; Harvey Unna & Stephen Durbridge Ltd for the extract from *Love Is A Many Splendoured Thing* by Alan Bleasdale; Martin Cuffs and Chrissie Maher (editors) for the extract from *Gobbledygook*; *The Times Newspapers* for the articles 'English as she tends to be writ' by Bob Doe, 15 May 1981, '£500 allowance to lure new staff' by TES Reporters, 5 September 1986, 'Too young to last' by John Hopkins, *The Sunday Times*, 21 November 1982, 'Steve, they said, is going to be fine' by Simon Brown, *The Sunday Times*, 23 March 1986, 'Police besieged by marchers', *The Sunday Times*, 28 April 1985, and 'Bird Table Treats' by Liz Hodgkinson, *The Sunday Times Magazine*, 29 November 1981; *The London Evening Standard* for the Letter of 18 March 1987; Boglée-L'Ouverture Publications Ltd for the poem 'Yuh Hear Bout?' by Valerie Bloom; Curtis Brown Ltd for the extract from *The Hidden Persuaders* by Vance Packard © Vance Packard, 1966; André Deutsch Ltd for the extracts from *North of South* by Shiva Naipaul and from 'Getting It Wrong' by Rhodri Jones; Longman Imprint and Bill Naughton for the extract from 'Spiv in Love' in *Late Night on Watling Street*; Wigan Metropolitan Borough Council for the advertisement 'Fast Forward'; 16th Daily Mirror Children's Literary Competition for the poems '35 Portman Street' by Esther-Yanne Lee-French and 'Eleven Plus and Minus' by Lynette Halewood; *The Observer* for the articles 'Police in race protest siege' by Arlen Harris, 28 April 1985 and 'She pops home' by Cal Clothier, and the Letter of 17 March 1985; *The London Evening News* for the 24-hour weather report of 16 October 1987; *The New Statesman* for the extract from 'Life in a Colour Supplement' by Malcolm Muggeridge; Longman Resources Unit and SCDC Publications for the extract from *Resources for Multicultural Education* by Gillian Klein © 1982; Ray

Bradbury for extracts from 'The Shave' and 'Marionettes, Inc'.

We should also like to thank the following for supplying copyright photographs:

Barnaby's Picture Library; *The Guardian* for 'Boy, aged 8, passes O level', 22 August 1986, and 'All the Fun of the Fair', 31 March 1970; *The Daily Telegraph* for 'Tottenham Protest', 22 March 1987 and '33 arrested in race demo', 28 April 1985; BBC/Hulton Press for 'Early polling', 11 January 1987; *The Observer* for 'Police in race protest siege', 28 April 1985, and 'Charlie left Liverpool to work in the South', 11 January 1987.

It has not been possible in all cases to contact copyright holders. The publishers and author would be pleased to hear from any unacknowledged source and full acknowledgement will be made at the first opportunity.